RESEARCH METHODS

RESEARCH METHODS
Exploring the Social World in Canadian Contexts

Second Edition

Diane G. Symbaluk

CANADIAN
SCHOLARS

Toronto | Vancouver

Research Methods: Exploring the Social World in Canadian Contexts, Second Edition
By Diane G. Symbaluk

First published in 2019 by
Canadian Scholars, an imprint of CSP Books Inc.
425 Adelaide Street West, Suite 200
Toronto, Ontario
M5V 3C1

www.canadianscholars.ca

Library and Archives Canada Cataloguing in Publication

Title: Research methods : exploring the social world in Canadian contexts / Diane G. Symbaluk.
Names: Symbaluk, Diane G., 1967- author.
Description: Second edition. | Includes index.
Identifiers: Canadiana (print) 20190144718 | Canadiana (ebook)
        20190144734 | ISBN 9781773381541
        (softcover) | ISBN 9781773381558 (ebook) | ISBN 9781773381565 (PDF)
Subjects: LCSH: Sociology—Research—Methodology. | LCSH: Sociology—Research—Canada—Methodology. |
LCGFT: Textbooks.
Classification: LCC HM571 .S96 2019 | DDC 301.072—dc23

Page layout by S4Carlisle
Cover design by Rafael Chimicatti

Printed and bound in Ontario, Canada

Canada

This book is dedicated to curious students, many of whom will come to realize that research methods are more than a practical means for finding answers to questions of interest. Research methods are also an integral part of an interesting and challenging process of discovery that involves learning skills through practice, in some cases career-determining skills you might wish you had developed sooner.

BRIEF TABLE OF CONTENTS

TABLE OF CONTENTS

PART I   PREPARING FOR RESEARCH

PART II   APPROACHES TO RESEARCH

PART III   WRITING UP RESEARCH AND THE DISSEMINATION OF FINDINGS

PREFACE

GOALS AND APPROACH OF THE BOOK

The purpose of this book is to introduce post-secondary students in Canada to a variety of social research methods as framed by research questions and objectives, rather than preferred qualitative, quantitative, mixed, or multiple method approaches. Students are more apt to want to learn about research methods and practise them if they are personally relevant and interesting. By introducing research topics within a Canadian context and drawing upon research conducted by Canadian scholars at universities and research institutes in Canada, students will be able to better identify with the learning material. While primarily directed at students in second-, third-, or fourth-year sociology classes who have yet to conduct research, this book is of equal benefit to students in anthropology, criminology, social work, psychology, or political science who are interested in learning more about social research through examples drawn from their disciplines. Also, given its emphasis on current ethical standards, this book is also instrumental for anyone who plans to carry out research and write research proposals or reports as part of an honours program, independent study, or graduate school requirement.

Through my teaching experience, I have discovered there is substantial variation in the way individuals learn. Accordingly, I have incorporated multiple learning strategies into this textbook. I hope my passion for teaching is evident and the pedagogy in this book helps readers succeed in research methods. I firmly believe that one of the best ways to learn about research methods is to practise them. Reading about recommendations for how to structure survey questions may help you prepare a draft survey, but a pilot test will confirm whether you are asking the right questions and whether people understand them. Similarly, while you can create an interview guide with key questions to indicate what you plan to do for an in-depth interview, it is only through experience that you will learn how to listen and create impromptu follow-up questions while the interview unfolds. Although this book provides you with steps for applying different methods, please appreciate that research is a process, and as such, it seldom conforms to ideal types in the real world. Again, it is only through experience that you will begin to understand the subtleties that underlie research processes.

I am the first to admit I have learned more about research from being engaged in it than reading about it, and I have similarly learned more about research processes through my errors and omissions than my initial successes. The Learning through Practice exercises and step-by-step instructions for planning and designing studies provide a starting point for inexperienced researchers. Beyond this book, you can continue to develop your research skills through educational pursuits such as a thesis-based master's program or through work-related experiences such as a research assistantship.

CHANGES IN THE SECOND EDITION

Revisions to this edition are largely based on reviewer feedback from instructors who teach research methods at post-secondary institutions throughout Canada, as well as suggestions made by students attending a Canadian university who used the earlier edition of this book. First, the title has changed to reflect the increased emphasis on Canadian content throughout, including research by Canadian scholars, examples framed within a Canadian context, and the use of Canadian research resources. In addition, contemporary issues, data, and research are prioritized over classic and historical case studies, and new sections and boxes highlight emerging methods and online resources. Additional theory and explanation are incorporated, including a section on Indigenous worldviews and the need for decolonizing research methods. The appendix now contains a student-authored research report from 2018 based on content analysis, and this section was expanded to include a sample poster designed to mentor students in the dissemination of research findings.

ORGANIZATION

Part I: Preparing for Research

The first part of the book prepares you for research by outlining considerations and processes that take place in the planning stage prior to the collection of data.

- Chapter 1 is on research foundations, and it begins with a consideration of the various strategies we have for finding things out. Chapter 1 also discusses the limitations to alternatives to social research methods and the common errors associated with reasoning processes. Finally, chapter 1 introduces you to social research, helps you to understand the goals of social science research, and distinguishes between qualitative and quantitative approaches to research.
- Chapter 2 details the importance of theory, beginning with the main assumptions of positivist, interpretive, critical, and pragmatic

paradigms, and then explains why decolonization is necessary for learning about Indigenous knowledges. This chapter differentiates between theoretical frameworks and theories, and deductive and inductive forms of reasoning. Chapter 2 helps you to formulate research questions and explains the importance of existing literature for framing research assumptions. Finally, this chapter teaches you how to locate appropriate literature and evaluate sources of information found on the internet.

- Chapter 3 introduces you to research ethics through historical examples of the unethical treatment of humans in military and medical cases, along with the regulatory outcomes. This chapter also discusses classic research examples to help you understand how ethical considerations arise in studies that include human participants. Ethical issues that relate to social science research are discussed in detail in this chapter, along with the core principles of the current Tri-Council Policy Statement (TCPS2 2014) on ethically responsible research.

- Chapter 4 covers the main components of a research design and explains conceptualization and operationalization processes. In addition, this chapter differentiates between levels of measurement, explores techniques used to assess reliability and validity, and identifies sources of measurement error. Finally, this chapter explores means for achieving rigour in qualitative research.

- Chapter 5 teaches you about sampling techniques including when and under what circumstances a researcher might choose a probability or a non-probability-based sampling method. This chapter distinguishes between probability-based methods including simple random sampling, systematic sampling, stratified sampling, and cluster sampling, and it also explores non-probability methods including convenience sampling, snowball sampling, purposive sampling, and quota sampling.

Part II: Approaches to Research

With the who, what, where, when, and why components of research covered, part II centres on how to collect data using a variety of research methods beginning with quantitative approaches.

- Chapter 6 explores the rationale underlying an experimental method and teaches you about the criteria needed to establish causality and how to test hypotheses using experimental designs. This chapter also examines potential threats to internal and external validity.

- Chapter 7 focuses on asking questions through survey methods. This chapter examines the key methodological considerations that precede survey research, describes the two main survey methods used by quantitative researchers, and provides survey construction guidelines.

- Chapter 8 introduces four indirect methods used to gather information about people: physical trace analysis, archival analysis, content analysis, and secondary analysis of existing data. These methods are unobtrusive because the source of data is something created by or for people, as opposed to information obtained directly from people. Chapter 8 ends with a discussion of digital media and how the internet has changed the nature of social research and the methods used to examine social issues.

- Chapter 9 moves into qualitative approaches for learning about people through a direct method called qualitative interviewing. This chapter describes the structure of qualitative interviews and explains how to conduct an in-depth interview. In addition, this chapter outlines focus groups and how they differ from qualitative interviews.

- Chapter 10, on ethnography, outlines the main features of ethnographic studies and explains the main roles of ethnographers engaged in fieldwork. In addition, this chapter looks at techniques used by ethnographers to blend into a group under investigation and the ethical issues raised in fieldwork.

- Chapter 11 examines the merit of including both qualitative and quantitative approaches within a single study and introduces mixed-methods research designs. In addition, this chapter shows how researchers can combine multiple methods to collect information on people and organizations using case study research, evaluation research, and action research.

Part III: Writing Up Research and the Dissemination of Findings

Finally, chapter 12 explains how to write research proposals and reports. The book concludes with an appendix containing a sample research report and poster to illustrate research dissemination.

- Assuming you have a firm understanding of the preliminary chapters and have settled on the most appropriate method or methods needed to answer a research question of interest, chapter 12 helps you translate your research ideas into a technical plan that can be submitted to a research ethics board or your supervisor for approval or grading. If you have already carried out research as part of a class project or thesis requirement, the chapter also provides guidance and suggestions for how to structure and write a report that can later be submitted to a journal for consideration.

- The appendix includes a research report written by a student as part of her course work in social research methods. The report demonstrates that students can and do carry out research projects. Readers benefit from being able to follow the same topic through the stages of basic research, report writing, and the dissemination of findings in a poster presentation.

PEDAGOGY

Opening Quotes

Each chapter begins with a selected quote or overview by a methodologist, scholar, or research-based organization to provide you with focal insight into the material covered in the chapter.

Canadian Content

Students and instructors at Canadian colleges and universities will be pleased to learn this book is written from the ground up with intentional emphasis on Canadian content. In most cases, research examples are based on empirical research carried out in Canada by Canadian scholars.

Learning Objectives

Each chapter begins with a brief set of learning objectives, consisting of statements that spell out the core skills or knowledge students should be able to demonstrate after carefully reviewing the chapter.

Test Yourself

Test Yourself questions are built-in open-ended review questions designed to help students gauge their understanding of a learning objective before proceeding to the next section of the book.

Research on the Net

Research on the Net boxes contain information on recommended websites and online resources useful for understanding key concepts and expanding on key ideas in the chapter.

Research in Action

Research in Action boxes include descriptions of research, documentaries and feature films, news stories, YouTube videos, and other examples that illustrate the relevance of methods and research concepts in everyday life.

Key Terms

Throughout each chapter, key terms are indicated in boldface font and defined at the end of the textbook in a glossary.

Chapter Summary

Chapter summaries consist of brief statements that are illustrative of the kinds of responses students should be able to provide as evidence that they have achieved the learning objectives.

Research Reflection

Research reflection questions provided at the end of the chapter are designed to help students think critically about the material. Reflection questions can be used in any number of ways, including as a basis for class discussion, for use by instructors as short assignment questions, and/or by students to help them prepare for short-answer and essay questions on exams.

Learning through Practice

Each chapter contains a practice exercise designed to help students understand the chapter material through direct engagement. Some instructors may assign this exercise as a short laboratory assignment, a research assignment, a class demonstration, or as part of group work.

Research Resources

References to articles, book chapters, and websites that provide a more in-depth understanding of the key concepts and issues are included as recommended resources at the end of each chapter.

Instructor Resources

Textbook supplements including lecture PowerPoint slides, a test bank, and research assignments that can also serve as laboratory exercises or tutorials are available for instructors who adopt this textbook for classroom use. Please visit https://www.canadianscholars.ca/books/research-methods to access these supplements.

ACKNOWLEDGEMENTS

This text is the result of a collective effort put forth by many individuals. Special thanks to Nick Hilton (Editorial/Production Manager) at Canadian Scholars for his ongoing assistance with my many queries and his contribution to the overall development, editing, and production of this book. Additional appreciation is extended to Kerrie Waddington (Acquisitions Editor) for her encouragement and support in the early stages of manuscript planning and peer review and Cindy Angelini (Copyeditor) for her wise counsel on grammar and keen eye for detail.

I was fortunate to have Jessica Gillard as a student in my research methods course during the winter of 2018. Jessica gave me permission to include an adapted version of her final report as the appendix in this book to assist others in the development of a research project using content analysis. She turned her report into a poster presentation (also included) to disseminate her findings at MacEwan University's 2019 student research conference. At the time of writing, Jessica was a fourth-year Bachelor of Arts student at MacEwan University majoring in sociology and psychology.

Finally, I wish to acknowledge those students from whom I continue to learn valuable teaching and research lessons.

PART I

Preparing for Research

CHAPTER 1

Research Foundations

The most beautiful thing we can experience is the mysterious. It is the source of all true art and science.
 —Albert Einstein[1]

Learning Objectives

After reading this chapter, students should be able to do the following:

LO1 Explain why it is important to learn about social research methods.

LO2 Identify various "ways of knowing" and note their limitations.

LO3 Recognize common errors in reasoning.

LO4 Define social research, distinguish between primary and secondary research, and differentiate between basic and applied research.

LO5 Explain the goals of research.

LO6 Differentiate between qualitative and quantitative research methods.

INTRODUCTION

Many students enroll in an introduction to social research course only because the course is required for their program of study. Some dread the thought of having to read about and carry out academic research, and others worry about how they will perform in what they perceive is going to be a highly laborious and boring course. I know this because students routinely admit these reservations, and they also ask why they need to take such a course and what value the course will have for them in their everyday lives. My response is this: though you may be skeptical now, what you will learn about in this research methods book and in a methods course is interesting, and it has practical and relevant implications for you—for understanding people and events around you, for earning a living, and especially for making informed choices. After taking a research methods course, one of my students wrote in the course evaluation, "This class should be the last one that anyone completing an undergraduate degree takes . . . the skills learned and the knowledge acquired directly translate into the real world."

Research informs practice. Regardless of the career path you take, research has already played and continues to play an integral role in the proficiency of the skill set practised within that occupation. For example, healthcare professionals such as family physicians, nurse practitioners, and dentists rely upon best practices as identified by researchers in the discipline. Similarly, teachers base lesson plans on an established curriculum that is continually monitored and evaluated, peace officers interview eyewitnesses based on methods that are designed to maximize recall and minimize errors, social workers employ proven crisis-intervention strategies to assist families and individuals in need, and lawyers argue points based on their prior research into similar cases with specific outcomes. Moreover, successful businesses frequently invest in research to learn about existing customers, satisfaction with current products and services, and the potential for market growth (e.g., this is how Apple comes up with ideas for its newest iPhones).

In addition to describing people and processes, applied research also helps us evaluate whether the course of action we take is the most appropriate in a given circumstance, and it provides direction for how we might make improvements in the future. Summing up, research methodology can be best viewed as a practical means for acquiring relevant knowledge that is used to make informed decisions. As implied by Einstein's opening quote, anybody who is curious about people or events around them can be considered a potential social researcher. This book is specifically designed to help these individuals use the most appropriate methods in their quest to find answers.

Research on the Net

Statistics Canada

One of the leading sources for information on Canada and Canadians is Statistics Canada. Statistics Canada, originally called the Dominion Bureau of Statistics, was established in 1918 as a federal government department that is mandated under the Statistics Act to "collect, compile, analyze, abstract and publish statistical information relating to the commercial, industrial, financial, social, economic and general activities and conditions of the people of Canada" (Statistics Canada, 2016a). Here, various economists, mathematical statisticians, programmers, demographers, sociologists, senior methodologists, and others are employed in a realm of social research describing Canada and its people. For example, you can learn about the population and characteristics of Indigenous people; the health and well-being of children and youth; the economic viability of Canada's economy; the average annual income of families; trends in labour; energy supply and demand; and commuting patterns.

One of the most important functions of Statistics Canada is to generate research to help inform policy that is developed at the provincial and federal levels of government. The information collected about Canadian citizens, businesses, departments, and programs helps decision making involving the prioritization of issues, the allocation of funding, and the development of rules and strategies. This occurs through the analysis of economic performance, the shaping of trade negotiations, the monitoring of the effectiveness of the justice system, the assessment of program funding, the maintenance of education and health-care policies, and other regulatory systems involving the government. For more information on Statistics Canada and its research-based career opportunities, visit the Statistics Canada website at www.statcan.gc.ca.

Statistics Canada is the main federal government source for economic, social, and census data.

Source: xtock/shutterstock.com

WAYS OF KNOWING AND THEIR LIMITATIONS AS SOURCES OF KNOWLEDGE

Each one of us has accumulated knowledge based on ideas and events we have heard about, read about, witnessed, and/or experienced that we use at different times to make choices. As you will discover, many of these ways of knowing have limitations that detract from our ability to make sound and informed choices.

Tradition, Common Sense, and Authority

One of the earliest ways of knowing lies in **tradition**—the compilation of beliefs and practices passed down from one generation to the next that everyone knows about and often adheres to, though rarely questions. Without delving into any- one's personal preferences or religious views about what marriage should or might entail, consider what our gendered tradition tells us about the main performers in wedding ceremonies in Western culture. We know, for example, that there is usually a bride and a groom who are part of a larger wedding party consisting of a maid of honour, a best man, bridesmaids, and groomsmen. Similarly, there are various well-established customs associated with weddings, including the groom asking the bride's father for permission to marry his daughter, the bride wearing a white dress, a bridal veil, a garter belt, and other articles that represent something old, something new, something borrowed, and something blue. Other common features include the exchange of wedding vows and the placing of wedding bands, the first kiss as a newlywed couple, the bouquet toss, the cutting of a wedding cake, the first dance as a couple, and the departure for a honeymoon. While trad- ition as a form of knowledge might be important for teaching religious doctrine or helping maintain certain cultural practices, it is often passed on and adhered to without a consideration of what the practices mean historically or even in the present-day context. For instance, it is unlikely that a modern groom seen tossing the bride's garter belt into a crowd on their wedding day would be trying to stave off a group intent on tearing at his bride's clothing. Instead, the couple is highly likely to be mindlessly observing the norms of tradition.

Another source of information is **common sense**, which is a form of practical knowledge based on adaptive prior learning that can generalize to novel situations. Common sense is often relied upon to make sound judgments that will benefit us or that will help to keep us out of harm's way, often through recognition of our physical, emotional, and/or cognitive limits. For example, my common sense tells me to opt for intermediate (or blue) down-hill ski runs over expert (black dia- mond) trails given my current abilities at this stage in my life. And, if I felt out of

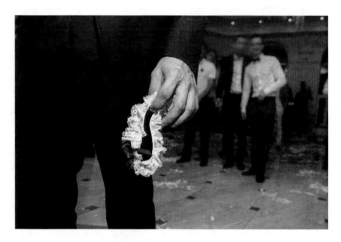

Wedding couples continue to follow the norms of tradition.

Source: Bogdan Sonjachnyj/shutterstock.com

control while skiing down an intermediate run, as might be the case if I picked up too much speed or slid on an icy patch and was thrown off course, I would again rely upon my common sense to help guide me back to safety by perhaps seeking out deeper-looking snow that might provide some traction or by looking for ways to traverse across the mountain. Common sense also plays a role in the establishment and maintenance of intimate relationships, where a person might end a relationship with too many "red flags" or obstacles to overcome. Of course, our common sense might also be misguided, such as when we believe that "opposites attract for a reason" and stay in an unfulfilling relationship. A limitation of common sense is that it doesn't articulate when and under what specific circumstances our generalized beliefs hold true. Sometimes opposing traits foster attraction in a partner; however, research shows that people who are alike (e.g., in looks and with respect to values) fare much better in relationships (Berscheid & Reis, 1998). Common sense may even provide false hope as we cling to the belief that "absence makes the heart grow fonder," while research indicates that long-distance relationships seldom work. Instead, proximity is the key antecedent in the establishment of relationships (Aronson, Wilson, Fehr, & Akert, 2017).

We also learn new things through the teachings of **authority** figures or experts who share their knowledge and experience with us. Beginning with early socialization in our families of origin, we receive imparted wisdom from our parents and relatives, who teach us about the importance of eating well-balanced meals, of looking both ways before we cross the road, of respecting our teachers

Half of Canadian adults do not eat enough fruits and vegetables.
Source: Aleksandar Mijatovic/shutterstock.com

and peers, and of obeying the rule of law. Of course, the same authorities may pass on erroneous information and/or model less appropriate forms of conduct, such as poor eating habits and disregard for the law. Beyond the family, we also obtain information from various credentialed professionals, academics, institutions, and organizations (e.g., a dentist who indicates root canal therapy is necessary, a political science professor who predicts provincial budget cuts, and Health Canada's food guidelines for healthy eating). Although many of the teachings offered by authority figures are helpful and even necessary to our well-being, we often fail to follow expert advice. For example, the World Health Organization informs us how an inadequate intake of fruits and vegetables is linked to 1.7 million deaths per year on a global basis, while a Canadian Community Health Survey indicates that half of Canadian adults do not eat enough fruits and vegetables (Symbaluk & Bereska, 2019). In addition, some authority figures offer opinions on issues outside their realm of expertise, as in the case of professional athletes who are paid to endorse viewpoints and products.

Finally, we tend to over-rely on the mass media as a source of authority without questioning the legitimacy of the messages provided. The mass media is an authority for informing us about local and international events in the form of communications we receive in newspapers, on television, and especially over the internet. However, the media is also a profit-based business with highly concentrated ownership. For example, Bell Media owns more than 200 websites, the CTV Network and its affiliates, including 30 TV channels and 30 specialty channels (e.g., RDS and TSN), and it is Canada's largest radio broadcaster, with 109 stations including Virgin Radio (Bell Media, 2018). Québecor Media is also a big contender, owning daily and local newspapers, Quebec's largest cable company and French-language TV network, book and magazine publishers, and music recording interests (CRTC, 2018). Media giants set the agenda, thereby determining what we are exposed to when we watch television, listen to music, or read newspapers. Thus, it is important to critically assess the messages we are exposed to, as well as their originating sources.

Experience

Lastly, much of what we believe we gain through first-hand **experience**. You probably understand more about the complexities of single parenthood or divorce if this is something you personally have experienced. Similarly, if you are considering whether divorce is becoming increasingly common in Western culture, you may rely upon your own personal knowledge of couples who have divorced. While you may be able to recall several recent instances of divorce among friends, family members, and work associates, does this really provide evidence for a claim that

Source: ©Aaron Warner, www.Cartoonstock.com

divorce is becoming more common? It could be that you are better able to remember recent cases of divorce than ones that occurred much earlier on. It could also be that your friends are not representative of the general population (e.g., they may possess shared characteristics by association that put them at greater risk for divorce, such as being of an age where they are more likely to have young children, having fewer financial resources, or holding an occupation that is less conducive to a stable marriage or family life).

Test Yourself

- What are the four ways of knowing that do not involve scientific research?
- Why might it be problematic to rely upon common sense as a source of knowledge?
- Why is it especially important to critically assess information gleaned from the mass media?

COMMON ERRORS IN REASONING

First-hand experience, common sense, authority, and tradition are all important sources of knowledge that help inform what we know about the social world. However, each has limitations that can lead to a narrow or even inaccurate understanding. As humans we are subject to errors in reasoning, since we pay more careful attention to certain people and events than to others. Some of the more common errors in reasoning that result from reliance on unscientific or everyday ways of knowing include imprecise observation, illogical reasoning, overgeneralization, selective observation, and premature closure.

Imprecise Observation

Although we do pay attention to the people and events going on around us, there is so much information that it is impossible to take in everything at once, let alone process that information accurately, store the details, and recall it at a later point in time. **Imprecise observations** are the inevitable result. As you will learn in later chapters, our ability to observe can be greatly improved when we use a careful, systematic process in which we look for things that are precisely defined ahead of time. In addition to our tendency to make errors while observing, humans are also prone to making errors in their consideration of what they have observed. For example, people over-rely on what can be recalled (i.e., what is available in memory) as an indication of the frequency for that event (Tversky & Kahneman, 1973).

Gamblers often fail to consider the true probability of an event occurring.

Source: PIRO4D/pixabay.com

Illogical Reasoning

Another of the more common errors has to do with **illogical reasoning,** where people make decisions based on faulty logic. This underlies what is referred to as a "gambler's fallacy," where a gambler will place a bet believing that an outcome is *due,* such as a red number on a roulette table following a run of several black numbers. Odds of a red number coming up are based on the overall quantity of numbers (i.e., there are 18 red numbers, 18 black numbers, and two green numbers [i.e., a zero and a double zero] in most North American versions). The probability of a red (or black) number occurring is 47.4 percent every time, regardless of previous events. Illogical reasoning results from a failure to consider the true odds or probability of an event occurring.

Overgeneralization

Overgeneralization refers to the tendency to assume the existence of a general pattern or trait based on a limited number of observations (Babbie & Roberts, 2018). For example, during the global Occupy movement against economic and social inequality initiated by the Canadian activist organization Adbusters Media Foundation in September of 2011, reporters highly sensationalized the fact that a few of the students in attendance at New York's financial district protests were from highly privileged backgrounds as evidenced by their clothes and belongings, including expensive laptop computers and cellphones. This led to overgeneralizations about who the protestors were, reflected in headlines such as "The Rich Kids Occupy Wall Street" and stories depicting protestors as sharing "more in common with that top one percent than with the bottom one percent" (Flynn, 2011). This type of faulty logic is the basis for stereotypes, which involve overgeneralizations made about entire groups of people based on shared group characteristics such social class, race, or ethnicity.

Selective Observation

A related error is made when the search for a pattern is undertaken by specifically seeking out instances that confirm an existing belief. **Selective observation** refers to the tendency to assume a general pattern exists based on factors other than objective frequency. For example, suppose you recently purchased a new car. After deliberating for days, you decide to purchase one that is red. During the first couple of weeks, it may appear to you that most vehicles on the road are red! This is because your attention is drawn to that colour (i.e., it is now salient for you) and you are inadvertently seeking out red vehicles while ignoring the higher prevalence of other vehicles that are not red. Due to its high visibility, white is the most common colour for vehicles that display business signs. Moreover, white is also the most popular colour for vehicles of any build in North America, followed by black, and then grey or silver (PPG, 2018). Similarly, when seeking to support a viewpoint, observers may be biased (even unknowingly) toward certain observations in their quest to find confirming evidence.

Research in Action

Selective Observation

If you don't believe you are prone to selective observation, try completing Christopher Chabris and Daniel Simon's two-minute "Original Selective Attention Test," found under videos and demos on a website for their book, *The Invisible Gorilla*, at http://www.theinvisiblegorilla.com.

1. Try it: Click on the YouTube clip of the "Original Selective Attention Test," located at the author's site. (The instructions are provided at the start of the clip, wherein you are asked to count the number of basketball passes made by players wearing white.)
2. Hint: Concentrate only on the players wearing white shirts and ignore those who are wearing black shirts to see whether you can obtain the correct answer, which is one of the following: 13, 14, 15, 16, or 17 passes.
3. Were you correct? Where you surprised by what you learned from completing this test? Are you, in fact, prone to selective attention?

To learn more about the processes underlying perception and attention, review Christopher Chabris's 2010 Authors@Google talk. The YouTube video for this fascinating lecture is posted at the web address indicated above under the title "Chris's 2010 presentation at Google."

Premature Closure

Premature closure refers to a tendency to stop searching for necessary observations due to an erroneous belief that an answer has already been determined. This is like overgeneralization and selective observation because, in all three cases, a social perceiver fails to locate the most appropriate answer by short-cutting the process and limiting a search to a small number of observations. In an analysis of one hundred medical cases of injuries and deaths involving diagnostic errors, the most common error made by internists was premature closure, or the failure to search for alternatives after making an initial (albeit incorrect) diagnosis (Graber, Franklin, & Gordon, 2005). Premature closure can also foster what Chambliss and Schutt (2019) call "resistance to change," where people are reluctant to modify their assumptions in the face of new information.

Test Yourself

- What are the five common errors that result from reliance on unscientific forms of reasoning?
- What does overgeneralization refer to?
- In what way is selective observation like premature closure?

SCIENTIFIC REASONING

What sets scientific reasoning apart from the other ways of knowing with their corresponding limitations is the reliance on empirical methods. **Empirical methods** refer to data collection techniques carried out using systematic procedures that are widely recognized by other researchers and produce verifiable findings (Symbaluk & Bereska, 2019). Researchers in the social sciences use empirical methods to study individuals, groups, societies, and social processes in a manner that helps to overcome the limitations of other ways of knowing. Specifically:

- Social researchers seek to find answers through a careful examination of the social world. They do not assume that their initial beliefs or ideas are necessarily correct, and this reduces the likelihood of unquestioning faith in the teachings of tradition or authority. Similarly, while common sense and prior experience can aid scientific inquiry, these forms of knowledge do not substitute for observations that take place in the social world. The importance of theory and prior research for informing the development of new research is the topic of chapter 2.
- Social researchers also rely upon systematic procedures and processes that contribute to quality observations focused in areas of interest. These lessen the likelihood of imprecise observation, selective observation, and illogical reasoning since researchers are very clear about what it is they are studying and how they will go about collecting, analyzing, and making sense of their observations. The main components of a research design and the features of sound measurement are covered in detail in chapter 4.
- Social researchers limit the tendency to make overgeneralizations by ensuring they collect information from individuals or sources that appropriately represent the group or targeted area of interest (see chapter 5 on sampling). In addition, their findings are also open to scrutiny and verification by other researchers in their field of study.

Social Research

Both the social and natural sciences use empirical methods in their endeavour to understand and explain the world around us. The *natural sciences* focus on laws that govern nature (e.g., plants and animals) from within various branches, such as the biological sciences, physical sciences, and earth and planetary sciences. In contrast, the *social sciences* study human nature and society from within various disciplines, such as economics, education, criminology, sociology, psychology, political science, anthropology, and archaeology. **Social research** is "a process in which people combine a set of principles, outlooks, and ideas (i.e., methodology) with a collection of specific practices, techniques, and strategies (i.e., a method of inquiry) to produce knowledge" (Neuman & Robson, 2018, p. 2). The generation of new knowledge is often the result of **primary research**, or first-hand data collection and data analysis that are undertaken to answer an original research question. Primary research is the focus of much of this book and most courses on research methods. Primary research can be contrasted with **secondary research**, which is the summarizing or analysis of research already collected by others. An essay you write on a topic that summarizes what is already known about an issue or a published review of research findings in an area would be examples of secondary forms of research. Regardless of whether it is collected first- or examined second-hand, all research in the social sciences is conducted in a manner that attempts to reveal knowledge and increase our understanding, while minimizing the likelihood of errors. Generally, social research takes one of two broad forms, as described in the next section.

Applied and Basic Research

Applied research refers to scientific research that is conducted to specifically address a problem or issue. Applied research has a practical and often immediate intention, such as when it is initiated on behalf of an employer or business to learn how to improve services at a location or how to better advertise a specific product. Applied research may be carried out within post-secondary institutions to evaluate internal programs, policies, or services (e.g., How could we improve a registration process or service for students?). In addition, a government or social agency may sponsor applied research to evaluate a program, a policy, or a community service (e.g., Is this treatment program working or not working?). Finally, applied research is also carried out to find a solution to an issue of concern. For example, Genome Canada, a not-for-profit organization that manages applied research projects dealing with large-scale issues, is currently seeking applications for studies on ways to mitigate the effects of climate change and improve disease resistance in crops (Genome British Columbia, 2018).

Basic research, in contrast, is research that is conducted to advance knowledge for its own sake. Most of the research conducted in universities and published in academic journals is a form of basic research. Basic research usually stems from a researcher's own curiosity, interest, and area of expertise, as opposed to the commercial interests of a business or the agenda of an organization-sponsored project. Basic research can span an infinite number of topics and issues. For example, researchers interested in home births assisted by midwives studied the views and birthing experiences of 559 Canadian women who chose this practice (Janssen, Henderson, & Vedam, 2009); those interested in identity and appearance interviewed Canadian men about their experiences with cosmetic surgery (Ricciardelli & White, 2011); researchers wanting to learn more about how sexuality is constructed for older adults looked at portrayals of later-life online dating in Canadian newspapers and magazines (Wada, Clarke, & Rozanova, 2015); and researchers interested in patterns of illicit drug use following the cessation of injection drug use studied street-involved youth in Vancouver over time (Lake, Kerr, Nosova, Milloy, Wood, & DeBeck, 2018).

Research on the Net

Social Sciences and Humanities Research Council

The Social Sciences and Humanities Research Council (SSHRC) is a federal government agency that promotes research in the humanities and social sciences on a diverse range of social, cultural, economic, environmental, technological, and wellness issues (SSHRC, 2018). SSHRC funds basic research projects at post-secondary institutions through graduate scholarships, postdoctoral fellowship programs, and research grants. When you are entering a master's or doctoral program, you can apply to SSHRC for a potential scholarship to assist you financially while you design basic research. Since the awarding of scholarships is a highly competitive process, it might be helpful to note that SSHRC prioritizes research in certain areas (e.g., the experiences and aspirations of Indigenous peoples, emerging technologies, and new ways of learning in higher education). SSHRC also funds applied research through partnership development grants where industry partners with universities. For more information on the Social Sciences and Humanities Research Council and its funding, you can visit its website at www.sshrc-crsh.gc.ca.

Test Yourself

- What sets scientific research apart from other ways of knowing?
- How can social science methods reduce the risk of selective observation?
- What is social research?
- What is the main difference between basic and applied research?

GOALS OF SOCIAL RESEARCH

Social research is usually conducted to accomplish one of the following four goals: to explore, to describe, to explain, or to critically evaluate a phenomenon of interest.

Exploration

Exploratory research is undertaken to learn about an area of interest that is relatively new or not well understood or to find out more about an existing area using a novel approach. An underlying question of interest in an exploratory study centres on the notion of "What is X?" (where *X* can be anything of interest, such as "What is forced marriage?"). Data collected from frontline workers revealed that there are several kinds of forced marriages in Canada. For example, a person may be forced into marriage in a country of origin and then come to live with a spouse in Canada, or a person may be born in Canada or live in Canada and be forced into marriage by family members to someone already established in Canada (Bendriss, 2014).

Even areas of interest that are well established can benefit from the fresh perspective afforded by exploratory research, which Stebbins (2001) claims is designed to examine an issue using "broad" and "unspecialized terms." For example, Bansal and Eiselt (2004) conducted exploratory research to learn more about tourist motivation and planning in New Brunswick. Although previous research had already established various highly specialized reasons for travel, often linked to complex concepts such as "socioeconomic status," the authors opted for an exploratory approach to reassess vacation motives using five broad categories: climate, relaxation, adventure, personal, and education. The researchers selected these categories because they were readily amenable to field research and they would be easily understood by an average tourist (Bansal & Eiselt, 2004). As it turned out, many of the tourists vacationing in New Brunswick claimed they were primarily seeking adventure—an area in which vacation/tour companies might benefit from further exploratory research. Listed below are additional examples of research questions that underlie exploratory forms of research:

- What is the experience of maternal attachment like for mothers in Canadian stepfamilies? (Gosselin & Gosselin, 2016)
- What is the relationship between perceived and actual water quality in Newfoundland? (Ochoo, Valcour, & Sarkar, 2017)
- What factors affect individual food choice and availability in Inuit communities in Nunavut? (Mead, Gittelsohn, Kratzmann, Roaches, & Sharma, 2010)
- What barriers to employment are experienced by disabled Canadians? (Shier, Graham, & Jones, 2009)

Description

While most research has a descriptive component, **descriptive research** is specifically undertaken to establish the main traits or characteristics of a population or phenomenon. A question of interest within descriptive research is "What are the main features of X?" For example, McDonald and Reeder (1997) undertook descriptive research to learn more about obesity in Canada. By examining the body mass of Canadians between the ages of 18 and 74, the researchers were able to describe the prevalence of obesity in the adult population. Results showed that obesity increased with age, and that men had higher rates of obesity (35 percent) than women (27 percent). Additional examples of research questions examined using descriptive research include the following:

- What are Canadian athletes' experiences with and attitudes toward hazing behaviours? (Johnson, Guerrero, Holman, Chin, & Signer-Kroeker, 2018)
- What is the quality of the emotional health and well-being of Canadian caregivers for persons with health or addictions problems? (Slaunwhite, Ronis, Sun, & Peters, 2017)
- What are the social, health, and drug use characteristics of crack cocaine users in British Columbia? (Fischer, Rudzinski, Ivsins, Gallupe, Patra, & Krajden, 2010)
- What features describe the sexual offending committed by Canadian teachers? (Moulden, Firestone, Kingston, & Wexler, 2010)

Rookie athletes are often subjected to degrading forms of hazing.

Source: cherylholt/pixabay.com

Explanation

Explanatory research is conducted to clarify the variation found between groups on some dimension of interest. The central question underlying explanatory research is "why?" or "how?" and the goal is to explain an outcome. For example, in trying to explain why some people are more likely than others to become compulsive gamblers, Callan, Ellard, Shead, and Hodgins (2008) found support for a hypothesis that gambling served a justice-seeking function in certain people. That is, compulsive gamblers try to obtain rewards through gambling that they feel they deserve since they have not obtained success through more conventional means, such as earning a decent income and investing wisely over time.

In addition, explanatory research may be directed at better understanding the factors that influence or fail to influence some process, condition, or state of being. For example, Yang (2017) investigated the effects of a mandatory community service program on Ontario high school students' subsequent helping. Results showed increased volunteering during high school while in the program, but lower than anticipated volunteer efforts once students completed high school. Although the intent behind compulsory volunteering programs is to teach altruism, research shows that they, in fact, fail to positively impact long-term altruism. One explanation for this is a phenomenon known as "crowding out," where the intrinsic motivation to carry out a task is undermined by external rewards (Frey, 1997). Volunteering, then, is completed largely for grades and course expectations, not for the betterment of the recipients. The following are other examples of research questions from explanatory research:

- How does fluoride cessation impact tooth decay in children living in Alberta? (McLaren, Patterson, Thawer, Faris, McNeil, Potestio, & Shwart, 2017)
- How will most Canadians be able to maintain their standard of living in retirement? (Vettese, 2013)
- Why are US healthcare expenditures so different from Canadian healthcare expenditures? (Spithoven, 2011)
- Why don't boys like to read and why do girls outperform boys on Canadian reading assessment tests? (Canadian Council on Learning, 2009)

Evaluation

Evaluation research seeks to assess whether a program or policy is effective in reaching its desired goals and objectives. Central questions for evaluation research include "Is this policy working?" and/or "What is the impact of this program?" McDonald and colleagues (2009) evaluated a community-based group intervention strategy called Families and Schools Together (FAST), which was designed to help teenage mothers and their infants in 11 Canadian communities. Data collected from mothers and grandmothers before and after the intervention indicated an improvement in the original aims of the program, as a result of participation, including improved parent-child bonds, reduced stress and family conflict, and increased parental self-efficacy (McDonald et al., 2009). Evaluation research is sometimes more generally referred to as "critical research" when it is designed to assess an aspect of the social world rather than a program or policy. Examples of additional questions framed within evaluation research include the following:

- Is drug checking at a supervised injection facility in Vancouver a feasible intervention for reducing deaths caused by fentanyl overdoses? (Karamouzian et al., 2018)
- Does a health-promoting schools approach improve student well-being and health behaviours in elementary students in Nova Scotia? (McIsaac et al., 2017)
- Is methadone maintenance a cost-effective form of drug rehabilitation in Ontario? (Zaric, Brennan, Varenbut, & Daiter, 2013)
- Is the Continuing Medical Education program an effective approach for delivering road safety information to health professionals? (Dow & Jacques, 2012)

Test Yourself

- What is a central question of interest in exploratory research?
- Why is descriptive research undertaken?
- What central question underlies explanatory research?
- When would it be appropriate to use evaluation research?

QUALITATIVE AND QUANTITATIVE RESEARCH METHODS

Research methods are the specific tools or techniques used to carry out the research that obtains the information needed to answer questions of interest and achieve the goals discussed in the previous section. The information gathered through these techniques is collectively referred to as **data**. Chapters 6 through 10 each focus exclusively on specific data-gathering techniques used in the social sciences (e.g., experiments, surveys, unobtrusive methods, qualitative interviews, ethnography). At a broader level, consider for now that a **quantitative research method** is one that seeks to describe, explain, or evaluate some phenomenon using numerical data that are amenable to statistical analyses. In contrast, a **qualitative research method** is one that seeks to explore, interpret, explain, or evaluate a phenomenon of interest using non-numerical data, often in the form of words, patterns, and/or themes that are generally not amenable to statistical analyses. Let's look at both types in more detail, beginning with quantitative methods.

Quantitative Methods

Quantitative methods are often used to obtain information or data that can be counted or "quantified" in some way. The findings from a quantitative study usually tell us the percentage of people who feel a certain way about a topic, the number of times a certain event occurred, or the amount of time it took the average person to complete a task under certain conditions. The most commonly used quantitative methods are experiments and surveys, followed by a few unobtrusive methods. Experiments are studies carried out in carefully designed environments that allow researchers to test cause–effect relationships where one variable of interest is believed to be the cause and the other is believed to be the effect or outcome (see chapter 6). Surveys are studies used to gather people's views or opinions on a range of issues (see chapter 7). Unobtrusive methods are techniques that do not directly involve people as research participants in the data collection process (see chapter 8). For example, we can systematically observe people from a distance without asking them directly for information, we can conduct secondary data analysis on existing forms of primary data, and we can examine various social media such as television programs or song lyrics for the presence or absence of some phenomenon of interest (e.g., alcohol, violence, or gender stereotypes). Note that each of these methods will be discussed in detail in later chapters. For now, just try to associate these techniques with the quantitative realm of the research world.

Qualitative Methods

In contrast, qualitative methods are particularly useful for learning more about the nature or "quality" of some phenomenon of interest. Qualitative techniques underlie a desire to better understand how people are experiencing events and why people feel the way they do or why they do the things they do. The form of

Qualitative methods include observations in natural settings.

Source: Miss Nuchwara Tongrit/shutterstock.com

the data collected tends to be words as opposed to amounts or counts. Commonly used techniques include qualitative interviewing and ethnography, as well as un-obtrusive methods. Qualitative interviewing is used to gather in-depth informa-tion from the perspective of the participant to reveal meaning (e.g., what is it like to be a single parent of a child with special needs?) (see chapter 9). Ethnography is a multi-method approach that combines techniques such as participant obser-vation and qualitative interviewing to learn about a group in its natural setting (e.g., what can be learned about interactions among group members by joining a religious cult?) (see chapter 10). Finally, qualitative methods also include unobtru-sive methods such as content analysis, where the purpose is often exploratory and involves looking for patterns and themes; archival analysis, which involves look-ing at existing information including written documents (e.g., letters, records); historical analysis, which involves an examination of historical documents; and/ or secondary analysis of other phenomena that can be considered a data source, including traces left behind by people (e.g., garbage and graffiti). Refer to table 1.1 for a comparison and overview of the two main methods.

Qualitative versus Quantitative: An Unnecessary Divide

I do not wish to leave you with the impression that all research is qualitative or quantitative and that researchers necessarily should be of one type or the other. Re-search interests may be amenable to both quantitative and qualitative techniques,

Table 1.1: Overview of Qualitative and Quantitative Methods

	Method	
	Qualitative	**Quantitative**
Objective	• to learn about the nature of some phenomenon • to "qualify" or explain • to explore • to interpret	• to describe some phenomenon • to quantify • to count • to explain
Aim	• understanding • meaning	• description • cause–effect relationships
Focus	• human-centred	• objective reality
Research techniques	• qualitative interviews • ethnography/field research • unobtrusive methods (e.g., content analyses, naturalistic observation)	• experiments • surveys • unobtrusive methods (e.g., secondary analysis of existing data)
Data	• words • pictures • patterns • themes	• numerical • counts • ratings • amenable to statistical analyses

Source: Created by author

and some researchers may use both approaches within the same study. For example, Dr. Andrew Howell and I surveyed faculty and students at a Canadian university to determine views toward published student ratings of instruction. Using a primarily quantitative approach, we asked faculty and students to rate their level of agreement with items on a questionnaire to describe views (e.g., whether instructor ratings should be published and whether different forms of published ratings jeopardize instructor privacy). To provide answers, respondents mainly checked boxes that corresponded to their level of agreement with each statement (e.g., strongly disagree, disagree, neutral, agree, or strongly agree). Most of the data collected were coded into numbers and analyzed using descriptive and inferential statistics. Results indicated widespread support for disclosure of all forms of evaluation by students and widespread opposition from instructors (Howell & Symbaluk, 2001).

However, the survey also included open-ended items where respondents were asked to list advantages and disadvantages of published ratings. Faculty and student comments in their own words constituted qualitative data. Patterns and themes in the data highlighted the nature of potential benefits for students who, for example, were interested in learning more about an instructor's teaching style. Qualitative data also identified the main concerns of instructors, who, for example, worried that an instructor's reputation could be tarnished by a posted negative evaluation that might persist over time even if an instructor changed (Howell & Symbaluk, 2001).

Qualitative methods are not better or worse than quantitative ones. There is an ongoing and even sometimes highly contentious debate concerning the relative merit of quantitative versus qualitative methods, where some quantitative researchers dismiss qualitative approaches as being less scientific and qualitative researchers accuse quantitative approaches of being unable to tell us about the true nature of things. I, along with several other authors of textbooks on research methods, find this dichotomy to be unwarranted and unnecessary (e.g., see also Bouma, Ling, & Wilkinson, 2016; Palys & Atchison, 2014). While it is common practice to determine in advance whether you are using a more qualitative or quantitative approach, it is the nature of the research issue itself (e.g., an interest in understanding the experiences of a group versus a desire to quantify the prevalent views of a group on an issue), as well as many other aspects of any given study (e.g., the availability of resources, time restraints, and the willingness of the participants), that determine the exact method(s) used. Refer to chapter 11 for a comprehensive overview of the use of mixed methods and multiple methods within a single study.

Research in Action

The Blonde Mystique

The Blonde Mystique (Telefilm Canada, 2006) is a documentary that provides a light-hearted, fun look at research by showing us how just about any topic can underlie a research question, including whether there is such a thing as a "blonde mystique." Over the course of their study, three women set out to test whether a blonde mystique exists, using research techniques from interviews with men on the street, to field research conducted in bars, to staged roadside experiments. They even change their own hair colour to study how people treat them when they go from blonde to brunette or brunette to blonde!

Test Yourself

- Which type of research method typically produces numerical data?
- Which type of research method is best suited to revealing the meaning of events as experienced by individuals?
- Which type of research method utilizes experiments to test causal relationships?
- Which type of research approach is more appropriate for studying groups in natural settings?

CHAPTER SUMMARY

LO1 **Explain why it is important to learn about social research methods.**
Research methods are a practical means for acquiring knowledge and developing an informed opinion that is useful in a range of contexts, from everyday curiosity to skills that underlie most forms of employment.

LO2 **Identify various "ways of knowing" and note their limitations.**
Four common ways of knowing include the use of tradition, common sense, authority, and personal experience. While highly informative and convenient, sources of knowledge are also fraught with errors as we learn accurate and inaccurate information as part of tradition; common sense fails to hold true under many circumstances; authority figures often speak well beyond their level of experience; and personal experience is restricted to our recollections of observations.

LO3 **Recognize common errors in reasoning.**
Imprecise observation refers to the everyday errors we make as a function of our ability to take in, store, and later recall an overwhelming amount of information accurately. Illogical reasoning refers to decision making based on a failure to consider the most important sources of information. Overgeneralization is the tendency to assume a general pattern or trait exists based on a limited number of observations, while selective observation is the tendency to assume a general pattern exists based on factors other than objective frequency. Premature closure refers to a tendency to stop searching for necessary observations due to an erroneous belief that an answer has already been determined.

LO4   Define social research, distinguish between primary and secondary research, and differentiate between basic and applied research.

Social research is a process where a set of principles, outlooks, and ideas are combined with a collection of specific practices, techniques, and strategies to produce knowledge. Primary research refers to first-hand data collection and data analysis that are undertaken to answer an original research question. Secondary research refers to the summarizing or analysis of research already collected by others. Applied research refers to scientific research that is conducted to specifically address a problem, while basic research is conducted to advance knowledge for its own sake.

LO5   Explain the goals of research.

Social research is usually conducted to explore, to describe, to explain, or to critically evaluate a program or phenomenon of interest (i.e., evaluation or critical research). Exploratory research is carried out to learn more about an area of interest. Descriptive research is undertaken to establish the main traits of a population. Explanatory research is conducted to clarify the variation found between groups on some dimension of interest. Evaluation research assesses whether a program or policy is effective.

LO6   Differentiate between qualitative and quantitative research methods.

Quantitative research methods are techniques that seek to describe, explain, or evaluate a phenomenon of interest, while qualitative research methods are tools that seek to explore, interpret, explain, or evaluate a phenomenon of interest. Quantitative methods produce numerical data amenable to statistical analyses, while qualitative methods produce non-numerical data, often in the form of words, patterns, or themes.

RESEARCH REFLECTION

1. Identify one traditional belief or idea that was passed on to you from a family member or close friend as a form of advice. Are there any obvious limitations to that information as a means of knowing about the world? Do any of the common errors in reasoning apply to this example? If you were going to examine this assumption using a scientific approach, what is one technique you could use to test it in the real world? Describe how you would carry out such a study.

2. Suppose you were interested in studying homelessness in a large city such as Toronto, Montreal, Calgary, Vancouver, or Ottawa. Develop one research question you could attempt to answer in this study. Which of the four goals of social research is most closely aligned with the question you created? Defend your answer.

3. Starting with the general topic area of health, develop a specific research question to highlight each of the four distinct goals of social research. Which of the questions holds the most interest to you? Which research technique is best suited to gather data to answer your preferred question of interest?

LEARNING THROUGH PRACTICE

Objective: To familiarize students with social research

Directions:

1. Locate and print a scholarly article of interest based on primary research in an academic journal from a social science database (e.g., Social Sciences Citation Index, JSTOR, Web of Science, ScienceDirect, PsychINFO, SocINDEX with full text, Criminology: A SAGE Full-Text Collection, Family and Society Studies Worldwide, or Anthropology Plus).

2. Describe the social issue that underlies the research interest of the article. How is the main research question framed?

3. Are the researchers conducting mainly qualitative, mainly quantitative, or both types of research? How do you know?

4. Which main goal of social research does the objective of this study best align with? Explain your answer.

5. Describe one of the techniques used by the researchers to obtain information on their question of interest.

RESEARCH RESOURCES

1. For an overview of qualitative research techniques, I recommend van den Hoonaard, D. K. (2019). *Qualitative research in action: A Canadian primer* (3rd ed.). Don Mills, ON: Oxford University Press.

2. For an overview of quantitative research techniques, I recommend Cozby, P. C., & Bates, S. C. (2018). *Methods in behavioral research* (13th ed.). New York, NY: McGraw-Hill.

3. To find scholarly research articles, refer to Thomson Reuters' Social Sciences Citation Index. You can likely access this database for free through the library at the post-secondary institution where you are taking classes.

4. For the most comprehensive source of data on virtually all aspects of Canadian lives, refer to Statistics Canada, located at www.statcan.gc.ca.

NOTE

1. Retrieved October 2, 2018, from www.quotationspage.com.

CHAPTER 2

The Importance of Theory

There is nothing more practical than a good theory.
—Kurt Lewin, 1951, p. 169

Learning Objectives

After reading this chapter, students should be able to do the following:

LO1   Outline the main assumptions of positivist, interpretive, critical, and pragmatic paradigms.

LO2   Explain why decolonization is necessary for learning about Indigenous knowledges.

LO3   Define and differentiate between theoretical frameworks and theories.

LO4   Distinguish between deductive and inductive reasoning and explain how the role of theory differs in qualitative and quantitative research.

LO5   Formulate social research questions.

LO6   Explain the importance of a literature review.

LO7   Locate appropriate literature and evaluate sources of information found on the internet.

INTRODUCTION

In chapter 1, you were introduced to scientific reasoning as a desirable alternative to learning about the social world through tradition, common sense, authority, and personal experience. In addition, you learned to distinguish between basic and applied research, and that research methods are used to collect data for a variety of purposes (e.g., to explore, describe, explain, or evaluate some phenomenon). In this chapter, you will learn about paradigms that shape our views of social research and that there are alternative worldviews in the form of Indigenous knowledges, you will learn about theoretical frameworks, and you will find out about the importance of theory and prior research for informing the development of new research. Finally, this chapter helps you locate and evaluate sources of information you find in the library and on the internet.

INQUIRY PARADIGMS IN THE SOCIAL SCIENCES

At the most general level, a **paradigm** is a set of "basic beliefs" or a "worldview" that helps us make sense of the world, including our own place in it (Guba & Lincoln, 1994). Earl Babbie and Lance W. Roberts (2018) define a paradigm as "a theoretical perspective including a set of assumptions about reality that guide research questions" (p. 29). As a broad framework, a paradigm includes assumptions

Research findings may alter shared worldviews, bringing about what philosopher Thomas S. Kuhn (1962) termed a "paradigm shift."

Source: B Calkins/shutterstock.com

about the nature of knowledge (a branch of philosophy called epistemology), assumptions about the nature of reality or the way things are (a branch of philosophy called ontology), and assumptions about how we go about solving problems and gathering information (a system of principles or practices collectively known as methodology). The assumptions are interrelated in the sense that how one views the nature of reality (an ontological stance) influences beliefs about one's relationship to that reality (an epistemological stance) and how one would go about examining that reality (a methodological stance) (Guba & Lincoln, 1994). This will become clearer as we compare the assumptions of four distinct and competing inquiry paradigms.

Positivist Paradigm

French philosopher Auguste Comte (1798–1857) first used the term *social physics* (later called *sociology*) to describe a positivist science of society that could teach us about the social world through research and theorizing (Ritzer & Stepnisky, 2018). The **positivist paradigm** is a belief system aimed at discovering universal laws based on the assumption that a singular reality exists independent of individuals and their role in it. Positivism rests on a worldview like that of the natural sciences, which stresses objectivity and truth as discovered through direct empirical methods. Discounting subjective interpretations of events and accounts that cannot be proven by empirical tests, in its most extreme form, "only phenomen[a] and regularities confirmed by the senses (sight, hearing, etc.) can be accepted as knowledge" (Bryman & Bell, 2016, p. 9). The goal of positivism is to explain events and relationships via a search for antecedent causes that produce outcomes. Within a positivist paradigm, the search for empirical truth begins with what is already known about an area. From that starting point, probable causes are "deduced" using logical reasoning, and then theories are tested for accuracy. Systematic observation and experimental methods are commonly employed modes of inquiry and the data obtained are quantifiable.

Interpretive Paradigm

The **interpretive paradigm** (also called constructivism) arose in part as a critique of positivism for its failure to recognize the importance of subjectivity in human-centred approaches. The interpretive paradigm worldview rests on the assumption that reality is socially constructed in the form of mental representations created and recreated by people through their experiences and interactions in social contexts (Lincoln, Lynham, & Guba, 2018). As such, "multiple realities exist"

The interpretive paradigm emphasizes the constructed nature of reality for individuals.

Source: ljcor/pixabay.com

for any given individual (Guba, 1996), and these individual realities are largely "self-created" (Guba & Lincoln, 1994). The focus of the interpretive paradigm is on understanding individuals' perceptions of reality, including how events and interactions come to have meaning for them, rather than identifying objective phenomena or social facts that exist outside individuals and relationships. This generally necessitates a qualitative research strategy, such as ethnography, which brings the researcher into close contact with those being studied for prolonged periods of time; as a result, relationships develop and insight is gained from within those relationships. As Palys and Atchison (2014) put it, "good theory is not imposed; rather, it emerges from direct observation and contact with people in context" (p. 23).

Critical Paradigm

Another worldview that emphasizes interpretation and understanding is the **critical paradigm**. The critical paradigm rests on an assumption that "human nature operates in a world that is based on a struggle for power" (Lincoln et al., 2018, p. 115). The critical paradigm focuses specifically on determining the role power plays in the creation of knowledge, frequently using qualitative strategies. The critical approach is more of a critique concerning how and why particular views become the dominant ones and how privilege and oppression interact, often as the result of defining characteristics such as gender, race and ethnicity, and social class (Lincoln et al., 2018). Beyond examining inequality, there is also an emphasis on "praxis," whereby scholars provide knowledge that can help to end powerlessness (Symbaluk & Bereska, 2019). To the extent that research can identify ways in which groups are disadvantaged and identify the causes of subordination, it can also be used to help resolve the inequities. Various theoretical perspectives and theories stem from a critical-interpretative stance including feminism, critical race theory, cultural studies, and queer theory.[1]

Pragmatic Paradigm

Finally, in contrast to the dichotomy between the objectivity of positivism and the subjectivity of interpretive approaches, an impartial outlook is offered by a more recent paradigm called the **pragmatic paradigm**. The pragmatic view "arises out of actions, situations, and consequences rather than antecedent conditions" and is concerned with what is the most practical route to fully understanding a problem and finding a solution that will work for that problem at that time (Creswell & Creswell, 2018, pp. 10–11). This problem-centred worldview is not based in any philosophy, nor does it necessitate the use of a certain form of reasoning or research technique. It does, however, emphasize the importance of methodology for solving problems and advocates for the use of combined qualitative and quantitative approaches for a more complete understanding. Historically, combining qualitative and quantitative approaches has proven problematic given the opposing assumptions upon which each approach is based. The pragmatic paradigm offers

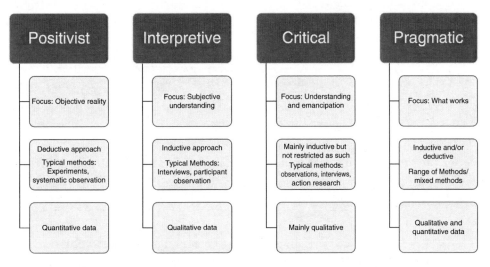

Figure 2.1: Comparison of Inquiry Paradigms in the Social Sciences

Source: Created by author

a solution to the dichotomy. As John W. Creswell and J. David Creswell (2018) note, "pragmatists do not see the world as an absolute unity. In a similar way, mixed methods researchers look to many approaches for collecting and analyzing data rather than subscribing to any one way (e.g., quantitative or qualitative)" (p. 10). Thus, the starting point is the issue or research problem, which itself suggests the most applicable means for further research exploration. Mixed-methods approaches to research that are grounded in a pragmatic paradigm are discussed in more detail in chapter 11.

Test Yourself

- Which paradigm seeks to discover universal laws?
- Which paradigm is most concerned with objective reality?
- Which paradigm is problem-centred?
- Which paradigm rests on the assumption that reality is socially constructed?

INDIGENOUS KNOWLEDGES AND RESEARCH PARADIGMS

It is important to note that the paradigms discussed thus far have philosophical and research underpinnings based on dominant Euro-Western modes of thought. Indigenous scholars highlight the value of reclaiming alternative worldviews stemming from the silenced cultural perspectives of groups that are marginalized, underprivileged, and/or have suffered European colonization (e.g., see Battiste, 2000; Belanger, 2018; Smith, 2012; Warrior, 1995). "**Indigenous knowledges** are diverse learning processes that come from living intimately with the land, working with the resources surrounding the land base, and the relationships that it has fostered over time and place. These are physical, social, and spiritual relationships that continue to be the foundations of its world views and ways of knowing that define their relationships with each other and others" (Battiste, 2013, p. 33). These Indigenous, sometimes called "traditional," knowledges contain a wealth of pragmatic lessons in diverse areas from environmental conservation to cultural protocols and familial relationships.

The loss of language stemming from forced assimilation via structural mechanisms such as residential schools and Eurocentric educational systems poses challenges for the maintenance of Indigenous knowledges, though elders continue to play a vital role in the verification and transmission of Indigenous cultures.

Elders play an important role in the verification and transmission of Indigenous cultures and knowledges.

Source: ©MacEwan University/Roxanne Tootoosis, Indigenous Knowledge Keeper and Facilitator, performing a smudging with Keestin O'Dell and Shawn McCarthy-Daniels at the Metis & Treaty 6 Flag Raising on October 18, 2017.

Note that researchers and the methods used to research Indigenous knowledges have historically been mainly non-Indigenous, and hence even the discourse of the colonized is shaped "through imperial eyes" (Smith, 2012). By employing decolonized methods, involving Indigenous researchers, including Indigenous peoples as active participants in research processes, listening to the teachings of elders, and recognizing the role that non-Indigenous researchers and Western methodologies have played in shaping the discourse on colonized Others, we can begin to remove the Euro-centric lens. The term *colonized Other* is used here to refer to Indigenous peoples in Canada who have experienced European colonization, but it can also be used more collectively to include those who are "disenfranchised" and "dispossessed" elsewhere in the world (e.g., those living in marginalized communities in underdeveloped countries) as described by Chilisa (2012, p. 12).

Decolonization is not one type of methodology, but rather is "a process of conducting research in such a way that the worldviews of those who have suffered a long history of oppression and marginalization are given space to communicate from their frames of reference" (Chilisa, 2012, p. 14). For example, instead of asking volunteers to complete a questionnaire worded by the researcher to learn about participants' views and experiences as prescribed by traditional social science methods, a former student of mine named Reith Charlesworth (2016) spent several months developing relationships and establishing trust with program attendees before participating in a *sharing circle* she co-facilitated with an Indigenous social worker. The sharing circle included a feast and provided the opportunity for women to tell stories that ultimately helped Reith better understand social and structural barriers experienced by young Indigenous mothers in a parenting program at iHuman Youth Society in Edmonton, Alberta.[2]

Since Indigenous knowledge structures encompass a dynamic array of beliefs and lived experiences held by various individuals identifying with vastly different groups in many different locations, it is difficult to identify common features. The United Nations Educational, Scientific, and Cultural Organization defines local and Indigenous knowledge as the "understandings, skills and philosophies developed by societies with long histories of interaction with their natural surroundings. For rural and Indigenous Peoples, local knowledge informs decision-making about fundamental aspects of day to day life. This knowledge is integral to a cultural complex that also encompasses language, systems of classification, resource use practices, social interactions, ritual and spirituality" (UNESCO, 2017). In her book on Indigenous methodologies, Margaret Kovach (2010) notes, "when considering tribal epistemologies, there are many entry points, one of which is commentary on its holistic quality. Descriptive words associated with Indigenous epistemologies include interactional and interrelational, broad-based, whole, inclusive, animate, cyclical, fluid, and spiritual. Tribal knowledge is pragmatic and ceremonial, physical and metaphysical. Indigenous cultures have sophisticated and complex cultural practices to access that which comes both from the ordinary and extraordinary. It is difficult to define, deconstruct, or compartmentalize the different aspects of knowing ('science,' spirit, inward knowing) within an Indigenous context" (p. 56). Whereas the aim of a positivist paradigm is to discover universal laws, an Indigenous research paradigm seeks to challenge colonized ways of thinking and to employ decolonized research methods that enable a respectful reclaiming of Indigenous cultures and knowledges. Because Indigenous knowledges are largely maintained through oral transmission and cultural practices, Indigenous methodologies also include ceremonies and formal protocols, and they are amenable to narrative inquiry as in the case of sharing circles and storytelling (Kovach, 2010). When it comes to employing Indigenous research methods, the fundamental point to remember is that the research process and the resulting data and knowledge stemming from it are integrally based on "relational actions"—that is, the personal relationships and connections that are formed with Indigenous communities based on trust (Kovach, 2018).

- What are Indigenous knowledges?
- In research, what does decolonization mean?

THEORETICAL FRAMEWORKS AND THEORIES

Positivist, interpretive, critical, and pragmatic paradigms all offer a broad worldview from which theoretical frameworks emerge. **Theoretical frameworks** are perspectives based on core assumptions that provide a foundation for examining the social world at different levels. Theoretical frameworks that operate at the **macro level** tend to focus on "larger social forces," while those dealing with the **micro level** are aimed at understanding "individual experiences and choices" (Symbaluk & Bereska, 2019, p. 4).

Within the discipline of sociology, the functionalist, conflict, symbolic interactionist, feminist, and postmodern frameworks provide different lenses from which we can view society. The functionalist framework is a macro-level perspective that views society as being made up of certain structures—such as the family, education, and religion—that are essential for maintaining social order and stability. For example, a primary function of the family is to provide for the social, emotional, and economic well-being of its members and to serve as a key agent of socialization. The functionalist framework is rooted in positivism in its focus on observables in the form of social facts and universal truths. The conflict framework is also a macro-level perspective, but it is rooted in the critical paradigm in its examination

Source: ©Mike Flanagan, www.Cartoonstock.com

of power and its emphasis on the prevalence of inequality in society as groups compete for scarce resources. Karl Marx (1818–1883), considered a key founder of this perspective, emphasized the central role of the economy in the creation of conflict and explained how workers in society are exploited and alienated under systems of capitalism (Ritzer & Stepnisky, 2018).

The symbolic interactionist framework is a micro-level perspective attributed to the early work of sociologists George Herbert Mead (1863–1931) and Herbert Blumer (1900–1987). The symbolic interactionist framework depicts society as consisting of individuals engaged in a variety of communications based on shared understandings (Symbaluk & Bereska, 2019). The emphasis here is on how individuals create meaning using symbols and language. Note how this framework emerges from interpretivism, with its emphasis on the importance of subjective meaning for individuals that is constructed and interpreted within interactions. For example, although two siblings in a familial union understand and relate to each other based on common features, such as a shared language and upbringing, they also each experience and recall events somewhat differently, based on their unique perspectives and relations toward one another. The symbolic interactionist perspective often guides qualitative researchers as they design strategies for uncovering meaning in groups and contexts.

With roots in the critical paradigm, the feminist framework[3] rests on the premise that men and women should be treated equally in all facets of social life (e.g., family, employment, law, and policy). The feminist framework includes a diverse range of perspectives (e.g., radical, socialist, post-colonial), operates at both the micro and macro levels, and is especially helpful for demonstrating ways in which society is structured by gender and how gender roles differentially impact males and females. For example, feminist scholars are quick to point out that women in relationships with men continue to adhere to traditional gender role expectations, doing more than their share of housework and experiencing less free time compared to their partners (e.g., Bianchi, 2011; Guppy & Luongo, 2015). Even in egalitarian relationships (based on equality in principle) where both partners are Canadian academics working outside the home, women assume more of the caregiving and household obligations at the expense of work-life balance (Wilton & Ross, 2017).

Finally, emerging post–World War II, the postmodern framework emphasizes the ways in which society has changed dramatically, particularly in relation to technological advances. The postmodern framework speaks out against singular monolithic structures and forces. It traces the intersectional features of inequality, including race, class, and gender, and focuses specifically on the effects of the digital age. This framework complicates dualistic boundaries between the micro and macro (arguing that they are one and the same) and calls into question the singular truths of earlier frameworks such as Marxism and functionalism. Postmodern perspectives are especially helpful for guiding research in areas of media literacy, globalization, and environmental studies.

Drilling down another layer, within broader theoretical perspectives, we can locate particular theories. Within the functionalist framework, for example, we find Robert Merton's (1938) strain theory of deviance, which explains how people adapt when there is a discrepancy between societal goals (what we are supposed to aspire to) and the legitimate means for obtaining them. Or, within the symbolic interactionist perspective, we can locate Edwin Lemert's (1951) labelling theory of deviance, which explains a process whereby people may come to view themselves as lifelong deviants. Theories are discussed in more detail in the next section.

Test Yourself

- Which level of theorizing focuses on broad social forces?
- How does a theoretical framework help us to examine the social world?

THE ROLE OF THEORY IN RESEARCH

A **theory** "is a set of propositions intended to explain a fact or a phenomenon" (Symbaluk & Bereska, 2019, p. 9). The propositions are usually expressed as statements that reflect the main assumptions of the theory. For example, Edwin Sutherland's (1947) differential association theory is a theory about crime, and it is explained in nine propositions. To give you a sense of the theory, the first proposition is that "criminal behaviour is learned"; the second is that "criminal behaviour is learned in interactions with other persons in a process of communication" (p. 6). Taken together, the propositions in differential association theory explain how crime is learned through interactions with others in much the same way as non-criminal behaviour is learned. That is, members of small groups with whom we spend time and who we feel are important may teach us the techniques and motives needed to develop criminal tendencies.

Deductive Forms of Reasoning

Theory doesn't happen in isolation from research; it can both inform the research process and develop from it. Theory that informs the research process is known as deductive reasoning. **Deductive reasoning** is a "theory-driven approach that typically concludes with [empirical] generalizations based on research findings" (Symbaluk & Bereska, 2019, p. 24). A deductive approach to social research is often a "top-down" linear one that begins with a research idea that is grounded in theory. A **hypothesis** or "testable research statement that includes at least two variables" is derived from the theory and this sets the stage for data collection (Symbaluk & Bereska, 2019, p. 28). A **variable** is a "categorical concept for properties of people or entities that can differ and change" (Symbaluk & Bereska, 2019, p. 24; as discussed in more detail in chapter 4). In a study on crime, criminal behaviour (e.g., the presence or absence of it) or a certain type of crime is likely to be a main variable of interest, along with another variable regularly associated with crime, such as age, gender, or race. For example, based on a theory of aggression, a hypothesis could be that men are more likely than women to commit physical assaults.

Testing Hypotheses Derived from Theories

Based on the tenets of Sutherland's (1947) differential association theory, Reiss and Rhodes (1964) "deduced" that delinquent boys are likely to engage in the same acts of deviance as their closest friends, since these are the people from whom they learn the techniques, motives, and definitions favourable to committing crimes. Specifically, they tested a hypothesis that the probability of an individual committing a delinquent act (e.g., auto theft, an assault, and vandalism) would be dependent upon his two closest friends also committing that act. The researchers looked at six different delinquent acts among 299 triads (i.e., groups of three), wherein each boy reported on his delinquency and indicated whether he committed the act alone or in the presence of others. In support of the theory, Reiss and Rhodes (1964) found that boys who committed delinquent acts were more likely to have close friends that committed the same acts. Figure 2.2 summarizes the logic of a typical research process based on deductive reasoning.

Inductive Forms of Reasoning

An **inductive** approach is more "bottom-up," beginning with observations and ending with the discovery of patterns and themes that are usually informed by theory or help establish and thereby "induce" new theory (see figure 2.3).

For example, Lowe and McClement (2011) examined the experience of spousal bereavement through interviews with young Canadian women whose husbands passed away. Over the course of data collection, the researchers identified various common themes including "elements of losses" such as the loss of companionship

Figure 2.2: A Research Process Based on Deductive Reasoning

Source: Created by author

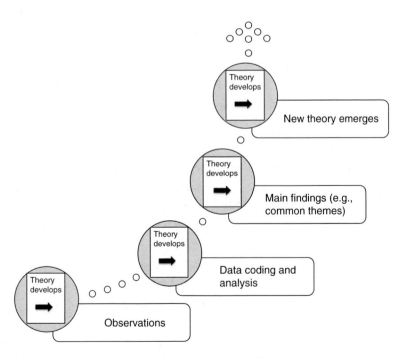

Figure 2.3: A Research Process Based on Inductive Reasoning

Source: Created by author

and the loss of hopes and dreams for the future. They also identified a notion of "who am I?" as the widows relayed their attempts to redefine themselves as single, in relation to other men, with their friends, and as parents. Although the lived experience of young Canadian widows as a specific group of interest had not been previously explored, the researchers interpreted their findings within the context of previous studies and theoretical frameworks, such as Bowman's (1997) earlier research on facing the loss of dreams and Shaffer's (1993) dissertation research on rebuilding identity following the loss of a spouse. Lowe and McClement (2011) also identified the importance of making connections through memories as a means of adapting, suggesting a direction for additional research and the potential for an eventual theory on the development of relationships following the loss of a spouse.

The Role of Theory in Quantitative and Qualitative Research

Note that the role and use of theory differs depending on whether the study is quantitative (i.e., based on deductive reasoning) or qualitative (i.e., based on inductive reasoning). Recall from chapter 1 that qualitative research often seeks to provide an in-depth understanding of a research issue from the perspective of those who are affected first-hand. The research process begins with an interest in an area such as cannabis use and a research question (e.g., What do parents perceive their role to be in the education of cannabis use?). Data collection is often undertaken through a technique such as qualitative interviews, where researchers ask open-ended questions to learn as much as possible from interviewees. For example, Haines-Saah, Mitchell, Slemon, and Jenkins (2018) asked parents of adolescent drug users what their experiences were like talking to their children about drug use. Theory is usually brought into an analysis to help make sense of the responses collected. In some cases, new theory develops out of the research findings. The "discovery of theory from data systematically obtained from social research" is better known as **grounded theory** (Glaser & Strauss, 2007, p. 2) since it is intricately linked to the data and context within which it developed. In most instances of qualitative research, theory plays a central role at various stages (e.g., in the formulation of the research question, in the initial stages of data coding, and especially toward the end of the data-analysis process). Findings from the cannabis study were interpreted in theoretical frameworks of risk and responsibility, as parents discussed cannabis use largely from a health narrative of drugs negatively impacting a developing brain, or a blame narrative where parents viewed themselves as the primary agents of prevention (Haines-Saah, Mitchell, Slemon, & Jenkins, 2018).

Qualitative research is a good starting point for learning about existing resources (or lack thereof) for assisting parents in the prevention of cannabis abuse among youth.

Source: angie3888/pixabay.com

In contrast, theory is the starting point for most quantitative studies. On one hand, a theory provides a set of interrelated ideas that organize the existing knowledge in a meaningful way and help to explain it (Cozby & Bates, 2018). For example, demographic transition theory helps to identify universal stages of population change as countries progress from pre-industrial societies through to post-industrial economies (Landry, 1934; Notestein, 1945). In countries characterized by the more advanced industrial stage of development, birth rates are low, corresponding to people having fewer children due to various considerations (e.g., birth control, female participation in the workforce, reliance on exported manufactured goods, greater emphasis on higher educational attainment). Despite the specificity of economic and social issues that vary from one country to the next, we can still identify broader commonalities such as a declining birth rate coupled with an already low death rate in all countries that have reached the industrial stage of development, including Canada. Hence, this early theory is still useful today for explaining differences between countries in early industrial, industrial, and post-industrial stages of development.

In addition, a theory provides a focal point that draws our attention to issues and events in a manner that helps to generate new interest and knowledge (Cozby & Bates, 2018). For example, conflict theorists showed us how capitalism and its focus on economic productivity is linked to major environmental issues, including the high extraction of natural resources and the high accumulation of waste

Conflict theories help us appreciate how capitalism plays a central role in current environmental crises.

Source: Skeeze/pixabay.com

(Schnaiberg, 1980). Schnaiberg's early framing of capitalism as a "treadmill of production" spawned additional interest in the study of modern industry, highlighting ways in which environmental issues are constructed as "proeconomic" measures in part because of alliances formed between capitalists, workers, and the state (Gould, Pellow, & Schnaiberg, 2008). Conflict theorists now direct our attention to the capitalist "treadmill of accumulation," which, in its reliance on ever-increasing amounts of expansion and exploitation, may render any attempts at sustainable capitalism unattainable from an environmental standpoint (Foster, Clark, & York, 2010).

Using theory as a starting point necessitates the development of specific propositions and the prior classification of key concepts and assumptions before data collection begins. As Mathew David and Carole D. Sutton (2011) explain, "there are advantages and disadvantages here. Those who seek to classify their qualities prior to data collection can be accused of imposing their own priorities, while those who seek to allow classifications to emerge during the research process are thereby unable to use the data collection period to test their subsequent theories. They too can then be accused of imposing their own priorities because it is hard to confirm or disprove their interpretations as no 'testing' has been done" (p. 92). You will learn more about the criteria used to evaluate research in chapter 4. For now, consider that both approaches, while different, have equal merit and drawbacks. Inductive and deductive approaches are probably best viewed as

different components of the same research cycle, with some researchers beginning with theories and ending with observations, and others doing the reverse
(Wallace, 1971).

Research on the Net

SocioSite

SocioSite is an online social science information system that is based at the
University of Amsterdam and was initiated and maintained until 2018 by the
now-deceased Albert Benschop. Here, you can explore sociological theories
and perspectives as well as find links to research centres, data archives, associations, and a multitude of resources on a range of social issues (e.g., gender
studies, population studies, research methodology and statistics, power, poverty, and racism). For an online tour of various internet resources on social
theories and perspectives, visit the SocioSite at www.sociosite.net.

Test Yourself

- What is theory?
- What does a hypothesis contain?
- In what ways is a research process based on deductive reasoning diffe-
  rent from one based on inductive reasoning?
- How do the role and use of theory differ in a qualitative versus quantita-
  tive study?
- What is grounded theory?

FORMULATING RESEARCH QUESTIONS

Although most of this chapter has focused on the role of theory for guiding the
development of research and helping to inform research outcomes, research begins
even before this, with a general area of interest. Every research study begins with
a topic of interest. As a general worldview can be narrowed into a specific theory,
a general area of interest can be shaped into a specific research question. Think
about the last time you were asked to write an essay on a topic of interest or, if you
are considering continuing your studies into graduate school, what a general area
of interest might entail. For a student in sociology, a broad area of interest could be

the family, gender and sexualities, deviance, globalization, or social inequality. A student in psychology is more likely to consider the areas of developmental psychology, cognition, neuropsychology, or clinical testing, to name a few. Someone in anthropology may have a starting interest that lends itself more to archaeology, physical anthropology, cultural anthropology, or linguistics.

Locating a Topic of Interest

Within a broad area of interest, there are topics or issues that are focus points for research. For example, a sociologist specializing in social inequality might wish to learn more about the distribution of poverty in Canada or the barriers to housing experienced by those who are homeless. A developmental psychologist may be studying the intellectual, emotional, or perceptual development of children. Someone in anthropological linguistics might be interested in the evolution of language dialects or the loss of a mother tongue over time. Regardless of the topic you choose, your research interest is likely to centre on social groups (e.g., homeless people, children with developmental delays, Indigenous peoples who speak an endangered language) or social structures, policies, and processes that affect groups (e.g., barriers to housing, definitions of poverty, cannabis legislation, health benefits coverage).

Framing an Interest into a Social Research Question

Recall from chapter 1 that a social research question is designed to explore, describe, explain, or critically evaluate a topic of interest. This means as you develop your topic of interest, you need to consider how the wording of the question suggests the most appropriate course of action for answering it. A **social research question** is "a question about the social world that is answered through the collection and analysis of firsthand, verifiable, empirical data" (Schutt, 2019, p. 30). A question beginning with "What is it like to . . ." often implies an exploratory purpose, inductive reasoning, and a qualitative research method. A question beginning with "Why" may presuppose a search for causes, and this is generally undertaken for an explanatory purpose based on deductive reasoning and a quantitative method, such as an experiment. Alternatively, "Why" might also imply inductive reasoning that is designed to get the essence of a first-hand experience using a qualitative approach. Research questions that are designed to evaluate a program or service are likely to be formulated along the lines of "Is this working?" Program evaluations are often based on qualitative methods, but the approaches and methods vary considerably and may include mixed methods, depending on the nature of the program or policy. Descriptive studies, often resting on a research

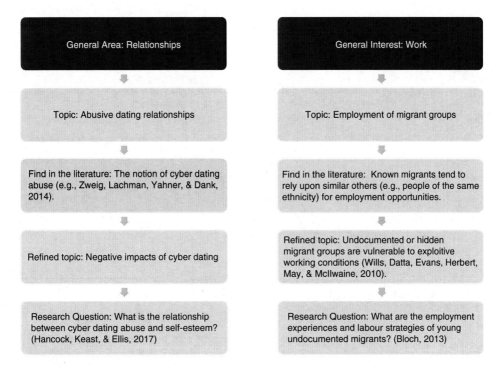

Figure 2.4: Developing an Area of Interest into a Research Question

Source: Created by author

question such as "What are its main features?," tend to be heavily represented in the quantitative realm (especially when the data are gathered through surveys). However, like evaluation research, descriptive studies are amenable to qualitative methods, especially in the case of field observation, which can produce highly descriptive forms of data.

Framing an interest is not a process that occurs instantly; rather it is one that you develop over time, eventually shaping your interest into a manageable research question that will direct a study that contributes to the existing body of knowledge. You will need to start with a general area, select a topic, issue, or focus within that area, and then look at the literature before refining your topic into a central social research question. Figure 2.4 provides two examples of the progression from a general area to a more specific question.

Test Yourself

- What does a research study begin with?
- What is a social research question?

THE IMPORTANCE OF A LITERATURE REVIEW

Just as every study originates with a topic of interest, every research-based study that is published in an academic journal is based on at least one central research question. The odds are very high that you will be able to find existing research on any topic you wish to learn more about. In fact, if you plan to conduct research, you will need to be familiar with what is already known about your research interest *before* you finalize your research question. It is important that you at least examine the literature before you commit to a specific research question. You are likely to modify your research question once you learn more about the topic from a literature review.

A literature review is essential for these reasons:

1. First, a literature review tells you how much has already been done in this area. For example, if you are interested in carrying out a study on the portrayal of gender stereotypes in the media, it is important for you to know that you are going to be delving into an area that has been heavily researched for decades. There are literally millions of previous studies on the gender stereotypes in movies, on television, in magazines, and on the internet. In this case, your research question would not be exploratory in nature. One of your next steps with this topic would be to narrow your focus (e.g., perhaps you are more interested in male stereotypes portrayed in magazine advertisements).

2. Second, a literature review helps familiarize you with what is already known in the area. Continuing with an interest in stereotyped depictions of males, the literature can help you learn more about the construction of masculinity and how the male body is depicted in advertising. For example, Mishkind, Rodin, Silberstein, & Striegel-Moore (1986) note that advertising has increasingly come to celebrate a young, lean, and highly muscular body. This helps you choose an area that most interests you and that you can build upon with your own research (or that you can identify as an area of future research).

3. Third, a literature review helps you understand the debates and main points of interest within an area of study. Existing literature can inform you about how the portrayal of gender stereotypes in the media can lead people to become dissatisfied with their body image or engage in extreme practices and measures designed to obtain an ideal body image (e.g., dieting, fitness, cosmetic surgery). The literature can also help you understand similarities and differences in the ways in which men and women

are portrayed, or how depictions of men have changed over time. These considerations may further shape the direction you elect to take with a current or future research project.

4. Fourth, a literature review highlights what still needs to be done in an area of interest. By examining previous research, you can find out researchers' suggestions for additional studies, where replications would be helpful, or areas that still need to be addressed. The discussion section at the end of most academic articles typically includes a few sentences that explicitly address how the current study could have been improved upon and/or point out a direction for future research. This is where you will obtain a sense of how you could design a study that builds on the existing literature but also contributes something new.

5. Lastly, a literature review can help you define important concepts and establish guidelines for how you will need to carry out your own study. For example, if you wish to clarify how male bodies are shown in magazine advertisements, it would be practical to locate examples by other researchers that have already established standard ways to describe and code the body of a central character in a magazine advertisement.

Test Yourself

-   In what ways is a literature review essential in the development of a research question?

LOCATING RELEVANT LITERATURE

Resist the temptation to simply search the internet with your preferred browser for any available resources you can find on your topic of interest. Search engines prioritize links that are from paid sponsors, so the resources that appear first are likely not the most relevant or even appropriate references for your area of interest. In addition to commercial interests, the internet also suffers from a lack of quality control; the information you glean from web pages and articles you find on the internet can be obsolete, and worse, fraught with errors.

Searching for Books

The best sources of information for a literature review include periodicals, e-books, books, and government documents located in or accessed through a library in a post-secondary institution. You can probably browse an online catalogue system for your post-secondary institution's library from any computer, if you can access the internet and you are officially registered as a student. The library home page will direct you to library resources and provide you with more specific instructions on how to search for holdings by subject, title, and/or author. Subject areas tend to correspond with main concepts or key words in an area of interest. If you find you are obtaining too many resources using a general search term, try combining two terms joined by *and*. For example, if you try searching for a book using the combined subject search terms *male and stereotypes*, you will probably locate a list of starting resources. If there are more than 50 books on this topic, you might try *male and stereotypes and media* to narrow your search a bit further. Conversely, if you are finding too few resources with even just one search term, try using two concepts joined by *or* to broaden the search.

Searching for Periodicals

Periodicals (including magazines, newspapers, and scholarly journals) are publications that contain articles written by different authors. Periodicals are released at regular intervals such as daily, weekly, monthly, semi-annually, or annually. Popular press periodicals (e.g., *Maclean's, Reader's Digest*, newspapers, and news websites) contain articles that are less scientific and more general-interest focused than scholarly articles published in peer-reviewed periodicals. Scholarly journals published by academic and professional organizations (e.g., universities) are the form of periodical most often cited by your instructors as credible sources for you to use in writing essays and research reports. Scholarly journals contain articles on basic research authored by academics and researchers with expertise in their respective areas. Articles found in scholarly journals have undergone considerable scrutiny in a competitive selection process that rests on peer review and evaluation prior to publication. This helps to ensure that only up-to-date, high-quality research based on sound practices makes it to the publication stage. Examples of Canadian sociological periodicals include the *Canadian Journal of Sociology* and the *Canadian Review of Sociology and Anthropology*. Note that there are hundreds of periodicals spanning a range of related disciplines (e.g., *Canadian Journal of Criminology, Canadian Journal of Economics, Canadian Journal of Political Science,* and *Canadian Psychology*) and more specialized topics (e.g., *Sex Roles, Child Abuse and Neglect, Contemporary Drug Problems, Educational Gerontology*).

In many cases, you can access journals online through a database. If it is available in "full-text," you can usually download the entire article onto a storage device, so you can later retrieve it for further reading. Comprehensive databases for locating articles on research in the social sciences include Academic Search Premier, Social Sciences Full Text, PsycINFO, JSTOR, and the Social Sciences Citation Index. For example, Academic Search Premier is dubbed the most comprehensive multidiscipline full-text database, containing more than 9,300 full-text journals on a range of subjects, including psychology, religion, and philosophy (EBSCO Industries, 2018).

Research in Action

Evaluating Sources Found on the Internet

It is not enough to simply locate sources of information on an area of interest and assume that you have appropriate materials for learning about the area of interest. While academic journals undergo a peer-review process that helps to provide a check on the quality, accuracy, and currency of the published materials, the internet has little or no quality control. If you use the internet to find sources of information, such as web pages with links to various articles and other resources, it is important to evaluate that information before using it to inform your research. MacEwan University's (2018) library suggests you assess the quality of information you find on the internet by answering the following questions about the site's source, timeliness, accuracy, and relevance (i.e., its STAR quality information).

Source

Choose sources that are credible and relatively objective.

- Who is the author?
- Who is making the information available?
- What are their credentials or qualifications?
- What makes them an authority on this subject?
- Is the source biased or expressing opinion?

Timeliness

If you are working on a current event, or a science or health topic, you will need something that has been published recently. If you are working on a historical topic, currency may not be as important.

- When was the information published or last updated?
- Does the date of the publication matter to your assignment?

Accuracy

Look for information or references that can be verified.

- Is the information free of spelling, grammatical, and technical errors?
- Where did the information come from?

Relevance

Choose information that will help you build a strong argument, illuminate concepts, or provide the best evidence.

- Does this information meet the requirements of your assignment?
- How will it help answer the question you are asking?

Source: ©MacEwan University, 2018. "Evaluating Information Sources." Retrieved November 5, 2018, from https://library.macewan.ca/research-help/evaluating

Test Yourself

- What are the best sources of information for a literature review?

CHAPTER SUMMARY

LO1   **Outline the main assumptions of positivist, interpretative, critical, and pragmatic paradigms.**

The positivist paradigm emphasizes objectivity and the importance of discovering truth using empirical methods. The interpretive paradigm stresses the importance of subjective understanding and discovering meaning as it exists for the people experiencing it. The critical paradigm focuses on the role of power in the creation of knowledge. The pragmatic paradigm begins with a research problem and determines a course of action for studying it based on what seems most appropriate given that research problem.

LO2   **Explain why decolonization is necessary for learning about Indigenous knowledges.**

For Indigenous knowledges to be derived from Indigenous sources in an authentic and respectful manner, those who have suffered colonization need to be given the space to communicate on their own terms from their frames of reference, as opposed to trying to obtain information via research methods that are based on Euro-Western influences.

LO3   **Define and differentiate between theoretical frameworks and theories.**

Theoretical frameworks are perspectives based on core assumptions that provide a foundation for examining the social world at different levels. For example, theoretical frameworks at the macro level tend to focus on broader social forces, while those at the micro level emphasize individual experiences. Theories develop from theoretical perspectives, and they include propositions that are intended to explain a fact or phenomenon of interest.

LO4   **Distinguish between deductive and inductive reasoning and explain how the role of theory differs in qualitative and quantitative research.**

Deductive reasoning is a top-down theory-driven approach that concludes with generalizations based on research findings. Inductive reasoning is a bottom-up approach that begins with observations and typically ends with theory construction. Inductive approaches to reasoning guide qualitative research processes, while deductive approaches guide the stages of quantitative research. Theory tends to be the starting point for quantitative research, while it is interspersed throughout and emphasized more in the later stages of qualitative research.

LO5   **Formulate social research questions.**

Based on a broad area of interest and a careful literature review, a researcher eventually shapes a research interest into a social research question, which is a question about the social world that is answered through the collection and analysis of data. For example, a researcher might begin with an interest in gender that develops into an examination of the effects of body size on income for male and female workers.

LO6   **Explain the importance of a literature review.**

A literature review is the starting point for formulating social research questions. A literature review helps to identify what is already known and still needs to be done in an area of interest. A literature review also points out debates and issues in an area of interest, along with the most relevant concepts and means for going about studying the issue in more depth.

LO7   **Locate appropriate literature and evaluate sources of information found on the internet.**

Appropriate literature sources include periodicals, books, and government documents, most of which can be accessed online through the library at a post-secondary institution. You should evaluate the quality of information gleaned from websites prior to using that information as a primary source in a literature review. Evaluating information on the internet generally takes the form of asking questions that centre on the source, timeliness, accuracy, and relevance of the site. For example, in assessing accuracy, you can ask "Is the information free of spelling, grammatical, and technical errors?" and "Where did the information come from?"

RESEARCH REFLECTION

1. Read Margaret Kovach's (2018) chapter titled Doing Indigenous methodologies: A letter to a research class in N. K. Denzin & Y. S. Lincoln (Eds.), *The Sage handbook of qualitative research* (5th ed., pp. 108–150). Thousand Oaks, CA: Sage. Based on your reading, explain why the author claims it is not possible to do Indigenous methodologies. Also note the ways in which Indigenous methodologies are relational in nature.
2. Identify a general area of interest to you. Within that area of interest, develop two social research questions—one that implies an exploratory purpose and one that implies an explanatory purpose. Which paradigm introduced at the beginning of the chapter do you think best represents the research questions you developed? Explain why this is the case.
3. In what ways is an article found in a scholarly journal likely to be more appropriate as a reference source for a research topic than one located using a search engine such as Bing or Google?

LEARNING THROUGH PRACTICE

Objective: To assess information on the internet

Directions:

1. Use a search engine to locate a website that contains relevant information on a topic of interest.

2. Assess the website and associated resources using the following 10 questions:
   a. Who created the site and what are their credentials?
   b. What are the qualifications of authors of key sources associated with the site?
   c. Is it possible to verify the accuracy of any of the claims made on this site?
   d. Is an educational purpose for this site evident?
   e. Is the site objective (or free from bias)?
   f. Is the site free of advertisements?
   g. Can you tell when the site was created?
   h. Was the site updated recently?
   i. Are there properly cited references on the site?
   j. Are there any errors on site (e.g., spelling, grammatical)?
3. What rating would you give this site out of 100, if 100 percent is "perfect" and 0 stands for "without any merit." Explain why you think the site deserves this rating, based on its overall source, timeliness, accuracy, and relevance (STAR) quality.

RESEARCH RESOURCES

1. To learn more about social theorists and the underpinnings of social theory, refer to Ritzer, G., & Stepnisky, J. (2018). *Classical sociological theory* (7th ed.). Thousand Oaks, CA: Sage.
2. For an introduction to Indigenous ways of knowing, as well as historical and contemporary issues involving Indigenous Peoples in Canada, refer to Belanger, Y. D. (2018). *Ways of knowing: An introduction to Native studies in Canada* (3rd ed.). Toronto, ON: Nelson Education.
3. To understand how Indigenous knowledges have been negatively impacted by the education system, refer to Battiste, M. (2013). *Decolonizing education: Nourishing the learning spirit.* Saskatoon, SK: Purich.
4. To learn how Indigenous knowledge structures inform research conducted by Indigenous scholars, see Kovach, M. (2010). *Indigenous methodologies: Characteristics, conversations and contexts.* Toronto, ON: University of Toronto Press.

NOTES

1. For more information on paradigms based on feminism, critical race theory, cultural studies, and queer theory, refer to *The Sage Handbook of Qualitative Research* (5th ed.) (2018) edited by Norman K. Denzin and Yvonna S. Lincoln.

2.   The sharing circle was part of a larger community-based project carried out by Reith
     Charlesworth during the winter of 2016, under the supervision of Brianna Olson, an
     Anishnaabe (First Nations) Métis woman/social worker who was iHuman's program manager,
     and Associate Professor Dr. Alissa Overend, Reith's research mentor at MacEwan University.
     I taught the foundational research methods course for this project in the fall of 2015 and set
     up/oversaw student placements as the faculty coordinator for the 2015–2016 calendar year.
3.   An in-depth discussion of feminist perspectives is beyond the scope of this book. To learn
     about feminist standpoints and their relationships to research methodology, I recommend *The
     Handbook of Feminist Research: Theory and Praxis* (2nd ed.), edited by Sharlene Nagy Hesse-
     Biber (2012). For insight into conceptions of power, refer to *The Power of Feminist Theory:
     Domination, Resistance, Solidarity*, by Amy Allen (1999).

CHAPTER 3

Research Ethics

Many research textbooks explain research methods and their ethical aspects as logical processes that follow a given number of steps. Research, however, does not take place in a vacuum. It is imagined, designed, planned, funded (or not), executed and reported in a complex world by and with people with a whole range of viewpoints, values, needs, beliefs and agendas.
　　—Martin Johnson, 2007, p. 29

Learning Objectives

After reading this chapter, students should be able to do the following:

LO1　Define research ethics and provide examples of research-related ethical conduct.

LO2　Recognize links between early military and medical research and regulatory outcomes.

LO3　Discuss ethical considerations raised by classic studies in social research.

LO4　Discuss the potential for harm, risk-benefit analysis, informed consent, privacy and confidentiality, and debriefing as major ethical considerations in social science research.

LO5　Identify the core principles of the Tri-Council Policy Statement (TCPS2 2014).

LO6　Describe the role of an ethics review board and outline the process for undergoing an ethical review of research.

INTRODUCTION

From medical breakthroughs to technological innovations to discoveries in the social sciences, few would argue against the importance of including humans in research. Along with the need to involve humans in research is a corresponding ethical obligation on the part of physicians and researchers to treat participants in a safe, dignified, and well-informed manner. **Ethics** refer to "conduct that is considered 'morally right' or 'morally wrong' as specified by codified and culturally ingrained principles, constraints, rules, and guidelines" (Rosnow & Rosenthal, 2013, p. 41). Professionals in society are expected to adhere to ethics guiding their occupations. For example, physicians, residents, and medical students follow the Canadian Medical Association's Code of Ethics, which consists of 10 fundamental principles, including "Consider first, the well-being of the patient" (Canadian Medical Association, 2004). Similarly, all members of the Canadian Psychological Association, whether they are practitioners or not, are bound by the Canadian Code of Ethics for Psychologists (Canadian Psychological Association, 2017), just as members of the Canadian Sociological Association are guided by the Statement of Professional Ethics (Canadian Sociological Association, 2012).

Research ethics refer to an array of considerations that arise in relation to the morally responsible treatment of humans in research, including means for protecting the welfare and dignity of participants and procedures for assessing the overall risks and benefits. For example, where possible, researchers carefully explain the procedures, risks, and benefits of a study to potential participants prior to their participation in the study. Researchers also obtain informed consent from participants prior to their enlistment in a study, they make participants aware that their participation is voluntary, and they make sure participants understand that they are free to withdraw from the study at any time without penalty. Ethical conduct also includes designing research procedures in a manner that minimizes the potential for causing harm and maintains the privacy of individual participants. However, as implied by the opening quote, while ethical principles and procedures may appear straightforward from a moral perspective, researchers are people with divergent interests, agendas, and even flaws. They may intentionally or inadvertently place participants in situations that they are ill-informed about ahead of time, that inflict harm, that invade privacy, or that otherwise compromise human dignity.

This chapter examines historical and social science cases involving the unethical treatment of humans in research, along with the development of principles and procedures used to help guide ethical human-based research. In later chapters, you will see how particular research techniques may pose special ethical dilemmas for researchers, such as when researchers try to balance the trust established with participants against the research objectives in field studies where a researcher joins a group to study it (see chapter 10).

UNETHICAL TREATMENT OF HUMANS AND REGULATORY OUTCOMES

Numerous military and medical cases involve the unethical treatment of unsuspecting citizens, soldiers, prisoners of war, and various vulnerable populations. These cases provide a historical context for understanding the ethical principles that regulate and govern research involving humans today.

Military Research: Nazi Experiments 1939–1945

Medical experimentation on human prisoners was routinely conducted during World War II. German physicians, military officials, and researchers subjected men, women, and children from concentration and death camps to all sorts of torturous treatments to learn how to carry out medical practices, to find out more about the course of disease pathology, to test the limits of human suffering, and even to establish means for eliminating the Jewish race.

Famous examples include Professor Carl Clauberg, who developed a technique for the mass non-surgical sterilization of Jewish women using chemical irritants; SS-Sturmbannführer Horst Schumann, who induced sterilization by subjecting women's ovaries and men's testicles to repeated radiation via X-rays; Chief SS physician Dr. Eduard Wirths, who studied contagious diseases by first inflicting them upon prisoners (Auschwitz-Birkenau State Museum, 2019); and Dr. Josef Mengele (the "Angel of Death"), whose interest in genetic abnormalities led him to carry out often-fatal surgical procedures on sets of twin children, including the removal and exchange of internal organs and tissues (Lagnado & Dekel, 1991). Experiments were also routinely conducted to inform the German army about health issues, to help the government advance anti-Semitism plans involving racism and hatred toward people of Jewish descent, and to aid academics and physicians in furthering their own personal or professional agendas (Auschwitz-Birkenau State Museum, 2019).

The main entrance (or "Gate of Death") to Auschwitz-Birkenau, the largest network of German extermination camps during World War II.

Source: carlosftw/pixabay.com

The Nuremberg Code

Many of the physicians, political leaders, and researchers implicated in the inhumane studies discussed above were prosecuted for their actions in a series of military tribunals. The Nuremberg Trials, which commenced in 1945 at the Palace of Justice in Nuremberg, Bavaria, in Germany, defined the Nazi medical experiments as "war crimes" and "crimes against humanity," and resulted in lengthy prison and/or death sentences for guilty defendants. Another important outcome was the establishment of a set of 10 directives for human experimentation called the **Nuremberg Code**. The Nuremberg Code (1949) is among the first published sets of ethical guidelines, and is summarized in the excerpts below:

1. The voluntary consent of the human subject is absolutely essential.
2. The experiment should be such as to yield fruitful results for the good of society.
3. The experiment should be so designed and based on the results of animal experimentation.
4. The experiment should be so conducted as to avoid all unnecessary physical and mental suffering and injury.
5. No experiment should be conducted where there is an *a priori* reason to believe that death or disabling injury will occur.
6. The degree of risk to be taken should never exceed that determined by the humanitarian importance of the problem to be solved by the experiment.

Entrance to the Nuremberg Trials
courthouse, the Palace of Justice in
Nuremberg, Germany

Source: Yurlick/shutterstock.com

7. Proper preparations should be made and adequate facilities provided to
    protect the experimental subject against even remote possibilities of in-
    jury, disability, or death.
8. The experiment should be conducted only by scientifically qualified
    persons.
9. During the course of the experiment the human subject should be at lib-
    erty to bring the experiment to an end.
10. During the course of the experiment the scientist in charge must be pre-
    pared to terminate the experiment at any stage. (pp. 181–182)

Research on the Net

Canadian War Veterans Exposed to Mustard Gas

Military experimentation extends beyond Germany and prisoners of war to include Canadian soldiers who volunteered for studies designed to help military

warfare. Many participants kept oaths of secrecy despite long-standing suffering, and even eventual death in some cases, from related health implications.
In May 2004, the Canadian government released a $24,000 compensation pay-
ment to retired Master Corporal Roy Wheeler and retired Flight Sergeant Bill
Tanner (CBC News, 2004). The two soldiers were the first of about 2,500 remaining World War II veterans to receive reparation and an official apology on behalf
of the estimated 3,500 men exposed to mustard gas and other deadly chemicals.
Experiments on the effects of chemical warfare agents were conducted by the
Canadian military at Canadian Forces Base Suffield near Medicine Hat in Alberta
for a 30-year period from 1940 to 1970 (CBC News, 2004). While the compensation acknowledges unethical treatment, it cannot repair health implications suffered by the soldiers, including infertility, heart disease, and lung complications.
Learn more by going to CBC News Online at www.cbc.ca and searching for the
news article "Vets exposed to mustard gas receive compensation."

Biomedical Research: The Tuskegee Syphilis Study

The unethical treatment of patients is not limited to prisoners of war and military
personnel. In 1932, six hundred low-income African American men from Macon
County, Alabama, were recruited by the United States Public Health Service for a
study on the natural (i.e., untreated) progression of the sexually transmitted disease
syphilis (Tuskegee Syphilis Study Legacy Committee, 1996). Although 399 of the
men had syphilis at the onset of the study, they were never informed about their condition. Instead, the men were told they were being examined for "bad blood." They
were monitored over a period of almost 40 years, during which they were not given
the standard therapy for syphilis of the time nor the penicillin that was developed
as a cure in 1947. Researchers even persuaded local doctors to withhold standard
antibiotics (Stryker, 1997). In exchange for their willingness to participate, the men
were provided with free meals, free medical examinations, and free burials (Tuskegee Syphilis Study Legacy Committee, 1996). Note that the study continued long
after the establishment of the Nuremberg Code. In fact, the research went on for
four decades, until lawyer Peter Buxton took the case to the media. The Tuskegee
study came to an end in 1972, when Jean Heller of the Associated Press released the
story, making the true purpose of the research apparent (Stryker, 1997).

   An obvious implication of the withholding of knowledge of the disease in conjunction with the prevention of treatment was that the men suffered prolonged
physical symptoms and many eventually died, passed the disease on to their wives,

Participants in the Tuskegee syphilis study thought they were being treated for "bad blood."

Source: PublicDomainPictures/pixabay.com

and even, in some cases, passed it on to their children as congenital syphilis. Survivors and their families eventually received financial compensation resulting from a class action suit. On May 16, 1997, President Bill Clinton formally apologized on behalf of the government to the remaining survivors, their families, and the community for wrongdoings carried out at Tuskegee (Tuskegee University, 2019).

The Belmont Report

In response to the Tuskegee study, the United States Congress passed the National Research Act in 1974, which created the National Commission for the Protection of Human Subjects of Biomedical and Behavioral Research. Since medical practices and research often occur together, the Commission outlined boundaries between medical practices and research to help determine conditions under which the actions of physicians and researchers would require review (National Commission for the Protection of Human Subjects of Biomedical and Behavioral Research [NCPHSBBR], 1979). A summary of the recommendations by the Commission, called the Belmont Report, outlines three basic ethical principles meant to guide all future research involving humans:

- Principle 1: Respect for persons
- Principle 2: Beneficence
- Principle 3: Justice

Respect for persons is a moral principle stressing the importance of people being treated as "autonomous agents." This means all participants should be valued as individuals who are free to make choices for themselves, including whether they wish to participate in a study. **Beneficence** is a term that is used to describe the general personal safety and well-being of research participants. Beneficence as a moral principle refers to the dual notions of (1) "do no harm" and (2) "maximize possible benefits and minimize potential harms" (NCPHSBBR, 1979). **Justice** is a moral principle based on "fairness" attributed to common-sense adages such as "to each person an equal share" and "to each person according to individual need." In this case, it is expected that researchers will make decisions and behave in socially responsible ways. For example, "an injustice occurs when some benefit to which a person is entitled is denied without good reason or when some burden is imposed unduly" (NCPHSBBR, 1979, p. 5).

Research on the Net

Recruiting the Poor for Clinical Drug Trials

Unfortunately, the principles of respect for persons, beneficence, and justice are not always upheld, as evidenced by the ongoing exploitation of disadvantaged groups for the advancement of science and profits. On March 4, 2012, *Dateline NBC* correspondent Chris Hansen reported on the exploitation of poor people living in Ahmedabad, India, by US pharmaceutical companies who pay participants to undergo clinical trials. Some of the test subjects were recruited by Rajesh Nadia, who was also paid for every person he found on behalf of the drug companies. In his interview with Chris Hansen, Nadia admitted the recruits often disregard the potential health risks and sometimes even enlist in overlapping studies for financial incentives (Sandler, 2012). How can pharmaceutical companies get away with this? Satinath Sarangi, director of the Bhopal Group for Information and Action, noted that "you can do it cheaply, do it with no regulation, and even if there are violations, get away with it" (Sandler, 2012). India is one of many countries targeted by pharmaceutical companies. As another example, view the Journeyman Pictures 2016 production "Big Pharma Companies Are Exploiting the World's Poor" on YouTube to learn more about clinical trials involving children and infants in Argentina.

Test Yourself

- What do research ethics refer to?
- What is the name for the ethical guidelines that developed out of the Nazi war trials?
- What features of the Tuskegee study illustrate unethical biomedical research?
- What three ethical principles are highlighted in the Belmont Report?

UNETHICAL TREATMENT OF PARTICIPANTS IN SOCIAL SCIENCE RESEARCH

The unethical treatment of humans also extends into the realm of social research, as demonstrated in the following two studies.

Stanley Milgram's Experiments on Obedience to Authority

In what proved to be among the most controversial set of studies ever conducted in the social sciences, Yale University professor Stanley Milgram (1961) devised a procedure, while still in graduate studies, for examining obedience. In this study, a naïve participant followed orders to administer increasingly painful electric shocks to a fellow participant serving as the "learner." In one of the earliest versions of what turned out to be a series of experiments, Milgram (1963) recruited participants through a newspaper advertisement for a paid study on memory conducted at Yale University. When a participant arrived at the university, he was greeted by an experimenter and an accomplice posing as the other participant in a two-person study of the effects of punishment on learning. After a brief overview, participants were asked to draw slips of paper from a hat to determine who would assume the role of the "teacher" and who would become the learner. The draw was fixed so that both slips of paper said "Teacher," ensuring that the participant would always end up in the role of the teacher, while the accomplice would assume the role of the learner.

The participant and accomplice were then taken to adjacent rooms and the learner was hooked up to a shock-generating apparatus, making it apparent to the teacher that the victim would be unable to depart the experiment of his own accord. The apparatus consisted of a series of lever switches marked in increments of 15 and labelled with descriptors to indicate increasing voltage from 15 (slight), to 75 (moderate), to 135 (strong), to 195 (very strong), to 255 (intense), to 315 (extreme intensity), to 375 (Danger: Severe Shock), up to 420, where the descriptor was Xs. To add credibility, the teacher was then given a sample shock of 45 volts (Milgram, 1963).

Throughout the experimental task, the teacher was instructed to give a shock by pressing down a lever on the shock generator each time the learner provided an incorrect answer. Importantly, the teacher was also told to increase the shock level after each error and call out the value, such that the voltage increased by 15 and the voltage amount was salient to the teacher. At pre-planned intervals, according to a script, the victim (learner) protested the shock treatment using various forms of feedback, such as pounding on the wall and screaming out in pain, until the shock value of 300 volts was reached. After that, the learner no longer responded. If, at any point during the experiment, the teacher stopped giving shocks and/ or sought guidance on how to proceed, the experimenter followed a sequence of scripted prods, including "Please continue" or "Please go on," "The experiment requires that you continue," "It is absolutely essential that you continue," and "You have no other choice, you *must* go on" (Milgram, 1963, p. 374).

A participant in Milgram's study administers what he believes is a shock to the learner while carrying out a word task.

Source: From the film Obedience ©1965 by Stanley Milgram.

©Renewed 1993 by Alexandra Milgram. Distributed by

Alexandra Street Press.

Results indicated that participants believed they were administering real shocks, and they showed signs of extreme tension (e.g., sweating, stuttering, trembling). Of the 40 participants included in the original version, the first refusal to continue came at 300 volts, with five subjects terminating their participation. An additional four quit at 315 volts, two more stopped at 330 volts, and one more left the study at each level of 345, 360, and 375 volts, for a total of 14 who defied the experimenter and 26 who obeyed orders to the very end (Milgram, 1963).

This procedure was replicated by Milgram in more than 20 variations, including conducting the experiment in different countries (e.g., Norway and France), introducing group dynamics (e.g., the teacher was part of a small group obeying or breaking off from the orders of the experimenter), introducing varied elements of the assumed responsibility (e.g., the learner made it evident he did not wish to continue but was unable to get out of the study without help; the experimenter claimed full responsibility for the situation), and changing the salience or immediacy of the victim (e.g., the victim was placed within view of the teacher) (Russell, 2010). In most cases, large numbers of participants obeyed the experimenter, providing what would be severely painful shocks to an innocent victim (i.e., the learner), and completing the study to the end. The fact that about two-thirds of the participants obeyed orders to the end goes against what we might consider to be common sense, which tells us that only in rare cases involving a highly sadistic or evil sort of person should this happen. Zimbardo (2004) explains that even 40 psychiatrists who were given a description of Milgram's procedures ahead of time failed to account for situational determinants and predicted that fewer than 1 percent of participants would shock to the maximum of 450 volts.

Milgram's experiments were widely criticized for their use of deception that evoked prolonged periods of distress where participants believed they were harming another individual. Milgram (1963) reported that "in a large number of cases the degree of tension reached extremes that are rarely seen in sociopsychological laboratory studies. Subjects were observed to sweat, tremble, stutter, bite their lips, groan, and dig their fingernails into their flesh. These were characteristic rather than exceptional responses to the experiment" (p. 375). Milgram (1963) went on to say that "one sign of tension was the regular occurrence of nervous laughing fits. Fourteen of the 40 subjects showed definite signs of nervous laughter and smiling. The laughter seemed entirely out of place, even bizarre. Full-blown, uncontrollable seizures were observed for 3 subjects. On one occasion we observed a seizure so violently convulsive that it was necessary to call a halt to the experiment" (p. 375). Many readers are left wondering if the "friendly reconciliation" between the learner and teacher that Milgram arranged at the end of the study was enough to disengage the tension produced throughout the study. As Diana Baumrind (1964) noted in an article questioning the ethics of Milgram's research, "It would be interesting to know what sort of procedures could dissipate the type of emotional disturbance just described. In view of the effects on subjects, traumatic to a degree which Milgram himself considers nearly unprecedented in sociopsychological experiments, his casual assurance that these tensions were dissipated before the subject left the laboratory is unconvincing" (p. 422). Baumrind (1964) further points out that Milgram has no way of determining how this study might negatively impact the self-image of participants or their future views of authority figures.

In addition to the potential for lasting distress suffered by participants, the very topic of Milgram's studies (i.e., obedience) warranted a type of procedure that necessarily impinged on the voluntary nature of participation. That is, teachers were ordered to continue and told they must go on even when they said they wished to stop. This practice clearly goes against voluntary participation since the teachers were not free to withdraw from the study at any time without penalty.

Philip Zimbardo's Stanford Prison Study

To study the interpersonal nature of prison life, Philip Zimbardo, Craig Haney, and Curtis Banks set out in 1971 to design a simulated prison in which participants would be randomly assigned to the role of "prisoner" or "guard" (Haney, Banks, & Zimbardo, 1973). The procedures for this study were relatively straightforward. Participants were recruited through a newspaper advertisement seeking paid volunteers for a "psychological study of prison life." Of the 75 respondents, 21 were selected, based on extensive background screening to determine those with the most "stable," most "mature," and least "anti-social" tendencies. Participants were informed that they would be assigned to either a guard or prisoner role and that they would be paid $15 per day for a period of up to two weeks. They signed a contract "guaranteeing a minimally adequate diet, clothing, housing, and medical care, as well as the financial remuneration in return for their stated 'intention' of serving in the assigned role for the duration of the study" (p. 74). No instructions were given for how to carry out a prisoner role, although they were forewarned that they would have little privacy and they could expect to have their "basic civil rights suspended during their imprisonment, excluding physical abuse" (p. 74). Those serving as guards were given vague instructions to "maintain the reasonable degree of order within a prison necessary for its effective functioning" (p. 74).

With assistance from the Palo Alto City Police Department, participants assigned to the prisoner role were unexpectedly arrested at their homes and taken to the mock prison to begin the study, which took place in the basement of the psychology building at Stanford University. When the prisoners arrived, they were "stripped, sprayed with a delousing preparation (a deodorant spray) and made to stand alone naked for a while in the cell yard" (Haney, Banks, & Zimbardo, 1973, p. 76). Following this, they were issued a uniform, had their ID picture taken, were taken to a cell, and were "ordered to remain silent." As part of the administrative routine, the warden, played by an undergraduate assistant, then explained rules for prisoners that the guards and the warden had created. These rules included being referred to as only a number, the granting of minimal supervised toilet breaks and limited scheduled visits, and complying with regular "count" lineups, among other things.

Results showed that, over time, guards became increasingly negative, aggressive, and dehumanizing, while prisoners became increasingly passive and distressed. Haney, Banks, and Zimbardo (1973) noted that "extremely pathological reactions which emerged in both groups of subjects testify to the power of the

A marked distinction developed between prisoner and guard roles during the Stanford Prison Study.

Source: prisonexp.org

social forces operating" (p. 81) and "the most dramatic evidence of the impact of the situation is seen in the gross reactions of five prisoners who had to be released because of extreme emotional depression, crying, rage and acute anxiety" (p. 81). Anyone who has seen video footage from the study is likely to question why the study was not stopped sooner or why particular prisoners who showed signs of extreme distress and begged to be let out of the study were not immediately allowed to do so. Even Zimbardo admits that it should have been his "job to hold in check the growing violence and arbitrary displays of power of the guards rather than to be the Milgramesque authority who, in being transformed from just to unjust as the learner's suffering intensified, demanded ever more extreme reactions from the participants" (Zimbardo, Maslach, & Haney, 2000, p. 194). It was not until after his soon-to-be-wife's tearful admonishment, "What you are doing to those boys is a terrible thing!" (p. 216) followed by a heated argument, that Zimbardo detached from his role as the prison superintendent and more fully appreciated how the power of the situation had taken over those in it, including himself (Zimbardo, Maslach, & Haney, 2000). For more information on the prison study, along with lectures, articles, and media interviews related to the study, as well as recent criticisms and responses, refer to the official website for the Stanford Prison Study at www.prisonexp.org.

Test Yourself

- What features of Milgram's study posed ethical concerns?
- What features of Zimbardo's study posed ethical concerns?

ETHICAL ISSUES COMMON TO SOCIAL SCIENCE RESEARCH

The historical medical, military, and social science examples discussed thus far all help to illustrate key ethical issues that arise in research. Five recurring concerns are discussed in more detail in this section, including the potential for harm, risk-benefit analysis, informed consent, privacy and confidentiality, and debriefing. These issues are still prevalent today and they need to be specifically addressed by researchers who plan to apply for ethical approval for research involving humans as participants.

1. The Potential for Harm

Perhaps the most essential consideration in any study is its potential to produce harmful outcomes for participants. Any procedure that requires participants to engage in physical activity has the potential, even if slight, for someone to incur an injury. Similarly, a clinical drug trial might require participants to ingest a medicine that could produce physical side effects such as sweating, blurred vision, or an increased heart rate. In most cases where there is the potential for physical harm, researchers attempt to design their study in a manner that minimizes the risk. For example, in my research on factors influencing participants' willingness to endure the pain of an isometric sitting exercise, we included only physically active, healthy individuals aged 18 to 25 who were continuously monitored and whose heart rates were assessed every 20 seconds to ensure their ability to continue safely to a maximum of six minutes (Symbaluk, Heth, Cameron, & Pierce, 1997). Harmful studies such as those conducted by the Nazi doctors or the researchers in the Tuskegee syphilis study would never receive ethical approval today.

It is also possible for participants to experience psychological forms of harm, as in the case of the severe stress experienced by some of the subjects in Milgram's experiments, who believed they were giving painful electric shocks to an innocent victim, or the "prisoners" in Zimbardo's experiment, who were verbally abused and degraded by the "guards." Participants may also experience stress as a function of being asked personal questions during an interview or disclosing private information on a questionnaire. In addition, being provided with certain kinds of feedback during a study, as happens when participants determine they are performing extremely poorly relative to the other participants, can lead to feelings of stress. In cases where procedures have the potential to evoke high levels of stress (e.g., the roles of prisoners and guards), safeguards need to be built into the study, such as careful monitoring, the ability to readily terminate a study, and ways to assess the stress. Where stressful reactions become apparent, especially if they were unanticipated (e.g., as the result of a question being asked during an interview), the onus is on the researcher to respond in a timely and appropriate manner.

Harm can take even less obvious forms that may not be apparent prior to the onset of a study. For example, researchers may obtain approval from participants to include visual forms of data in their research projects—such as photographs, works of art, or films that represent participants, their perspectives, or cultural practices and ceremonies—that prove to be harmful to individuals or communities once the images are disseminated in the public domain. For example, imagine how you would feel if you consented to having your photo taken for a research project on

Visual forms of data can pose unanticipated ethical challenges for researchers.

Source: jarmoluk/pixabay.com

cellphone use and then it was included alongside negative findings on distracted driving practices? Marcus Banks and David Zeitlyn (2015) recount issues with an early ethnographic study on a tribe in northeastern Uganda carried out by Colin Turnbull (see Turnbull, 1973) where the researcher included photographs of individuals making hunting weapons in what had recently become a national park. While a researcher's intent may be to portray a group or a practice using photographs to capture the authenticity of the research, there may be a host of unanticipated consequences for the now identified individuals. Banks and Zeitlyn (2015) suggest it is not so much a question of whether researchers should have the right to visually represent others but more a case of "how and under what conditions do they negotiate that right with those who are represented?" (p. 123). Visual representation is discussed in more detail under Privacy and Confidentiality.

2. Risk-Benefit Analysis

Studies should be designed to minimize harm and maximize benefits. Through risk-benefit analysis, studies that necessitate the use of known harm but contribute little to our understanding are usually considered unethical, while studies that minimize the potential for harm or result in negligible harm but greatly improve programs, help to reduce suffering, or have widely applicable benefits are more apt to be deemed ethical.

While Milgram's experiments clearly caused harm, they must be evaluated in historical context. These studies were the only ones to examine obedience at a time when science had yet to explain how millions of innocent people had lost their lives at the hands of otherwise "ordinary" Nazi soldiers and officials, many of whom claimed they were simply following orders. Similarly, while participants in Zimbardo's study were also negatively affected by their experience, the researchers could not anticipate the severity of the situation or how they themselves would be carried away by situational forces. In both cases, the importance of the findings for teaching us about obedience and situational forces, as well as how to build in participant safeguards in subsequent research, cannot be understated. While much of the information presented above is in hindsight, the point is that all research has benefits and drawbacks that need to be carefully weighed to determine the merit of any given study at a point and place in time.

3. Informed Consent

Under no circumstances should people be coerced, misled, or otherwise forced to take part in research. The indictment of the physicians implicated in Nazi medical experiments during the Nuremberg Trials was less based on the harm incurred than the fact that victims were forced into the experiments against their will. **Informed consent** refers to a process where potential participants are provided with all relevant details of a study needed to make a knowledgeable judgment about whether to participate in it.

Informed consent is usually obtained with a written consent form that discloses all relevant details of the study and clearly establishes the voluntary nature of participation. The form contains a statement indicating that the study constitutes research; a description of the nature and purpose of the research; an outline of the procedures, including the anticipated timelines; a disclosure of any potential risks and benefits; alternatives to participation; measures taken to ensure privacy, anonymity, and confidentiality; details of any reimbursement or compensation for participating; assurances that participation is voluntary; and contact information for the researchers.

Note that various factors can challenge the process for obtaining informed consent. For example, participants with limited or impaired cognitive ability may lack the capacity to understand the risks and benefits of a study or what is required in the role of a participant. Similarly, consent cannot be obtained from children without both their approval and the approval of adults who are responsible for them. Finally, individuals in vulnerable positions, such as people who are serving time in prison or employees being asked to take part in a study by their employers, may be informed that participation is voluntary, but still may believe that a failure to participate could have negative repercussions.

According to Cozby and Bates (2018), informed consent should be obtained in a manner that is readily understood by the public and aimed at an education level of about grade six to eight. In addition, the form should be written as an informal letter to the participant as opposed to a legal document. The letter should be free of any kind of technical terms specific to a research area or discipline. Finally, it should be apparent to the potential participant that they are free to withdraw consent at any time, without penalty. Importantly, signing a consent form is not the same thing as signing a waiver form, where a person absolves all others of blame. A researcher remains responsible and may incur later legal liability for actions taken or not taken during a study that result in harm to the participant (see figure 3.1).

4. Privacy and Confidentiality

Another key ethical issue in research concerns the loss of privacy and confidentiality. Although researchers try to uphold the privacy of participants, in many instances social research itself necessitates an invasion of privacy. From the completion of a relatively harmless online survey that intrudes into a respondent's personal time to highly personal questions about one's private experiences asked by a qualitative researcher in a face-to-face interview, research spans a continuum when it comes to loss of privacy. Sometimes a researcher may be more interested in the responses than in the respondents in a given study. In such cases, researchers may be able to maintain the **anonymity** of participants by keeping their names off any of the documentation that contain responses. Anonymity exists if a researcher cannot link any individual response to the person who provided it. As an example, consider student evaluations of courses and instructors, where student responses are anonymous because students do not include their names or any other identifying information on the evaluation instruments.

Confidentiality is an ethical principle referring to the process enacted to uphold privacy (Sieber, 1992). For example, a researcher may be able to identify a person and their responses if an interviewer can clearly see who is providing the responses; however, the researcher promises not to disclose information that would identify that person publicly. Confidentiality can often be upheld by reporting collected data in an aggregate (i.e., grouped) rather than individual format. In other cases, information may need to be omitted to preserve privacy. For example, a published report that indicated that a participant held a position as mayor or was a director of human resources at a university would inadvertently reveal the identity of that participant. Researchers routinely use pseudonyms in place of actual names, and they may even change a few details, such as the gender or age of a participant, to respect privacy.

Sample Informed Consent Form

You are invited to participate in research by Dr. xxx in the Department of Psychology at xxx University. This research is examining people's views toward others and people's responses to different descriptions of others. Participants will be asked to complete a number of ratings, such as judging how much you like various newspaper headlines that describe people in different ways. Participants will also be asked to report their age, sex, and program of study; whether they were born inside or outside Canada; and their year of study.

Participation will be anonymous. Only aggregate (group) data will be examined and reported. The recording of your ID number for the purpose of receiving course credit for your participation will be kept entirely separate from your questionnaire responses.

You will be credited with 2 percent toward your final course grade by participating in this research. Participation is voluntary, and you are free to withdraw at any time, for any reason, without a loss of credit. Additionally, if you choose to participate and find a question you would prefer not to answer, you are free to skip that question and continue on with the rest of the items.

Participation will take about 30 minutes. If you choose to participate, not only will you make a valuable contribution to scientific advancement, but you will experience what it is like to be a participant in psychological research and come to more fully appreciate and understand the research processes fundamental to the field of psychology. There are no anticipated risks of participating in this research.

If you choose not to participate in this study, you can obtain the same course credit by participating in another study or by completing the alternative non-research activity.

If you have any questions about this study at any time, feel free to contact Dr. xxx by email at xx@xxx.ca or by phone at (xxx) xxx–xxxx. You can also contact the chair of the Research Ethics Board with any questions or concerns (Dr. xxx; email: xx@xxx.ca).

Consent to Participate

I hereby give my consent to participate in the research described above. I realize that by signing, I have not waived my right to legal action should I be harmed in any way by participating in this study.

Signature of Participant: _____   Date: _____

Figure 3.1: Sample Informed Consent Form

Source: Created by author

Finally, in some forms of research it may not be possible to guarantee anonymity or confidentiality. For example, in focus groups (discussed in more detail in chapter 9), participants who are introduced to one another may later disclose identifying details from a research session, irrespective of researcher intentions. As another example, in visual research, photographs that become part of the research data and process may depict a participant's identity, or they may depict the identity of other individuals who were not part of the research project, as in the case of a participant's photo collection, which might include photos of family members and friends, photos that show events involving groups of people, and even historical photos of now deceased individuals. Marion and Crowder (2013) identify seven key ethical issues raised in visual research, including (1) "representational authority," concerning who gets to decide how the image is depicted, in terms of the perspective created; (2) "decontextualization/circulation," concerning where the image ends up and how it gets used; (3) "presumed versus actual outcomes of image display"; (4) "relations with and responsibilities toward research subjects/communities"; (5) "balancing privacy versus publicity, depending on subject's wishes"; (6) "the importance of communication and consent of subjects and communities at every stage of the research process"; and (7) "the collection and dissemination of visual materials within the context of globally expanding media savvy and presence" (pp. 6–7).

It is not always possible to guarantee anonymity or confidentiality in social research.

Source: Free-Photos/pixabay.com

Research in Action

Canadian Researchers Take Confidentiality to Court

Confidentiality was first put to the test in early 1994 in a Canadian case in which a researcher was subpoenaed to appear in court to provide evidence that would identify research participants (Palys & Atchison, 2014). The researcher was Russel Ogden, a then–MA student in the School of Criminology at Simon Fraser University who was carrying out controversial research on assisted suicide among individuals suffering from HIV/AIDs. Ogden guaranteed his research participants "absolute confidentiality" and therefore refused to provide any identifying information, on ethical grounds. Although he was threatened with a charge of contempt of court, he eventually won his case. The riveting case, the legal and ethical implications, and the controversy involving Simon Fraser University for its initial lack of support are described by Palys and Atchison (2014) and are outlined in detail on a web page posted by Ted Palys found at sfu.ca/~palys/OgdenPge.htm.

More recently, in 2014, criminologists Colette Parent and Chris Bruckert, from the University of Ottawa, won a Superior Court ruling in Quebec for a case involving a participant-confidentiality agreement. They were able to successfully argue research confidentiality, outlined in the Tri-Council Policy Statement, as grounds for dismissing a warrant involving interview transcripts they had from a former research participant in a study involving the sex industry, who was later accused of murder (Samson, 2014). Although ethical principles are not a guarantee of legal immunity, in this case, the judge weighed heavily on the fact that the researchers had diligently followed the protocols of establishing confidentiality with participants representing a vulnerable population where exposing the transcripts might do irreparable damage to future relations.

5. Debriefing

Debriefing refers to the full disclosure and exchange of information that takes place upon completion of a study. Debriefing is required in most situations where participants are not provided with all the details of the study or are misled about details of the study prior to participating in it. In social psychological research, for example, deception is sometimes required to maintain the integrity of the main variable under consideration. For example, suppose you wish to conduct an experiment on helping and want to see how many students are willing to help classmates who request to borrow notes under the pretense of missing class due to an illness. If you informed participants ahead of time that someone was going to approach them at the end of class and ask to borrow notes, so you could measure whether they helped, this knowledge would likely affect their willingness to help, in a manner that would negate the purpose of the study. Note that deception or the misleading of participants in social psychological research either by misconstruing or omitting details is different than the concealment of a researcher's identity or research purpose within a covert role sometimes undertaken in ethnography or fieldwork (discussed in more detail in chapter 10). In the case of covert field research, it may be ethically necessary to conceal information in order to protect the researcher or participants from incurring harm (W. C. van den Hoonaard, 2019).

Test Yourself

- Is harm always of a physical nature? Explain your answer.
- How is beneficence a risk-benefit calculation?
- What is informed consent and what details are included in a consent form?
- How is anonymity different from confidentiality?
- What is debriefing and when is it a requirement?

TRI-COUNCIL POLICY STATEMENT

Research ethics regulations in Canada arose in the late 1970s, largely in response to US policies stemming from the Tuskegee study, controversies surrounding deception in social psychological experiments including Milgram's, and calls for greater accountability by government funding agencies (Adair, 2001). Canada's three federal research funding agencies are the Canadian Institutes of Health Research (CIHR), the Natural Sciences and Engineering Council of Canada (NSERC), and the Social Sciences and Humanities Research Council (SSHRC). In 1998, these agencies collectively adopted the Tri-Council Policy Statement: Ethical Conduct for Research Involving Humans (TCPS or the Policy). The Policy is meant to guide researchers in the design of their studies, to promote ethical conduct in the carrying out of research projects, and to establish a process for the ethical review of research involving humans. Research on animals is not considered in this policy,

The overarching value of the TCPS2 2014 is respect for human dignity.

Source: geralt/pixabay.com

although separate, extensive ethical guidelines exist with respect to animal rights, animal care, and the use of animals in research. The TCPS expanded into a second edition in 2010 and then was updated further in 2014. It is currently referred to as the Tri-Council Policy Statement: Ethical Conduct for Research Involving Humans (TCPS2 2014) and it serves as the guide to official policies at universities throughout Canada where research takes place.

The overarching value of the TCPS2 2014 is **respect for human dignity**. Respect for human dignity necessitates that "research involving humans be conducted in a manner that is sensitive to the inherent worth of all human beings and the respect and consideration that they are due" (Government of Canada, 2018). Respect for human dignity is expressed in the three principles introduced earlier in this chapter: respect for persons, a concern for welfare, and justice.

Respect for Persons

As noted in the Belmont Report, respect for persons recognizes the value of human worth as well as the dual need to respect autonomy and protect those with diminished autonomy. The TCPS2 2014 additionally includes as persons "human biological materials," such as "materials related to human reproduction." Respect for persons is demonstrated through the establishment of consent to participate in a study.

Establishment of Consent

There are three important principles that underlie the establishment of consent. First, consent is given voluntarily. This means a subject is freely choosing to participate in the research. Consent is not voluntary in cases where, for example, soldiers are coerced into a study by their superior officers or prisoners participate in a study for fear of negative implications that might result if consent is not provided.

Second, consent is informed by the disclosure of all relevant information needed to understand what participation entails, including all foreseeable risks and benefits. For research intended to involve individuals who lack the capacity to provide informed consent, the individuals must be involved—to the extent possible—in the consent decision-making process, consent must be obtained from "authorized third parties" who are not affiliated with the research team, and the research must have direct benefit for the intended participants (CIHR, NSERC, & SSHRC, 2014, p. 43).

Third, consent is an ongoing process. This does not imply that once a person signs a consent form, they have consented to finish the study. Rather, "the researcher has an ongoing ethical and legal obligation to bring participants' attention to any changes to the research project that may affect them" throughout the course of the study (CIHR, NSERC, & SSHRC, 2014, p. 31). A participant may or may not choose to start a study and may elect to discontinue their involvement at any time after starting, without penalty. In cases where a participant discontinues involvement, data collected up to the point may also be withdrawn at the discretion of the participant.

Concern for Welfare

Harm has already been discussed in detail, so I won't reiterate this issue here. In addition to minimizing harm, a **concern for welfare** entails efforts to mitigate other foreseeable risks associated with participation, such as to housing, employment, security, family life, and community membership. The protection of privacy also falls under a concern for welfare: "Privacy risks arise in all stages of the research life cycle, including initial collection of information, use and analysis to address research questions, dissemination of findings, storage and retention of information, and disposal of records or devices on which information is stored" (CIHR, NSERC, & SSHRC, 2014, p. 57). In this case, the promise of keeping data confidential is expanded to include an obligation on the part of a researcher to put safeguards in place for all "entrusted information" so that it is protected from "unauthorized access, use, disclosure, modification, loss, or theft" (CIHR,

NSERC, & SSHRC, 2014, p. 58). Typical security measures include the storage of data on password-protected computers and in locked file cabinets away from the public, such as in the private office of a researcher.

Another concern related to welfare is the special consideration of individuals or groups "whose circumstances may make them vulnerable in the context of research," as in the case of impoverished persons where even a slight participation incentive could negate the voluntary nature of consent given (CIHR, NSERC, & SSHRC, 2014, p. 54). An example of this is the use of paid participants from poor areas in India, as described in the Research on the Net box "Recruiting the Poor for Clinical Drug Trials." On the other hand, in certain types of research, including focus groups and qualitative interviews (discussed in chapter 9), it is commonplace to offer participants compensation for their time, such as gift certificates to a local coffee shop or grocery store.

A final application of welfare extends to research involving Indigenous peoples. As noted in chapter 2 and the TCPS2 2014, much of the research carried out on Indigenous peoples has been historically linked to forced assimilation; it was undertaken by non-Indigenous researchers following traditional research approaches, and it was without benefit to Indigenous communities. Differences exist between non-Indigenous and Indigenous value systems when it comes to research foundations, and these differences are apparent in the TCPS2 2014 ethical guidelines that largely focus on individuals (e.g., consent and harm in relation to individual participants), not holistic interrelationships based on trust that are integral to Indigenous communities and research practices. Since non-Indigenous researchers lack training and knowledge when it comes to understanding and adequately accounting for Indigenous community customs, concerns, relationships, and values, the TCPS2 2014 dedicates an entire chapter (i.e., chapter 9) to research involving First Nations, Inuit, and Métis peoples of Canada. While this is a starting point and the provisions are meant to serve as a dialogue for interpreting the ethics framework within Indigenous contexts, there are few practical suggestions for how researchers are to go about implementing key requirements, such as community engagement, respect for governing authorities (e.g., community leaders), recognition of diverse interests, and respect for customs (Bull, 2016).

Justice

Recall that justice refers to "the obligation to treat people fairly and equitably" (CIHR, NSERC, & SSHRC, 2014, p. 8). Fairness means equal concern and respect is shown to all research participants, while equity relates more to considerations of the overall distribution of benefits versus "burdens" incurred by participants in research. Stemming from this is a concern that certain groups are not given the opportunity to participate in research, based on attributes unrelated to the research. For example, women, children, and the elderly are sometimes inappropriately excluded from research because of gender, age, or disability (see chapter 4 in the TCPS2 2014). Notably, researchers seeking to carry out projects that will include Indigenous participants, impact Indigenous communities, or be conducted on First Nation, Inuit, or Métis lands must first be informed about rules and customs that apply to Indigenous peoples and their land, must engage directly with the implicated community in the design and implementation of the project, and must reach prior agreements concerning research expectations, commitments, and ethical considerations with the community involved (CIHR, NSERC, & SSHRC, 2014).

Test Yourself

- What is the all-encompassing value of the TCPS2 2014?
- What three principles underlie the consent process?
- In what ways might a concern for welfare extend beyond physical and psychological harm?
- What are privacy risks and when do they arise?
- Why are certain individuals and groups especially vulnerable in the context of research?

RESEARCH ETHICS BOARDS AND THE ETHICAL REVIEW PROCESS

The TCPS2 2014 mandates that all research involving humans be subject to an ethical review by an institutional **research ethics board**. A research ethics board (REB) is a committee whose role is to "review the ethical acceptability of research on behalf of the institution, including approving, rejecting, proposing modifications to, or terminating any proposed or ongoing research involving humans" (CIHR, NSERC, & SSHRC, 2014, p. 71).

Membership Requirements

REB members must be qualified to judge the ethical provisions of the research as guided by the TCPS2 2014. At least some of the members of the committee are required to have expertise in research methodologies of the relevant disciplines of the researchers likely to submit applications. In addition, the group must contain ethical and legal expertise, as well as someone who can represent the interests of the public, such as a community member not affiliated with the institution.

Ethical Review Process

All research that is conducted by individuals affiliated with an institution, such as faculty members or professors, is conducted at a university using that institution's assets (e.g., a classroom, equipment), or includes students or staff members from a university as participants in research needs to be approved in advance by the review board. Even research conducted using web-based sources needs to undergo review if it is deemed "engaged," where a researcher may, for example, join an online community to study it. However, other forms of research that are conducted using publicly available sources of information, such as Twitter tweets or the existing content repurposed from various forms of media, such as television episodes, are generally not subject to ethical review processes. The formal process begins with the researcher completing an application for review.

Ethical Review Application Form

As directed by the TCPS2, an ethical review application at a university in Canada includes background information on the main or principal researcher, the affiliated institution, and the other investigators on the project. Also included are details about the proposed project, including the start and end date, the location where the study will be conducted, and other relevant specifics, such as ethical approval received or sought from other institutions and applicable funding sources. Researchers are required to provide a summary of their proposed project objectives and a brief literature review of the topic, and indicate the main hypotheses or research questions examined. An application also includes detailed information about the research participants, such as the number sought, the characteristics relevant to recruitment, and the ways in which the participants will be solicited.

In keeping with concerns for harm, researchers must disclose details of all known risks as well as any other foreseeable concerns stemming from participation. Researchers also need to provide justifications for any harm incurred and need to explain how safeguards or resolutions will be built into the study. The procedures to be used in the study are described in detail, including how informed and voluntary consent will be secured, how privacy will be respected, and how consent will be obtained. In cases where information is withheld from participants, explicit justification must be provided. Researchers also include details regarding when and how participants will be debriefed, if applicable, and their plans for the retention and disposal of data.

The application is typically submitted to the chair of the REB or through a web-based portal to a research office, along with any other kind of supporting documents deemed relevant in relation to the particular study, such as an advertisement for participant recruitment, an indication of ethical approval from another institution, an interview script or set of interview question guidelines, a participant informed-consent form, and/or a questionnaire or survey items.

Research Ethics Board Decision

Research ethics board members typically meet on a published scheduled (e.g., once a month) to review research applications and render a decision about the ethical acceptability of the proposed research, as guided by the TCPS2 2014. A decision is provided in writing to the researcher on behalf of the institution. It generally takes the form of an approval with no conditions, an approval subject to the conditions or proposed modifications provided by the committee, or a rejection on the grounds that the research project is deemed unethical for the reasons indicated.

Test Yourself

- What is a research ethics board and what is its role in relation to research?
- What kinds of study details are essential to include in an ethical review application form?

CHAPTER SUMMARY

LO1   Define research ethics and provide examples of research-related ethical conduct.

Research ethics refer to an array of considerations that arise in relation to the morally responsible treatment of humans in research. For example, ethical conduct includes minimizing the risk of harm to participants; treating participants fairly, equitably, and with respect; ensuring participants have provided informed and voluntary consent; and safeguarding privacy.

LO2 **Recognize links between early military and medical research and regulatory outcomes.**

Much of the early research conducted by Nazi doctors and military personnel involved severe injury or death for victims, who were forced to participate in experiments against their will. The Nuremberg Code consists of 10 ethical guidelines outlining safeguards for experiments, including the importance of obtaining informed and voluntary consent, providing justification for a study based on its overall merits versus potential for causing harm, minimizing the potential for harm, and giving subjects the liberty to withdraw their participation at any time. The Belmont Report comprises three main principles: respect for persons (a principle recognizing the autonomy and worth of individuals), beneficence (a principle stressing the importance of maximizing benefits and minimizing harm), and justice (a principle underlying socially responsible behaviour).

LO3 **Discuss ethical considerations raised by Milgram's and Zimbardo's classic studies in social research.**

In Stanley Milgram's experiments on obedience to authority, participants were harmed by the belief that they were administering painful electric shocks to another participant. In Philip Zimbardo's simulated prison study, prisoners were harmed by the aggressive and abusive tendencies that developed in the guards.

LO4 **Discuss the potential for harm, risk-benefit analysis, informed consent, privacy and confidentiality, and debriefing as major ethical considerations in social science research.**

Researchers attempt to design studies in a manner that minimizes the risk of any form of harm, such as physical or psychological. Informed consent refers to an autonomous process whereby participants are provided with the relevant details needed to make a judgment about whether or not to participate in a study. Anonymity exists if a researcher cannot link individual responses to the person who provided them. Confidentiality is a process for maintaining privacy wherein the researcher ensures that a participant's identity will not be publicly disclosed. Debriefing refers to a full disclosure and exchange of information regarding all aspects of the study.

LO5   **Identify the core principles that underlie the Tri-Council Policy Statement (TCPS2 2014).**

The overarching value of the TCPS2 2014 is respect for human dignity, expressed as respect for persons (i.e., human worth), concern for welfare (i.e., quality of life), and justice (i.e., fair and equitable treatment).

LO6   **Describe the role of an ethics review board and outline the process for undergoing an ethical review of research.**

The role of an ethics review board is to review the ethical acceptability of research on behalf of an institution, including approving, rejecting, proposing modifications to, or terminating any proposed or ongoing research involving humans. Researchers submit an application that summarizes a proposed study, along with the relevant ethical considerations, to the chair of the REB, the REB reviews the application, and the researcher is provided with a written decision.

RESEARCH REFLECTION

1.   Imagine you are a member of a research ethics board and the chair of the REB has asked you to come up with criteria for assessing the level of risk in social research. Develop criteria and/or provide examples to illustrate "low or minimal risk," "moderate risk," and "probable harm or high risk."

2.   Watch the Hollywood movie *The Stanford Prison Experiment* (2015), directed by Kyle Patrick Alvarez, to familiarize yourself with the original prison experiment conducted by Philip Zimbardo, Craig Haney, and Curtis Banks in 1971. Using the movie replica as a case study, provide an assessment of the key ethical issues raised by the study. If you were going to replicate this study, what changes would you make to resolve or mitigate ethical issues?

3.   Become an expert on the TCPS2 2014. The Government of Canada's Interagency Advisory Panel on Research Ethics offers an online tutorial for free. This condensed Course on Research Ethics (CORE) is designed to help researchers, members of research ethics boards, educators, students, and others become familiar with the TCPS2 2014. Upon completion, you will receive an official certification. You can access the TCPS2 Tutorial at www.pre.ethics.gc.ca.

4.   To learn about responsible conduct for researchers in relation to conflicts of interest and competing interests, authorship and publication, intellectual property, research misconduct, and liability, read chapter 8 in Unger, D. (2011). *The Canadian bioethics companion: An online textbook for Canadian ethicists and health care workers*, online at canadianbioethicscompanion.ca.

LEARNING THROUGH PRACTICE

Objective: To evaluate ethical issues in social research

Directions:

1. Locate and read Burger, J. M. (2009). Replicating Milgram: Would people still obey today? *American Psychologist, 64*(1), 1–11.
2. Describe the central research question and summarize the main procedures used to carry out the study on obedience.
3. Explain how the replication attempts to resolve for specific ethical implications raised in Milgram's original experiment. Do you think the changes accomplish this? Why or why not?
4. If you were a member of an institutional ethics review board, would you grant approval to this study with no conditions, provide approval but require changes to the study, or fail to grant approval? Justify your answer by referencing the main ethical issues discussed in this chapter.

RESEARCH RESOURCES

1. For further guidance on ethical issues, including assessing risk and benefits, protecting privacy, obtaining informed consent, working with vulnerable populations, and navigating ethical review processes, see Anderson, E. E., & Corneli, A. (2018). *100 questions (and answers) about research ethics.* Thousand Oaks, CA: Sage.
2. For information on ethical issues as they relate to visual representations in research, I recommend "Ethics and visual research" in Banks, M., & Zeitlyn, D. (2015). *Visual methods in social research* (pp. 122–126). Thousand Oaks, CA: Sage.
3. To learn more about ethical dilemmas concerning qualitative research, refer to Gallagher, K. (Ed.). (2018). *The methodological dilemma revisited: Creative, critical, and collaborative approaches to qualitative research for a new era.* New York, NY: Routledge.
4. To read about the Tuskegee syphilis study in more detail, refer to Jones, J. H. (1993). *Bad blood: The Tuskegee syphilis experiment.* New York, NY: The Free Press or Gray, F. D. (1998). *The Tuskegee syphilis study.* Montgomery, AL: NewSouth Books.

CHAPTER 4

Research Design and Measurement

In any discussion about improving measurement, it is important to begin with basic questions. What exactly are we trying to measure, and why?
    —Christine Bachrach, 2007, p. 435

Learning Objectives

After reading this chapter, students should be able to do the following:

LO1   Describe the main components of a research design.

LO2   Explain what conceptualization and operationalization processes entail.

LO3   Explain how the purpose of a variable is directly related to how it is measured in research.

LO4   Outline the main techniques used to assess reliability and validity.

LO5   Distinguish between random and systematic errors.

LO6   Explain how rigour is achieved in qualitative research.

INTRODUCTION

After carefully considering research foundations, the importance of theory, and the ethics involving research with humans, you are almost ready to delve into the techniques used for obtaining answers to social research questions. But before you can start collecting data, you need to develop a research plan that outlines who or what it is you are studying and how you will go about measuring and evaluating the attitudes, behaviours, or processes that you want to learn more about.

MAIN COMPONENTS OF A RESEARCH DESIGN

Linked to a specific research question, a **research design** "is the plan or blueprint for a study and includes the who, what, where, when, why, and how of an investigation" (Hagan, 2018, p. 57). Beginning with the "who," researchers in the social sciences most often study people, so individuals are usually the focus of investigation, called the **unit of analysis**. Individuals are often studied as part of a collective or group. For example, the unit of analysis could be students, employees, single-parent-headed families, low-income earners, or some other group of interest. Researchers also compare groups of individuals along particular variables of interest, such as a sample of individuals with less than a high school education versus those who have a grade 12 diploma, single- versus dual-income families, or patients who completed a treatment program versus ones who dropped out. Social institutions and organizations that guide individuals and groups can also be the units of analysis for research, such as the university you are attending, a not-for-profit agency such as the Canadian Red Cross, or a healthcare organization such as the Canadian Medical Association. Finally, social researchers are sometimes interested in artifacts created by people rather than people themselves. For example, researchers might examine newspapers, television shows, motion pictures, personal diaries, profiles on an online dating site, YouTube videos, Facebook posts, or Twitter tweets.

The "what" component of research design refers to whatever is specifically examined and measured in a study, such as attitudes, beliefs, views, behaviours, outcomes, and/or processes. The measured component is usually referred to as the "unit of observation" since this is what the data are collected on. For example, a researcher might be interested in factors affecting instructors' views on published ratings of instruction. Instructors at a university who take part in the study constitute the unit of analysis from whom the views on published ratings are obtained (i.e., the more specific focus of the research that comprises the data). Similarly, a researcher might be interested in dating preferences of individuals who use online matchmaking sites such as EliteSingles or Zoosk. The individuals seeking dates online are the units of analysis, while their posted profiles containing the characteristics of interest in the study are the units of observation.

The "where" pertains to the location of a study. The possibilities are endless, from research conducted first-hand in the field to studies conducted in the home of participants or even in the office of the principal researcher. The location for a study is closely linked to the unit of analysis since the researcher often needs to go to the individuals, groups, or organizations to collect information from them or about them. For example, a researcher interested in interviewing couples who met online might set up appointments to visit dating couples in restaurants or coffee shops near to where the couples reside, at the discretion of the participants. Alternatively, a researcher interested in online dating relationships might choose to gather information in a virtual environment by posting a survey on the internet.

The "when" relates to an important time consideration in the research design. Some studies are conducted once at a single point in time, and others are carried out at multiple points over time. Most often, when social researchers carry out a study, it takes place at a single point in time or within a single time frame, such as when a researcher develops a questionnaire about internet dating and administers it to a group of people attending a singles' social function. This is called **cross-sectional research** because the study is made up of a cross-section of the dating population taken at a point in time, like taking a photo that captures a person or group at a single point in time. Alternatively, social researchers sometimes study individuals or groups at multiple points in time using what is called **longitudinal research**. For example, a sample of dating couples might be surveyed shortly after they meet and again after dating for one year to capture their initial viewpoints and to see how their perceptions change once they get to know each other better. Four longitudinal designs are discussed below.

A **panel study** is a longitudinal study in which a researcher observes the same people, group, or organization at multiple points in time. A new phase of a large-scale panel study called Alberta's Tomorrow Project was launched in 2017 to learn more about the causes of cancer. The study, active since 2000, includes 55,000 cancer-free Albertans (Alberta's Tomorrow Project, 2018a). Researchers from Alberta's Tomorrow Project collect information on participants' health and lifestyle through surveys and the occasional collection of other specimens, such as blood samples. Going back to the dating example, by collecting information on the same dating couples at various intervals, a researcher could use a panel study to examine how relations evolve or change over time.

A **cohort study** is like a panel study, except, rather than focusing on the same people, it focuses on comparable people over time. "Comparable" refers to a general category of people who are deemed to share a similar life experience in a specified period. The most common example of this is a birth cohort. Think about your classmates in school. Although there were individual differences between you and your classmates, you also shared some common life events, such as the music that topped the charts at that time, the clothing fads and hairstyles, and the political events that occurred during that era. Following the earlier example, a researcher might include people who met and married an online dating partner in 2015 as a unit of analysis. Several couples might be studied in 2015 shortly after they were married, several other couples who also married in 2015 might be studied in 2016, another group in 2017, another group in 2018, and so on over a period of five years.

A **time-series study** is a longitudinal study in which a researcher examines different people at multiple points in time. Every year, Statistics Canada gathers information from thousands of Canadians using what is called the General Social Survey. Although the participants are different each time, similar forms of information are gathered over time to detect patterns and trends. For example, we can readily discern that Canadians today are delaying marriage (i.e., getting married for the first time at a later age) and they are having fewer children relative to 20 years ago. Going back to the online dating example used throughout this section, a researcher might use a time-series study in order to gather information from new dating couples at an online site each year for five years. Looking at the data over time, a researcher would be able to determine if there are changes in the overall profiles of online daters at that site. For example, the use of the site might be increasing for groups such as highly educated women or single individuals over the age of 60 years.

Lastly, a **case study** is a research method in which a researcher focuses on a small number of individuals or even a single person over an extended period. You'll learn more about this method in chapter 11. For now, you can think of a case study as a highly detailed study of a single person, group, or organization over time. For example, a researcher might study an alcoholic to better understand the progression of the disease over time, or a researcher might join a subculture, such as a magic card club that meets every Friday night, to gain an insider's perspective of the group. Similarly, a researcher could examine the experiences of a frequent online dater over time to get a sense of how online dating works at various sites. See figure 4.1 for an overview of time considerations in relation to units of analysis.

Figure 4.1: Time Considerations by Units of Analysis

Source: Created by author

Research in Action

Longitudinal Panel Study on Smokers' Perceptions of Health Risks

Cho and colleagues (2018) examined changes in smokers' perceptions about health risks following amendments to warning labels on cigarette packages using a longitudinal panel study. Four thousand six hundred and twenty-one smokers from Canada, Australia, Mexico, and the United States were surveyed every four months for a total of five times to determine if their knowledge of health risks increased after toxic constituents were added to pictorial health warning labels. Results showed that knowledge of toxic constituents such as cyanide and benzene increased over time and was associated with a stronger perceived risk of vulnerability to smoking-related diseases, including bladder cancer and blindness, for participants in Canada, Australia, and Mexico, but not the United States (Cho et al., 2018).

Warning labels are designed to increase smokers' knowledge of health risks.
Source: Created by author

In addition to the time dimension, a research design also includes the "why" and the "how" plan for a study. "Why" relates to the purpose of a study as discussed in chapter 1. A study on internet dating could be focused on exploring ways in which people represent themselves in posted profiles; describing who uses internet dating sites; explaining the importance of including certain types of information, such as appearance or personality factors, for attracting dates; or evaluating the effectiveness of a given site in matching suitable partners. The nature of the study really depends on the interests of the researcher and the nature of the issue itself.

"How" refers to the specific method or methods used to gather the data examined in a study. With an interest in the merit of including certain items in a dating profile, a researcher might opt for an experimental design to explain, for example, whether certain characteristics in posted dating profiles are better than others for eliciting potential dates (see chapter 6 for a discussion of different types of experiments). An experiment is a special type of quantitative research design in which a researcher changes or alters something to see what effect it has. In the dating example, an experimenter might compare the number of responses to two profiles posted on an internet dating site. If the profiles are identical except for one trait—for example, one profile might contain an additional statement saying the person has a great sense of humour—it would be possible to determine the importance of that trait in attracting potential partners.

Recall from chapter 1 that the specific methods or techniques differ depending on whether a researcher adopts a qualitative or quantitative orientation, and the approach itself links back to the research interest. A researcher interested in learning more about why people make dates online or how people define themselves online is more apt to use a qualitative approach. Qualitative researchers tend to engage in research that seeks to better understand or explain some phenomenon using field research and in-depth interviews, as well as strategies involving discourse analyses and content analyses that can be used to help to uncover meaning. Regardless of the approach taken and specific methods used, all researchers must work through various design considerations and measurement issues in their quest to carry out scientific research. Similarly, both qualitative and quantitative researchers undertake a process of conceptualization and measurement—it just occurs differently and at different stages within the overall research process, as discussed in the next section.

Test Yourself

- What does a research design inform us about?
- What is the main difference between cross-sectional and longitudinal research?
- What is the name for research on the same unit of analysis carried out at multiple points in time?
- In what ways will a quantitative research design differ from a qualitative one?

CONCEPTUALIZATION AND OPERATIONALIZATION

Researchers in the social sciences frequently study social issues, social conditions, and social problems that affect individuals, such as environmental disasters, legal policy, crime, healthcare, poverty, divorce, marriage, or growing social inequality between the rich and poor, within a conceptual framework. Their quest is to explore, describe, explain, or evaluate the experiences of individuals or groups. A conceptual framework is the more concentrated area of interest used to study the social issue or problem, which includes the main objects, events, or ideas, along with the relevant theories that spell out relationships. Terms like *family* or *crime* are broad **concepts** that refer to abstract mental representations used to signify important elements of our social world. Concepts are very important because they form the basis of social theory and research in the social sciences. However, as often-abstract representations, concepts like family can be vague since they mean different things to different people. Consider what the concept of family means to you. Does your notion of a family include aunts and uncles or second cousins? What about close friends? How about pets? People have very divergent views about what a family is or is not. The concept of family also has very different meanings depending on the context in which it is applied. For example, there are rules about who is or is not considered eligible to be sponsored under family status for potential immigration to Canada, or who may or may not be deemed family for visitation rights involving prisoners under the supervision of the Correctional Service of Canada. Because concepts are broad notions that can take on various meanings, researchers need to carefully define the concepts (or constructs) that underlie their research interests as part of the conceptualization and operationalization process.

Conceptualization, in research, is the process where a researcher explains what a concept or construct means in terms of a research project. For example, a researcher studying the impact of education cutbacks on the family, with an interest in the negative implications for children, might adopt the broad conceptualization of family provided by Statistics Canada (2018c):

> Census family is defined as a married couple and the children, if any, of either and/or both spouses; a couple living common law and the children, if any, of either and/or both partners; or a lone parent of any marital status with at least one child living in the same dwelling and that child or those children. All members of a particular census family live in the same dwelling. A couple may be of opposite or same sex. Children may be children by birth, marriage, common-law union or adoption regardless of their age or marital status as long as they live in the dwelling and do not have their own married spouse, common-law partner or child living in the dwelling. Grandchildren living with their grandparent(s) but with no parents present also constitute a census family. (para. 1)

The concept of a family differs depending on the context in which it is applied.

Source: Monkey Business Images/shutterstock.com

Conceptualization is essential since it helps us understand what is or is not being examined in a study. For example, based on the conceptualization provided above, children being raised by their grandparents or living in homes headed by single parents would be included in the study, but might have otherwise been missed if a more traditional definition of family were employed.

Source: ©Betsy Streeter, www.Cartoonstock.com

The term *concept* is often used interchangeably with a similar term, *construct*. Both refer to mental abstractions; however, concepts derive from tangible or factual observations (e.g., a family exists), while **constructs** are more hypothetical or "constructed" ideas that are part of our thinking but do not exist in readily observable forms (e.g., love, honesty, intelligence, motivation). While we can readily measure and observe crime through different acts that are deemed criminal (the concept crime), we infer intelligence through measures such as test scores (the construct intelligence). Both concepts and constructs are the basis of theories and are integral components underlying social research. Like concepts, constructs undergo a process of conceptualization when they are used in research. Suppose a researcher is interested in studying social inequality, which we commonly understand to mean differences among groups of people in terms of their access to resources such as education or healthcare. We know some people can afford private schools, while others cannot. We understand that healthcare benefits differ depending on factors such as how old a person is, how much one pays for a health plan, what type of job one has, and where one lives. Social inequality is a construct that conjures up a wide range of examples and notions. To examine social inequality in a specific study, a researcher might opt to use personal finances as an **indicator** of social inequality. An indicator is "a measurable quantity which 'stands in' or substitutes, in some sense, for something less readily measurable" (Sapsford, 2006, para. 1). Personal finances can be further specified as employment income, since most of the working population is able to state how much they earn in dollars.

Note that in the case of employment income, people earn a certain amount of money (i.e., gross pay), but they receive a different amount as their take-home pay after taxes and various deductions (i.e., net pay). The process we use to examine with precision the progression of taking an abstract construct, such as social inequality, and conceptualizing it into something tangible, such as net income, is known as operationalization. **Operationalization** is the process whereby a concept or construct is defined so precisely that it can be measured. In this example, financial wealth was operationalized as net yearly employment income in dollars. Note that once a construct such as social inequality has been clarified as financial wealth and then measured in net yearly income dollars, we are now working with a variable, since net yearly income is something that can change and differ between people. Quantitative researchers examine variables. A researcher interested in implications of social inequality might test the hypothesis that among individuals who work full time, those with low net yearly incomes will report poorer health compared to people with high net yearly incomes. In this example, health (the second variable) might be operationalized into the self-reported ratings of very poor, poor, fair, good, or very good.

In contrast, qualitative researchers tend to define concepts based on the users' own frameworks. Qualitative researchers are less concerned with proving that certain variables affect the individual. Instead, they are more concerned with *how* individuals make sense of their own social situations and *what* the broader social factors are for such framing.

Research in Action

Online Dating and Variables

Students routinely have difficulty understanding what variables are, let alone how to explore research questions that contain them. A starting point is to examine what is contained in a typical "profile" posted on any internet dating site, such as EliteSingles or Zoosk. Registered members list certain attributes they feel best describe themselves and that may also be helpful in attracting a compatible dating partner, such as their age, physical features, and certain personality traits. For example, someone might advertise as a single male, 29 years of age, 5′11″, in great shape, with a good sense of humour, seeking men between the ages of 25 and 35 for friendship. These attributes are variables; many that are routinely used in social research! Variables are often defined using

Personal profiles on dating sites are largely made up of variables.

Source: www.pexels.com

categories. For example, the word *single* refers to a category of the variable "marital status." Marital status is a variable since it is a property that can differ between individuals and change over time, as in single, common-law, married, separated, widowed, or divorced. Other variables listed on dating sites include age (in years), gender and preference (e.g., man interested in men), height (in feet and inches), body type (slim, fit, average), eye colour (e.g., green, blue, or brown), and astrological sign (e.g., Virgo, Libra, Scorpio). Even the purpose or intent of the posting constitutes a variable, since a person may state whether they are seeking fun, friendship, dating, or a long-term relationship.

Test Yourself

- What is a concept? Provide an example of one that is of interest to social researchers.
- Why is conceptualization important to researchers?
- What is an indicator? Provide an example of one that could be used in a study on aggression.
- What are three variables you could examine in a study of online dating relationships?

MEASURING VARIABLES

Now that you better appreciate what is meant by a variable, you can also start to see how variables are operationalized in different ways. Some variables are numerical, such as age or income, while others pertain more to categories and descriptors, such as marital status or perceived health status. Decisions made about how to clarify a construct such as health have important implications for other stages of the research process, including what kind of analyses are possible and what kind of interpretations can be made. For example, the categories for the self-reported health variable described above can tell us whether someone perceives their health to be better or worse than someone else's (e.g., "very good" is better than "good," while "fair" is worse than "good" but better than "poor"). However, from how this variable is measured, we are unable to ascertain how much worse or how much better someone's health is relative to another.

Levels of Measurement

Variables mean different things and can be used in different ways, depending upon on how they are measured. At the lowest level, called the **nominal level**, we can classify or label cases, such as persons, according to marital status, eye colour, religion, or the presence of children. These are all qualitative variables. Even if we assign numbers to the categories for marital status, where 1 = single, 2 = common-law, 3 = married, 4 = separated, 5 = widowed, and 6 = divorced, we have not quantified the variable. This is because the numbers serve only to identify the categories so that a 6 now represents anyone who is currently "divorced." The numbers themselves are arbitrary; however, they serve the function of classification, which simply indicates that members of one category are different from another category.

At the next level of measurement, called the **ordinal level**, we can classify and order categories of the variables of interest, such as people's perceived health into levels, job satisfaction into ratings, or prestige into rankings. Note that these variables are measured as more or less, or higher or lower amounts, of some dimension of interest. The variable health, then, measured as very good, good, fair, poor, and very poor, is an ordered variable since we know that very good is higher than good and therefore indicates better health. However, as noted earlier, we cannot determine precisely what that means in terms of how much healthier someone is who reports very good health. Ordinal variables are also qualitative in nature.

At the next highest level of measurement, called the **interval level**, we can classify, order, and examine differences between the categories of the variables of interest. This is possible because the assigned scores include equal intervals between categories. For example, with temperature as a main variable, we know that 28°C is exactly one degree higher than 27°C, which is 7 degrees higher than 20°C, and so on.

Statisticians sometimes make a further distinction between an interval and **ratio level** of measurement. Both levels include meaningful distance between categories, as well as the properties from the lower levels. However, a true zero only exists at the ratio level of measurement constituting the additional property. In the case of temperature, 0°C cannot be taken to mean the absence of temperature (an absolute or true zero). At the ratio level, however, there is a true zero in the case of time, where a stopwatch can count down from two minutes to zero, and zero indicates no time left. Most variables that include the property of score assignment have a true zero. One way to determine if a variable is measured at the ratio level is to consider if its categories can adhere to the logic of "twice as." For example, an assessment variable where a person can achieve twice the score of someone else

Figure 4.2: Properties and Functions of Levels of Measurement

Source: Created by author

or net employment income where one employee can earn twice that of another are both measured at the ratio level. Interval- and ratio-level variables are quantitative, and they are amenable to statistical analyses such as tests for associations between variables. The properties of each level of measurement are summarized in figure 4.2.

Indexes versus Scales

Instead of using the response to a single statement as a measure of some construct, indexes and scales combine several responses together to create a composite measure of a construct. An **index** is a composite measure of a construct comprising several different indicators that produce a shared outcome (DeVellis, 2017). For example, in a study on gambling, Wood and Williams (2007) examined the extent to which internet gamblers manifest a "propensity for problem gambling" (i.e., the outcome). The propensity for problem gambling was assessed using nine items composing the Canadian Problem Gambling Index (CPGI). The CPGI consists of a series of nine questions, which follow prompts to consider only the preceding 12 months, including "Thinking about the last 12 months . . . have you bet more than you could really afford to lose?"; "Still thinking about the last 12 months, have you needed to gamble with larger amounts of money to get the same feeling of excitement?"; and "When you gambled, did you go back another day to try and win back the money you lost?" The response categories for all nine items are sometimes (scored as 1), most of the time (scored as 2), almost always (scored as 3), or don't know (scored as zero). The scores are added up for the nine items, generating an overall score for propensity for problem gambling that ranges between 0 and 27, where 0 = non-problem gamblers, 1–2 = a low-risk for problem gambling, 3–7 = a moderate risk, and 8 or more = problem gamblers (Ferris & Wynne, 2001). Although the index has several items, they all independently measure the same thing: the propensity to become a problem gambler. And while there are expected relationships between the items—for instance, spending more than one can afford to lose is assumed to be associated with needing to gamble with larger amounts of money to get the same feeling of excitement—the indicators are not derived from a single cause (DeVellis, 2017). That is, a person may gamble more than they can afford to lose due to a belief in luck, while the same person might need to gamble larger amounts due to a thrill-seeking tendency. Regardless of their origins, the indicators result in a common outcome: the tendency to become a problem gambler. The higher the overall score on an index, the more of that trait or propensity the respondent has.

In contrast, a **scale** is a composite measure of a construct consisting of several different indicators that stem from a common cause (DeVellis, 2017). For example, the Eysenck Personality Questionnaire–Revised (EPQR) is a 48-item questionnaire designed to measure an individual's personality (the construct) via extroversion and neuroticism (Eysenck, Eysenck, & Barrett, 1985). Extroversion and neuroticism are two underlying potential causes for certain behavioural tendencies. Extroversion is the propensity to direct one's attention outward toward the environment. Thus, extroverts tend to be people who are outgoing or talkative. Sample yes/no forced-choice items on the EPQR measuring extroversion include the statements "Are you a talkative person?"; "Do you usually take the initiative in making new friends?"; and "Do other people think of you as being very lively?" Neuroticism refers to emotional stability. For example, a neurotic person is someone who worries excessively or who might be described as moody. Sample questions include "Does your mood often go up and down?"; "Are you an irritable person?"; and "Are you a worrier?"

Note that there are some similarities between indexes and scales, and that these terms are often used interchangeably (albeit incorrectly!) in research. Both indexes and scales measure constructs—for example, dimensions of personality, risk for problem gambling—using nominal variables with categories such as yes/no and presence/absence, or ordinal variables depicting intensity such as very dissatisfied or dissatisfied. In addition, both are composite measures, meaning they are made up of multiple items. However, there are also some important differences (see figure 4.3).

While an index is always an accumulation of individual scores based on items that have no expected common cause, a scale is based on the assignment of scores to items that are believed to derive from a common cause. In addition, scales often comprise items that have logical relationships between them. Namely, someone who indicates on the EPQR that they "always take the initiative in making new friends" and "always get a party going" is also very likely to "enjoy meeting new people," but is very unlikely to be "mostly quiet when with other people." In addition, specific items in a scale can indicate varying intensity or magnitude of a construct in a manner that is accounted for by the scoring. For example, the Bogardus social distance scale measures respondents' willingness to participate with members of other racial and ethnic groups (Bogardus, 1933). The items in the scale have different intensity, meaning certain items show more unwillingness to participate with members of other groups than others. For example, an affirmative response to the item "I would be willing to marry outside group members" indicates very low social distance (akin to low prejudice) and scores 1 point, whereas an affirmative response to "I would have (outside group members) merely as speaking acquaintances" scores 5, indicating more prejudice. A scale takes advantage of differences in intensity or the magnitude between indicators of a construct and weights them accordingly when it comes to scoring. In contrast, an index assumes that all items are different but of equal importance.

Sometimes it can be difficult to determine if an instrument is better classified as a scale or an index. For example, the Eating Attitudes Test (EAT-26) was

Figure 4.3: Comparing an Index to a Scale

Source: Created by author

developed by Garner and Garkfinkel (1979) as a self-report measure designed to help identify those at risk for an eating disorder such as anorexia nervosa. Taken together, it can be considered an index since it is based on items that do not have a single underlying cause since eating disorders can result from many different individual causes. Importantly, as required by an index, the indicators are used to derive a composite score for a common outcome (risk of anorexia) by summing up the scores obtained for all 26 independent items. However, the EAT-26 also contains three sub-scales, where certain items can be used to examine dimensions of anorexia that are believed to be the result of dieting, bulimia and food preoccupation, and oral control (common causes).

Test Yourself

- What property distinguishes the ordinal level of measurement from the nominal?
- What are the main properties and functions of the interval level of measurement?
- What special property does the ratio level have that distinguishes it from the interval level of measurement?
- In what ways are indexes and scales similar and different?

CRITERIA FOR ASSESSING MEASUREMENT

Measurement often involves obtaining answers to questions posed by researchers. In some cases, the answers to questions might be very straightforward, as would be your response to the question "How old are you?" But what if you were instead asked, "What is your ethnicity?" Would your answer be singular or plural? Would your answer reflect the country you were born in and/or the one you currently reside in? Did you consider the origin of your biological father, mother, or both parents' ancestors (e.g., grandparents or great-grandparents)? Did you think about languages you speak other than English or any cultural practices or ceremonies you engage in? Ethnicity is a difficult concept to measure because it has different dimensions; it reflects ancestry in terms of family origin as well as identity in the case of more current personal practices. According to Statistics Canada (2017a), if the intent of the study is to examine identity, then a question such as "With which ethnic group do you identify?" is probably the best choice, since it will steer respondents to that dimension by having them focus on how they perceive themselves. To assess whether measures are "good" ones, you can evaluate their reliability and validity.

RELIABILITY

As a quantitative term, **reliability** refers to the consistency in measurement. A measurement procedure is reliable if it can provide the same data at different points in time, assuming there has been no change in the variable under consideration. For example, a weigh scale is generally considered to be a reliable measure for weight. That is, if a person steps on a scale and records a weight, the person could step off and back on the scale and it should indicate the same weight a second time. Similarly, a watch or a clock—barring the occasional power outage or worn-out battery—is a dependable measure for keeping track of time on a 24-hour cycle (e.g., your alarm wakes you up for work at precisely 6:38 a.m. on weekdays). Finally, a specialized test can provide a reliable measure of a child's intelligence in the form of an intelligence quotient (IQ). IQ is a numerical score determined using an instrument such as the Wechsler Intelligence Scale for Children—Fifth Edition (WISC-V), released by Pearson in 2014. The test consists of questions asked of a child by a trained psychologist who records the answers and then calculates scores to determine an overall IQ (Weschler, 2003). IQ is considered a reliable indicator of intelligence because it is stable over time. The average IQ for the general population is 100. A boy who obtained an IQ score of 147 on the WISC-V at age eight would be classified as highly gifted. If that same person took an IQ test several years later, the results should also place the person in the highly gifted range. While a child could have a "bad test day" due to illness or distraction and a lowered score, it is unreasonable to assume a score of 147 could result from fluke guesses. Four ways to determine if a measure is reliable or unreliable are discussed below, including test-retest, split-half, inter-rater, and inter-item reliability.

Test-Retest Reliability

Demonstrating that a measure of some phenomenon, such as intelligence, does not change when the same instrument is administered at two different points in time is known as **test-retest reliability**. Test-retest reliability is usually assessed using the Pearson product-moment correlation coefficient (represented by the symbol r). The correlation ranges between 0 and +1.00 or –1.00, representing the degree of association between two variables. The closer the value of r is to ±1.00, the greater the degree or strength of the association between the variables. For example, an

r of +.80 is higher than one that is +.64, 0 indicates no relationship between the two variables, and 1.00 indicates a perfect relationship. The positive or negative sign indicates the *direction* of a relationship. A plus sign indicates a positive relationship, where both variables go in the same direction. For example, an r of +.60 for the relationship between education and income tells us that as education increases, so does income. In 2015, Canadians aged 25 to 64 who worked full time and had a high school diploma earned about $55,774 per year, while those with a bachelor's degree earned $82,082 (Statistics Canada, 2016b). In the case of negative correlations, the variables go in opposite directions, such as an $r = -.54$ for education and prejudice. With increased education, we can expect decreased prejudice.

To evaluate test-retest reliability, the correlation coefficient denotes the relationship between the same variable measured at time 1 and time 2. The correlation coefficient (also called a reliability coefficient) should have a value of .80 or greater to indicate good reliability (Cozby & Bates, 2018). Test-retest reliability is especially important for demonstrating the accuracy of new measurement instruments. Currently, the identification of gifted children is largely restricted to outcomes determined by standardized IQ tests administered by psychologists (Pfeiffer, Petscher, & Kumtepe, 2008). Expensive IQ tests are only funded by the school system for a small fraction of students, usually identified early on as having special needs. This means most students are never tested, and many gifted children are never identified as such. An alternative instrument, the Gifted Rating Scales (GRS), published by PsychCorp/Harcourt Assessment, is based on teacher ratings of various abilities, such as student intellectual ability, academic ability, artistic talent, leadership ability, and motivation. Test-retest reliability coefficients for this assessment tool's various scales were high, as reported in the test manual. For example, the coefficient for the Academic Ability scale used by teachers on a sample of 160 children aged 12.00 to 13.11 years old and reapplied approximately a week later was .97 (Pfeiffer et al., 2008).

Split-Half Reliability

An obvious critique of test-retest reliability concerns the fact that since participants receive the same test twice or observers provide ratings of the same phenomenon at close intervals in time, the similarity in results could have more to do with memory for the items than the construct of interest. An alternative to the test-retest method that provides a more independent assessment of reliability is the **split-half reliability** approach. Using this method, a researcher provides exactly half the items at time 1 (e.g., only the odd-numbered items or a random sample of the questions on a survey) and the remaining half at time 2. In this case, the researcher compares the two halves for their degree of association.

Inter-Rater Reliability

Another way to test for the reliability of a measure is by comparing the results obtained on one instrument provided by two different observers. This is called **inter-rater reliability** (and interchangeably inter-judge, inter-coder, or inter-observer reliability). Inter-rater reliability is the overall percentage of times two raters agree after examining each pair of results. Using the IQ example above, two different teachers would provide assessments of the students on the various indicators of giftedness and then the two sets of responses would be compared. If two different teachers agree most of the time that certain children exhibit signs of giftedness, we can be more confident that the scales are identifying gifted children as opposed to showing the biases of a teacher toward their students.

A statistical test called Cohen's kappa is usually employed to test inter-rater reliability because it takes into account the percentage of agreement as well as the number of times raters could be expected to agree just by chance alone (Cohen, 1960).[1] Given the conservative nature of this test, Landis and Koch (1977) recommend considering coefficients of between .61 and .80 as substantial, and .81 and over as indicative of near-to-perfect agreement. Building on the earlier example, the test manual for the GRS reported an inter-rater reliability of .79 for the academic ability of children aged 6.00 to 9.11 years old, based on the ratings of two different teachers for 152 students (Pfeiffer et al., 2008).

Inter-Item Reliability

Lastly, when researchers use instruments that contain multiple indicators of a single construct, it is also possible to assess **inter-item reliability**. Inter-item reliability (also called internal-consistency reliability) refers to demonstrated associations among multiple items representing a single construct, such as giftedness. First, there should be close correspondence between items evaluating a single dimension. For example, students who score well above average on an item indicating intellectual ability (e.g., verbal comprehension) should also score well above average on other items making up the intellectual ability scale (e.g., memory, abstract reasoning). The internal consistency of a dimension such as intellectual ability can be assessed using Cronbach's alpha, a coefficient ranging between 0 and 1.00,

Test-Retest	Split-Half	Inter-Rater	Inter-Item
• renders the same findings at **two different times** using the same instrument	• renders the same findings provided by **two halves** of the same instrument	• renders the same findings as provided by **two different observers**	• renders the same findings as provided by **two or more indicators**

Figure 4.4: Distinguishing among Techniques Used to Assess Reliability

Source: Created by author

which considers how pairs of items relate to one another (co-vary), the variance in the overall measure, and the number of items there are (Cronbach, 1951).

In addition, since giftedness is a broad-ranging, multi-dimensional construct that is usually defined to mean more than just intellectual ability, students who score high on the dimension of intellectual ability should also score high on other dimensions of giftedness, such as academic ability (e.g., math and reading proficiency) and creativity (e.g., novel problem solving). Pfeiffer, Petscher, and Kumtepe (2008) reported a correlation coefficient of .95 between intellectual ability and academic ability, and one of .88 between intellectual ability and creativity using the GRS. The four approaches for assessing reliability that were discussed in this section are summarized in figure 4.4.

Research on the Net

Assessing Inter-Rater Reliability

Matthew Lombard, along with Jennifer Snyder-Duch and Cheryl Campanella Bracken, created a web resource to help researchers and students better understand inter-rater reliability, which stemmed from their earlier literature review (see Lombard, Snyder-Duch, & Bracken, 2002). The authors apply inter-coder (i.e., inter-rater) reliability to a specific research technique called content analysis and provide step-by-step instructions alongside screen shots to illustrate how to calculate the measures using software. The site, named "Practical Resources for Assessing and Reporting Intercoder Reliability in Content Analysis Research Projects," can be accessed at matthewlombard.com/reliability.

Test Yourself

- What is reliability? Provide an example of a reliable measure used in every-day life.
- What is the main difference between test-retest reliability and split-half reliability?
- What type of reliability renders the same findings provided by two different observers?
- What type of reliability refers to demonstrated associations among multiple items representing a single construct?

VALIDITY

Perhaps even more important than ensuring consistency in measurement, we need to be certain that we are measuring the intended construct of interest. **Validity** is a term used by quantitative researchers to refer to the extent to which a study examines what it intends to. Not all reliable measures are valid. We might reliably weigh ourselves with a scale that consistently tells us the wrong weight because the dial was set two kilograms too high. Similarly, we may depend upon an alarm clock that is consistently ahead of schedule by a few minutes because it was incorrectly programmed. In this section, you will learn about four methods for evaluating the extent to which a given measure is measuring what it is intended to using face validity, content validity, construct validity, and criterion validity.

Face Validity

First, in trying to determine if a measure is a good indicator of an intended construct, we can assess the measure's face validity. **Face validity** refers to the extent to which an instrument or variable appears on the surface or "face" to be a good measure of the intended construct. Grade point average, for example, appears to be a pretty good measure of a student's scholastic ability, just as net yearly income seems like a valid measure of financial wealth. Your criteria for determining whether something has face validity is an assessment of whether the operationalization used is logical. For example, in the case of giftedness, most teachers would agree that children who exhibit very superior intellectual ability (i.e., the ability to reason at high levels) also tend to exhibit very superior academic ability (e.g., the ability to function at higher than normal levels in specific academic areas, such as math or reading).

Content Validity

Content validity refers to the extent to which a measure includes the full range or meaning of the intended construct. To adequately assess your knowledge of the general field of psychology, for example, a test should include a broad range of topics, such as how psychologists conduct research, the brain and mental states, sensation, perception, and learning. While a person might not score evenly across all areas of psychology (e.g., a student might score 20 out of 20 on the questions related to sensation and perception and only 15 out of 20 on items about research methods), the test result (35/40) should provide a general measure of knowledge regarding introductory psychology. Similarly, the Gifted Rating Scale discussed earlier is an instrument designed to identify giftedness that includes not only items related to intellectual ability, but also content pertaining to the dimensions of academic ability, creativity, leadership, and motivation. This is not to say that a person scoring in the gifted range will achieve the same ratings on all items. For example, it is possible for a gifted child to score in the very superior range for intellectual and academic ability as well as creativity, but only superior for motivation and average for leadership. However, when taken together, the overall (i.e., full-scale) IQ score is 130 or greater for a gifted individual.

Construct Validity

Another way to assess validity is through **construct validity**, which examines how closely a measure is associated with other measures that are expected to be related, based on prior theory. For example, Gottfredson and Hirschi's (1990) general theory of crime rests on the assumption that a failure to develop self-control is at the root of most impulsive and even criminal behaviours. Impulsivity, as measured by school records, such as report cards, should then correspond with other impulsive behaviours, such as deviant and/or criminal acts. If a study fails to show the expected association (e.g., perhaps children who fail to complete assignments or follow rules in school as noted on report cards do not engage in higher levels of criminal or deviant acts relative to children who appear to have more self-control in the classroom), then the measures of missed assignments and an inability to follow rules may not be valid indicators of the construct. That is, the items stated on a report card, for example, incomplete assignments, may be measuring something other than impulsivity, such as academic aptitude, health issues, or attention deficit problems. In this case, a better school indicator of impulsivity might be self-reported ratings of disruptive behaviour by the students themselves or teachers' ratings of student impulsivity rather than the behavioural measures listed on a

Figure 4.5: Distinguishing among Techniques Used to Assess Validity

Source: Created by author

report card. Alternatively, behavioural measures from other areas of a person's life, such as a history of unstable relationships or a lack of perseverance in employment, may be better arenas for assessing low self-control than the highly monitored and structured early school environment.

Criterion Validity

Finally, a measure of some construct of interest can be assessed against an external standard or benchmark to determine its worth using what is called **criterion validity**. We can readily anticipate that students who are excelling are also more likely to achieve academic awards, such as scholarships, honours, or distinction, and go on to higher levels of education. Academic ability as measured by grades or grade point average is predictive of future school and scholastic success. Similarly, consider how most research-methods courses at a university or college have a prerequisite, such as a minimum grade of C– in a 200-level course. The prerequisite indicates basic achievement in the course. It is the cut-off for predicting future success in higher-level courses in the same discipline. The prerequisite has criterion validity if most students with the prerequisite end up successfully navigating their way through research methods. All four types of validity are summarized in figure 4.5.

Test Yourself

- Are all reliable measures valid? Explain your answer.
- What does it mean to say a measure has face validity?
- What does content validity assess?
- Which type of validity is based on the prediction of future events?

RANDOM AND SYSTEMATIC ERRORS

Researchers and research participants are potential sources of measurement error. Think about the last time you took a multiple-choice test and accidently entered a response of *d* when you intended to put *e*, or when you rushed to finish an exam and missed one of the items in your answer because you didn't have time to re-read the instructions or your answers before handing in the test. Similarly, errors occur in research when participants forget things, accidently miss responses, and otherwise make mistakes completing research tasks. Also, researchers produce inconsistencies in any number of ways, including by giving varied instructions to participants, by missing something relevant during an observation, and by entering data incorrectly into a computer program (where a 1 might become an 11). Errors that result in unpredictable mistakes due to carelessness are called **random errors**. Random errors made by participants can be reduced by simplifying the procedures (e.g., participants make fewer mistakes if instructions are clear and easy to follow and if the task is short and simple). Even researchers' and observers' unintentional mistakes can be reduced by using standardized procedures, simplifying the task as much as possible, training observers, and using recording devices or apparatus other than people to collect first-hand data (e.g., replaying an audio recording for verification following an interview). Random errors mostly influence reliability since they work against consistency in measurement.

In contrast to random errors, **systematic errors** refer to ongoing inaccuracies in measurement that come about through deliberate effort. For example, a researcher who expects or desires a finding might behave in a manner that encourages such a response in participants. Expecting a treatment group to perform better than a control group, a researcher might interpret responses more favourably in the treatment group and unjustifiably rate them higher. The use of standardized procedures, such as scripts and objective measures that are less open to interpretation, can help reduce researcher bias. In addition, it might be possible to divide participants into two groups without the researcher being aware of the groups until after the performance scores are recorded.

Study participants make other types of intentional errors, including ones resulting from a social desirability bias. Respondents sometimes provide untruthful answers to present themselves more favourably. Just as people sometimes underestimate the number of cigarettes they smoke when asked by a family physician at an annual physical examination, survey respondents exaggerate the extent to which they engage in socially desirable practices (e.g., exercising, healthy eating) and minimize their unhealthy practices (e.g., overuse of non-prescription pain medicine, binge drinking). Researchers using a questionnaire to measure a construct sometimes build in a lie scale along with the other dimensions of interest. For example, in the Eysenck Personality Questionnaire–Revised (EPQR), there are 12 lie-detection items, including the statements "If you say you will do something, do you always keep your promise no matter how inconvenient it might be?"; "Are all your habits good and desirable ones?"; and "Have you ever said anything bad or nasty about anyone?" A score of 5 or more indicates social desirability bias (Eysenck et al., 1985).

Similarly, participants in experimental research sometimes follow what Martin Orne (1962) called demand characteristics or environmental cues, meaning they pick up on hints about what a study is about and then try to help the researchers and the study by behaving in ways that support the hypothesis. Systematic errors influence validity since they reduce the odds that a measure is gauging what it is truly intended to.

Test Yourself

- Who is a potential source of error in measurement?
- Which main form of errors can be reduced by simplifying the procedures in a study?
- What is the term for the bias that results when respondents try to answer in the manner that makes them look the most favourable?

RIGOUR IN QUALITATIVE RESEARCH

While it is important for anyone learning about research to understand the centrality of reliability and validity criteria for assessing measurement instruments, it is also imperative to note that much of what has been discussed in this chapter pertains mainly to quantitative research that is based in the positivist paradigm. Qualitative research, largely based in the interpretative and critical paradigms, is aimed at understanding socially constructed phenomena in the context in which it occurs at a specific point in time. It is therefore less concerned with the systematic reproducibility of data. In many cases, statements provided by research participants or processes studied cannot be replicated to assess reliability. Similarly, if we are to understand events from the point of view of those experiencing them, validity is really in the eyes of the individual actor for whom that understanding is real. That is not to say reliability and validity are not relevant in qualitative research; in fact, if we conclude that these constructs are not applicable to qualitative research, then we run the risk of suggesting that qualitative inquiry is without **rigour**. As defined by Gerard A. Tobin and Cecily M. Begley (2004), "rigour is the means by which we show integrity and competence; it is about ethics and politics, regardless of the paradigm" (p. 390). This helps to legitimize a qualitative research process.

Just as various forms of reliability and validity are used to gauge the merit of quantitative research, other criteria such as rigour, credibility, and dependability can be used to establish the trustworthiness of qualitative research. **Credibility** (comparable to validity) has to do with how well the research tells the story it is designed to. For example, in the case of interview data, this pertains to the goodness of fit between a respondent's actual views of reality and a researcher's representations of it (Tobin & Begley, 2004). Credibility can be enhanced through the thoroughness of a literature review and open coding of data. For example, in the case of a qualitative interview, the researcher should provide evidence of how conclusions were reached. **Dependability** is a qualitative replacement for reliability and this "is achieved through a process of auditing" (Tobin & Begley, 2004, p. 392). Qualitative researchers ensure their research processes, decisions, and interpretations can be examined and verified by other interested researchers through **audit trails**. Audit trails are carefully documented paper trails of an entire research process, including research decisions such as theoretical clarifications made along the way. Transparency, detailed rationale, and justifications all help to establish the later reliability and dependability of findings (Liamputtong, 2013).

Similarly, while questions of measurement and the operationalization of variables may not apply to qualitative research, questions concerning how the research process was undertaken are essential. For example, in a study using in-depth interviews, were the questions posed to the respondents in a culturally sensitive manner that was readily understood by them? Did the interview continue until all important issues were fully examined (i.e., saturation was reached)? Were the researchers appropriately reflective in considering their own subjectivity and how it may have influenced the questions asked, the impressions they formed of the respondents, and the conclusions they reached from the findings (Hennick, Hutter, & Bailey, 2011)? Qualitative researchers acknowledge subjectivity and accept researcher bias as an unavoidable aspect of social research. Certain topics are examined specifically because they interest the researchers! To reconcile biases with empirical methods, qualitative researchers openly acknowledge their preconceptions and remain transparent and reflective about the ways in which their own views may influence research processes.

Achieving Rigour through Triangulation

One of the main ways rigour is achieved in qualitative research is by using **triangulation**. Triangulation is the use of multiple methods to establish what can be considered the qualitative equivalent of reliability and validity (Willis, 2007). For example, we can be more confident in data collected on aggressive behavioural displays in children if data obtained from field notes taken during observations closely correspond with interview statements made by the children themselves. We can also be more confident in the findings when multiple sources converge (i.e., **data triangulation**), as might be the case if the children, teachers, and parents all say similar things about the behaviour of those being studied. Since the data comes from various sources with different perspectives, the data can also exist in a variety of forms, from comments made by parents and teachers, to actions undertaken by children, to school records and other documents, such as report cards.

Other Means for Establishing Rigour

Various alternative strategies to triangulation that help to establish rigour in qualitative studies include the use of member checks, prolonged time spent with research participants in a research setting, peer debriefing, and audit checking (Liamputtong, 2013; Willis, 2007). **Member checks** are attempts by a researcher to validate emerging findings by testing out their accuracy with the originators of that data while still in the field. For example, researchers might share observational findings with the group being studied to see if the participants concur with what is being said. It helps to validate the data if the participants agree that their perspective is being appropriately conveyed by the data. Whenever I conduct interviews with small groups (called focus groups, as discussed in chapter 9), I share the preliminary findings with the group and ask them whether the views I am expressing capture what they feel is important and relevant, given the research objectives. I also ask whether the statements I've provided are missing any information that they feel should be included to more fully explain their views or address their concerns about the topic.

Qualitative researchers also gain a more informed understanding of the individuals, processes, or cultures they are studying if they spend prolonged periods of time in the field. Consider how much more you know about your fellow classmates at the end of term compared to what you know about the group on the first day of classes. Similarly, over time, qualitative researchers learn more and more about the individuals and processes of interest once they gain entry to a group, establish relationships, build trust, and so on. Time also aids in triangulation as researchers are better able to verify information provided as converging sources of evidence are established.

In addition to spending long periods of time in the field and testing findings via their originating sources, qualitative researchers also substantiate their research by opening it up to the scrutiny of others in their field. **Peer debriefing** involves attempts to authenticate the research process and findings through an external review provided by another qualitative researcher who is not directly involved in the study (Creswell & Creswell, 2018). This process helps to verify the procedures undertaken and substantiate the findings, lending overall credibility to the study. Note that reflexivity and other features underlying ethnographic research are discussed in detail in chapter 10, while multiple methods and mixed-methods approaches are the subject matter of chapter 11.

Test Yourself

- What is the qualitative term for validity?
- How do qualitative researchers ensure their research processes and conclusions can be verified by other researchers?

CHAPTER SUMMARY

LO1   Describe the main components of a research design.
A research design details the main components of a study, including who (the unit of analysis), what (the attitudes or behaviours under investigation), where (the location), when (at one or multiple points in time), why (e.g., to explain), and how (the specific research method used).

LO2   Explain what conceptualization and operationalization processes entail.
Conceptualization is the process whereby a researcher explains what a concept, such as family, or a construct, like social inequality, means within a research project. Operationalization is the process whereby a concept or construct is defined so precisely it can be measured in a study. For example, financial wealth can be operationalized as net yearly income in dollars.

LO3   Explain how the purpose of a variable is directly related to how it is measured in research.
Variables are measured at the nominal, ordinal, interval, and ratio level. The nominal level of measurement is used to classify case, while the

ordinal level has the property of classification and rank order. The interval level provides the ability to classify, order, and make precise comparisons as a function of equal intervals. The ratio level includes previous properties and a true zero. An index is a composite measure of a construct comprising several different indicators that produce a shared outcome, while a scale is a composite measure of a construct consisting of several different indicators that stem from a common cause.

LO4   Outline the main techniques used to assess reliability and validity.

Reliability refers to consistency in measurement. *Test-retest* reliability examines consistency between the same measures for a variable at two different times using a correlation coefficient. *Inter-rater* reliability examines consistency between the same measures for a variable of interest provided by two different raters, often using Cohen's kappa. *Split-half* reliability examines consistency between both halves of the measures for a variable of interest. *Inter-item* reliability involves demonstrated associations among multiple items representing a single construct. *Validity* refers to the extent to which a measure is a good indicator of the intended construct. *Face* validity refers to the extent to which an instrument appears to be a good measure of the intended construct. *Content* validity assesses the extent to which an instrument contains the full range of content pertaining to the intended construct. *Construct* validity assesses the extent to which an instrument is associated with other logically related measures of the intended construct. *Criterion* validity assesses the extent to which an instrument holds up to an external standard, such as the ability to predict future events.

LO5   Distinguish between random and systematic errors.

Random errors are unintentional and usually result from careless mistakes, while systematic errors result from intentional bias. Sources of both types of errors include participants, researchers, and observers in a study. Errors can be reduced through training, the use of standardized procedures, and the simplification of tasks.

LO6   Explain how rigour is achieved in qualitative research.

Rigour refers to a means for demonstrating integrity and competence in qualitative research. Rigour can be achieved using triangulation, member checks, extended experience in an environment, peer review, and audit trails.

RESEARCH REFLECTION

1. Suppose you want to conduct a quantitative study on the success of students at the post-secondary institution you are currently attending. List five variables that you think would be relevant for inclusion in the study. Generate one hypothesis you could test using two of the variables you've listed above. Operationalize the variables you included in your proposed hypothesis.
2. Studies on the health of individuals often operationalize health as self-reported health using these five fixed response categories: poor, fair, good, very good, and excellent. What level of measurement is this? Provide an example of health operationalized into two categories measured at the nominal level and three categories at the ordinal level. Is it possible to measure health at the interval level? Justify your answer.
3. Consider some of the variables that can be used to examine the construct of scholastic ability (e.g., grades, awards, and overall grade point average). Which measure do you think best represents scholastic ability? Is the measure reliable and/or valid? Defend your answer with examples that reflect student experiences.
4. Define the construct of honesty and come up with an indicator that could be used to gauge honesty. Compare your definition and indicator with those of at least three other students in the class. Are the definitions similar? Consider how each definition reflects a prior conceptualization process.

LEARNING THROUGH PRACTICE

Objective: To construct an index for students at risk for degree incompletion

Directions:

1. Item selection: Develop 10 statements that can be answered with a forced-choice response of *yes* or *no*, where *yes* responses will receive 1 point and *no* responses will be awarded 0 points. Select items that would serve as good indicators of students at risk for failing to complete their program of study. Think of behaviours or events that would put a student at risk for dropping out or being asked to leave a program, such as failing a required course. Make sure your items are one-dimensional (i.e., they only measure one behaviour or attitude).
2. Try out your index on a few of your classmates to see what scores you obtain for them. Is there any variability in the responses? Do some students score higher or lower than others?

3. Come up with a range of scores you feel represent no risk, low risk, moderate risk, and high risk. Justify your numerical scoring.

RESEARCH RESOURCES

1. To locate and learn more about a cohort-based longitudinal National Population Health Survey (NPHS), search "National Population Health Survey" on Statistics Canada's home page: statcan.gc.ca.
2. To learn more about the longitudinal panel study on cancer called Alberta's Tomorrow Project, discussed near the start of this chapter, visit the website myatp.ca.
3. For an in-depth look at scale development, see DeVellis, R. F. (2017). *Scale development: Theory and applications* (4th ed.). Thousand Oaks, CA: Sage.
4. To learn more about how rigour is achieved in qualitative research, see Tobin, G. A., & Begley, C. M. (2004). Methodological rigour within a qualitative framework. *Journal of Advanced Nursing, 48*(4), 388–396.

NOTE

1. Cohen's kappa is generally used only with nominal variables. If the variables of interest are at the ordinal or interval/ratio level, Krippendorff's alpha is recommended (Lombard, Snyder-Duch, & Bracken, 2002).

CHAPTER 5

Sampling

"The Census Program provides a statistical portrait of the country every five years" (Statistics Canada, 2018b). While the national census of population collects information such as age and income on everyone in Canada, a survey collects information from only a portion (a sample) of the targeted population.

Learning Objectives

After reading this chapter, students should be able to do the following:

LO1   Define sampling and differentiate between a population and a sample.

LO2   Explain why a researcher might choose a probability-based sampling method and distinguish between simple random, systematic, stratified, and cluster sampling techniques.

LO3   Identify the main advantages and disadvantages of probability-based sampling techniques.

LO4   Explain why a researcher might choose a non-probability-based method and distinguish between convenience, snowball, purposive, and quota sampling techniques.

LO5   Identify the main advantages and disadvantages of non-probability-based techniques.

LO6   Explain how theoretical sampling differs from probability- and non-probability-based sampling techniques.

INTRODUCTION

Recall from chapter 4 how a research design details the plan for a study, beginning with whom the study is about. In addition to identifying the unit of analysis—such as individuals, groups, or organizations—a design also provides details on how the unit of analysis was selected. **Sampling** is the technique used to acquire the unit of analysis from a population of interest. You already use sampling in everyday life as you "sample" a grape or a cherry at a local supermarket before buying the entire bunch. Similarly, you might try a couple of food samples offered to you at a local market before choosing an item to purchase in greater quantity. If you are a parent, perhaps you have tried out or sampled several babysitters for short periods of time before settling on one that you feel is best suited for looking after your child for extended periods of time. Finally, you probably hang out with a select group of friends as opposed to everyone in your class, and you invite only certain people over from your place of work. In social research, an investigator sometimes selects a sample of individuals, or chooses a group or an organization to study, in hopes of generalizing the findings to a wider population of interest. In other cases, a sample is chosen because that group best suits the research problem, interest, and/or needs of the investigator. In this chapter, you will learn why it is important to sample, what the relationship is between samples and populations, and how to conduct probability- and non-probability-based sampling.

A buyer samples candies before making a purchase.
Source: Askolds Berovskis/shutterstock.com

POPULATIONS AND SAMPLES

A **population** is "the total collection of all cases in which the researcher is interested and that [they wish] to understand better" (Healey, Prus, & Lieflander, 2019, p. 8). As noted in the opening passage, Statistics Canada's census population is every single person living in Canada, while another population of interest to Statistics Canada researchers is all employed Canadians. Statistics Canada's Labour Force Survey questions about 56,000 households across Canada every month (a sample) to estimate the total population of employed and unemployed Canadians (Statistics Canada, 2018g).

As another example, all students enrolled at the University of Toronto might compose a population for a researcher interested in views on tuition costs. Universities keep records on registered students, including their status as full-time or part-time, their home mailing addresses and phone numbers, and so on. From fall 2017 to winter 2018, the University of Toronto had an enrolment of 90,077 students (University of Toronto, 2018). While the population is "known," it would be difficult to locate every student since some students change addresses and phone numbers without updating their contact information. In addition, some of the students who can be located may be too busy or otherwise uninterested in participating in the study. Finally, it could take years to complete a study with tens of thousands

A sample is a subset of the population of interest.

Source: lamnee/shutterstock.com

of participants and it might be too costly to do so. An important question, then, is whether it is necessary to include the entire student body. The short answer is "no." Using techniques discussed in this section, a smaller **sample** of students can be obtained for use in a study and their views can be indicative of the larger population.

Finally, Toronto's homeless might constitute a population of interest to a social worker from the University of Toronto interested in the daily challenges faced by individuals who are living on the street. It is generally not possible to identify or locate all homeless people living in Toronto; therefore, it would be very difficult to even determine who composes the population of interest. Instead, a researcher could examine homelessness using secondary resources, such as reports from local agencies that deal directly with homeless individuals in the area or conduct interviews with employees of agencies that work with homeless people. Alternatively, the researcher might opt to speak with a small number of homeless individuals who agree to participate in the study. While not representative of the entire population of interest, such a sample is available for inclusion in a study and it will still constitute an important unit of analysis, especially as a starting point, to learn about challenges facing homeless individuals.

SELECTING A SAMPLE

Researchers use two main types of procedures to obtain a sample: **probability sampling** and **non-probability sampling**. Probability sampling is a method in which every individual or element in the population has a known chance of being selected. Non-probability sampling is a method in which the chance of selection of an individual or element in the population is unknown.

Test Yourself

- What is sampling and when might you use this in everyday life?
- What is the relationship between a sample and a population?
- What is the difference between probability and non-probability sampling?

PROBABILITY SAMPLING

Probability sampling is used when a researcher wants a **representative sample**: "A sample is representative of the population from which it is selected if the aggregate characteristics of the sample closely approximate those same aggregate characteristics in the population" (Babbie & Roberts, 2018, p. 155). For example, if a population consists of students who are mainly enrolled full-time and taking classes in the day, then those students who end up in the sample should also be mostly full-time students who attend day classes. To the extent that this is true, the findings obtained from the sample will generalize to the larger population. This is very important when the researcher wants to accurately capture the views of the entire population but the population is so large it would be difficult if not impossible to include every member in a study. A survey on the views of people living in the province of Ontario or a survey on the views of all Canadians are examples of projects best carried out with probability sampling. Most surveys conducted by Statistics Canada utilize probability sampling (Statistics Canada, 2018i). Probability sampling relies upon known probabilities concerning the pro-portion of times an event will occur. For example, when you roll a die and you hope for a five, the probability of obtaining a five is one chance in six, since there are six possibilities on the die (1, 2, 3, 4, 5, 6). Similarly, when you flip a coin and you hope for "heads," the probability of obtaining heads is one out of two (or 0.5), since there are two possible outcomes (heads or tails). With probability sampling, the population must be known (i.e., every member is identifiable to the researcher). In the example used earlier, it is possible to identify all 90,077 students attending the University of Toronto via a list generated by the registrar's office. The complete list of 90,077 students is called a **sampling frame**. If a sampling frame can be made available, then the researcher can calculate probabilities, and probability sampling is possible. Four types of probability-based sampling techniques are de-scribed here.

Simple Random Sampling

Simple random sampling is a method used to obtain individuals (or cases) that make up a sample based on chance alone. For example, if we randomly select one student from the U of T sampling frame, this means that student, like any other student at U of T, has a 1 in 90,077 chance of being selected. Note that the term *random* is not to be confused with *haphazard*, as in any method will work. Random only means that chance alone determines the selection based on probability. For example, imagine 10 people attend a meeting and all 10 people write their names on little slips of paper of the same size, which are then put into a hat and mixed around, and one is randomly drawn for a prize. Each person in attendance has an equal chance of winning, with a probability of 1 out of 10. But what if two or three prizes are to be given out? "Sampling with replacement" means the first person

HARDIN

"Do you really care about my opinion or am I just a random sample?"

Source: ©Patrick Hardin, www.Cartoonstock.com

drawn would be put back into the hat for another try at a prize, keeping the odds at 1:10 for all members in attendance, including the person who already won a prize. However, research in the social sciences (like many door prize raffles) is usually carried out using "sampling without replacement." This means that after the first person wins the prize, they are taken out of the draw. The odds for the next prize winner then change to 1:9, and for a third prize to 1:8. While the probability of selection for each case (or element) from the population is always known, the probability of selection for each case is not always identical.

To obtain a random sample without replacement, a researcher would need to follow these steps:

1.   Generate a complete list of all individuals in the population.
2.   Number every individual in the sampling frame.
3.   Use a random numbers table to randomly select the sample of a specific size as described below.

A random numbers table is a computer-generated listing of random numbers. There are various internet sites that contain tools for generating random number

100 Random Numbers
54243 07462 57727 20932 83471 76008 56167 01689 75046 59054 83107 10946
71197 70599 48470 24781 71926 20568 42333 67115 35000 65191 40773 47872
02652 72159 67713 57129 88880 83705 33076 70964 23454 33673 26938 47143
52683 78296 25379 27901 44257 61342 52319 13235 40408 72888 17681 50992
41137 22857 77699 03249 04211 01325 09984 74083 61940 74448 36924 59418
58091 85994 02287 07098 82743 35962 62304 49432 21894 80585 84667 30189
79623 87553 21530 39446 75774 09022 76970 53281 10349 49068 46910 05538
63500 03614 69273 76372 31151 76736 06136 85629 27303 22128 61576 09387
51954 38251 31516 51721

Figure 5.1: A Random Numbers Table Generated Using Stat Trek

Source: Stat Trek (2019)

tables (e.g., stattrek.com). These are straightforward to use: simply enter how large a sample you wish to include in your study (e.g., 100), which numbers represent the sampling frame (e.g., for the University of Toronto example above, the minimum possible value is 1 and the maximum value is 90,077), and that you wish to use sampling without replacement. When the table is generated, it will include *only* 100 randomly selected non-repeating numbers within that range. For example, the first number might be 54243, meaning the first person included in the sample will be the student whose name is beside the number 54243 on the sampling frame. Going across the first row, the second number listed is 07462, indicating that the second person included in the sample would be whoever was numbered 7462, and so on until the 100th person, corresponding to whoever is listed as 51721 in the sampling frame (see figure 5.1).

Systematic Sampling

As a potentially more efficient alternative to simple random sampling, some researchers opt for **systematic sampling**. Systematic sampling is a method used to obtain individuals that compose a sample based on a fixed interval, representing every nth listed case. For example, using an interval of size five, a random starting point is selected that is between 1 and 5, and then every fifth person listed in the sampling frame would be selected for inclusion in the sample. The fixed interval is called a **sampling interval** and it is calculated by dividing the population size by the desired sample size. Using our earlier example, $90{,}077 \div 100 = 900.77$

or, rounded to the nearest whole number, is every 901st student. The steps are summarized as follows:

1. Generate a complete list of all individuals in the population.
2. Number every individual in the sampling frame.
3. Calculate the sampling interval by dividing the population by the desired sample size.
4. Randomly select the first case. It should be a number between 1 and the size of the sampling interval. For the example above, it would involve randomly selecting a number between 1 and 901, such as 10.
5. Use every nth number after that (as denoted by the sampling interval) until the number of cases selected reaches the desired sample size. In this example, the sampling interval is 901. The first person included in the sample would be whoever is listed at 10, then 911, then 1,812, 2,713, and so on until the desired sample size is reached.

Stratified Sampling

Stratified sampling is a method used to obtain a sample based on known population characteristics. Researchers using stratified sampling are trying to ensure that certain characteristics of the population, such as age, gender, ethnicity, education, location, or any other attribute deemed especially relevant to a given study, end up in the sample. To accomplish this, researchers divide the population into subgroups based on known characteristics and then randomly (or systematically) sample for a certain number of cases from each group (see figure 5.2).

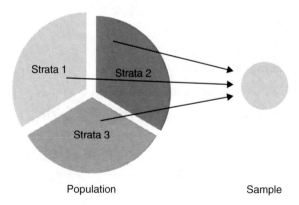

Population   Sample

Figure 5.2: Stratified Sampling

Source: Created by author

For example, a researcher interested in 1,200 instructors' views on abolishing student ratings of instruction might want a sample that includes full-time instructors, as well as those who teach on a part-time basis (often called sessional or term instructors). In this example, the instructors would first be grouped based on their teaching status (full-time or part-time). Each of the two groups is considered a "strata." If the goal is a sample size of 100 instructors, 50 can be randomly selected from the part-time strata and 50 can be randomly selected from the full-time strata. While even subgroups are desirable for some statistical tests, this practice can detract from representativeness, depending on how the characteristic of interest is distributed in the population. For example, there are likely to be more part-time instructors overall, meaning that the sample obtained through the stratified technique is now somewhat less representative than what was obtained using simple random and systematic sampling. Researchers can, instead, opt for a "proportionate" sample that includes an equivalent ratio of relevant characteristics as exists in the population. For example, if 750 of the 1,200 instructors teach part-time, then 62.5 percent of the sample would also need to be made up of part-time instructors. This can be achieved if the researcher randomly selects for 63 part-time and 37 full-time instructors.

Finally, in some instances, a researcher may wish to specifically examine certain characteristics of importance and might purposely oversample for these traits. For example, if part-time instructors are known to have more reservations about student ratings of instruction because they hold only limited appointments without job security, a researcher might intentionally oversample part-time instructors to learn as much as possible about their concerns. **Disproportionate sampling** is the term used to describe a sampling method used deliberately to obtain a different ratio of relevant characteristics than what exists in the population.

Research in Action

Statistics Canada Sampling Methods

Most of the national surveys conducted by researchers at Statistics Canada include representative samples based on one or more of the probability-based techniques. For example, the Canadian Community Health Survey (CCHS), designed to assess the health and well-being of Canadians through a series of questions on health status, health determinants, and utilization of healthcare services, targets everyone 12 years of age and over living in the ten provinces and three territories (Statistics Canada, 2018a). Although the survey excludes a few groups, such as persons who are living on reserves, those serving in the Canadian Forces, and institutionalized populations, the sample has 130,000 respondents and represents about 97 percent of the Canadian population. The CCHS is based on a cross-sectional design and uses multi-stage stratified cluster sampling. First, clusters are selected based on geographic location, and then they are adjusted for the population size to ensure adequate representation from individuals of various ages. Finally, systematic sampling is used to obtain dwellings within the clusters (Statistics Canada, 2018a). The data collected by the survey are used by various organizations and individuals, including Health Canada, mental health services, and universities. It is also used by researchers who conduct additional analyses. For example, Nowrouzi-Kia, Li, Nguyen, and Casole (2018) used the CCHS to look for trends in heart disease based on occupational risk factors such as long working hours. Findings revealed no association between hours worked and heart disease (Nowrouzi-Kia, Li, Nguyen, & Casole, 2018).

Cluster Sampling

In contrast to simple random, systematic, and stratified sampling methods, which all rely on the selection of cases one individual at a time, **cluster sampling** is a method for selecting groups based on their geographic location. Sometimes, even with a sampling frame it might not be feasible to reach every person who might end up in a sample, as might be the case if they are thinly spread across a huge geographic area. In such cases, a researcher might randomly sample a few clusters (or locations), and then everyone in the selected clusters would be included in the sample (see figure 5.3).

For example, a researcher wishing to interview people about their summer vacation spots by lakes in Alberta would be unable to obtain a complete sampling frame of individuals with campers, trailers, or cabins near lakes in Alberta. Even if it were possible to create such a listing, it would not be feasible for a researcher to locate everyone in the vast area including Peace River, Grand Prairie, Hinton, Red Deer, Canmore, Jasper, Wainwright, and Lethbridge. Instead, the population of interest can be divided into mutually exclusive clusters based on geographic location. The Alberta Fishing Guide (2019) divides Alberta lakes into 14 main geographic zones (Eastern Slopes 1; Eastern Slopes 2; Eastern Slopes 3; Eastern Slopes 4; Parkland-Prairie 1, etc.). Within each of the 14 zones (or clusters), there

Sample =
Randomly
selected clusters
(e.g., 2 & 3)

Figure 5.3: Cluster Sampling

Source: Created by author

are several lakes (e.g., Eastern Slopes 1 includes 159 lakes). A researcher can randomly sample one lake from each cluster and then attempt to conduct interviews with everyone in those 14 lake communities. If every person or instance from a cluster is included in the sample, the overall process is called "one-stage cluster sampling." Even though the researcher in this example limited the study to only 14 lake communities, there might be several hundred lake dwellers within each community, resulting in a sample size into the tens of thousands. To decrease the sample size, a researcher might utilize random or systematic sampling within each lake community. For example, the researcher might randomly sample for 20 members within each of the lakes chosen, for a total sample size of 280. Further sampling within clusters is called "two-stage cluster sampling." For an overview of the four probability-based sampling techniques, refer to figure 5.4.

Research in Action

Understanding Sampling

For additional information on sampling techniques with numerous straightforward examples, view Dr. Manishika Jain's lecture titled "Sampling and Its 8 Types: Research Methodology" posted on YouTube on May 26, 2017. You can access this video at youtube.com by searching the title.

Simple Random	Systematic	Stratified	Cluster
• Used when there is a known sampling frame • Equal chance of selection (unbiased) • Considered the ideal since the sample will be highly representative of the population • There is still some sampling error, but this can be reduced by increasing the sample size	• Used when there is a known sampling frame • Every *n*th element after a random start • Is more straightforward to carry out than simple random sampling • Could be problematic if there is any special order to the sampling frame	• Used when there is a known sampling frame • Based on subgroups that contain important attributes • Good for ensuring certain strata are represented in the sample • Used with simple or systematic sampling • May not be representative, depending on the distribution of the strata in the population	• Used when the complete sampling frame is not readily available or accessible • Practical when there are readily identifiable subgroups spread across diverse geographic locations • Results in a fairly large overall sample size, which could be costly to study

Figure 5.4: Overview of Probability-Based Sampling Techniques

Source: Created by author

Test Yourself

- When is probability sampling used in research?
- What is a sampling frame?
- Is sampling usually carried out with or without replacement in social research?
- Which sampling method is especially practical when subgroups are spread across diverse geographic locations?
- Which sampling method relies upon a fixed sampling interval?

ADVANTAGES AND DISADVANTAGES OF PROBABILITY SAMPLING

Representativeness

The biggest advantage of a probability-based sampling method is that the sample generated is a fair representation of the population of interest. This means information obtained from the sample, often in the form of opinions of respondents who complete a survey or provide answers during an interview, is generalizable to the larger population. As a result, when a sample of students expresses their desire for published instructor ratings, we can be reasonably assured that the points raised are relevant to the wider study body. For example, if students in the sample noted that they wanted ratings published so that they could be used in the selection of courses and instructors, we can be certain that most students would identify the same benefits stemming from the disclosure of student ratings of instruction (Howell & Symbaluk, 2001). A population that has very little variability, as is the case if members of a population hold similar views or have similar characteristics, is considered "homogenous." The more homogenous a population is, the more confident we can be that a sample drawn from it represents that population. For example, if most students believe student ratings of instruction accurately measure teaching effectiveness, and most students support the public disclosure of ratings, then it doesn't really matter if the sample contains one hundred or five hundred students, since their responses are likely to repeatedly express the same position. Alternatively, if there is variation in views toward student ratings of instruction, as is the case with instructors—where some consider student ratings to be valid measures of teaching excellence, while others perceive them to be biased measures of teaching that are highly influenced by things like grades or level of course difficulty—a larger sample of instructors would be necessary to ensure that the appropriate variation was similarly captured in the study.

Sampling Error and Sample Size

Although the overall purpose of using a probability-based sampling method is to obtain a sample that is representative of the population, a sample generally does not contain the exact same parameters as the population of interest. For example, imagine your methods class of 30 students constitutes a population and your teacher randomly selects five students from the class list. While the class or population average on a midterm might be 78 percent, with a range of marks from 48 percent to 100 percent, the average for a sample of only five students might be quite different, depending on the exact students selected. If one of the top students ends up in the sample, even if the remaining four are "average," the mean for the sample is likely to be quite a bit higher than 78 percent. Similarly, if even just one student is quite a bit below average, the sample mean will be substantially lower than what exists for the population. The difference between the sample mean ($\bar{x}$) and the population mean (μ) is called **sampling error**. When researchers rely upon a sample to tell them about a population, they account for the likely amount of error using what is called a **confidence interval**. A confidence interval is an estimated range that is likely to contain the true population value, based on the sample value. A confidence level tells you how sure you can be that the results obtained using the sample are accurate. For example, an analyst might report that a survey's findings are accurate within 4 percentage points (the confidence interval) with 95 percent accuracy (the confidence level). If the survey found that 56 percent of Canadians sampled support raising the Goods and Services Tax (GST) back to the pre-2006 level (i.e., from 5 percent to 7 percent), this means that the analyst is 95 percent sure between 52 percent and 60 percent of all Canadians support the tax increase.

Research on the Net

Random Sampling and Sampling Error

To help make the notion of sampling error clearer, complete the very quick interactive activity that is part of a math tutorial provided by Annenberg Learner at learner.org/courses/learningmath/data/session1/part_d/random_noflash.html.

   Goal: To select five circles (a sample) to accurately represent all 60 circles (the population)

   Instructions:

1. Click on the start button.
2. Read the instructions under "Your Selection," where you are invited to select 5 circles from a population of 60 circles of various diameters. The goal is to select circles that you think, taken together, would represent the average size of the circles in the population. When you are ready to begin, click on the "Make a Selection" button.
3. Note the average diameter for your selection.
4. Now click on the "Random Selection" tab. Note any differences between the randomly selected diameter and the one that was generated when you "eyeballed" the data. Also note that if you redo steps 2 or 4, you will get different values.
5. Finally, select the "All 60 Circles" tab to discover the true diameter of the 60 circles.
6. If the sample size was increased from 5 to 15, how do you think it might influence the average diameter for the sample?

Source: Annenberg Learner. (2017). Random sampling. In *Data analysis, statistics, & probability.* Session 1, Part D: Bias in Sampling. Annenberg Foundation.

One way to be more confident in the findings based on a sample (i.e., to re-duce sampling error) is to increase the size of the sample used. That is, the larger the sample, the more confident we can be that it will contain the same features as the population. Clearly, selecting only two students from a methods class is less likely to give you an accurate sense of how 30 students are doing than if the sample contained 10 students. But does a larger sample always increase accuracy? In other words, how big is big enough? The needed sample size can be determined using a statistical formula based on probability theory, which accounts for the confidence level, the size of the confidence interval, and the population size. While such calculations are beyond the scope of this chapter, most introductory statistics text-books include the formula in a chapter on sampling distributions. As an example, if a population has 2,000 people, you only need 92 in your sample to be within 10 percentage points of accuracy, but you will need 322 in the sample to be within 5 points (Cozby & Bates, 2018, p. 153).

Research on the Net

Sample Size Calculator
Creative Research Systems, a survey software developer, offers a free online sample size calculator as a public service. Using the calculator at surveysystem.com/sscalc.htm, you can determine the sample size you need for a represen-tative sample by selecting a preferred confidence level, entering a confidence interval, and indicating the population size. For example, using a 95 percent confidence level and choosing an interval of 5 (to represent the number of percentage points we could be "off" the population mean), if we were using a sample of students' views toward publishing instructor ratings at the University of Toronto, where the population size is 90,077, we would need a sample size of 383. Try it!

Test Yourself

- What is the main advantage of using probability-based sampling methods?
- What is sampling error?
- Why does increasing a sample size lead to improved accuracy?

NON-PROBABILITY SAMPLING

Thus far I have discussed techniques based on probability, or the known chance of being selected. All sampling that is not based on known probabilities is a form of non-probability sampling. In non-probability sampling, the likelihood of selection of an individual or element in the population is unknown. This is usually because the sampling frame cannot be readily identified, such as the opening example of homeless people in Toronto. Members of many subgroups of interest to researchers are difficult to identify or locate, including survivors of natural disasters and people living in remote communities. Others may wish to avoid detection for any number of reasons, as might be the case for individuals who live in polygamous marriages. Those who are identifiable and willing to participate in a study are very important and relevant contributors to our understanding of the subgroup or community of interest. Four common non-probability sampling techniques are discussed in more detail here: convenience, snowball, purposive, and quota sampling.

Convenience Sampling

Convenience sampling is a non-probability method used to obtain individuals or cases that make up a sample based on availability. A newspaper reporter who is developing a story about a fire in an apartment building might ask anyone who is present outside the apartment building if they have any information on the fire. Similarly, a researcher interested in community responses to fire evacuations after a state of emergency is declared might interview anyone who can be reached from the community of interest. In both cases, the sample will not be representative of the entire population; however, the reporter is likely to find out something about the fire in the apartment building and learn about select resident concerns, just as the researcher will find out how some members of the community are faring following the fire-related evacuation. Convenience sampling is sometimes called "haphazard sampling" and "accidental sampling" due to the way the sample is obtained. However, I prefer convenience sampling since the other terms imply disorganized research practices. A research question or the characteristics of a population of interest may necessitate the use of a sample that was obtained based on its availability. In this sense, availability only means potential accessibility or obtainability, not an easy route to acquiring a sample.

Convenience sampling is often used in exploratory qualitative research where one group of interest is studied as a starting point for learning more about an area. For example, Globerman (1996) conducted a study to learn more about the motivations of family members caring for relatives with Alzheimer's disease, a form of dementia. Specifically, she was interested in questions such as "How do in-laws take responsibility for their spouses' parents?" To obtain the sample, Globerman sent a letter to family contacts for patients diagnosed with Alzheimer's who were residing in the community and were registered with a geriatric psychiatric clinic. The letter of request specified that Globerman wanted to interview at least three members of the family, all of whom would need to be living within 60 miles of the city. Of the 60 requests she sent out, 38 families agreed to participate in the study. Although not generalizable to all Canadian caregivers of elderly family members with Alzheimer's, Globerman (1996) identified various patterns of interaction that could be explored in future research, including one in which sons-in-law tended to act as "performers," who helped out when needed or directed to do so by their wives, and daughters-in-law acted more as "directors," taking more of the initiative to get things done.

Snowball Sampling

Another type of convenience sampling is **snowball sampling**. Snowball sampling, also called "chain sampling" and "referral sampling," is a non-probability method used to obtain a sample based on one or two available cases, followed by referrals that come from the original cases. For example, a researcher identifies one person who is suitable for the study, and that individual refers the researcher to another suitable individual, usually based on shared group membership. The next recruited participant then introduces the researcher to other potential participants, who then provide additional contacts. The process continues until a large enough sample is secured, like how a snowball collects surrounding snow and grows larger as it is moved along.

This technique is often used by researchers studying deviant or "hidden" populations. For example, as part of a larger study on drug-using street-involved youth in Vancouver, British Columbia, Stoltz et al. (2007) identified associations between early forms of child abuse and later involvement in sex work. Clearly, a sampling frame for homeless youth who are drug addicts is non-existent. The starting point for such a sample is usually whoever can be obtained through a convenience strategy, in this case involving what the researchers refer to as "extensive street-based outreach." Willing participants are eventually located and recruited into the study, often with the help of social workers or members of agencies that already have an established rapport with members of the hidden population. For example, outreach organizations provide free condoms and clean needles to homeless individuals to reduce the transmission of diseases, and through their interactions, workers come to know some of the individuals living on the street. The snowball aspect of sampling comes into play through efforts to get initial participants to recruit their drug-using homeless peers and friends into the study (Stoltz et al., 2007).

Purposive Sampling

Purposive sampling involves a combination of sampling techniques used to obtain all possible cases that possess elements or characteristics of interest to the researchers. For example, McIntyre et al. (2003) were interested in finding out why disadvantaged women in Canada had lower than required dietary intakes but their children did not. The researchers used purposive sampling to obtain a sample of mothers living in Atlantic Canada who were lone parents of at least two children and whose income was at or below Statistics Canada's low-income cut-off. With this sampling technique, the goal is to obtain a certain type of sample using a combination of strategies. To locate as many cases as possible of the desired population, the researchers first developed community clusters based on geographical representation and community size (like cluster sampling). Then, within each cluster, the researchers tried to recruit participants via referrals from personnel working for parent resource centres, public health units, and community organizations who could identify low-income families headed by lone females (sampling by convenience). Finally, the researchers relied on snowball sampling to obtain additional participants once they had some initial recruits, until they achieved a final sample of 141 families. In case you are curious, results indicated that mothers' dietary intakes were consistently poorer than their children's. Further, the differences in dietary adequacy and intake between mothers and children widened as money for food dwindled, suggesting that mothers compromise their own nutritional needs to provide for their children (McIntyre et al., 2003).

Quota Sampling

Finally, **quota sampling** is a method in which cases are selected based on specified characteristics believed to represent the population of interest. Quota sampling is like stratified sampling, except that the sampling frame is unknown. As a result, the population is not first divided into the groups or strata of interest, and the actual sampling method rests with the individual researcher. For example, a researcher might post an online survey, choose a sample size (e.g., 100), and then select for inclusion in the study the first 50 part-time instructors and the first 50 full-time instructors who complete the survey. While this method is an improvement over convenience sampling since an expected population characteristic is being replicated, the result still might bear little resemblance to the population of interest due to the non-random selection process. For example, what if the 50 part-time instructors are mostly from biology, while the 50 full-time instructors are from psychology? In this case, any differences found between the full- and part-time instructors might more accurately reflect differences in views based on the discipline of study rather than their employment status.

Research in Action

RCMP Use Quota Sampling in Affirmative Action Hiring

To overcome disproportionate white male police officer prevalence in the workforce, the Royal Canadian Mounted Police endorses affirmative action practices in their recruitment of new officers. The underlying principle is that a modern and effective police force should be diverse and representative of the communities it serves (Royal Canadian Mounted Police, 2018a). Using a method like quota sampling, certain members of the population are over-emphasized in recruiting practices, including women, visible minorities, and Indigenous people. For example, one strategic priority of the RCMP involves contributing to safer and healthier Indigenous communities, including efforts to recruit Indigenous police officers (Royal Canadian Mounted Police, 2018b). As a result, the RCMP currently sponsors a Pre-Cadet Training Program, specialized police education through the Aboriginal Policing Professional Development Fund, and a paid special constable position to train alongside RCMP posted in Indigenous communities. For more information, visit the RCMP home page at www.rcmp-grc.gc.ca.

Royal Canadian Mounted Police.
Source: KeithJJ/pixabay.com

ADVANTAGES AND DISADVANTAGES OF NON-PROBABILITY SAMPLING

Practicality

The main advantages of using non-probability-based sampling techniques include the fact that they are generally convenient and inexpensive, and are often efficient for getting access to a sample needed to carry out research on a topic of interest. Non-probability sampling is important because, from a practical standpoint, it can enable a researcher to carry out a study in cases where probability sampling is not possible. A population can be hidden or difficult to reach, as might be the case if a researcher is interested in illegal drug users, homeless individuals, HIV positive people, outlaw motorcycle gang members, street prostitutes, same-sex couples, families living in poverty, and/or individuals with an abusive family history. Non-probability sampling is especially effective for qualitative forms of exploratory research aimed at an in-depth understanding of small groups (Chambliss & Schutt, 2019).

Generalizability

One of the main challenges non-probability-based sampling poses is that the techniques produce samples that are not representative of the population. This means the findings generated by the sample, such as the responses given on a survey, answers provided during an interview, or observations made on the group, pertain only to that group. In addition, samples obtained through non-probability methods are prone to errors such as bias because they are not randomly selected. It is impossible to even ascertain how the sample is biased because it is unclear which characteristics of the population ended up or did not end up in the sample (Bouma, Ling, & Wilkinson, 2016). Think about what would happen if you only included your closest friends in a study on matters of interest to you. It is likely that you and your friends share common interests, such that any findings obtained from the sample will closely correspond to your personal views but not the views of other individuals in your class, your city, or your home province.

While it is true that qualitative research poses issues for generalizability, it is just as important to note that qualitative research is not conducted for this explicit purpose. Instead, qualitative researchers examine a specific group or process at a time and location to learn more about it or to explain what is going on in that setting. That is not to say the findings cannot extend beyond that group. Scott and Garner (2013) suggest it may be more appropriate to use the term *relevance* in place of *generalizability*. They use an example of a researcher who studies episodes of violence carried out by members of a gang and concludes that there is more violence enacted toward fellow gang members (intra-gang victimization) than against rival gang members (inter-gang violence). If the goal is to understand a more generic process, then, "a study (or scientific story) of a specific set of gang members might not be generalizable to all gang members in all cities across the planet, but it might have relevance to the way many or most or a significant number of gangs operate" (Scott & Garner, 2013, p. 35). Similarly, Robert Yin (2018) argues that the logic that pertains to the kind of probability sampling discussed earlier on is suited to survey research but does not apply in the same way to case study designs. However, he also claims if it is possible to isolate what is happening in one case, then a researcher can later examine other cases to see if the findings extend. Yin (2018) calls this "replication logic," more like experimental designs, where additional case studies are used to test theories developed in the initial one.

Test Yourself

- What type of population is especially suited for non-probability sampling methods?
- What is the main disadvantage of using a non-probability sampling technique?

THEORETICAL SAMPLING

In concluding this chapter, I want to note that sampling is not just a technique that is decided upon prior to beginning a study. In certain forms of qualitative research, sampling can be an ongoing process that occurs largely at the data collection and analysis stage. In fact, sampling can produce findings that prompt additional and even different sampling techniques. This special type of sampling, called **theoretical sampling**, is a concept-driven method for obtaining data used in qualitative research (Corbin & Strauss, 2015). Theoretical sampling occurs as data gathering processes uncover important concepts, which then dictate how subsequent data gathering will take place to develop the emerging theory (Corbin & Strauss, 2015). For example, while conducting interviews with Vietnam War veterans, Corbin noted that one participant (a nurse) identified the war experience as "not too bad," leading the researcher to ask, "How come?" The vet indicated he was not a "combatant" (p. 138). The concept "combatant" then prompted the researchers to immediately seek out a combatant who might offer a different perspective on what the war experience was like. The second interviewee brought

Table 5.1: Comparing Sampling Methods

Probability	Non-Probability	Theoretical
• Sampling frame is generally known	• Sampling frame is unknown	• Sampling frame is unknown
• Certain characteristics of the population are known	• Certain characteristics of the population may be anticipated	• Population characteristics are unknown
• Probability of selection is known	• Probability of selection is unknown	• Probability of selection is unknown
• Sample size is known and is calculated for representativeness	• Sample size is defined based on convenience	• Sample size is not defined in advance
• Sampling occurs prior to data collection and analysis	• Sampling occurs prior to data collection and analysis	• Sampling occurs during data collection and follows the data analysis
• Sampling ends when the sample size is met	• Sampling ends when a sufficient sample size is located	• Sampling ends when theoretical saturation is achieved
• Sample may be representative of the population	• Sample is not representative of the population	• Sample is not representative of the population

Source: Created by author

up the centrality of "survival" and a "lack of healing"—issues that were part of the combatant experience and were still evident more than 30 years after the original ordeal. These findings then prompted the researcher to read memoirs written by combatants for more information on the "war experience" that was shared by combatants, and the process continued to unfold from there (Corbin & Strauss, 2015, p. 138). In theoretical sampling, the population and its central features are not known in advance. Instead, the sampling criteria are defined or created with each new step involving data collection and analysis. The process ends once an in-depth exploration and understanding of the main concepts is achieved. This is called "theoretical saturation" (Corbin & Strauss, 2015; Flick, 2014). Table 5.1 summarizes the sampling methods.

Test Yourself

- What is theoretical sampling?

CHAPTER SUMMARY

LO1 **Define sampling and differentiate between a population and a sample.**
Sampling is a technique used to acquire the unit of analysis from a population of interest. The sample is a subset of the population, which contains the complete set of individuals, scores, or objects of interest to the researcher.

LO2 **Explain why a researcher might choose a probability-based sampling method and distinguish between simple random, systematic, stratified, and cluster sampling techniques.**
A researcher will likely employ a probability-based sampling method when a representative sample is desired and when a sampling frame can be made available. *Simple random sampling* is used to obtain a sample based on chance. A random sample is usually obtained using a random numbers table after a sampling frame is identified. *Systematic* sampling is also based on probability, except the sample is selected based on a fixed interval. First, the sampling frame is identified, and then a sampling interval is determined. After randomly selecting the first case, every *n*th case is chosen after that until the desired sample size is reached. *Stratified* sampling relies upon known population characteristics of interest. A researcher divides the

population into groups based on features such as age, employment status, or location and then randomly samples for a certain number of cases from each group. Finally, *cluster* sampling involves selected groups rather than individual cases, often to accommodate a population that is spread over a vast geographic area from which it is not feasible to randomly sample individual cases. For example, to obtain a sample of individuals living in remote communities, a researcher might first create a sampling frame of remote community clusters based on geographic area and then randomly select clusters that will be included in the sample.

LO3 **Identify the main advantages and disadvantages of probability-based sampling techniques.**

The advantage of probability-based techniques is that they produce representative samples that closely resemble populations of interest. This means generalizations or inferences can be more readily made from samples to populations of interest. However, since samples are not exact replicas of populations, generalizations need to be made with caution, as there are still differences that result from measurement error. Larger samples help to increase accuracy and confidence that the sample will contain the relevant population parameters.

LO4 **Explain why a researcher might choose a non-probability-based sampling method and distinguish between convenience, snowball, purposive, and quota sampling techniques.**

Sometimes populations are hard to locate or are hidden, making it impossible to identify the needed sampling frame used in probability-based techniques. *Convenience* sampling is a non-probability method in which individuals (or cases) are selected based on availability. *Snowball* sampling is a non-probability method that begins with a few cases selected by convenience, followed by referrals resulting from the original cases. *Purposive* sampling involves a combination of techniques used to obtain all possible cases that possess characteristics of interest to researchers. Finally, *quota* sampling is a method in which certain individuals are selected to try and replicate characteristics that are known to exist in the population of interest.

LO5 **Identify the main advantages and disadvantages of non-probability-based techniques.**

Overall, non-probability sampling methods are practical in many cases, as they are less costly and less time consuming than probability-based techniques. It is also not always possible or even desirable to use probability sampling. In some cases, a sampling frame is unknown and therefore a non-probability method must be employed to study a hidden or hard-to-reach population. The main disadvantage is that the sample is not representative of the population. This means findings are generally limited to the sample itself.

LO6   **Explain how theoretical sampling differs from probability- and non-probability-based sampling techniques.**

Theoretical sampling is a concept-driven method for obtaining data in qualitative research. Data collection and analysis sometimes uncovers important concepts that warrant further exploration in a process that leads to eventual theory development. To learn more about the concepts, additional research is necessary, which entails additional sampling methods to acquire new participants or cases. Since the sampling emerges out of data analysis, the population is not identified ahead of time, as is the case with probability-based techniques. There is also no prior intent to obtain a sample of a certain size or with certain features.

RESEARCH REFLECTION

1. Think of a topic of interest that would be suitable to examine if students at your university constituted the population under investigation. Write three questions that would help you learn more about your topic of interest. Interview a couple of students in class to obtain information on your topic. Did the sample of students you talked to make up a suitable sample? Why or why not? Given your specific topic and interests, which sampling method would be ideal? Defend your answer.

2. Identify a practice in everyday life that involves simple random sampling. Explain your answer.

3. Suppose your post-secondary institution has 2,400 instructors. The president decides to systematically sample two hundred instructors for suggestions on how to improve office space and working conditions.

    a. What would be the sampling interval?

    b. If the number 6 was randomly drawn for a starting point, what would be the next five numbers for inclusion in the sample?

LEARNING THROUGH PRACTICE

Objective: To review sampling concepts in an applied context

Directions:

1. Locate Statistics Canada's 2017 *Survey on Opioid Awareness*, released on January 9, 2018. You can find the survey if you go to Statistics Canada's home page, located at statcan.gc.ca, and click on the tab "Surveys and statistical programs." Under that tab, select "Surveys and statistical programs—Main page." You will see two options: one for survey participants and the other dealing with survey results. Select the link "Results and documentation of surveys and statistical programs" and then choose "Survey on Opioid Awareness" dated January 9, 2018.
2. Locate the survey's information on "Data sources and methodology." Read the description of the target population, instrument design, and sampling sections to answer the following questions:
   a. Who is the target population?
   b. Was a probability- or non-probability-based sampling method used?
   c. Which specific sampling technique was used?
   d. What was the sample size?
3. Why do you suppose this sampling technique was utilized?
4. What are some of the potential challenges Statistics Canada researchers likely encountered using this technique?

RESEARCH RESOURCES

1. For an overview of probability and non-probability sampling techniques, see uploads *4.2 Probability Sampling Techniques* and *4.3 Non-probability Sampling Techniques* by MeanThat posted on YouTube on April 3, 2016.
2. To learn more about probability-based sampling techniques and sampling issues beyond the scope of this chapter (e.g., ratio estimation), I recommend Levy, P. S., & Lemeshow, S. (2011). *Sampling of populations: Methods and applications* (4th ed.). Hoboken, NJ: John Wiley & Sons.
3. For additional information on non-probability sampling methods, refer to Emmel, N. (2013). *Sampling and choosing cases in qualitative research: A realist approach.* Thousand Oaks, CA: Sage.
4. For a detailed discussion on theoretical sampling, see chapter 7 in Corbin, J., & Strauss, A. (2015). *Basics of qualitative research* (4th ed.). Thousand Oaks, CA: Sage.

PART II

Approaches to Research

Experiments

Doubt the conventional wisdom unless you can verify it with reason and experiment.
  —Steve Albini[1]

Learning Objectives

After reading this chapter, students should be able to do the following:

LO1   Describe the rationale underlying an experimental method.

LO2   Identify the criteria needed to establish causality and explain which features of an experiment support the testing of cause–effect relationships.

LO3   Differentiate between basic and classic experimental designs; explain how exposure to the independent variable differs in between-subjects versus within-subjects designs; and explain why some designs are classified as quasi-experimental.

LO4   Define internal and external validity.

LO5   Identify and describe potential threats to internal validity.

LO6   Identify and describe potential threats to external validity.

INTRODUCTION

In chapter 4, you learned that a research design is a template for a study detailing who, what, where, when, why, and how an investigation will take place. In addition to distinguishing between designs based on "when" a study takes place, as in a cross-sectional study at one point in time versus a longitudinal design conducted at multiple points in time, researchers in the social sciences sometimes classify designs as "experimental" or "non-experimental" based on their ability to determine causality. Also recall from chapter 1 how explanatory research is conducted with the aim of answering the question of "why" something occurs the way it does or to clarify why there is variation between groups on some dimension of interest. Experimental methods provide a means for testing causal relationships through the manipulation and measurement of variables. In an **experiment**, at least one **independent variable** is manipulated by a researcher to measure its effects (if any) on a **dependent variable**. For example, a researcher interested in the effects of sleep deprivation on scholastic performance might manipulate the amount of sleep obtained by participants. Half the participants in the experiment might be allowed only three hours of sleep. In other words, half the participants experience the treatment (independent variable), which in this example is sleep deprivation. The other half might be allowed to experience a normal night's sleep of about eight to nine hours, with no sleep deprivation. The independent variable is the presumed cause of some outcome. In this example, the researcher might hypothesize that sleep deprivation will lower academic performance on a memory-based word task. In this case, participants who experience sleep deprivation should remember fewer words than participants with normal amounts of sleep, since sleep deprivation is believed to cause impaired performance. The measured performance on the memory task is the dependent variable, or the outcome.

Research on the Net

iScience Internet Experiments

The iScience group consists of researchers from the University of Konstanz in Germany who study methodologies for internet-based research and have a special interest in experimental psychology (iscience, 2019). If you would like to participate in an experiment that is currently being conducted over the internet or wish to examine opportunities for students to develop research as part of a master's or bachelor's degree, visit the home page at iscience.deusto.es. This site also contains resources such as software for conducting experiments online and tools for navigating statistics associated with various experimental designs.

CAUSALITY, CONTROL, AND RANDOM ASSIGNMENT

The study of cause–effect relationships rests on the assumption that one variable of interest is the cause of another; that is, changes in one variable produce changes in another. To establish a causal relationship, three criteria must exist. First, the variables must be related in a logical way. For example, education and income are associated, as people with higher levels of education also tend to earn more. This is sometimes referred to as the "covariance rule" (Beins, 2017, p. 151). Second, the cause must precede the effect in time, establishing "temporal order." A person acquires an education and then enters the workforce to earn an income. Finally, the presumed cause should be the most plausible one and rival explanations should be ruled out. Although education contributes to income, there are other factors that help to explain one's income, including age, years of experience, family socioeconomic status (i.e., how well off a person's family of origin is), and type of employment. These factors cannot be completely ruled out from this example. While we have established an association, we have yet to prove causation. This can only be done by conducting an experiment.

Experimental methods common to the natural sciences are also regularly employed by psychologists and used to a lesser extent by sociologists, such as social psychologists and criminologists. Although experiments often conjure up images of scientists wearing white lab coats working with beakers in research laboratories, they can be conducted anywhere a researcher has control over the environment. Just as an instructor can close a classroom door and lock it, thereby preventing people from entering the room during a lecture, a researcher can follow standardized procedures, use scripts, and take precautions to turn a classroom, office, and/or some other area on campus into a carefully controlled laboratory setting.

Experiments constitute the only method that can demonstrate causation due to the strict environmental control and the random assignment of cases to the treatment. **Random assignment** is a method for assigning cases to the experimental group (the one that receives the independent variable) based on chance alone. This is important because, going back to the original example on sleep deprivation, some individuals require more sleep than others, some have better working memories than others, and some have higher overall scholastic aptitude than others—all of which can influence performance on the word task, as can mood, time of the day, and whether the person has recently eaten. If participants are randomly assigned to a sleep deprivation group or a normal sleep group, then any existing individual differences will also be randomly assigned across the groups, making them equivalent at the onset. The group exposed to the independent variable is called the **experimental group** and the group that does not experience the independent variable is called a **control group**. The control group provides a measure of what would "normally" happen in the absence of the experimental manipulation. In the example used earlier, the control group tells us how many words on average people can recall during a word task. We can then compare the results for the sleep-deprived experimental group to the results for the control group to see if the experimental group fares worse, as hypothesized.

Therefore, with random assignment and strict control over the environment, where both groups receive identical instructions and undergo the exact same experience except for the independent variable, we can be reasonably sure that any differences found between the two groups on some measure result solely from the manipulation. Using the previous example, if the sleep-deprived group performs worse on the word task, we can attribute the difference to the independent variable.

Students routinely confuse random sampling (discussed in chapter 5) with random assignment. Try to remember that random sampling has to do with how a sample is selected from a population of interest. This process permits a researcher to generalize from the sample to the population. For example, one of the probability-based sampling methods is simple random sampling, where a sample of a given size is obtained using a random-numbers generator. This means chance alone determines who is selected to take part in a study. Random assignment, on the other hand, has to do with how participants are put into groups in experimental research. In this case, chance alone determines who from the collection of sample subjects ends up receiving the manipulation (see figure 6.1). Random assignment helps ensure the experimental and control groups are identical before the experimental manipulation.

Since the hallmark of an experiment is the manipulation of an independent variable presumed to be the cause of a change in the dependent variable, researchers often incorporate a "manipulation check" into their study procedures to be certain the experimental group experienced the independent variable as intended. For example, participants might be asked to report on how much sleep they received. Those in the experimental group should say they received about 3.0 hours sleep, while those in the control condition should indicate about 8.5 hours, on average. Similarly, an experimenter studying the effects of watching a video on subsequent attitudes might ask participants a question or two about the video to gauge whether they watched it. This is an important check to see that the procedures of the experiment unfolded as intended.

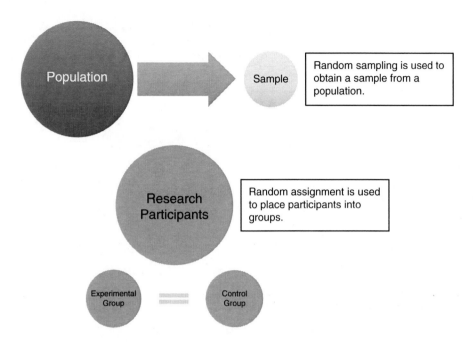

Figure 6.1: Random Sampling and Random Assignment

Source: Created by author

Test Yourself

- Which variable is manipulated in an experiment?
- What three criteria must exist to establish a causal relationship?
- How can random assignment be distinguished from random sampling?

TYPES OF EXPERIMENTAL DESIGNS

There are many different types of experimental designs. What makes any experiment a "true" experiment is the presence of four core features: (1) random assignment, (2) an experimental and a control group, (3) the manipulation of an independent variable experienced by the experimental group, and (4) the measurement of a dependent variable (i.e., the outcome) to see what (if any) effect the independent variable had. This is usually referred to as a "post-test." An experimental design that includes these four features and only these four features is referred to as a **basic experimental design** (see figure 6.2).

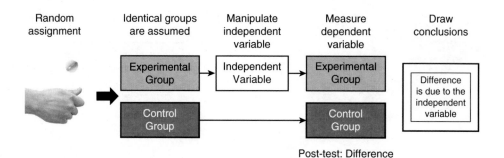

Figure 6.2: Steps in a Basic Experimental Design

Source: Figure created by author. Coin Toss ©grey_and/shutterstock.com

Classic Experimental Design

A **classic experimental design** includes the four basic features from the basic design (random assignment, an experimental and a control group, the manipulation of an independent variable, and a post-test measurement of the dependent variable), along with a pre-test of the dependent measure. This design is also commonly called a pre-test–post-test design. Even when random assignment is used to place participants into groups, there may be differences between the groups starting out. For example, perhaps some of the participants who end up in the experimental group have exceptional memories or are great at word tasks. If a basic experimental design is used, then the dependent variable is measured only once following exposure to the independent variable, during the post-test. Due to the exceptional qualities of the participants in the experimental group, the researcher might find no differences in word recall between the experimental and control groups. It appears that the independent variable, sleep deprivation, had no impairing effect on performance. But what if the experimental group had done even better had they not been sleep deprived? With only one measure of the dependent variable, an experimenter will never know the answer. However, if performance is measured before and after exposure to the independent variable, we can see how much performance is impaired by sleep deprivation. In a classic experimental design, participants are randomly assigned to an experimental or control group and then given a pre-test, where the dependent variable is measured prior to exposure to the manipulation (i.e., the independent variable). The participants in the experimental group then receive the manipulation (i.e., are sleep deprived), and both groups are reassessed (i.e., given a post-test) on the dependent variable, as outlined in figure 6.3.

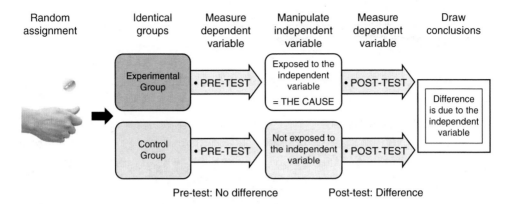

Figure 6.3: Steps in a Classic Experimental Design

Source: Figure created by author. Coin Toss ©grey_and/shutterstock.com

Between-Subjects and Within-Subjects Designs

In the designs discussed thus far, the experimental group is exposed to an independent variable and the control group is not. The experimental group can experience an independent variable in two ways: it can be assigned either to one or all levels of the independent variable. In a **between-subjects design**, participants in the experimental group are exposed to only one level of the independent variable. For example, in an experiment on the effects of music on personality, undergraduates at a Canadian university were randomly assigned to one of three possible conditions where they (1) listened to a classical song while reading the English translation of the lyrics, (2) listened to a classical song and followed along with the text provided in German, or (3) listened to an English translation of the lyrics (Djikic, 2011). This is called a between-subjects design because there are differences between participants (also known as subjects) in how they experience the independent variable. This type of design is also called an "independent groups design" since each fraction of the experimental group independently receives one treatment. One-third of the participants heard the song while reading the English translation (a music and lyrics condition), one-third listened to the song while looking at German lyrics (described as a music only condition since no one in the study understood German), and one-third listened to the English translation (lyrics only without the music). In case you are curious, Djikic (2011) found that listening to classical music changed the participants' personalities for the better, leading to a self-reported enhanced variability in overall personality, while exposure to lyrics but no actual music produced a diminished variability in personality.

In a **within-subjects design**, the participants in the experimental group are exposed to all levels of the independent variable. For example, in an experiment on participants' willingness to endure a painful exercise for money, Cabanac (1986) paid 10 participants varying amounts of money to endure an isometric sitting exercise. Isometric sitting is akin to sitting without a chair, with one's legs at a 90-degree angle, causing lactic acid to build up in the thigh muscles to produce a painful sensation. Using a within-subjects design, all participants were exposed to the six different levels of the independent variable, wherein they were paid 0.2, 0.5, 1.25, 3.125, or 7.8125 French francs (FF) per 20 seconds of exercise or a lump sum, presented in a random order. For example, participant number one attended their first session and might receive 0.2 FF for every 20 seconds of exercise during that session, 1.25 FF at the next session, 7.8125 FF at the third session, 3.125 FF at the fourth session, a lump sum on the fifth session, and 0.5 FF at their last session. All participants experienced the same conditions; however, the order of presentation differed (e.g., participant number two might receive the lump sum during their first session and the highest pay amount during their second). In this case, the difference in how the independent variable occurs is within the participants themselves, who each receive the treatments in random order. Cabanac (1986) found that money motivated participants' willingness to endure pain up to a certain point: participants lasted longer for increasing amounts of money, but eventually were unable to continue the exercise due to physical limitations beyond their desire to continue to withstand the pain for money.

A within-subjects design is also called a repeated measures design since participants are exposed to the independent variable repeatedly at multiple points in time. In a within-subjects/repeated measures design, participants may receive exposure to the same condition repeatedly as opposed to encountering different levels of the independent variable at different times. For example, McConville and Virk (2012) used a repeated measures design to examine the effectiveness of game-playing training using the Sony PlayStation 2 and EyeToy combination with the Harmonix AntiGrav game for improving postural balance. Participants were randomly assigned to either the control group (no training) or the experimental group (attended nine scheduled training sessions over a period of three weeks). During each 30-minute training session, the participants played the game four times using the controls and incorporating necessary head, body, and arm movements. Participants who underwent game training showed significant improvement on two different facets of balance (McConville & Virk, 2012).

One potential drawback of this type of design is its tendency to create order effects. **Order effects** are differences in the dependent variable that result from the

To prevent order effects in a cola test, a researcher can counterbalance the order in which participants receive the cola brands.

Source: Created by author

order in which the independent variable is presented (as opposed to the manipulation itself). For example, imagine you are interested in learning whether people state a preference for a brand of cola (e.g., Pepsi versus Coke) in a blind taste test. If, as the researcher, you always gave participants Coke first, it could be that the initial brand tasted lingered in a participant's mouth, confounding or interfering with the taste of the next cola; that is, effects from trial number 1 have carried over into trial number 2. To control for this, the researcher could increase the time between trials 1 and 2 (to ensure the taste of the first cola has dissipated) or the experimenter could offer water in between trials to eliminate the traces left from trial 1. Alternatively, the researcher could employ a technique called "counterbalancing," where all possible ways to order the independent variable are included in the design. For example, in half the trials Coke would be presented first, and in half the trials Pepsi would be presented first.

Quasi-Experimental Designs

Although you might be inclined to infer that a more complicated design is always a better one, there are many instances in which even a basic experimental design cannot be used.

For instance, a counsellor who works with clients in a Manitoba-based treatment program for adolescents, such as the Edgewood Program (for male youth who have committed a sexual offence) or the Mutchmor Program (for adolescent males with aggressive tendencies), might be interested in examining the effects of program completion on reoffending. It would be unethical and potentially unsafe to randomly offer treatment to certain offenders and not others to see if the treated group is less likely than the untreated group to reoffend at some point in the future. However, some offenders voluntarily enter treatment programs, while others do not. And, similarly, some offenders who enter treatment programs complete treatment, while others fail to complete the full course of the treatment (e.g., they fail to comply with the rules and are asked to leave the program or they decide to quit the program). While random assignment to the independent variable (treatment) is not possible, naturally occurring groups sometimes become available for studying, such as treatment completers and non-completers. These groups might be compared to see if those who complete treatment have lower reoffending rates (the dependent variable) than those who fail to complete the treatment program.

Experimental designs lacking in one or more of the main features of a true experiment are commonly referred to as **quasi-experimental designs** (also called pre-experimental designs). Quasi-experimental designs are especially prevalent in research projects designed to examine the effectiveness of treatment programs in areas such as clinical psychology, sociology, and social work. One of the most common types of quasi-experimental design is a **static group comparison**, where there are two groups and a post-test measure, but random assignment was not an option for the placement of participants into the two groups. Instead, participants typically end up in the two groups as a function of self-selection. For example, a static group comparison might be used to examine treatment completers versus non-completers in a rehabilitative program for sexual offenders (see figure 6.4). Allowing time for reoffending to occur following treatment (e.g., a period of up to five years), the research question of interest, then, could be "Is reoffending (called recidivism) lower in treatment completers compared to non-completers?" A static group comparison is also useful for examining the differences between groups in situations wherein one group receives a novel treatment or when one group receives a placebo (or simulated treatment) while the other does not (Thyer, 2012). In evaluating the merit of a static group comparison, it is important to note that this design is often used in research that is more of a starting place for determining if a program or intervention appears to be effective. While static group comparisons are frequently employed to compare groups to see if a treatment helps, without random assignment, causal inferences are difficult to establish. For example, there could be important differences between offenders who complete treatment and those who do not, which account for the lower recidivism, irrespective of what went on in a given treatment program.

Figure 6.4: Static Group Comparison

Source: Created by author

Figure 6.5: One-Shot Case Study

Source: Created by author

Another common quasi-experimental design is a **one-shot case study,** where a group receives exposure to an independent variable and then is measured on a dependent variable. This design lacks a control group (see figure 6.5). One-shot case studies are commonly employed in social work and educational research. In his book on quasi-experimental designs, Bruce Thyer (2012) notes that one-shot case studies play an especially important role in answering questions concerning the effectiveness of various interventions and programs, such as "What is the status of clients after they have received a given course of treatment?" and "Do clients improve after receiving a given course of treatment?"

Research in Action

Impression Formation

In a classic study on impression formation, Solomon Asch (1946) read a list of peripheral character traits used to describe someone's general disposition— intelligent, skillful, practical, etc.—to a group of participants and then had participants describe the sort of person to whom the traits might apply. All participants heard the same list read except for one word. Half the participants heard the word *warm*, while the other half heard the word *cold* included among the descriptors. Results showed that participants exposed to the word *warm* created much more favourable impressions than those who were exposed to the word *cold*. Asch (1946) explained that only certain words (such as warm and cold) are "central traits" that have an overall effect on impression formation, as demonstrated in his early study. In this example, only an experimental group was exposed to the independent variable (the warm or cold descriptor) and then measured on the dependent variable (i.e., their impression). This allowed the researcher to examine for an overall main effect, the difference between the warm and cold condition. However, without a control group, it was not possible to say which condition accounts for the effect. It could be that the warm descriptor produced a favourable impression and this alone accounted for the difference between the warm and cold condition, with the cold condition perhaps not having any effect. Conversely, it could be that the cold descriptor negatively impacted the impression to create the difference between the cold and warm condition, and the warm condition on its own did not produce an effect. Finally, it could be that both the warm and cold descriptors produced separate main effects.

Test Yourself

- What four features underlie a true experimental design?
- What main feature distinguishes a classic experimental design from a basic design?
- Which type of quasi-experimental design lacks a control group?

INTERNAL AND EXTERNAL VALIDITY

Recall how validity is an important consideration in evaluating whether a study is properly measuring/assessing the central concepts and constructs of interest. In other words, is a study properly examining what it is supposed to? In an experiment, validity takes on an even greater level of importance as a researcher tries to prove causation and generalize the findings beyond the confines of that study. **Internal validity** refers to the capacity to demonstrate an experimental effect and to rule out rival explanations for that effect. Campbell and Stanley (1963) coined the term *internal validity*, referring to it as "the basic minimum without which any experiment is uninterpretable: Did in fact the experimental treatments make

"Well, I guess we're the control group."

Source: ©Loren Fishman, www.Cartoonstock.com

a difference in this specific experimental instance?" (p. 5). In other words, internal validity pertains to whether a causal relationship has been established. A study has high internal validity if a researcher can demonstrate that it is highly likely an independent variable produced the outcome (i.e., the differences between groups observed on the dependent variable were due solely due to the independent variable) and it is highly unlikely that alternative explanations can account for the effect. Random assignment to an experimental and a control group helps to establish internal validity by minimizing differences between the groups prior to the experimental manipulation.

External validity refers to the generalizability of the effect or outcome beyond an experiment. In other words, do the results generalize to other people in other settings at other times? Does sleep deprivation impair performance in general, such as other cognitive or behavioural areas of functioning in the real world for most people, or is it limited to the results found in this study measuring performance on a word task with these participants? Random sampling helps to establish external validity because it eliminates bias generalizing from the sample to the population (Dorsten & Hotchkiss, 2005).

Internal and external validity are related in a manner that is considered a trade-off in experimental research. With high internal validity, a researcher can be sure the independent variable is the cause of any differences found between the experimental and control group on the dependent measure. However, the greater the control over the environment, which is high for most laboratory experiments, the more artificial and less lifelike the study becomes and the less likely the experiment will generalize to the real world (external validity). This can be countered by using a **field experiment**, where the experiment occurs naturally in a real-life context. For example, the Smithsonian Tropical Research Institute conducts field experiments in different locations on the effects of global climate change on tropical plants, such as by looking at plant responses to various levels of carbon dioxide concentrations. Similarly, social researchers examine variations in the behaviour of groups that take place in actual social situations, such as performance on a sports team, shopping behaviour in a supermarket, motorist responses at busy intersections, and student engagement in a classroom. Although field experiments have higher generalizability because they take place in the real world, there is very little control over that environment, and the isolation of variables can be quite problematic. As a result, high external validity corresponds to low internal validity and vice versa.

Test Yourself

- What is the term for the generalizability of an experimental effect?
- How are internal and external validity related?

THREATS TO INTERNAL VALIDITY

In their pioneering work on experimental design, Donald Campbell and Julian Stanley (1963) identify eight considerations they refer to as "classes of extraneous variables" that need to be carefully controlled for within an experimental design or ruled out as possibilities via careful consideration. Otherwise, these unintentional variables can confound or interfere with the effects of the independent variable and make it difficult to properly assess the findings. The eight classes of extraneous variables are now more commonly recognized as "threats to internal validity" and they include selection, history, maturation, selection by maturation interactions, experimental mortality, testing, instrumentation, and statistical regression.

Selection

As a threat to internal validity, **selection** refers to methods used to obtain groups that can result in differences prior to the experimental manipulation. Recall how true experimental designs rely upon random assignment to achieve identical groups at the onset of the study. The first threat to validity concerns any practices that can lead to a selection bias, where the two groups are not identical at the beginning of the study. For example, allowing participants to self-select into groups can produce differences between the experimental and control groups since certain individuals opted for the treatment, while others chose to avoid it (Mitchell & Jolley, 1996). Using my earlier example, if participants who normally need a lot of sleep opt to be in the control condition because they would prefer to avoid sleep deprivation and those who end up in the sleep deprivation treatment choose it because they do not feel they require the normal amount of sleep, the effects of the independent variable may be nullified. This is because those least impacted by sleep deprivation self-selected themselves into the study, while those likely to be most impacted opted out. A similar problem would occur if a researcher purposely assigned participants to the groups in a manner that appeared arbitrary but was in fact not, as would be the case if a teacher assigned students in the front of the class to one group and the back of the class to another (Mitchell & Jolley, 1996). To help assess whether selection is a threat to internal validity in a given study, ask yourself, "Can I be sure the experimental and control groups are identical at the onset of the study?" This threat can be prevented by using random assignment.

History

Another potential threat to internal validity concerns what is called **history**, which refers to changes in the dependent measure that are attributed to external events other than the independent variable and that occurred between the first and second measurement. This threat pertains to classic experimental designs or other designs containing a pre-test and post-test measurement of the dependent variable. For example, suppose a researcher is interested in the effects of exposure to information on government cutbacks on students' attitudes toward tuition hikes. If large-scale student tuition protests take place during the testing periods, it is unclear whether changes in students' attitudes toward tuition from time one to time two result from learning about government cutbacks (the experimental manipulation) or the coinciding historical event. To help assess whether history is a threat to internal validity in a given study, ask yourself, "Is it possible that some other event outside the study produced these findings?" This threat cannot be avoided, but random

Historical events such as riots can influence findings in an experimental study.

Source: parameciorecords/pixabay.com

assignment will help ensure that both groups experience its effects similarly. In addition, the inclusion of a pre-test will indicate if a history effect may have occurred, since there will be a difference between the pre-test and post-test for both groups, even the control group that did not experience the independent variable. Note that the difference will only indicate that history is a potential problem. The difference could also be the result of maturation, as discussed next.

Maturation

A third potential threat to internal validity pertaining to experimental designs containing a pre-test and post-test is maturation. In the context of experimental research, **maturation** refers to changes in the dependent measure that result from processes within the research participants themselves over the period of treatment, such as growing older, gaining experience, or growing fatigued. For example, Palys and Atchison (2014) provide a simplistic case of a researcher interested in whether the administration of pills will help children learn to walk. If the participants are one-year-olds and none of them are walking at time 1 but all of them are walking at time 2, it is impossible to determine if the pill administered on a monthly basis for a year (as the treatment or independent variable) facilitated walking or if a natural biological process attributed to maturation resulted in all of the children walking at age two (p. 238).

Although none of the features of the designs discussed in this section protect against maturation, you can question whether this threat might be operating in studies showing a difference in the dependent measure at time 1 and time 2 for a control group. It cannot be the experimental manipulation that accounts for the unexpected change because this group is not exposed to the independent variable. To help assess whether maturation is a threat to internal validity in a given study, ask yourself, "Is it possible that naturally occurring changes within the participants are responsible for the findings?" Like history, this threat cannot be avoided, but random assignment will evenly distribute the effects across the experimental and control groups, and a pre-test will provide evidence of a difference that may be attributed to maturation.

Selection by Maturation Interaction

The influence of maturation can sometimes be driven by the initial selection of the experimental and control groups. In a **selection by maturation interaction**, there is a combined effect of initial differences in the groups at the onset of the study alongside maturation effects. For example, suppose a researcher assigned six-year-old boys to an experimental group and six-year-old females to a control group for a study on spatial skills. The experimenter believes that they can design an exercise program that will improve spatial skills. Both groups are measured at time 1, then the researcher spends a few months designing the program and places the boys in the exercise program where they do special drills once a week for an hour over the course of three weeks. Both groups are measured about a month after completing the program, and the boys show marked improvement in spatial skills compared to the girls. In this example, several factors could account for the findings. First, there could be differences in spatial skills between boys and girls to begin with. In addition, even if there are no initial differences between boys and girls, it could be that over a course of several months, the boys engaged in a variety of activities that the girls did not that inadvertently led to improvements in their spatial skills, irrespective of the specialized exercise program. For example, some may have participated in organized sports such as baseball or soccer, while others perhaps played sports during their recess breaks and over the lunch hour.

To help assess whether a selection by maturation interaction is a threat to internal validity in a given study, ask yourself, "Is it possible that the two groups would have eventually become different, irrespective of the independent variable?" Again, random assignment helps to improve internal validity by eliminating biases that could otherwise be present at the onset, and a pre-test for the

A selection by maturation effect could account for the improved spatial skills observed in boys.

Source: StartupStockPhotos/pixabay.com

control group helps to establish whether maturation is a possibility that could otherwise be mistaken for a treatment effect.

Experimental Mortality

A fifth potential threat to internal validity is **experimental mortality**, referring to the loss of participants due to a discontinuation of voluntary participation over time. Simply stated, the longer a study carries on, the greater the odds that participants will drop out of the study for any number of reasons (e.g., they move, they lose track of the study, they lose interest). Mortality, also called attrition, is an inherent problem in longitudinal studies, particularly ones conducted over many years and ones that involve time-consuming and even unpleasant contributions from participants. For example, although highly important to our eventual understanding of the development of cancer among Canadians, Alberta's Tomorrow Project periodically requests that participants complete detailed documents on their food intake, activity levels, and body measurements. In addition, they are asked to go to a health clinic to provide saliva samples, urine samples, and blood samples (Alberta's Tomorrow Project, 2018b). What if the participants who are most motivated or healthiest choose to remain in the study and those who are least motivated or least healthy drop out? To help assess whether mortality is a threat to internal validity in a given study, ask yourself, "Did more participants drop out of the experimental compared to

The more time-consuming or unpleasant a study is, the greater the likelihood of participant drop-out.

Source: RobinHiggins/pixabay.com

the control group (or vice versa)?" While mortality cannot be prevented by an experimental design feature, it can be reduced, where possible, by limiting the overall time frame for a study or by taking the pre-test and post-test measures at close intervals in time. By examining the pre-test and post-test measures for the control group, a researcher can see if a change in the group size has potentially influenced the results of a study. Finally, it is especially important to monitor the number of participants in each group to see if more participants drop out of one group relative to the other.

Testing

Although a pre-test is very important for indicating the presence of potential threats, such as mortality or maturation, **testing** itself can even pose a threat to the internal validity of an experimental design. Just as students in a class sometimes perform better on a second midterm once they have gained familiarity with how a professor designs and words the questions on exams, participants may improve from a first test to a second test, regardless of the experimental manipulation. In this case, a researcher would expect both the experimental and control group to show improvement. If the independent variable has an effect, the change should be greater for participants in the experimental condition. To help assess whether testing is a threat to internal validity in a given study, ask yourself, "Is it possible that participants' test scores changed due to experience or familiarity gained from

Practice tests help students improve their scores on exams such as the timed Law School Admissions Test (LSAT).

Source: lecroitg/pixabay.com

taking a pre-test?" The necessary feature for determining whether testing is a potential threat is the inclusion of a control group.

Instrumentation

Instrumentation refers to any changes in the way the dependent variable is measured that can lead to differences between Time 1 and Time 2. For example, a researcher might change a measuring instrument such as a scale or index because a newer or more improved version becomes available between Time 1 and Time 2. Alternatively, an observer or rater might fall ill or otherwise be unable to obtain measurements at both time periods, and there may be differences between how the first and second observer interpret events that influence the results. To help assess whether instrumentation is a threat to internal validity in a given study, ask yourself, "Were there any changes to the way the dependent variable was measured between the pre-test and post-test that might account for the findings?"

Statistical Regression

Finally, as Mitchell and Jolley (1996) point out, "even if the measuring instrument is the same for both the pre-test and post-test, the amount of chance measurement error may not be" (p. 143). Extreme scores are sometimes inflated by measurement error. That is, with increased measurement (as in testing someone at two points in time), extreme scores or outliers tend to level off to more accurately reflect the construct under investigation. In statistical terms, this is a phenomenon known as **regression** toward the mean. For example, researchers interested in helping people overcome phobias, obsessions, or behavioural disorders such as attention deficit might try to include participants likely to display extreme scores on a pre-test because extreme scores are indicative of those who are out of the range of normal and therefore have an actual disorder that needs to be managed. However, it is also likely that participants with extreme scores will show some improvement (their scores will go down from Time 1 to Time 2) regardless of the treatment, as they cannot really go any higher (since they are already extreme), and they are likely to have some good days and some bad days. There is a change in the dependent measure, but "the change is more illusory than real" (Palys & Atchison, 2014, p. 239). To help assess whether regression is a threat to internal validity in a given study, ask yourself, "Is it possible that participants were on the outlier or extreme end of scoring on the pre-test?" To help control for statistical regression, a researcher can try to avoid the use of participants with extreme scores.

Test Yourself

- What is the name for the threat to internal validity that results from methods used to obtain participants that result in differences prior to the experimental manipulation?
- Which threat to internal validity results from processes occurring within the participants?
- What is the name for the threat resulting from the combined effect of initial differences in the groups at the onset of the study alongside maturation effects?
- Which threat is assessed by asking "Were there any changes to the way the dependent variable was measured between the pre- and post-test that might account for the findings?"
- What question should be asked to see if regression toward the mean is a threat to validity?

THREATS TO EXTERNAL VALIDITY

Recall that external validity pertains to the ability to generalize beyond a given experiment. While a psychologist might utilize a convenient sample of introductory psychology students who consent to participate in a study on jury deliberations, the psychologist ultimately hopes the findings will be indicative of how Canadian jurors deliberate during trials. Just as there are threats to internal validity, there are features of experimental designs that can jeopardize the generalizability of findings beyond the experimental settings and participants on which they were based. In this section, I discuss the three common threats to external validity: experimenter bias, participant reactivity, and unrepresentative samples.

Experimenter Bias

In an earlier chapter, you learned about sources of error in measurement and how a researcher might try to help along a study in order to get a desired outcome. **Experimenter bias** "exists when researchers inadvertently influence the behavior of research participants in a way that favors the outcomes they anticipate" (Marczyk, DeMatteo, & Festinger, 2005, p. 69). For example, a researcher who expects sleep deprivation to hinder performance might distract participants in the experimental condition or fail to give them the full instructions for how to complete the task, whereas those in the control condition might receive additional cues that aid performance. Although experimenter bias is one of the most common and basic threats to external validity (Kintz, Delprato, Metteee, Persons, & Shappe, 1965), there are ways to minimize its occurrence. First, procedural control in an experiment can include the use of scripts to ensure a researcher reads the exact same instructions to each participant. Alternatively, control can even be removed from the researcher such that participants might receive typed instructions, watch a video clip, or hear an audio recording that describes how to carry out the task that is being measured in the study. Anything that can be done to standardize the procedures to help ensure identical treatment for the control and experimental group (except for the independent variable) will reduce the likelihood of experimental bias.

In addition to standardized instructions and procedures, where possible, experimenters should not be allowed access to the outcome measure while it is taking place. For example, in Symbaluk et al.'s (1997) pain experiment, the dependent variable was how long participants lasted at an isometric sitting exercise. Participants ended a session by sitting down on a box that contained a pressure plate that stopped a timer. The experimenter was not in the same room with the participants while they performed the exercise and therefore could not influence how long they lasted at the exercise. Further, a recording device (not the experimenter) indicated how long each participant lasted.

Finally, in some studies it is possible to keep an experimenter or research assistant "blind" to the important features of the study until after the dependent variable is measured. For example, in the pain experiment, an assistant was in the room with the participants while they performed the exercise. The assistant recorded pain ratings at regular intervals and noted when participants ended the exercise. The assistant was never informed about the hypothesis or the independent variable, or whether any given participant was in an experimental or control condition. As a result, the assistant had no reason to create an experimenter effect. It may even be possible to utilize a "double-blind" technique, where both the researchers/assistants and the participants are unaware of which participants are assigned to the experimental and control conditions. In the pain experiment discussed above, participants were not informed about the other conditions until the completion of the study, so they could not form an expectation about whether they should or should not do well based on features of the study, such as the amount of money they were being paid relative to others. Participant bias is discussed in the next section.

Research in Action

Basic Instincts, Part 5. The Milgram Experiment Re-Visited

Recall the now classic experiments on obedience conducted by Stanley Milgram in the 1960s that were discussed in detail in chapter 3 as an example of unethical research due to the prolonged psychological harm experienced by participants who believed they were giving painful electric shocks to a learner. Professor Jerry Burger, an emeritus social psychologist from Santa Clara University, partially replicated Milgram's studies in an experiment that was broadcast on January 3, 2007, as part of an ABC News Primetime television program called *Basic Instincts*. Surprisingly, participants were almost as obedient in this study as they were in Milgram's original versions. To learn how Burger created a "safer" version of Milgram's procedures and to find out if there are differences in obedience between males and females, check out the video published by ABC News Productions. For more information on the video and Burger's (2009) article summarizing this study, called "Replicating Milgram: Would People Still Obey Today?" published in *American Psychologist*, refer to scu.edu/cas/psychology/emeritus/jerry-burger/.

Participant Reactivity

A second source of bias rests with participants themselves. **Participant reactivity** refers to the tendency for research participants to act differently during a study simply because they are aware that they are participating in a research study. This sometimes occurs because participants try to "look good," suggesting a social desirability bias, or they pick up on what the study is about and try to help the researchers prove their hypothesis by following demand characteristics, as discussed in chapter 4. One way to lessen participant reactivity is to withhold details regarding the hypothesis and/or experimental manipulation from the participants until after the dependent variable is measured. For example, suppose I was interested in whether students would help a fellow classmate get caught up on missed lecture notes. The dependent variable is whether students agree to loan their notes. Perhaps I hypothesize that students will be more willing to loan notes to someone who was sick versus someone who skipped class. I can manipulate the independent variable by sending one request to half of the class asking if anyone is willing to loan their notes to a fellow classmate who was recently ill, and a request to the other half of the class asking if anyone is willing to loan their notes to a student who missed class to attend a Stanley Cup playoff game. If I told the class ahead of time I was studying their willingness to help a classmate, they might react to my request in order to appear helpful, irrespective of the independent variable.

Participant effects are also sometimes controlled for with the use of deception, where participants are led to believe the experimenter is investigating something different than the true purpose of the study. In the example above, I might use a cover story in which I tell the students I am studying aspects of internet usage and have them complete a short questionnaire asking about their familiarity with and time spent on sites such as Facebook and Twitter. As they complete the short survey, I might pass out the request for help. The request might be in the form of a handout that has a spot at the bottom where they can check a box if they want to lend notes and leave a contact. I could then collect the handout along with the completed questionnaires.

In cases where participants are not informed about the hypothesis under investigation or they are misled about the hypothesis, at the completion of the study the investigators may ask participants if they can guess the hypothesis under investigation. A participant who accurately states the hypothesis under investigation despite the researcher's attempts to conceal it would be considered "suspicious," and the results for the experiment would be examined with and without suspicious cases as a further check to determine if reactivity was a problem. Deception and the withholding of information is used only rarely in experimental research—typically involving social psychological processes that would be negated by full disclosure (e.g., willingness to help) because the practice goes against the participants' ethical rights to informed consent. In all cases where information is withheld from participants or they are deceived by a cover story or misled in any way by procedures used in the experiment, a detailed debriefing must occur as soon as possible. The debriefing should include full disclosure of the nature and the purpose of any form of deception and allow the participant to seek further clarification on any aspect of the study.

Unrepresentative Samples

Researchers at universities across Canada regularly conduct studies using students enrolled in introductory psychology classes as a common pool of available research participants. In many cases, the students receive a small course credit as a direct incentive for their participation so that psychologists and graduate students can obtain the needed participants to further the interests of science, their own research agendas, and important degree requirements. To ensure voluntary participation from an ethical perspective, students who do agree to participate in research must be allowed to withdraw their participation at any time without penalty (i.e., they would still obtain credit or be able to complete a comparable project for course credit). While clearly a convenient sample, a group of psychology majors seeking an arts or science degree is unlikely to represent the broader university population enrolled in any number of other programs, such as commerce, communication studies, or contemporary popular music. Similarly, Canadian residents who volunteer as experimental research participants tend to be different in important ways from the general population. Rosenthal and Rosnow (1975), for example, found that the typical volunteer in experimental research was more intelligent, more sociable, and from a higher social class.

Unrepresentative samples are especially problematic for claiming the effectiveness of programs for things like drug treatment since the participants who self-select into treatment tend to be the most motivated and most likely to benefit from treatment. Campbell and Stanley (1963) refer to this threat as a **selection by treatment interaction** effect since those most susceptible to the independent variable have placed themselves in the study. That is not to say that unwilling participants should be coerced into treatment just to balance out the sample. Research ethics aside, research has also shown that court-ordered participants are more resentful and less committed to the objectives of drug treatment programs (Sullivan, 2001).

Test Yourself

- What is experimenter bias and how can this be minimized in an experiment?
- What is participant reactivity and how can this be controlled for in an experiment?
- Why is a volunteer sample unlikely to be representative of the larger population from which it was drawn?

CHAPTER SUMMARY

LO1   **Describe the rationale underlying an experimental method.**

In an experiment, at least one independent variable is manipulated by a researcher to measure its effects (if any) on a dependent variable.

LO2   **Identify the criteria needed to establish causality and explain which features of an experiment support the testing of cause–effect relationships.**

To establish causality, two variables must be related in a logical way, the presumed cause must precede the effect in time, and the cause should be the most plausible, ruling out rival explanations. Strict control over the environment and random assignment to the experimental group and the control group helps to ensure that the only difference between the two groups results from the independent variable.

LO3   **Differentiate between basic and classic experimental designs; explain how exposure to the independent variable differs in between-subjects versus within-subjects designs; and explain why some designs are classified as quasi-experimental.**

A *basic experimental design* includes random assignment, an experimental group and a control group, the manipulation of an independent variable experienced by the experimental group, and the measurement of a dependent variable. A *classic experiment* includes these features along with a pre-test measure of the dependent variable prior to the manipulation of the independent variable. In a *between-subjects design*, participants in the experimental group are exposed to only one level of the independent variable. In a *within-subjects design*, participants in the experimental group are exposed to all levels of the independent variable. A *quasi-experimental design* lacks one of the features of a true experiment, such as random assignment or a control group.

LO4   Define internal and external validity.
Internal validity is the capacity to demonstrate an experimental effect and to rule out rival explanations for that effect. External validity refers to the generalizability of the effect beyond a given experiment to other people in other settings at other times.

LO5   Identify and describe potential threats to internal validity.
This chapter discusses eight threats to validity: (1) *selection* refers to methods used to obtain groups that can result in differences prior to the experimental manipulation; (2) *history* refers to changes in the dependent variable attributed to external events occurring between the first and second measurement; (3) *maturation* refers to changes in the dependent measure that result from processes within the research participants; (4) *selection by maturation interaction* refers to a combined effect of initial differences in the groups and maturation; (5) *experimental mortality* refers to the course of participant drop-out over time; (6) *testing* refers to changes in the dependent variable that result from experience gained on the pre-test; (7) *instrumentation* refers to any changes in the way the dependent variable is measured; and (8) *statistical regression* refers to differences produced by the tendency for extreme scores to become less extreme.

LO6   Identify and describe potential threats to external validity.
This chapter discusses three threats to external validity: (1) *experimenter bias* exists when researchers influence the behaviour of research participants in a manner that favours the outcomes they anticipate; (2) *participant reactivity* refers to the tendency for research participants to act differently during a study simply because they are aware that they are participating in a research study; and (3) *unrepresentative samples*, such as introductory psychology students or other groups that self-select into experiments, are likely different in important ways from the population of interest.

RESEARCH REFLECTION

1. Visit the home page for Psychological Research on the Net, located at psych. hanover.edu/research/exponnet.html. This website, maintained by John H. Krantz, Ph.D., lists ongoing web-based psychology experiments by general

topic (e.g., mental health, gender, relationships). Select a recently added study of interest to you and do the following:

   a. List the name of the study and the affiliated primary researcher(s).

   b. Describe the purpose of the study as identified in the associated consent form.

   c. Outline the procedures for potential participants.

   d. Based on details provided about the study, describe one potential threat to internal or external validity discussed in this chapter that could impact the results of your selected study.

2. Visit YouTube's official site, at youtube.com. Search the title "Sheldon and Amy's Date Night Experiment—The Big Bang Theory" to locate and watch a short clip from the popular television series. In this clip, Amy sets up an experiment to test whether events associated with fond memories for Sheldon can be directed toward her, so she can accelerate their intimate relationship.

   a. Does the experimental design used by Amy fit the criteria for a true experimental design? Why or why not?

   b. Why is it impossible to prove causality in this instance?

   c. What recommendations would you make to Amy to improve upon her design, so she could be more confident that her manipulation is working?

3. Read the following article: Morisano, D., Hirsch, J. B., Peterson, J. B., Pihl, R. O., & Shore, B. M. (2010). Setting, elaborating, and reflecting on personal goals improves academic performance. *Journal of Applied Psychology, 95*(2), 255–264. You can download a PDF version of the article at individual.utoronto.ca/jacobhirsh/publications/GoalSettingJAP2010.pdf.

   a. Which type of experimental design discussed in this chapter was employed by the authors?

   b. What is the main independent variable and how was it manipulated?

   c. What is the main dependent variable and how was it measured?

   d. Does setting goals improve academic performance? What features of this study increase your confidence in the findings?

   e. Are there any potential threats to internal or external validity relevant to this study? Explain your response.

LEARNING THROUGH PRACTICE

Objective: To design an experimental taste test

Directions:

1. Pair up with someone in class.

2. Discuss whether you believe people can accurately identify their preferred food or beverage brand from among a sample of competitors' brands.
3. Come up with two testable hypotheses of interest related to specific taste preferences. For example, H1: Participants will be able to identify their stated cola preference in a blind taste test between Pepsi and Coke.
4. Reflecting on threats to internal validity, identify factors that you think might influence taste and how you might control for these in your experimental design.
5. Write a detailed procedure section describing how you would design a study to test one of your hypotheses. Provide enough detail so that others could replicate it. See below for some considerations to address in your procedures section:
    -   What materials will you need to carry out this study?
    -   How will you order the presentation of the beverages or food items?
    -   What sort of instructions will you give participants?
    -   How will you measure preference?

RESEARCH RESOURCES

1. For students and researchers with statistical proficiency who want to learn more about experimental designs, refer to Kirk, R. E. (2013). *Experimental design: Procedures for the behavioral sciences* (4th ed.). Thousand Oaks, CA: Sage.
2. To learn about independent-groups, dependent-groups, and single-participant designs, I recommend chapters 7 to 9 in Rooney, B. J., & Evans, A. N. (2019). *Methods in psychological research* (4th ed.). Thousand Oaks, CA: Sage.
3. For an overview of 19 issues that can potentially jeopardize the strength of causal claims and the interpretation of experimental findings, refer to Peter Norvig's (2012) Warning Signs in Experimental Design and Interpretation page, located at norvig. com/experiment-design.html.
4. For advice on how to conduct research over the internet, I recommend Gosling, S. D., & Johnson, J. A. (2010). *Advanced methods for conducting online behavioral research.* Washington, DC: American Psychological Association.

NOTE

1. Opening quote retrieved December 3, 2018, from www.brainyquote.com.

CHAPTER 7

Surveys

Users of surveys require solid, reliable data. The cliché "garbage in, garbage out" applies to surveys. If a survey contains the wrong questions, good decisions cannot be based on the information.
—George Gray & Neil Guppy, 1994, p. 7

Learning Objectives

The line below is a divider.

After reading this chapter, students should be able to do the following:

LO1 Describe the purpose of a survey and the kinds of questions asked using surveys.

LO2 Explain why research objectives need to be clarified prior to the onset of research.

LO3 Outline key methodological considerations that precede survey research.

LO4 Compare and contrast questionnaires and interviews.

LO5 Identify recommended "do's" and "don'ts" in the construction of surveys.

INTRODUCTION

From customer satisfaction surveys to public opinion polls to market research, a wealth of information can be obtained by asking questions. Surveys outnumber other data collection methods in the leading journals of various disciplines, including economics, sociology, political science, and social psychology (Saris & Gallhofer, 2014). "**Surveys** are information collection methods used to describe, compare, or explain individual and societal knowledge, feelings, values, preferences, and behaviour" (Fink, 2017, p. 2). Statistics Canada's census surveys the entire population to describe Canadians by asking questions on housing (e.g., whether people rent versus own their dwelling), personal attributes (e.g., age and marital status), and economic characteristics (e.g., yearly income and employment status), among other topics (Statistics Canada, 2018b). Because the data are collected every five years, comparisons can be made to gauge trends over time, such as population growth or changes to the employment rate. Census data are also grouped so we can note, for example, the percentage of those 14 years of age and under, 15 to 64 years, and 65 years of age and older for Canada, as well as within and between provinces and territories.

THE PURPOSE OF SURVEYS

Simply put, the purpose of a survey is to find out things by asking questions. Researchers use survey methods to describe individuals and groups and to learn more about their existing knowledge, their thoughts and feelings about certain issues, and their actions—what they do, why they do it, or how they are likely to behave under specific circumstances. Similarly, surveys are routinely employed by psychologists, social workers, and healthcare professionals in the identification, assessment, and treatment of people for various conditions and disorders, such as anxiety, depression, attention deficit, drug abuse, and anger management. Importantly, survey methods enable researchers to describe populations and examine relationships among and between variables of interest.

Surveys are a popular method for obtaining feedback.
Source: Suhsam/pixabay.com

Asking Questions

One of the more common types of information collected through surveys is demographic. **Demographic questions** help describe a population by collecting "facts about a respondent's age, race/ethnicity, education, job, gender, marital status, geographic place of residence, type of residence, size of family, and so on" (Fink, 2003, p. 79). Demographic information helps us better understand the population, and it can serve as an indicator for why people think or behave the way they do or why they experience events as they do. For example, we know that certain groups such as Indigenous Peoples, single parents, children, individuals with work-limiting disabilities, unattached individuals aged 45 to 64, and recent immigrants are at greatest risk for poverty in Canada (Government of Canada, 2016).

In addition to demographic questions, most surveys include questions that measure knowledge, attitudes, and/or behaviours. **Knowledge questions** gauge whether respondents can retrieve and correctly report facts. Political knowledge, for example, can be assessed through questions pertaining to respondents' understanding of election procedures and the rights and responsibilities of Canadian citizens, Canada's social and cultural history, and/or Canada's political system (Government of Canada, 2017b). In an Institute for Research on Public Policy survey conducted in 2006, Henry Milner found that Canadians were lacking in their knowledge of politics and government. A series of questions was used to assess political knowledge, including one in which respondents were asked, "Which of the following best describes who is entitled to vote in federal elections?" Response options included the fixed categories "residents," "taxpayers," "legal residents," "citizens," and "don't know." Respondents were also asked open-ended questions, including "Please name two members of the Federal Cabinet and identify the department they are in charge of." Results for seven main questions assessing political knowledge showed that the average number correct for Canadians was 2.57 for those aged 15 to 25 and 2.93 for those 26 years of age and older. Only 33 percent correctly named one cabinet minister (Milner, 2007). Stockemer and Rocher's (2017) more recent analysis of electorate survey data attributes decreasing political knowledge to declining levels of voter turnout among younger Canadians over time.

Attitude questions measure respondents' views toward a person, event, institution, or whatever the attitude object happens to be, such as "Are you in favour of abortion?"; "Do you consider yourself to be healthy?"; or "Is your instructor effective?" Attitudes are believed to consist of cognitive, affective, and behavioural components (Aronson, Wilson, Fehr, & Akert, 2017). The cognitive component has to do with what people think about the attitude object (e.g., "I think that political candidate is honest"). The affective component has to do with one's feelings toward the object (e.g., "I like that political candidate"), and the behavioural component involves a person's intended actions based on the attitude (e.g., "I plan to vote for that candidate"). Surveys are also used to compare the attitudes and opinions of various subgroups. For example, are students in business as satisfied with their educational outcomes as students who are in health and community studies, and if not, why might this be the case?

Finally, **behaviour questions** ask about respondents' actions or experiences and they are typically stated with reference to "time, duration, or frequency" (Fink, 2003, p. 71). For example, "Which of the following radio stations do you usually listen to?"; "How often do you eat out at restaurants?"; "When was the last time you had a physical examination by a medical doctor?"; or "In the last year, have you been a victim of an identity theft?" Behaviour questions often measure the central constructs or dependent variables (i.e., outcomes) in a study. For example, researchers might examine whether respondents act a certain way or experience certain events because of other characteristics they possess, such as demographic variables or attitude measures that serve as independent variables (i.e., the presumed causes). Figuring out what type of questions to include and which constructs need to be measured in a survey becomes possible only after a researcher has clarified the overall purpose of the study.

Research on the Net

Institute for Research on Public Policy

The Institute for Research on Public Policy (IRPP) is an independent, non-profit organization dedicated to research aimed at helping Canadians and government make informed public policy decisions. For example, the IRPP is currently conducting research on the challenges of an aging Canadian population for healthcare, retirement income, and end-of-life care. Downie and Chandler's (2018) IRPP report, titled *Interpreting Canada's Medical Assistance in Dying Legislation*, identifies problems with key phrases in the legislation, including what is meant by "reasonably foreseeable natural death" and "serious and incurable condition." You can download this report at irpp.org.

Test Yourself

- What is the purpose of a survey?
- What are the main types of questions typically included in surveys?

PREPARING FOR SURVEY RESEARCH

The first step in any survey project is clarifying the research objectives. The research objectives are the underlying aims of the study, or what the study is about. The objectives provide direction for how to create the questions that will provide the relevant information on the topic of interest. Otherwise, as noted in the opening quote, a researcher may ask questions that are the wrong ones, making the data meaningless. Guppy and Gray (2008, p. 13) offer five essential questions a researcher can ask to help clarify a study's objectives *before* designing or beginning to carry out a study:

1. What needs to be known?
2. Why does it need to be known?
3. What else needs to be known? Why?
4. What will the results of the survey accomplish? What decisions will be based on the results of the survey?
5. Is a survey the best method?

Once the research objectives are clarified and a survey method is decided upon, a researcher can begin designing a survey instrument to collect the information to answer the main research question of interest. However, several decisions still need to be made and various steps will need to be followed before a survey gets to the data collection stage.

Methodological Considerations

In addition to clarifying the main research question, a researcher also needs to decide whether to employ a longitudinal or cross-sectional design, which sampling method is most appropriate, who or what will comprise the units of analysis, and how the central variables are to be measured. In other words, how should the researcher design survey questions that will produce the relevant answers given the overall purpose and more specific objectives of the study? In addition, a researcher needs to determine if the survey will be administered using a questionnaire or interview format, how relevant ethical concerns will be addressed, and the best means for administering the survey (i.e., in person, by mail, over the internet, or by telephone).

Choosing a Design
In chapter 4, you learned that some studies are conducted at a single point in time, while others take place at multiple points over time. Survey researchers are likely

to choose a cross-sectional design when they are interested in describing a phenomenon of interest as it currently exists. For example, a researcher might want to know how Canadians feel about the oil sands mining projects being carried out in Fort McMurray, Alberta. A cross-sectional design is especially suitable for revealing differences in views based on respondent attributes such as occupation, educational level, ethnicity, political affiliation, and/or the province a respondent resides in.

In contrast, a researcher is likely to choose a longitudinal design for studies concerned with changes in variables of interest over time. For example, do people's views toward the Athabasca oil sands mining projects change after learning about the greenhouse emissions and the destruction of ecosystems as identified by environmentalists? Using a longitudinal design, a researcher could measure views before and after exposure to environmental campaigns to see if attitudes change. Note that this follows the same logic as experimental designs with a pre-test and post-test measure, enabling researchers to identify influences on attitudes and explain how and why they change over time.

Sampling Considerations

After settling on the time dimension for the design, a researcher also needs to consider which of the sampling techniques discussed in chapter 5 is most suitable for obtaining an appropriate sample. Remember that if one of the aims is to have a sample that is representative of the larger population from which it was drawn, then a probability-based method such as simple random sampling is likely to be employed. However, if the sampling frame cannot be readily identified or certain characteristics of the population are of interest, then a researcher is more apt to rely on one of the non-probability sampling techniques, such as purposive sampling. While survey research is most often associated with the quantitative realm and an aim of describing a population of interest with a representative sample using statistical or numerical terms such as percentages, qualitative surveys do exist and are used to examine diversity in a population through more open-ended questioning (Jansen, 2010).

Finally, a researcher needs to consider the size of the sample to be included in the survey. Time and cost permitting, a quantitative researcher may wish to include a large sample to maximize generalizability while minimizing error. For example, a random sample of 15,519 respondents was included in the Canadian Financial Capability Survey conducted in 2009 to represent the financial knowledge, savings, and debt patterns of all Canadians aged 18 years of age and older (Chawla & Uppal, 2012). In contrast, a relatively small sample might be enough for certain research purposes. For example, Hägelli (2005) surveyed only 75 people to learn about winter backcountry use in Western Canada. In this case, the sample consisted of carefully selected avalanche professionals who were included because of their highly specialized experience and knowledge of non-commercial backcountry recreation in the study area.

Note that a preferred sample size does not in any way guarantee the size of, or even the quality of, the sample that ends up taking part in the study. The **rate of response** for a survey refers to "the percentage of those sampled for whom data are actually collected" (Fowler, 2014, p. 6). The rate of response is calculated by dividing the number of completed questionnaires (or interviews) by the intended sample size (i.e., those initially targeted for inclusion). In general, the higher the response rate, the more likely the respondent sample will be representative of the population. However, perfect response rates are unlikely, and even what is considered a "good" response rate is dropping all the time as individuals become more difficult to locate (e.g., some people have a cellphone but no land line) and even if reached are often unwilling to participate. This is partly because potential respondents are

"This is interesting, 70% of the respondents to our survey said they don't respond to surveys."

Source: ©Larry Lambert, www.Cartoonstock.com

becoming increasingly mistrustful of surveys—particularly ones conducted over the telephone—due to the prevalence of computer-generated telemarketing efforts and unsolicited telephone calls involving identity theft and fraud scams. As a rule of thumb, a response rate of at least 50 percent is deemed adequate for analysis and reporting, one that is 60 percent is good, and one that is 70 percent or higher can be considered very good (Babbie, 1990).

Measurement Errors

In addition to design and sampling considerations, a researcher needs to be mindful of errors that can affect the reliability and validity of the information obtained by a survey. Groves (1989) identifies the following four main types of errors that pose problems for survey research: coverage error, sampling error, nonresponse error, and measurement error.

1. **Coverage error:** Coverage error "occurs when the list from which sample members are drawn does not accurately represent the population on the characteristic(s) one wants to estimate with the survey data (whether a voter preference, a demographic characteristic, or something else)" (Dillman, Smyth, & Christian, 2014, p. 3). For example, coverage error occurs when researchers surveying Canadians interview residents of the ten provinces and exclude those living in the three territories. Coverage error can also be a problem if a sampling frame is constructed from a telephone directory, since it will not include residents with cellphones but no land line, those who have unlisted telephone numbers, and people who have moved recently or recently acquired a telephone listing.

2. **Sampling error:** As described in chapter 5, sampling error is the difference between the sample statistic and population parameter. Generally speaking, the larger the sample size, the lower the sampling error, or the better a sample statistic will approximate the true population value.

3. **Non-response error:** Non-response error results from inaccuracies stemming from a failure to get everyone sampled to complete the survey as intended. Specifically, non-response error "is the difference between the estimate produced when only some of the sampled units respond compared to when all of them respond. It occurs when those who do not respond are different from those who do respond in a way that influences the estimate" (Dillman, Smyth, & Christian, 2014, p. 3). To try and minimize this, survey researchers may employ strategies to increase overall

response rates, including the use of reminders, personalized contacts, and various incentives (Smyth & Pearson, 2011).

4. **Measurement error**: Systematic errors in measurement occur when a questionnaire contains poorly worded instructions, questions, and/or response categories. For example, suppose a survey on criminal activity includes items that ask respondents how often they have done something, such as carry a concealed weapon or steal from a department store. If the response options are "never," "two to three times," and "more than three times," someone who has carried out an act only once will either leave that item blank, resulting in a missing response, or provide an inaccurate response. In this case, the respondent is much more likely to choose zero since there is a greater tendency for respondents to skew estimates of infrequent behaviours toward zero (Bradburn, Sudman, & Wansink, 2004). This is highly problematic since respondents who commit a criminal offence once are likely to be different than respondents who never commit the act.

Test Yourself

- Why is a cross-sectional design especially suitable for survey research?
- How is the rate of response for a survey calculated?
- What are the four main types of errors that pose problems for survey research?

SURVEY METHODS

Quantitative researchers use two main survey methods: questionnaires and structured interviews. A **questionnaire** is a survey data collection tool in the form of a series of questions, items, and/or prompts to which a respondent provides the information of interest to the researcher. A respondent may complete the instrument entirely on their own, called a self-administered questionnaire, or may complete an assisted questionnaire, where a researcher or other trained staff member guides the respondent through it. The questionnaire itself can be in hard-copy (paper) format or, if it is administered online, it can be in a soft-copy (screen image) that is accessed using a survey software program. Surveys can also take the form of highly structured **survey interviews** where respondents answer a series of prescribed (i.e., prearranged) questions posed directly by researchers or trained research assistants

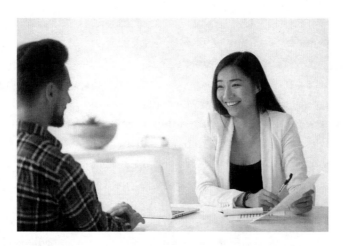

A respondent provides answers to survey questions posed by an interviewer.

Source: fizkes/shutterstock.com

who record the responses. This can be done in person, over the telephone, or as an email exchange. Note that interviews can also be open-ended, unstructured, and highly intensive. These are designed to allow the researchers to learn more about events from the perspective of participants. Such interviews are discussed in detail in chapter 9 on qualitative interviewing. This chapter is dedicated to the more quantitative forms.

Surveys are popular methods for describing groups of interest and finding out more about their knowledge, attitudes, and behaviours. As a method, surveys are an efficient means for collecting a huge amount of information from large samples. Every question is potentially a different variable, except in the case of indexes and scales where multiple questions measure the same construct. This means researchers can examine relationships among variables and look at numerous social issues at one time. Unfortunately, survey methods also raise validity concerns since responses are obtained from respondents who provide information that may or may not be accurate. Respondents make mistakes, forget relevant information, distort information, and give false answers. As noted in an earlier chapter, a social desirability bias, for example, can prompt respondents to give "good" answers as opposed to accurate ones. There are also ethical concerns raised by survey data collection methods.

Ethical Concerns

All surveys pose ethical concerns. Respondents provide informed consent prior to participating in a survey based on a detailed description about the study, including information on the objectives and the type of questions they can expect to be asked. However, they need to be reminded that their participation is voluntary, they are free to refrain from answering any question, and they may withdraw altogether at any time without penalty. Asking questions of any nature can produce potentially harmful psychological outcomes for respondents, who may feel bad about characteristics they possess or about actions that they are being asked to report on. In addition, respondents may feel uneasy about providing information that is requested, particularly if it involves highly personal issues or deals with sensitive topics. Respondents may even become upset by what they learn about themselves after providing answers to the questions posed by researchers.

In addition to the ongoing potential for harm, anonymity can rarely be achieved in survey research. For example, in a face-to-face interview, the interviewer clearly knows who is providing the responses. Even for telephone, mail-out, or internet-based surveys, the number, address, or email account can be used by the researcher to identify the respondent. Identifying information is generally important only for sampling purposes. A researcher usually does not need to link up individual answers to the respondent who gave them and can, instead, code the responses under an assigned number (e.g., Respondent #1, #2) rather than an actual

While anonymity is not always possible, a researcher can uphold confidentiality by not revealing information that could identify participants publicly.

Source: geralt/pixabay.com

identity to help protect respondents' privacy. Also, while anonymity cannot always be guaranteed, confidentiality usually can. A researcher can uphold confidentiality by never revealing identifying information publicly. A more detailed comparison of the specific data collection formats is provided next.

Face-to-Face Interviews

Prior to the 1960s, most quantitative surveys were conducted in person by an interviewer who usually visited respondents at their place of residence. One of the main advantages of this method is that sought-after potential respondents are highly likely to agree to participate in the study, producing high response rates. This is also beneficial for reducing response bias since all types of respondents are equally likely to participate at high rates (Czaja & Blair, 1996). In an in-person interview, a trained interviewer asks questions and the respondent provides answers, which are recorded by the interviewer. Skilled interviewers establish rapport and trust while remaining neutral, so they do not influence the respondents' answers in any way. Interviewers carefully manage the conversation such that the respondent follows the instructions, does most of the talking, and provides appropriate answers to the questions of interest. Interviewers can assist in clarifying questions and explaining response categories to aid in the validity of responses obtained. In addition, interviewers can probe for responses and prompt respondents to provide additional details for increased accuracy in reporting. This also enables the researcher to explore topics in a bit more depth and complexity than is possible through a self-administered questionnaire.

While face-to-face interviews are still conducted today because they yield such high-quality data and they have the highest response rates of the survey methods, in-person surveys are rarely used for quantitative research purposes, largely due to their inherent drawbacks. Face-to-face interviews are the most expensive and time-consuming form of data collection (Czaja & Blair, 1996). Imagine interviewing one thousand of the more than 705,244 people who live the city of Winnipeg, Manitoba. There are 281,050 private dwellings, spanning an area of about 464 square kilometres (Statistics Canada, 2017b). It would take a very long time—likely more than two thousand hours—for one researcher to complete the interviews. Even assuming the assistance of multiple trained interviewers who can conduct interviews simultaneously, if each interviewer conducted 50 interviews, the research project would require 20 interviewers. Each interviewer would need to travel to the location of their randomly assigned respondents and then spend an hour or so interviewing each person individually. Estimating a time of two hours per interview, including travel, at a rate of $25 per hour, each interviewer would be paid $2,500, amounting to $50,000 for data collection alone. And this is for a survey conducted only within the city of Winnipeg. A cross-national survey involving cities throughout Canada would be costlier and more time consuming.

In addition to cost, in-person surveys also run the risk of interviewer bias, an interviewer-based effect that can creep into a study in various subtle forms (Gray, 2018). First, despite efforts to remain neutral, how an interviewer behaves toward the respondent (intentionally or unintentionally) can affect that respondent's willingness to answer any given question. In addition, the interviewer is the person asking the questions; therefore, how a question is asked might affect how it is interpreted and subsequently answered by the respondent. Also, how an actual response is recorded is determined by the interviewer, who may "interpret" responses in a manner that is more consistent with the interviewer's own views than those of the respondent. While interviews pose many difficulties for quantitative researchers, they are especially beneficial to qualitative researchers seeking in-depth understanding with small samples (see chapter 9).

Mail-Out Questionnaires

Beginning in the 1960s and 1970s, researchers routinely mailed out questionnaires to intended respondents at their place of residence. A mail-out survey is a self-report questionnaire containing a series of items to be completed by the respondent and then sent back to the researcher. One main advantage of this method lies in its efficiency since researchers can send the questionnaires out at the same time, to be completed by respondents on their own, without having to pay interviewers. In a few short hours, envelopes can be filled, labelled, and stamped accordingly. Although they are less expensive overall when compared to interviews, there are still substantial costs associated with mail-out surveys. For example, mail-out survey costs are likely to include paper, questionnaire printing, envelopes, and postage at two or three times the usual rate since most questionnaires exceed the size and weight of a regular letter. These costs are incurred even for surveys that fail to be returned or are returned unopened due to inaccurate mailing addresses. To increase the likelihood that a respondent will return a completed questionnaire, it is practical to also include return postage with an envelope addressed to the researcher.

One of the main advantages of a mail-out questionnaire is the absence of the potential for interviewer bias. Another advantage afforded by the absence of an interviewer is anonymity. Respondents generally feel more comfortable and are therefore more inclined to answer sensitive questions and give accurate answers while completing a questionnaire alone than while being interviewed by a stranger (Fowler, 2014). Mail-out questionnaires can also include visual aids such as maps, charts, or other examples built into the design of the questionnaire. Visual aids help to explain instructions, can be used to illustrate points, and can provide additional guidance on how to answer questions using the response format provided for greater clarity and accuracy. In addition, respondents completing mail-out questionnaires can take the time to think about and even verify their answers before providing them.

As a disadvantage, mail-out questionnaires are easy to ignore or forget about, so they have a much lower rate of return than surveys involving some form of personal contact. Without additional follow-up, mail-out surveys are likely to yield a return rate of less than 50 percent (Heberlein & Baumgartner, 1978). Researchers relying on mail-out surveys, then, need to consider ways to increase response rates. Fowler (2014) notes that anything researchers can do to make a questionnaire

Mail-out surveys are efficient and they allow for respondent anonymity.

Source: MrPuffin/pixabay.com

appear more personalized, professional, and attractive will increase response rates. It is also important to make sure the questionnaire has very clear instructions and layout for how to complete it, is formatted in an attractive, easy-to-read manner, and consists of relatively simple response tasks (Fowler, 2014). This means, where possible, it is better to use closed-ended questions where a respondent can readily choose an answer from a small number of selections rather than have them try to generate more effortful answers to open-ended items. Although open-ended responses are rich in detail, respondents will often leave open-ended questions blank (Dillman, Smyth, & Christian, 2014). In addition, the response categories need to be straightforward and easy to complete without making errors, such as the use of large boxes the respondent can check to indicate a choice or numbers that a respondent can easily circle as an answer. Aside from the design of the instrument, researchers can increase response rates with incentives provided in advance, such as an enclosed gift card, as well as mailed out reminders sent out more than once to those who have failed to respond (Fowler, 2014).

Telephone Surveys

One way to retain most of the advantages of face-to-face interviews but reduce costs is by using telephone surveys. Gaining popularity in the 1980s and 1990s, telephone-based surveys are interviews conducted over the phone. Because many people today have unlisted phone numbers, researchers often substitute the use of phone directories for a sampling method called **random digit dialing**. Random digit dialing is a process where a computer randomly generates a sample of phone numbers from a sampling frame created using the assigned area codes for a given location. The interviewer can make the telephone calls to prospective respondents, or a computer can make the calls and transfer the call to an interviewer only if someone answers. Many phone surveys take the form of **computer-assisted telephone interviews** (CATI). In a CATI, the interviewer wears a headset and sits in front of a computer. The computer screen displays the question or item, which is read according to a script to the respondent. The respondent's answers are then directly inputted as they are provided. Note that computer-assisted methods are also used in face-to-face interviews, called computer-assisted personal interviewing (CAPI). In this case, responses are input into laptops or mobile devices during the in-person interview (Dillman, Smyth, & Christian, 2014).

In a telephone survey, a trained interviewer reads questions to a respondent and records the answers provided. As in the case of in-person surveys, telephone interviewers can clarify instructions and questions for greater validity of responses.

An interviewer inputs answers provided by a respondent during a computer-assisted telephone interview.

Source: goodluz/shutterstock.com

In addition, telephone surveys permit more anonymity than face-to-face interviews, which helps to increase the likelihood of providing truthful answers and decrease response bias, and it allows for the inclusion of more sensitive topics.

Telephone surveys are generally less time consuming and more cost efficient than in-person surveys. However, trust and credibility are difficult to establish over the phone. As a result, respondents are less inclined to participate in a telephone survey than one that is conducted face-to-face. It is also easier to ignore a phone call, especially when call display indicates an unrecognized phone number. Nonetheless, with repeated callbacks—which are relatively cost effective when using telephone surveys—response rates can eventually reach as high as 90 percent (Neuman & Robson, 2018). However, more and more people are opting for cellphones over land lines, and new technologies will continue to enable end-users to block and screen unwanted calls—including those from unknown sources such as computers—thereby limiting the future viability of telephone surveys.

Research in Action

Citizens' Panel on Energy and Climate Challenges

Researchers in Alberta recruited participants for an intensive panel on energy and climate change challenges designed as an alternative to public opinion polls. Panelists deliberated for 42 hours over a period of six days before voting on policy recommendations to promote energy-efficient travel, renewable energy, energy-efficient buildings, greater urban density and less expansion, and the reduction of greenhouse gas emissions. While optimistic at the onset, panelists' views of policy options became more critical over time and were close to those expressed in an earlier public opinion poll (Boulianne, Loptson, & Kahane, 2018). The study is available at publicdeliberation.net/jpd/vol14/iss1/art4.

Internet Surveys

From 2000 to present, internet surveys have become an increasingly popular data collection tool. Internet surveys can be conducted in one of two ways: a respondent is sent a questionnaire as an email attachment to save, complete, and return, or, more typically today, a respondent is asked to visit a website where a questionnaire is made available for completion (Dillman, Smyth, & Christian, 2014). Various web-based companies offer survey support to individuals and organizations wishing to develop and administer online surveys. User-friendly templates make formatting and question construction relatively straightforward, even for novice researchers and those with less-than-ideal computer programming skills. For only a modest monthly fee for a software licence or subscription, internet surveys can be readily developed and sent out. Most people today have access to the internet, and respondents can reply almost immediately. Feedback given to open-ended questions on internet surveys is much more detailed than what is given through more traditional data collection formats (Dillman, Smyth, & Christian, 2014). Moreover, the results for closed-ended items are often tabulated with the software program, making this the most efficient and inexpensive form of survey data collection compared to the other methods that require ever-increasing expenses related to travel, postage, printing, and/or long-distance telephone bills, followed by data coding, data entering, data analysis, and then data interpretation.

Unfortunately, the many advantages are overshadowed by some of the drawbacks. One of the biggest drawbacks unique to this form of survey is the lack of a random sample. The people who choose to complete an internet survey are generally not determined from a sampling frame, and even in cases where they are, those who respond are not likely to constitute a representative sample, due to high rates of non-response. Internet surveys have the greatest variance in response rate. Some studies obtain a very low response rate, while others can secure a modest rate. They also have a lower overall rate of response compared to the other data

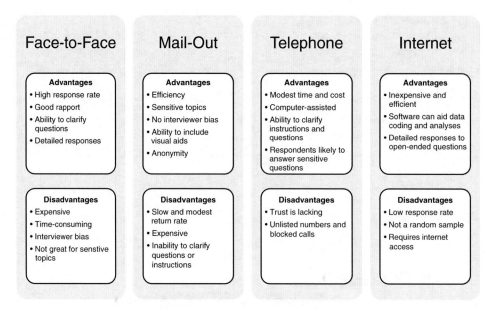

Figure 7.1: Advantages and Disadvantages of Survey Data Collection Methods

Source: Created by author

collection methods (Smyth & Pearson, 2011). Given the lack of personal contact and connection, internet surveys are the easiest to delete or otherwise ignore. Dillman, Smyth, and Christian (2014) recommend using highly tailored internet survey approaches that increase response rates through a careful consideration of all aspects of the survey process, from the targeted sample, to the form of initial contact, to the benefits of participation, to the sampling procedures, as well as the many features of the questionnaire design. For a summary of the advantages and disadvantages of survey methods, see figure 7.1.

Test Yourself

- What is the overarching limitation of data collected from survey respondents?
- Under what circumstances might it be preferable to use a self-report questionnaire rather than a face-to-face interview?
- Which of the survey data collection methods produces the highest response rate?

Research on the Net

SurveyMonkey

One of the more well-established survey software programs is provided by SurveyMonkey, an internet-based company. The program helps users create their own surveys, such as Facebook surveys or telephone surveys, using a variety of question formats, such as multiple choice, open-ended, and so on. SurveyMonkey also provides support for data collection and analysis. At the home page for the site, you can find all kinds of survey templates (e.g., customer satisfaction surveys, market research surveys, student feedback) that will help you design survey questions. While you can create good questions with this software, there are some limitations to how you can ask certain types of questions and how you can set up the response formats. Visit the site at surveymonkey.com.

SURVEY CONSTRUCTION

A survey is only as good as the questions asked. Keeping in mind the overall purpose and objectives of the study, a researcher aims to develop valid and reliable measures of the sought-after concepts or constructs. While the exact wording of questions will differ from survey to survey, good questions are "clear, short, unbiased, [current] and relevant to the target respondents" (Ritter & Sue, 2007, p. 29). In addition, effective surveys avoid the pitfalls associated with the use of double-barrelled items, negative questions, technical terms, and jargon. This section discusses established practices that can be considered the essential "do's" and "don'ts" of survey construction, including aspects of question wording, response formats, and design layout.

Question Wording

Be Clear

First, and foremost, the questions need to be clear so that respondents readily understand what is being asked of them. If the goal is to find out what students think of courses and instructors, the evaluation tool should include items focused specifically on aspects of the course, such as course content, assignments and tests, and level of difficulty, as well as aspects of the instructor, such as communication style, clarity, and knowledge. One way to help make the objectives of questions clear is to state items in complete-sentence form. For example, course evaluation surveys prompt students to rate their level of agreement with statements, such as "The course met my learning objectives" and "Overall, my instructor was effective." Note that an item such as "office hours" on its own is vague and therefore inadequately worded since respondents cannot tell whether they are being asked to comment on whether there were office hours, whether the office hours attended were helpful, or something else entirely. A much better item, stated in a complete sentence, makes the point clear: "My instructor was available during regularly scheduled office hours."

Another way to make questions clear is to define central concepts and constructs so that respondents similarly interpret items as intended before they provide an answer. For example, rating "health" can entail aspects of well-being (e.g., perceived mental health, perceived life stress), health conditions (e.g., mood disorders, asthma, cancer incidence), as well as non-medical determinants of health including living and working conditions, resources, or environmental factors (Statistics Canada, 2018e). Similarly, asking respondents if they have experienced "aggressive driving" from other motorists necessitates a common understanding of what this includes, such as aggressive tailgating, lights flashed at them because the other motorist was annoyed, rude gestures, and/or being deliberately obstructed or prevented from moving their vehicle (Neuman et al., 2003).

Finally, one way to be sure you are writing clear questions is to assume a lack of knowledge about the subject matter. For example, a criminologist interested in public opinion toward crimes and associated penalties should not assume that respondents understand anything about crime from a legal perspective (e.g., how Canada's legal system originated) or how specific crimes are categorized in Canada (e.g., based on their perceived seriousness and depending on the intended victim of harm). All relevant background information should be provided, along with definitions for all crime-related terminology that would not be considered general knowledge.

Keep It Short

Words, questions, and the survey itself should all be kept relatively short. In most cases, word concepts should be stated at the most basic level possible. For example, the term *job* or *where you work* is more straightforward than *employer* or *place of employment*, and a prompt for the *city where you live* is much easier to interpret than the *locality where you currently reside*. Similarly, long questions are more difficult to interpret since they may raise several points or include multiple concepts, and this increases the likelihood that different respondents will hear or read different things into the question being asked. Even the overall length of the survey itself is a concern. The longer it takes to complete a questionnaire or interview, the greater the likelihood that respondents will lose interest, potentially leading to more errors. For example, respondents may give inaccurate answers because they are no longer paying close attention to what is being asked or are rushing to finish. In addition, length can contribute to a greater tendency for respondents to leave items blank or choose to end their participation before completing the survey.

Minimize Bias

Minimizing bias is also an important goal in the creation of good survey questions. Bias exists when a question is worded in such a way that a response appears to be the most appropriate one or is favoured in some way. For example, it would be difficult for a respondent to disagree with an item stating "To ensure the highest quality education for Canadian children, a greater portion of tax dollars must be spent on education." From a social desirability standpoint, few respondents would admit they fail to endorse a practice tied to quality education. Similarly, an item asking "As a proud Canadian, do you plan to vote in the next federal election?" implies that only those who are ashamed to be Canadian would respond in anything but the affirmative. A question is considered leading if it suggests the appropriate answer. Instead, questions should be worded in a neutral, value-free manner, as in "Do you support giving more tax dollars to education?" and "Do you plan to vote in the next federal election?" or "Did you vote in the last federal election?"

A question can also be biased by the inclusion of endorsements by high-ranking individuals. For example, knowing the president or senior manager of a company supports a position makes employees more likely to provide similar opinions. Similarly, a question can be biased by references to prestigious institutions, organizations, or professions, such as "Do you agree or disagree with the Canadian Medical Association's decision?" or "Do you agree or disagree with the proposed solutions suggested by researchers at McGill University?" While there is no guarantee of an endorsement, in these examples, the prestige of the organization biases the likelihood that respondents will provide support (Babbie, 1990).

Ensure Relevancy and Currency

Surveys also need to be relevant to most participants. That is, if a researcher is interested in attitudes toward some topic, it should be a topic that the respondents know about and are likely to have an informed opinion on. Most students, for example, can tell a researcher about the quality of instruction they received in a course they have taken. Course evaluation surveys are especially relevant to students more so than they are to administrators, who may know something about the class and instructor based on the course outline, a peer review, or the instructor's employment history, but lack the overall knowledge of what occurs in the classroom on a regular basis. Similarly, a student resource centre looking for ways to improve its services to students with disabilities should ask its client base, not the more general student body, for direction.

Even with a carefully selected sample, not all questions on a survey will apply equally to all participants. Consider the case of a criminologist who is interested in learning more about variables associated with aggressive driving. Rather than ask a series of questions about each aggressive form of driving that may only apply to a very small fraction of the respondents, the researcher can include **contingency questions**. Contingency questions are questions answered only if an item is relevant to the respondent. This is usually determined by an affirmative response to a main question on the issue. If the item does not apply, the respondent is supposed to skip over to another part of the survey. If the item applies, the respondent is prompted to answer one or more subsequent questions. Figure 7.2 shows how a main question about one form of aggressive driving with a contingency question could appear on a questionnaire.

Finally, to help increase accuracy, survey questions should be limited to events occurring now or events that happened in the not-too-distant past or will happen in the not-too-distant future. For example, if I asked you what classes you plan to enroll in next semester, I would obtain more reliable results than if I asked

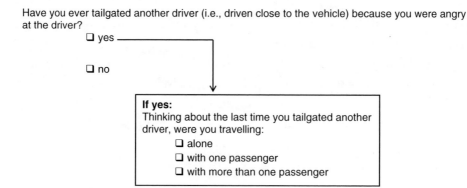

Figure 7.2: A Contingency Question Based on a Previous Item

Source: Created by author

you what you plan to enroll in two years from now. Similarly, asking respondents about daily events, such as what they had to eat or drink in the last 24 hours, is likely to produce a much more accurate recollection than asking them what they did last month, or even last week. Therefore, course evaluations occur near to the end of the term while students are still in the classes they are evaluating. Imagine rating a class you took several years ago. How many details can you recall pertaining to how the instructor organized the class or whether course materials were appropriately reflected on exams? An exception to this rule are rare but highly salient events, which are likely to be recalled for a much longer period. For example, people can readily recall victimization experiences: "Within the last year, were you the victim of a motor vehicle theft?" Significant experiences are also likely to be inaccurately reported by respondents who tend to bring important events forward in time, a survey response error known as "telescoping." That is, a respondent might say "yes" to victimization involving a motor vehicle theft even though their car was stolen three years ago, not within the last year. This occurs because the event is salient to the respondent, not because the respondent is intentionally fabricating a response.

Avoid Double-Barrelled Questions

In addition to suggestions for what researchers should do, there are also practices researchers should try to avoid in question construction. First, researchers should avoid double-barrelled questions. A **double-barrelled question** is a question prompting a "single answer to a combination of questions" (Babbie, 1990, p. 128). The question contains more than one idea, often identified by the conjunction *and*. For example, an item asking respondents to agree or disagree with the statement "The Canadian government should spend more money on healthcare *and* the environment" contains two separate opinions, one related to healthcare and one about the environment. What if the respondent feels more money should go to healthcare but not the environment (or vice versa)? In either case, a respondent would likely provide a neutral response to reflect a combination of agreement and disagreement, even though their response is not neutral toward either item.

Avoid Negative Questions

Researchers should avoid the use of negative questions. A **negative question** is a question comprising the negative or opposing form of a statement. In everyday usage, a negative question generally prompts a favourable response. "Don't you hate it when it rains on golf night?" "Yes, I do hate it." "Aren't you going to accept your award in person?" "Yes, I am." "Isn't this cheesecake excellent?" "Yes, it is." If you have encountered one of these questions on a multiple-choice exam, it likely took the form of an item asking you to pick out the exception: "All of the following statements are part of this theory except . . ." or "Which of the following is not part of this theory. . . ." Although commonly used in the English language, negative questions on surveys are difficult to understand and should be reworked into the affirmative form. Consider the case of motorists in Ontario who are caught eating or texting while driving and fined $490 (Ontario Ministry of Transportation, 2018). A negative question on a survey by the transportation ministry might be "Don't you support the distracted driving law?" In the positive format, it is much easier to understand as "Do you support the distracted driving law?"

Avoid Technical Terms, Abbreviations, and Other Jargon

Researchers should also steer clear of highly technical or specialized terms, abbreviations, and informal jargon. Every group, organization, profession, culture, and subculture develops its own specialized language over time. At a Canadian university, students might be able to learn more about becoming an RPN (registered psychiatric nurse), find out about a BSC degree (Bachelor of Communications Studies), attend a meeting of the AGC (Academic Governance Council), apply to the REB (research ethics board), and see what the SIFE (Students in Free Enterprise) club is up to. While convenient for those directly involved in such groups, abbreviations are meaningless to those outside the group and/or can be readily misinterpreted. For example, AGC also stands for Associated Gospel Churches of Canada, and it is the name of a Canadian automotive glass assembly company. Researchers should always include the full name the first time an identifying term is used and, when necessary, explain what the term refers to.

Slang terms, sometimes called idioms or jargon, are words or phrases that are widely used and understood within the culture or group in which they originated. For example, an anger scale that asks about a respondent's tendency to "fly off the handle," meaning "lose one's temper," is unlikely to be understood by someone whose first language is anything but English. Similarly, regular users of marijuana may refer to their drug of choice as pot or weed. Pot smokers understand how to roll a joint and inhale by taking a toke. They might also save the roach (i.e., the butt left from a joint) if they are running low on supply. If a survey is directed at a subgroup, the slang for that subgroup might be relevant to incorporate. However, if the survey is aimed at a more general population, avoid slang terms.

Developing Response Formats

Sometimes a survey respondent is asked to provide any answer that comes to mind, while in other cases a respondent is asked to choose a response that best approximates their view.

Open- and Closed-Ended Questions

Open-ended questions prompt any response a participant deems appropriate in their own words, such as "In your opinion, what are the advantages of published ratings of instruction?" This could be answered in an infinite number of ways. One student might answer that question by noting "I would use them to help me choose courses," while another student might respond with "They help students match their learning styles with particular instructors." Open-ended questions are advantageous for obtaining highly detailed responses, learning about unanticipated views, and finding out how respondents think about certain issues (i.e., their thought processes). Open-ended questions are used most often in cases where the response categories are not well known in advance, as might be the case in a more exploratory study. For example, in looking for effective ways to reduce prostitution, a criminologist might ask sex-trade offenders if there are any potential consequences for their actions that would lead them to stop using the services of sex-trade workers.

Closed-ended questions prompt a participant to respond using a predetermined or a fixed-choice set of responses, usually consisting of four, five, or seven choices. Closed-ended questions often require carefully worded instructions that help the participant understand how to respond, much like you might be instructed to choose the one best option from a set of four potentially correct responses on a multiple-choice test. By using the same response choices and by limiting the number of possible responses across participants, researchers can readily code, analyze, and compare the answers provided. A drawback is that respondents can select answers to questions they know little or nothing about (much like a student might guess on a multiple-choice exam). In addition, the answer a respondent wishes to provide may or may not be included in the provided set of response choices.

The most commonly used response format for questionnaires are closed-ended ordinal categories because they are easy to complete, they allow for a range of intensity in responses, and they lend themselves well to the measurement of attitudes and behaviours (Dillman, Smyth, & Christian, 2014). For example, Howell and Symbaluk (2001) asked students to provide views on potential outcomes of published ratings of instruction. One question asked, if instructor evaluations were made accessible to students, how likely is it that this practice would "increase the likelihood that students will participate in student ratings of instruction"? Students were asked to rate the likelihood using an ordinal measure ranging from not at all likely, to slightly likely, to moderately likely, to very likely, to extremely likely.

Another especially popular response category arrangement is the use of a Likert format depicting levels of agreement with the ratings strongly disagree, disagree, neutral, agree, and strongly agree. For example, students might be asked to indicate their level of agreement pertaining to the statement "Overall, my instructor is effective" by checking the appropriate response box:

☐ strongly disagree ☐ disagree ☐ neutral ☐ agree ☐ strongly agree

The five-point response categories listed above are preferred for a number of reasons: they are balanced, in terms of positive and negative options; they allow for sufficient discrimination among responses; they are readily understood by most respondents; they have a neutral midpoint that is preferable over the use of "don't know"; they are especially amenable to use in online surveys; and they are easy to score for the purpose of analysis (Brace, 2018).

Response categories for closed-ended questions should always be **exhaustive** and **mutually exclusive**. Exhaustive signifies that the choices are comprehensive enough to cover the range of all possible responses. For example, asking participants in an internet survey to select their age from a set of age categories—for example, 19 and under, 20 to 29, 30 to 39, 40 to 49, 50 to 59, and 60 to 69—doesn't

Survey respondents are frequently asked to rate their opinions using closed-ended ordinal response categories.

Source: mg Park/shutterstock.com

allow for the appropriate selection by individuals 70 years of age and older. To remedy this so the categories are exhaustive, the researcher should add additional categories and/or include an open-ended final category, such as 70 and over. Mutually exclusive indicates that all response categories are separate and distinct from each other. Age responses would not be mutually exclusive if one category included those "20 and under" while the next category was "20 to 30" because the categories overlap. A respondent's age should correspond to one and only one response category. Due to the limited number of responses, closed-ended items are much easier to code for and interpret than open-ended items at the data analysis stage of research.

In addition to the wording of questions and response categories, a survey researcher needs to think through a few other considerations before finalizing a survey instrument.

Appealing Format and Design

Every effort should be made to make a questionnaire as professional looking and appealing as possible to the potential respondent. This can include decisions about the type of font used, the size of the lettering, the arrangement of the questions, the style of the question numbering, and the format of the responses. While there is no exact formula for what works and doesn't work, the objective is to strike a balance between design appeal and ease of completion. Respondents are more apt to complete a questionnaire that is easy to navigate. This means the questions should be well spaced (uncluttered) and the response formats should be clearly laid out and be relatively easy to complete.

Perhaps the questionnaire can be divided into three sections with 10 questions in each. Answering this seems less daunting than answering 30 questions in a row. Related questions on the same topic should generally be grouped together. Also, by using the same response formats for a series of questions or items, respondents can provide answers quite quickly and will be less discouraged by survey length. That said, there should also be some variation in question and response formats to prevent respondents developing the tendency to provide the same answer throughout, regardless of the specific question. For example, if a person agrees with one item, that person may agree with most items without reading them carefully.

Clear Instructions

Whether in questionnaire or interview format, a respondent completing a survey needs to be provided with clear instructions for how to provide responses.

Are respondents supposed to indicate their opinion by checking a box, circling a number, or providing a written response? Are respondents supposed to choose all responses that apply to a given question or only the one that most closely approximates their view? In the case of an interview, are respondents supposed to choose from a range of answers provided or say anything that comes to mind? Even trained interviewers need carefully laid out instructions for how to proceed with the survey and how to give standardized responses to potential questions raised by the respondents.

Question Order

Researchers also need to be careful about the order in which specific questions are included. It is a good idea to include a few relatively simple non-threatening questions at the beginning of a survey, such as demographic questions designed to describe the respondent, like "Are you a full- or part-time student?" and "On which campus do you mainly attend classes?" Sensitive questions tend to be ones that involve personal attributes or issues (e.g., income, mental health, ethnicity, relationships), private behaviour (e.g., sexual behaviour, alcohol consumption), or socially undesirable practices (e.g., aggressive driving, racism)—all of which are likely to form the basis of research in the social sciences. Non-threatening questions are especially important at the start of interviews, where developing good rapport with the respondent can be critical to securing participation. Sensitive questions should be left until near the end of a survey because, by this point, the respondent has already developed a rapport with the interviewer or has already invested time on the questionnaire and will be more likely to provide answers. Also, placing threatening questions near the end helps to ensure that most of the survey will be completed even if respondents choose not to respond to these items (Brace, 2018; Rea & Parker, 2005).

Pre-Testing the Instrument

The best way to obtain feedback about the design, length, wording, formatting, instructions, or any other survey feature is to pre-test it. A pre-test is a trial run using a different group of respondents than those who will be included in the final sample. Just as having someone proofread a paper of yours before you turn it in to your professor can identify errors, a pre-test can help identify problems with the survey. At the minimum, a pre-test will help determine if respondents can readily follow the instructions as intended, if the questions are worded clearly, if the responses are appropriate, if there are any obvious errors, and how long it takes to complete the survey.

Test Yourself

- What features make for good survey questions?
- What practices need to be avoided in the construction of good survey questions?
- When would it be appropriate to use an open-ended question?
- Why is question order important in the creation of a survey?

Research on the Net

Web Survey Methodology (WebSM)

Today, cellphone owners and users of popular social media such as Facebook are the latest sought-after population of potential survey respondents (Blair, Czaja, & Blair, 2014). Of course, with most advantages come drawbacks, including response and non-response biases based on attributes of cellphone and social media users, such as the fact that they tend to be younger. To learn more about the advantages and disadvantages of conducting surveys over the internet as well as how social media can be used in research, visit Web Survey Methodology at websm.org. The site is maintained by the University of Ljubljana, Faculty of Social Science, Centre for Social Informatics, in Slovenia. It contains a current bibliography of more than 7,600 articles on methodological issues related to internet surveys (Vehovar, Manfreda, & Berzelak, 2019).

CHAPTER SUMMARY

LO1   Describe the purpose of a survey and the kinds of questions asked using surveys.

The purpose of a survey is to find something out by asking questions. A researcher might choose this method to describe a population, to learn more about people's feelings about some issue, to determine the frequency of certain behaviours, and/or to examine ways in which various variables are related. Common types of questions include demographic questions that help describe a population's features, knowledge questions about facts, attitude questions comprising opinions about people and events, and behaviour questions about respondents' actions and experiences.

LO2   **Explain why research objectives need to be clarified prior to the onset of research.**

The research objectives outline what the study is about, and they provide direction for the creation of appropriate questions for obtaining answers on the topic of interest. Questions that help facilitate this process include "What needs to be known?", "Why does it need to be known?", "What else needs to be known?", "What will the results of the survey accomplish?", "What decisions will be based on the results of the survey?", and "Is a survey the best method?"

LO3   **Outline key methodological considerations that precede survey research.**

A researcher needs to decide upon the type of design for the survey (e.g., a longitudinal or cross-sectional design), which sampling method is most appropriate (e.g., a probability- or non-probability-based technique), who will be included in the sample, and how the central variables are to be measured or how to design the survey. In addition, a researcher needs to determine if the survey will be administered using a questionnaire or interview format, how relevant ethical concerns will be addressed, and how the survey will be administered, such as in person, by mail, over the internet, or by telephone.

LO4   **Compare and contrast questionnaires and interviews.**

A *questionnaire* is a data collection tool consisting of a series of questions or items to which a respondent provides answers. An *interview* is also a structured data collection method, but in this case an interviewer asks the questions and records the answers provided by the respondent. *Face-to-face interviews* produce the highest response rate and result in rich, detailed information, but also constitute the most expensive and time-consuming survey data collection method. Interviewer bias is also problematic in the case of in-person interviews and is alleviated using mail-out questionnaires. *Mail-out surveys* also afford greater anonymity to the respondent, who is more likely to provide answers to sensitive questions but less likely to complete or send back the survey. *Telephone surveys* are good for establishing rapport (like face-to-face interviews), they are less costly than in-person surveys, and they take less time to conduct. However, sampling frames are likely to be incomplete, and it is difficult to establish trust and credibility over the phone. *Internet surveys* can reach a vast number of respondents and collect information inexpensively in a short period of time. The greatest drawback to internet surveys is their lack of a random sample and their low overall response rate compared to the other data collection formats.

LO5   **Identify recommended "do's" and "don'ts" in the construction of surveys.**

Good survey questions are clear, short, free from bias, relevant, and time-sensitive. Poor questions that need to be avoided contain terms and phrases that are double-barrelled, negative, highly technical, abbreviated, or full of jargon. Open-ended questions prompt any response deemed appropriate by the participant, whereas closed-ended questions force the respondent to choose an answer from a fixed set of responses. Surveys should also have appealing designs and clear instructions, be carefully ordered, and undergo pre-testing.

RESEARCH REFLECTION

1. For each of the following statements, indicate why it is not suitable as a survey question and then re-write it to correct for the error. Assume that students were instructed to rate their level of agreement with the following statements.
   a. The instructor was helpful and organized.
   b. The instructor posted lectures notes on BB for students to access online.
   c. The instructor didn't always start class on time.
   d. The instructor used effective pedagogy to facilitate student engagement.
   e. The dean's offer of full-time employment to this instructor is a good decision.
2. Suppose a researcher wished to describe the prevalence of dangerous driving among motorists in the province of Ontario. Design five closed-ended survey questions that could help meet this research objective.
3. Have you ever consumed an energy drink, such as Red Bull or Monster Energy? Suppose you were going to develop an internet survey on the effects of caffeinated energy drinks for consumers. List five questions you would ask respondents. Compare your questions to those posed by researchers in Ontario who examined the adverse effects of caffeinated energy drinks on Canadian youth and young adults using a web-based survey (see Hammond, Reid, & Zukowski, 2018).
4. Researchers at Queen's University and York University examined coping mechanisms among youth who experience cybervictimization. Cybervictimization was operationalized as "being threatened, embarrassed, singled out, gossiped about, or made to look bad through the Internet, text messages, or pictures" (Hudson, Lambe, PREVNet National Youth Advisory Committee, Pepler, & Craig, 2016, p. 6). If you were designing a similar study, how would you operationalize coping mechanisms?

LEARNING THROUGH PRACTICE

Objective: To evaluate a service provider on campus

Directions:

1. Pair up with someone in class.
2. Identify various service providers on campus (e.g., the library, a lunch vendor, the computer help desk).
3. Select one of the service providers and discuss ways in which it could be evaluated (e.g., speed of service, quality of service).
4. Design a questionnaire consisting of four closed-ended questions and one open-ended question that could be used to evaluate different aspects of the services provided.
5. Pilot test the five questions with another pair from the class. Make any necessary revisions to the questionnaire based on information provided during the pilot test. For example, are you measuring what you intend to? Were the questions clear to the pilot testers?

RESEARCH RESOURCES

1. To learn more about survey design, data collection and analysis, and presentation of findings, refer to Atkeson, L. R., & Alvarez, R. M. (2018). *The Oxford handbook of polling and survey methods.* New York, NY: Oxford University Press.
2. For information on question types, effective questions, and appropriate response categories, see Brace, I. (2018). *Questionnaire design: How to plan, structure and write survey material for effective market research* (4th ed.). London, UK: Kogan Page.
3. For a guide on how to conduct surveys and organize survey data, I recommend Fink, A. (2017). *How to conduct surveys: A step-by-step guide* (6th ed.). Thousand Oaks, CA: Sage.
4. For information on access panels used in official statistics and for managing non-response and missing data, see Engel, U., Jann, B., Lynn, P., Scherpenzeel, A., & Sturgis, P. (Eds.) (2015). *Improving survey methods: Lessons from recent research.* New York, NY: Routledge.

CHAPTER 8

Unobtrusive Methods

A major confounding factor in social research is eliminated in non-reaction studies because the observed person or group is not able to react to the measurement process— that is, is not able to manipulate presentation-of-self for the researcher.
    —Winston Jackson & Norine Verberg, 2007, p. 143

Learning Objectives

After reading this chapter, students should be able to do the following:

LO1   Define unobtrusive methods and explain what is meant by reactive and non-reactive research methods.

LO2   Explain what physical trace analysis is used for and differentiate between erosion and accretion measures.

LO3   Differentiate between public and private archives and note a main advantage and disadvantage of archival analysis.

LO4   Define content analysis and outline the steps for conducting a content analysis.

LO5   Explain what secondary analysis of existing data entails, identify key sources for secondary data analysis, and note a main advantage and disadvantage of secondary data analysis.

LO6   Define digital media and explain how the internet has changed the nature of social research and the methods used to study it.

INTRODUCTION

Most methods rely upon participants who provide the data of interest to researchers through their actions or words, such as experiments, surveys, ethnographic studies, or qualitative interviews. These methods are considered obtrusive because they necessitate an intrusion into the lives of participants to obtain the data. They are also considered to be reactive because participants are responding or reacting to the research instrument (e.g., the questions posed on a questionnaire or an experimental manipulation), the researcher (e.g., a qualitative interviewer), and/or to the study itself (e.g., demand characteristics). In contrast, non-reactive methods, called **unobtrusive research methods**, are ones in which "the researcher examines evidence of people's behaviour or attitudes, rather than interacting directly with those being studied" (Strand & Weiss, 2005, p. 161). This evidence takes the form of a variety of sources of information created by and for people (e.g., government statistics, official documents, newspaper stories, personal diaries, song lyrics, and television scripts), and it can also include things left behind by people (e.g., litter, belongings, patterns of erosion). Notably, the information is originally produced for a particular purpose (e.g., song lyrics might be designed in order to express an artist's creativity and to make money for producers), but it is later examined by social researchers for a different purpose (e.g., to determine the prevalence of gender stereotypes in a music genre), thereby circumventing issues of reactivity (the song is already written and produced).

As early as 1966, Gene Webb and Don Campbell (joined by Richard Schwartz and Lee Sechrest in 1981) wrote about the need for innovative, non-conventional means for finding things out, which they originally dubbed "oddball research" and "oddball measures." For example, they noted how the careful examination of children's drawings, library withdrawals, and worn floor tiles could be used to inform researchers about children's interests, the potential effects of new forms of media, and the popularity of museum exhibits (Webb, Campbell, Schwartz, & Sechrest, 2000). Unobtrusive methods include any number of non-reactive measures or techniques. This chapter examines four types of unobtrusive measures that are classified based on characteristics of the data studied: (1) forms of physical evidence examined using physical trace analysis; (2) public and private records that are observed using archival analysis; (3) written, spoken, or visual messages examined using a technique called content analysis; and (4) official statistics and other forms of existing data studied through secondary analysis. This chapter explains how physical trace analysis, archival analysis, content analysis, and secondary analysis can be used to examine data unobtrusively; that is, in a manner that is independent from the original processes that produced it (Lune & Berg, 2017).

PHYSICAL TRACE ANALYSIS

Physical traces are the "remnants, fragments, and products of past behaviour" (Shaughnessy, Zechmeister, & Zechmeister, 2015, p. 107). Just as a criminal investigator might examine a crime scene for remaining clues such as finger prints, blood stains, or clothing fibres, researchers can examine locations for physical evidence that helps them to better understand humans based on their past behaviour. This is not unlike what archaeologists and anthropologists have been doing for centuries as they study bones, artifacts, and other aspects of material culture left behind by humans to learn more about earlier civilizations. Physical traces are usually one of two types. First, physical traces can take the form of **erosion measures** or use traces "where the degree of selective wear on some material yields the measure" (Webb, Campbell, Schwartz, & Sechrest, 2000, p. 36). Erosion measures indicate patterns of human use, as in the case of heavily worn and dirty carpets or flooring in high-traffic areas on a university campus. Similarly, pathways woven through the grass between buildings can indicate frequently used routes or desired walkways.

Physical traces can also take the form of **accretion measures**, "where the research evidence is some deposit of materials" (Webb, Campbell, Schwartz, & Sechrest, 2000, p. 36). Accretion measures are products left behind due to prior activity, such as waste or graffiti. For example, the accumulation of empty beer,

Erosion measures such as well-worn paths reveal what people have done, and this may differ from what they were expected to do.

Source: Bliss Images/shutterstock.com

liquor, and wine bottles in a recycle bin can help to establish the level of alcohol consumption in a given household. The analysis of waste in trash bins can reveal information about people's habits such as their nutrition and dietary practices, material use and misuse, and waste disposal and recycling efforts.

Garbology

The term **garbology** is frequently used today to refer to the study of behaviour based on the analysis of waste. Garbology as an academic pursuit can be traced to William Rathje (1945–2012), an archaeologist at the University of Arizona who founded the Garbage Project, which lasted from 1973 to 2005. In an earlier independent studies project, two of Rathje's students examined the correspondence between stereotypes and "physical realities" through a comparison of the trash collected from two affluent and two poor families (Humes, 2012). Results showed that all four homes consumed similarly, with the same amounts and types of foods and drinks. However, the poorer households spent more on educational items for their children and they bought more household cleaners than the affluent ones (Rathje & Murphy, 2001). Although questionable due to the small sample size and limited time frame for analysis, the findings nevertheless sparked an interest in Rathje that resulted in a career-long exploration into the assumptions and potential misconceptions related more generally to consumption and waste disposal.

Instead of going out on archeological "digs," Rathje and his students excavated carefully sampled garbage that was re-routed by the sanitation department and dumped at the University of Arizona (Humes, 2012). For more than three decades, Rathje and his students surveyed, itemized, counted, and weighed garbage, dispelling popular myths about what is most commonly thrown away and what happens to trash after it gets thrown away. For example, while the American public believed that the most common forms of solid waste were diapers and take-out food containers, more prevalent forms of waste turned out to be newspaper and building materials. Another interesting finding was that consumption increased, as opposed to decreased, during food shortages, especially when red meat was scarce. The Garbage Project also showed how many forms of organic waste were unexpectedly preserved by plastics rather than broken down over time in landfills. Finally, how people behave is very different from how they claim to behave, as evident in the under-reporting of unhealthy consumption (e.g., chips, bacon, and alcoholic beverages) and the

Garbology helps us learn about human consumption, excess, and waste management.

Source: Mr. Nirun Chanadis/shutterstock.com

over-reporting of healthy intake (e.g., cottage cheese, high-fibre cereals, and skim milk) (Rathje & Murphy, 2001).

Graffiti

Graffiti is a special kind of accretion measure that takes various forms and is interpreted in just as many ways. For example, Decker and Curry (2017) define graffiti as a "form of visual communication, usually illegal, involving the unauthorized marking of public space by an individual or group. Although the common image of graffiti is a stylistic symbol or phrase spray-painted on a wall by a member of a street gang, some graffiti is not gang-related. Graffiti can be understood as antisocial behaviour performed in order to gain attention or as a form of thrill seeking, but it can also be understood as an expressive art form." As a means of self-expression, graffiti commonly takes the form of "tagging," which involves personalized signatures, or "piecing" and "bombing," which includes much more highly specialized forms of artwork created with spray cans to embody names and symbolize subcultures (Alonso, 1998). Graffiti also consists of written phrases and statements that express viewpoints and positions (Abel & Buckley, 1977). For example, predominant themes include gang graffiti denoting territories, political graffiti, or derogatory forms of graffiti directed at groups (Alonso, 1998).

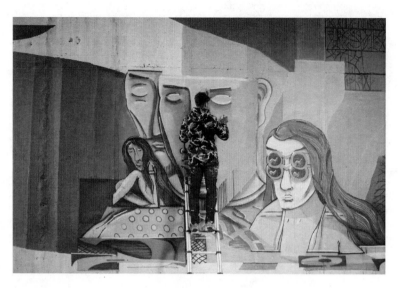

Graffiti can be considered a criminal act, a form of art, or an accretion measure that provides important insight into subcultures.

Source: sashafolly/shutterstock.com

Graffiti can also take the form of ongoing dialogue as one graffiti writer responds to what another has written, as in the case of bathroom graffiti. The graffiti that appears on the stalls inside bathrooms is usually referred to as "latrinalia" (Abel & Buckley, 1997; Melhorn & Romig, 1985).

Graffiti also occurs within subcultures and in response to historical events. Rawlinson and Farrell (2010), for example, examined construction site graffiti at 10 large-scale construction projects and identified various common subcultures of graffiti producers (e.g., subcontractors, trades, and football fans), as well as various predominant themes within the graffiti itself, such as celebrations of ownership and personal immortalization. Hagan, Ender, Tiemann, and Hagen (2005) studied disaster graffiti following a major flood, which they coined "catastroffiti." The Red River Valley flood of 1997 took place along the Red River in North Dakota, Minnesota, and southern Manitoba. The most dominant theme in the graffiti following the flood was humour as a coping mechanism. Even within the humorous graffiti, several themes emerged, including jocular humour (e.g., "1-800-big-mess"), sarcasm (e.g., "Are we having fun yet? Keep it up!"), and satirical humour (e.g., "49 FEET MY ASS") in response to a nearby dike that was supposed to be fortified to 52 feet (Hagan, Ender, Tiemann, & Hagen, 2005).

Research in Action

Bomb It

Bomb It (2007) is an award-winning documentary about graffiti directed by Jon Reiss. This film documents the history of graffiti and street art and highlights the work of various artists, including graffiti writers Taki 183, Cornbread, Stay High 149, T-Kid, Cope 2, and Shepard Fairey. Filmed on five different continents, the documentary tracks controversies around the definition and use of public space in major cities, including Los Angeles, New York, Tijuana, London, Paris, Cape Town, and Tokyo. *Bomb It 2* (2010) broadens Jon Reiss's investigation of graffiti to previously unexplored areas of Asia, Southeast Asia, the Middle East, Europe, the United States, and Australia. For more information on these films, go to bombit-themovie.com.

Advantages and Disadvantages of Physical Trace Analysis

The biggest advantage of using physical trace analysis pertains to the use of non-reactive measures. Because the traces already exist, they are not subject to the problems inherent in surveys and experiments where participants may alter their responses as a function of being studied, such as trying to please the researcher or appearing socially desirable. In most cases, the originators of the physical evidence will never even know it was examined for research purposes. This means the physical traces are likely to have occurred naturally. As a result, the garbologist studying what was thrown out can be reasonably sure that the data reflect true habits versus what would or would not be thrown away if people knew ahead of time their waste was going to be examined, perhaps to see how many items could have been diverted from a landfill through recycling efforts. In addition, except for graffiti deliberately designed in some instances to identify its authors, physical traces are anonymous because the originators are long gone from the scene when researchers arrive to examine the remaining evidence.

Although free from participant biases common to reactive measures, physical trace measures raise questions concerning the validity of the inferences drawn from the measures. For example, does the presence of lots of cleaning products in a trash bin indicate that a residence is likely to be clean or dirty? Similarly, does the absence of cleaning products mean little cleaning is taking place or something else, such as hired house cleaners bringing in and taking supplies with them? In addition, since the researcher cannot determine who the originator of the data is, it is difficult to generalize with certainty the findings to any given group or subculture. This is compounded by the fact that only certain kinds of traces are likely to persist long enough to make it into a study (e.g., worn carpets get cleaned or replaced, floors can be polished, rain can wash away footprints, and graffiti can be painted over). Webb, Campbell, Schwartz, and Sechrest (2000) point out that especially in the case of accretion measures, some physical traces have a higher probability of being established in the first place, while others have a higher probability of surviving over time. They refer to these drawbacks as **selective deposit** and **selective survival** biases. Thus, while physical trace measures can constitute a novel means for studying past behaviour, researchers need to be aware of the potential for biases. One way to help establish the validity of the measures as true indicators of behaviour is to combine physical trace analysis with other methods to see if they all point to similar conclusions, thereby demonstrating convergent validity of the measures.

Test Yourself

- Physical traces usually take the form of which two measures?
- What can we learn through an analysis of waste?
- Which type of physical trace measure is graffiti?
- Which two biases are of concern to researchers using physical trace measures?

ARCHIVAL ANALYSIS

Archives are historical documents, records, or collections of information that detail the activities of businesses, agencies, institutions, governments, groups, or individuals. To help you understand what archives consist of, consider the various organizations or institutions that can be considered archival sources for information pertaining to you, such as the current school you attend as well as any previous schools, employers, creditors, doctors' offices, and perhaps even a hospital or police agency. Now think of the different ways that information about you and others can be collected and stored, such as in files, as journal entries, and in electronic format. Finally, consider that archival data can be public or private in nature.

Public and Private Archives

Public archives are public records that are prepared specifically to be examined by others. Public archives tend to be continuous and ongoing, as in the case of running records, such as monthly budgets or annual reports; official documents, such as school attendance records or hospital intake records; and library collections, such as periodicals and books. Public records are also prepared, collected, or organized in standard ways, such as arranged alphabetically, organized by date, indexed, and so on.

Research on the Net

Library and Archives Canada

The largest collection of Canadian public archives is Library and Archives Canada. As of 2004, the collection brings together what used to be the National Archives of Canada (established in 1872) and the National Library of Canada (founded in 1953). The vast collection includes Canadian films and documentaries; architectural drawings, maps, and plans; periodicals and books; photographic images; video and sound recordings; works of art, including watercolours, sketches, miniatures, oil paintings, and caricatures; sheet music; postal archives; medals, seals, posters, and coats of arms; textual archives; national, provincial, and territorial newspapers; periodicals, microfilms, and theses; and portraits of Canadians (Library and Archives Canada, 2017). To conduct an archives search, visit collectionscanada.gc.ca.

Researchers sometimes further categorize public archival data based on characteristics of the data. For example, Lune and Berg (2017) modernized the original archival categories first described by Webb and his colleagues into three main groups: commercial media accounts, actuarial records, and official documentary records. Commercial media accounts "represent any written, drawn, or recorded (video or audio) material produced for general or mass consumption" (Lune & Berg, 2017, p. 138). These public archives can include books, newspapers, periodicals or magazines, television program transcripts, film scripts, photographs, music lyrics, radio broadcasts, Twitter tweets, YouTube videos, website information, and so on. Actuarial records are "produced for special or limited audiences but they are typically available to the public under certain circumstances" (Lune & Berg, 2017, p. 139). Examples of actuarial records include birth, death, marriage, and divorce records, as well as things like land titles and credit histories. Official documentary records are those "originally produced for some special limited audiences, even if they eventually find their way into the public domain" (Lune & Berg, 2017, p. 140). Official documentary records can include school, hospital, dentist, or medical records, as well as court documents, police records, minutes from meetings, annual reports, sales records, and so on.

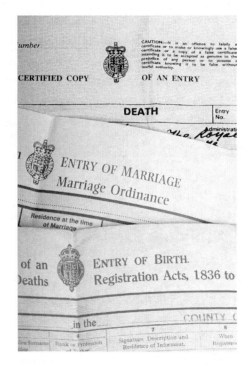

Actuarial records include birth, death, marriage, and divorce records.

Source: Brian Maudsley/shutterstock.com

Researchers may later examine public archives, such as official records collected for one purpose, for a completely different purpose. For example, Moulden, Firestone, Kingston, and Wexler (2010), from the University of Ottawa in Ontario, examined official documentary records collected on convicted sexual offenders to learn more about patterns of sexual offending involving teachers. Specifically, the researchers analyzed archival Violent Crime Linkage Analysis System reports obtained from the Royal Canadian Mounted Police to describe the offending of 113 Canadian teachers who committed a sexual offence against a child in their care between 1995 and 2002. Archival analysis indicated that most offenders abused a position of trust to initiate contact with the victim (84 percent). In addition, many of the offenders befriended the victim (40 percent), offered a form of assistance to the victim (16 percent), or offered the victim money, treats, toys, or work (14 percent). In addition, findings showed that many of the offences occurred at school (44 percent), the offender's residence (41 percent), the victim's residence (19 percent), in a religious facility (14 percent), or in another residence (12 percent).

Private archives, in contrast, are personal records created for use mainly by the originating author. These are sometimes directed at a narrow known target, such as a friend or loved one. Examples of private archives include personal items such as diaries, letters, or journal entries. The internet is now changing what would traditionally be considered a private archive into what is probably better considered a **social domain personal archive**. For example, some people post videos depicting their (otherwise) private, personal events on YouTube, while others post highly personal information on websites such as Facebook.

Research in Action

Online Dream Diary

As a further illustration of a social domain personal archive, one young man posted a detailed description of his dreams on a personal website. Psychologist Jayne Gackenbach from MacEwan University in Alberta, along with her research team, studied a video game player's 13-year-long online dream diary (consisting of 831 dreams), as well as his daily activity blogs, to see if the reported dream content was consistent over time and whether it corresponded to what is already known about dreams in video game players. In addition, the researchers examined the correspondence between daily blog activity and subsequent dreams to see if prior everyday events were incorporated into dreams. Results for the 447 dreams included in the analysis from the archive showed that the dream content was consistent over time (e.g., similar characters appeared, similar social interactions took place) and there was some incorporation of elements of the daily blog into subsequent dreams. The video game player's dreams also contained themes consistent with other gamers, including the prevalence of dead and imaginary characters (Gackenbach, Sample, Mandel, & Tomashewsky, 2011).[1]

Advantages and Disadvantages of Archival Analysis

Like trace measures, archives are beneficial to researchers largely because they are non-reactive. In addition, archives often provide a low-cost means for researchers to access a multitude of existing records. Since archives can be collected indefinitely, archival analysis is especially suited for longitudinal analysis where pattern and trends can be examined over time.

The main drawback of archival analysis relates to validity because, as with trace measures, selective deposit and selective survival biases may determine who or what ends up in the records and which records have a better chance of persisting over time (Webb, Campbell, Schwartz, & Sechrest, 2000). For example, because records are sometimes created for the benefit of an organization or agency (e.g., sales records, annual reports), biases may be built into how the data were collected in the first place. In addition, records may be incomplete, they may get lost, and/or certain records may be destroyed over time. One way to increase validity and lessen the likelihood of errors due to missing data is to use archival analysis in combination with other data collection methods.

Finally, since unobtrusive methods involve means of obtaining evidence indirectly, people are usually unaware that data about them have been used for research purposes, and therefore informed consent was never obtained. While we may learn important insights and historical facts through the analysis of private records such as diaries and letters often found only after people pass on, should this knowledge come at the expense of the privacy of the originator? In many cases it may be difficult to even establish the accuracy of existing documents—especially personal ones such as biographies.

Test Yourself

- What kinds of records are accessible as public archives?
- What are the main advantages and drawbacks of archival analysis?

CONTENT ANALYSIS

Another main source of non-reactive data comes from visual and print-based forms of media, such as television shows, films, photographs, books, and newspapers, which contain messages studied by social scientists about race, class, violence, and gender, for example. Although **content analysis** can be traced to propaganda techniques employed by the media (e.g., see Lasswell, 1927), it has also been used to examine the meaning of messages in a variety of archival records including messages delivered by the words, phrases, and passages in books, articles, and news stories; in song lyrics; in information found on websites; in representations shown in magazines; and in character portrayals as shown in television commercials, television programs, and major motion pictures. Similarly, while some researchers view content analysis as an objective, quantitative means for looking at message characteristics (e.g., see Neuendorf, 2002), others view interpretations of text as largely an interpretive, qualitative endeavour involving techniques such as

Content analysis is a popular method for examining messages contained in print and visual forms of media.

Source: geralt/pixabay.com

discourse analysis or narrative analysis (e.g., see Van Dijk, 1997). Discourse analysis is directed more at how language is used in a social context, while narrative analysis focuses more on stories provided by individuals. It is probably most accurate, at this point, to "say that content analysis has evolved into a repertoire of methods of research that promise to yield inferences from all kinds of verbal, pictorial, symbolic, and communication data" (Krippendorff, 2019, p. 23).

Conducting a Content Analysis

Any number of topics can be studied using content analysis. Popular topics that students in my classes have studied using this method include gender stereotypes, humour in advertising, violence in the mass media, themes in children's books, sports injuries, cancer resources, and representations of groups in the media. A sample of topics investigated by Canadian researchers using content analyses include the following:

- Teen depression groups on Facebook (Lerman et al., 2017)
- Gendered research in the *Canadian Journal of Counselling and Psychotherapy* (Bedi, Young, Davari, Spriner, & Kane, 2016)
- Settlement service organizations' inclusivity of LGBTQ immigrants (Giwa & Chaze, 2018)
- #cheatmeal images on social media (Pila, Mond, Griffiths, Mitchison, & Murray, 2017)

- Canadian newspaper articles and readers' comments related to schizophrenia (Shigeta et al., 2017)

As is the case with any research method, the first step in a content analysis is to clarify the research objectives (see figure 8.1).

Once the objectives for a study are clarified and the researcher has deemed content analysis the most appropriate method for obtaining the data of interest, the next step is to determine the most relevant archival source. For example, a researcher interested in the representation of Indigenous people in the mass media might narrow the project to an exploration of whether Indigenous people are over- or under-represented in media stories involving Canadian crime. Similarly, a researcher might compare how more-or-less liberal news outlets report on stories involving crimes committed by Indigenous youth. My students have selected a range of archival sources for research projects involving content analyses, including local newspapers, national newspapers, primetime television shows, television shows aimed at preschool children, television commercials for children's products, car magazines directed at young and older audiences, and songs within music genres such as hip-hop. The appropriateness of any given archival source is largely determined by the research questions and objectives. For example, one former student of mine examined representations of Indigenous women in online advertisements for Halloween costumes (O'Dell, 2016). Another student looked at user comments on YouTube about hip-hop/rap music videos featuring sexually objectified depictions of women (Knish, 2018).

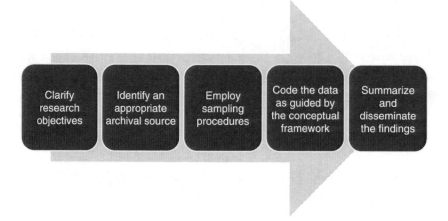

Figure 8.1: Main Steps for Conducting a Content Analysis

Source: Created by author

After locating an appropriate source, a researcher needs to employ a sampling procedure. Will the study include all available records, a sample obtained using a probability-based technique, or a sample obtained using a non-probability-based technique? Again, it will depend on what the specific study is about. A researcher interested in the portrayal of gender in magazine advertisements might begin by examining a random sample of 10 magazines from the 100 top-selling Canadian magazines, such as *Reader's Digest, Chatelaine, Canadian Living,* and *Maclean's.* Within the selected magazines, another simple random sample of advertisements could be obtained. As noted in chapter 4, it is sometimes helpful to distinguish between units of analysis (the magazines) and the more precise units of observation (the advertisements). Once sampling procedures have been worked through, a researcher can begin to code the data.

Coding is the "process of transforming raw data into a standardized form" (Babbie & Roberts, 2018, p. 249) and it is used to help make sense of the data collected. If a researcher takes a quantitative approach, hypotheses are developed and a precise coding scheme is established according to some conceptual framework in advance of data collection. The researcher defines specific variables for use in analyzing the content of a message to test the hypotheses. For example, a researcher might code the advertisements in magazines to test a hypothesis that females will be more likely than males to be portrayed in gender-stereotyped ways for certain products. The literature is replete with established coding schemes for examining gender portrayals in advertisements. A coding scheme might include the variables sex, type of product sold, role depicted by the main character, and type of portrayal depicted by the main character. Each one of these variables would be precisely defined, such as operationalizing sex as male or female, type of product as food, clothing, service, and so on. Using the coding scheme, the researcher codes each advertisement for each variable and then examines the data collected to see if females are portrayed in gender-stereotyped roles for certain products; for example, as traditional housewives to sell cleaning products. Quantitative content analysis usually involves coding the presence or absence of some event, determining the frequency of a variable, or counting the number of times a word or theme appears in text as described in numbers 1 through 3 on the list of indexes. In each of these cases, the researcher is most likely recording the **manifest**, or more obvious, stated content in the message, such as words or phrases.

Qualitative content analysis, in contrast, is directed more at understanding the underlying meaning or **latent** content of a message. It is therefore more likely to involve coding text or images for implied themes and the repetition of constructs, as explained in numbers 4 and 5 on the list of indexes. From a qualitative approach, the researcher begins with a research question (as opposed to a hypothesis) and looks for themes to emerge from the data, which are then reinterpreted using theory, as opposed to coding for specific variables at the onset. For example, in an exploratory study, Mezzana, Lorenz, and Kelman (2012) were interested in learning more about how rock music lyrics portray islands. Theory is still important for developing a conceptual framework that informs the data collection. In this case, the researchers examined what previous researchers had to say about the constructs of "islands," "islandness," and "island features" in rock music. However, the purpose was not to test theories, but to try to uncover the meaning of islands as related to the lyrics of rock songs. The researchers looked at five decades of rock music—412 songs containing island references—to see how island references were used in the songs. They ended up identifying broader categories (themes) to help qualify the more specific observations. The 24 themes included the notions of loneliness and despair, seclusion, fear, depression, spirituality, love and romance, adventure, and intimacy, among others. The 24 themes adapted from the data and corresponding literature were then further coded under five main meta-themes of space (e.g., seclusion), lifestyle (e.g., adventure), emotions/psychology (e.g., fear), symbolism (e.g., spirituality), and social-political relations (e.g., dominance) (Mezzana, Lorenz, & Kelman, 2012).

To summarize, in content analysis, researchers examine messages contained in visual and print media for measurable indicators of more abstract constructs and ideas such as aggression, love, "islandness," or gender stereotyping. According to Krippendorf (2019, pp. 65–66), these five indexes are typically employed in content analyses:

1. The *presence or absence* of a reference or concept as an indication of some phenomenon of interest. For example, DeJean, Giacomini, Schwartz, and Miller (2009) examined 608 Canadian health technology assessment reports produced from 1997 to 2006 for the presence or absence of ethics content. They found that only a minority incorporated any form of ethical consideration into the documents.

2. The *frequency* with which a symbol, idea, reference, or topic occurs generally as an indicator of a concept's importance or emphasis. A content analysis on 150 top-selling video games, for example, revealed a high frequency of the use of profanity (Ivory, Williams, Martins, & Consalvo, 2009).

3. The *number* of favourable or unfavourable characteristics attributed to a symbol, idea, or reference that indicates an attitude toward some phenomenon of interest. For example, in Symbaluk and Howell's (2010) study,

students' posted ratings of instructor attributes at RateMyProfessors. com were coded as positive or negative, depending on the nature of the comment. For example, "knows nothing" would be considered a negative comment about intelligence, while "really knows his stuff" would be positive. The study showed that teaching-award winners receive more positive ratings than research-award winners.

4. The *kinds* of qualifications used in statements about a symbol, idea, or reference that are indicative of the intensity associated with the belief signified by the symbol, idea, or reference. Weitzer and Kubrin's (2009) content analysis of misogyny in rap music revealed five prevalent kinds of misogyny, including derogatory naming and shaming of women, sexual objectification of women, distrust of women, legitimization of violence against women, and a celebration of prostitution and pimping.

5. The repeated *co-occurrence* of two concepts that indicates the strength of association between them. Singer's (1982) content analysis of Ontario newspaper coverage of Indigenous people revealed an association between "Indian identification" and words depicting conflict, especially in relation to unresolved land claims.

Research in Action

Teen Depression Groups on Facebook

Researchers from the University of Guelph in Ontario studied teen depression by examining content disclosed in Facebook depression-support groups targeting youth (Lerman et al., 2017). Five hundred and eight "wall" posts from six public Facebook groups containing the terms *teen* and *depression* in the title or descriptions were coded for main themes. Lerman et al. (2017) found that posts largely consisted of self-disclosures involving depression, feedback between posters, and suggestions for help.

Advantages and Disadvantages of Content Analysis

Content analysis, like the other unobtrusive measures, is a great economical and non-reactive means for learning more about the messages conveyed in print and visual forms. Content analysis is free from biases that can lead to distortion in data obtained from participants, such as in a carefully controlled laboratory experiment or with a highly structured survey. Content analysis also maintains the data as originally conceived. The songwriter did not write the lyrics for a content analysis, nor did an author write a book for such purposes. As content analysis expert Klaus Krippendorff (2019) puts it, "the chief advantage of the unstructuredness of content analysis data is that it preserves the conceptions of the data's sources, which structured methods largely ignore" (p. 49). While it may be more difficult to examine text and messages that come in a range of unstandardized formats and types, the structure is not imposed and therefore exists as envisioned by the originator. As a related point, this also means that the "context sensitive" nature of the data can be considered during content analysis (Krippendorff, 2019).

Content analysis is also beneficial because it can be applied to a multitude of topics and it can also manage large amounts of data. For example, recall how Gackenbach et al. (2011) analyzed the content of 447 dreams and DeJean et al. (2009) examined 608 health technology assessment reports. Since the data for content analysis are archival in nature, there is also the potential for longitudinal analyses (e.g., are there fewer gender stereotypes portrayed in children's books that were written in the last 20 years compared to books from the 1980s and 1990s?). In addition, since the records already exist, they can be examined and re-examined to increase coder reliability.

A main limitation of content analysis is that the data originated for other purposes and hence it may be biased toward a viewpoint or perspective, as in the case of information contained in the mass media that is produced for profit. Also, it may be incomplete for examining certain hypotheses or questions of interest. Disadvantages of content analysis often relate to questions of validity. Once a coding scheme has been developed and constructs are operationalized into variables that can be readily measured by trained observers, will observers be able to use it properly? Manifest content is much more straightforward to code than latent content since manifest coding generally only involves counting the number of times a word appears or noting the presence or absence of a theme. However, the way in which a message is understood by a coder may not be the way in which the original producer intended the message to be interpreted (Richardson, 2007). Moreover, especially in the case of latent content, different coders are likely to interpret the same message in different ways, resulting in disagreements over what is or is not identified as a major theme in the message and a low inter-rater reliability.

Test Yourself

- What are the main steps for conducting a content analysis?
- How does manifest content differ from latent content?
- Which indexes are usually employed in qualitative content analysis?

SECONDARY ANALYSIS

As an alternative to collecting data first-hand directly from participants, as in the case of surveys and experiments, or indirectly, as in the case of trace, archival, and content analysis, researchers can also re-examine existing data using a method called **secondary analysis of existing data**. Secondary analysis involves the examination of data originally collected by someone other than the researcher for a different purpose. Secondary data can be quantitative or qualitative in nature, as in the case of archived survey data or interview transcripts.

Locating Secondary Sources

Examples of existing Canadian data include official census data and data obtained through national surveys, such as the General Social Survey and the National Population Health Survey. Various government departments and agencies (e.g., Environment Canada, the Correctional Service of Canada), institutes (e.g., Canadian Research Institute for Law and the Family, the Canadian Statistical Sciences Institute), and universities throughout Canada (e.g., the Institute for Social Research at York University, the Canadian Plains Research Centre at the University of Regina, and the Québec Inter-University Centre for Social Statistics) also collect a wealth of information.

Research in Action

Problematic Cannabis Use

Using existing cross-sectional data from the 2013 Canadian Tobacco, Alcohol and Drugs Survey (CTADS), researchers from the School of Public Health and Health Systems and Propel Centre for Population Health Impact at Waterloo University examined problematic cannabis use in Canada (Leos-Toro, Rynard, & Hammond, 2017). The CTADS is a biennial survey conducted by Statistics Canada on behalf of Health Canada (beginning in 2013) that collects information on tobacco, alcohol, and illicit drug use among Canadians 15 years of age and older (Statistics Canada, 2015). Using measures from the World Health Organization's Alcohol Smoking and Substance Involvement Screening Test, results showed only 2 percent of those who indicated use in the last three months could be classified as "high risk" for severe health or other problems (Leos-Toro, Rynard, & Hammond, 2017).

Determining the Appropriateness of a Source

It is one thing to know of potential sources of secondary data and quite a different thing to locate one that can be of use for a study. The starting point is always the narrowed research focus. For example, one of my students was interested in a phenomenon in sports known as the "Myth of the Contract Year" where professional athletes purportedly play harder in their final contract year to secure more lucrative future contracts. To determine whether this is the case in hockey, the student examined statistics for hockey players made available by the National Hockey League (NHL). By comparing production measured in points per game (goals, assists) for well-known NHL players averaged over their contract year versus non-contract years, Janke (2012) showed that some players were as productive or even more productive in non-contract years, helping to dispel the myth.

Some sources may appear to be appropriate but may not actually contain the variables needed to answer a specific research question, and sometimes information exists in a format other than what is needed for a specific study. For example, suppose a researcher wanted to test the applicability of Gottfredson and Hirschi's (1990) general theory of crime for explaining differences in treatment completion rates for sexual offenders using indicators of self-control. In this case, offenders with higher levels of self-control are expected to be more likely to complete treatment, while those with lower levels are less likely to complete treatment. After gaining the necessary ethical and institutional permissions to access what would appear to be an appropriate secondary source (e.g., a data set on Canadian offenders who underwent treatment for sexual offending at a minimum-security institution), the researcher might discover that the data set only contains limited information collected on patients at the beginning and end of treatment. The information the researcher is interested in, such as background characteristics pertaining to early school years, the stability of relationships, and job histories, which would serve as indicators for self-control, might still exist, but may be contained in individual patient files as notes from various sources (e.g., the head psychiatrist, therapists who regularly interact with the client). How then can a researcher determine if a data set will be appropriate in advance of carrying out the research?

In most instances, a researcher can assess the merit of a potential secondary data set by examining available information that describes the data set, or data sources and methodology used to obtain the data. For secondary data stemming from Statistics Canada, there is published information on the purpose of the survey, the date the data were originally released, questionnaire(s) and reporting guides, description, data sources and methodology, and data accuracy. For example, Statistics Canada conducts a mandatory annual census of all registered

Canadian pension plans (RPPs). If you look up "Pension Plans in Canada Survey" at Statistics Canada, you will learn its purpose is to provide information on the terms and condition of RPPs, membership in them, and contributions made by and on behalf of members (Statistics Canada, 2018h). Additional information about a data set is sometimes included in a **codebook**, a listing of variables that details how they were operationalized in the data set. For example, a variable might be "gender" and it could refer to "the behavioural, cultural, or psychological traits associated with a particular sex, within a certain culture, at a given point in history" (Symbaluk & Bereska, 2019, p. 136). Gender, in the study, might be coded as 1 = male, 2 = female, and 3 = other. A variable such as "offence" might refer to the type of criminal offence committed by someone whose information is included in the data set. A codebook also includes details on how any scales and indexes were constructed and how missing data were dealt with. Note that for a qualitative study, a researcher may be able to access journal notes, audit trails, or other documents that detail the process by which the available data were transformed into the current format, which could be in the form of words, images, or even artifacts.

In addition to details about the purpose of the data and how the data were gathered, a researcher also needs to pay special attention to the data format and structure. The **data format** usually refers to "the statistical format in which data are saved or stored" (Pienta, McFarland O'Rourke, & Franks, 2011, p. 18). For example, quantitative data are likely to be in a numerical format amenable to statistical analysis using a software package designed especially for the social sciences, such as IBM SPSS Statistics. Qualitative data are more apt to be a collection of visual or textual statements (see chapter 9 for more information on how verbal information collected in interviews is turned into data). The **data structure** refers to "the number and organizational nature of distinct files that compose a data collection and the relationship among those data" (Pienta et al., 2011, p. 18). For example, secondary data are often contained in a single file in a table with rows of information that illustrate variables by participants, as shown in table 8.1. Each row except for the first row corresponds to the information from one case.

Statistics Canada as a Leading Data Source

Statistics Canada regularly collects data on virtually all aspects of Canadian life of interest to federal government agencies. For example, pertaining to criminal justice, Statistics Canada conducts various annual surveys such as the Adult Correctional Services Survey, the Adult Criminal Court Survey, and the Uniform Crime Reporting Survey (Statistics Canada, 2018d). The Adult Correctional Services Survey collects data from all institutions in the provincial and federal correctional

Table 8.1: Sample Data Structure

Case	Sex	Age	Offence	Risk
1	1	23	1	2
2	2	21	4	1
3	3	20	2	4
4	3	19	3	5
5	2	20	2	3
6	1	19	2	3

Source: Created by author

systems on new admissions, conditional releases, and financial/human resources. The Adult Criminal Court Survey collects information on criminal court appearances and charges. The Uniform Crime Reporting Survey is managed by the Canadian Centre for Justice Statistics, a division of Statistics Canada that is responsible for collecting national data on crime (Statistics Canada, 2018d).

Police agencies throughout the country use the Uniform Crime Reporting Survey (UCR) to report crime statistics in a standard way for criminal offences. Since 1962, the UCR has collected information on the number of criminal incidents, the clearance status of those incidents, and the persons charged. In 1988, a second survey was created (called the UCR2) to obtain additional details on the characteristics of incidents, victims, and accused (Statistics Canada, 2018j). The UCR and UCR2 provide available data on close to one hundred different offences. See table 8.2 for summary information on the number and type of homicides committed in Canada between 2013 and 2017. Crime data can be re-examined to test theories, look for patterns and trends, and explore relationships among variables.

It is important to note that Canadian crime data are the end result of crimes that were recorded as such by the police, as opposed to a "true" measure of the amount of crime committed, since many crimes go undetected, many go unreported, and many are not classified as crimes after being reported. Furthermore, there are concerns about how particular crimes are counted. For example, in the case of multiple offences committed at the same time, only the most serious offence is recorded. In addition, the data obtained by police may be shaped by other factors, such as policy decisions, policing practices, and public concerns (Evans, 2020). To try to gain a more accurate estimate of the true amount of crime, criminologists and other interested parties typically supplement official crime statistics with other measures, such as information obtained on surveys completed by offenders and/or victims of crime.

Table 8.2: Homicides by Method, 2013–2017

	2013	2014	2015	2016	2017
All methods	509	522	610	612	660
Shooting	134	155	179	223	266
Stabbing	195	189	216	175	201
Beating	102	101	135	116	108
Strangulation	45	33	39	39	26
Fire*	5	7	7	11	14
Other**	18	23	16	28	27
Not known	10	14	18	20	18

Note: Homicides include Criminal Code offences of murder, manslaughter, and infanticide. If multiple methods against one victim are used, only the leading method causing death is counted. Thus, only one method is scored per victim.

* Fire includes burns and suffocation.

** Other methods include poisoning, exposure, shaken baby syndrome, deaths caused by vehicles, and heart attacks.

Source: Statistics Canada. (2018f). CANSIM. Table 35-10-006901, and Homicide Survey, Canadian Centre for Justice Statistics.

Advantages and Disadvantages of Secondary Analysis

Secondary analysis is an inexpensive and time-saving method for looking at patterns and trends in official data, such as the information collected through surveys conducted by Statistics Canada. In addition to being non-reactive, secondary analysis may have built-in safeguards, including the protection of privacy pertaining to how the data were collected in the first place. Information collected in Statistics Canada surveys, for example, is confidential. That is, Statistics Canada will not release information (even to the Royal Canadian Mounted Police) that would identify individuals with the responses provided. Furthermore, the data collected are reported and released in aggregate form as grouped data. Secondary analysis is especially suited to longitudinal research since the data from multiple surveys can be examined and compared over time.

One of the main drawbacks of secondary analysis is that the data were collected for purposes other than the present research study. This means the data may be incomplete or not contain the essential variables of interest for the secondary analysis. Moreover, except for sources such as Statistics Canada, there may be no way to determine how the data were originally collected, calling into question whether ethical safeguards were put into place and whether the measures are reliable and valid.

Research on the Net

Open Data Pilot Project

As an effort to make Canadian data more available for commercial and non-commercial purposes, the Government of Canada launched its first-generation Open Data Portal in 2011, launched its second-generation Open-Government Portal in 2013, and is now part of an international Open Government Partnership (Government of Canada, 2017a). Open Data allows access to a catalogue of federal government data sets freely available to users for secondary analysis. Tens of thousands of data sets can be accessed using key word search terms such as *roads, immigration, law,* or *health.* You can access the home page at data.gc.ca.

Test Yourself

- What is secondary data analysis?
- Which agency serves as the main source of secondary data on virtually all aspects of Canadian life?
- Why does secondary data analysis pose ethical concerns?

VIRTUAL RESEARCH AND DIGITAL RESEARCH

Given the limitlessness of the internet today, this chapter concludes with a brief discussion of internet-based research methods and data that may fall within an unobtrusive or reactive realm, that may include public or private sources of information, and that may or may not require prior ethical approval. The internet has dramatically changed the way researchers conceptualize the social world, and it continues to shape the way social researchers conduct research. First, the internet is a "social space" that offers an endless array of social opportunities and interactions that have meaning for individuals who create virtual selves, participate in online communities, and engage with social media platforms (Hine, 2013). Historically, social researchers have employed traditional methods such as ethnographic fieldwork in online environments (called virtual ethnography) to study individuals or virtual selves created by individuals (Hine, 2000; Pink, 2001). The internet also includes digital technologies that expand the reach of traditional methods into virtual domains such as virtual experiments, online focus groups, or interviews conducted using email. Moreover, the internet contains a wealth of primary and secondary visual data sources as objects of study, in the form of pictures, videos, and graphics that enable researchers across disciplines to examine cultural arti-facts, social issues, interactions, and consumption patterns as they exist online (Ardévol, 2012). Networking services such as Twitter or Facebook have amassed such popularity that their "big data" sources have been mined for myriad purposes and have grown beyond what can be adequately examined with more traditional research methods. Consequently, the internet has responded by making available digital tools for examining social issues as digital data, using even more specialized technology. For example, software such as DiscoverText can be used to help sort and analyze textual data in the form of public comments and statements made in blogs and posted to sites such as Twitter (Discovertext, 2019).

Appreciating that the internet can be used in various ways as a source of data or as a facilitator for carrying out research, it should be becoming apparent that previous distinctions made between reactive and non-reactive forms of research, and between private versus public forms of information, are beginning to blur. Are an individual LinkedIn user's posts considered private information, shared information among a social network, or a form of primary data that exists in the public domain? Given one's ability to alter a virtual self, is an online representation best considered reactive or non-reactive? Even the distinction between digital forms of information as data sources versus data gathering methods is difficult to maintain if we consider digital media as the framework for both, as captured by Sarah Quinton and Nina Reynold's (2018) notion of **digital media**, which "encompasses all computer mediated internet and digitally enabled media through which data may be collected, shared and ana-lyzed, including, for example, blogs, online forums, QR codes, online questionnaires, emails, Skype interviewing, Youtube material, Instagram messages, Twitter content, geo-location and internet navigation" (p. 10). Alongside the internet's potential for ever-increasing research opportunities, the ethical challenges stemming from the use of digital media are similarly expansive, particularly in terms of potential risks to individuals and privacy considerations, and ethical issues arise at all stages of the research process, from the nature of the research and its aims, to how the data are conceptualized, to whether and how participants are involved in the research, to how the data are collected and analyzed, and to what is done with the data and findings that result from the study (e.g., see Quinton & Reynolds, 2018).

Test Yourself

- In what ways is the internet a source of data for social researchers?
- In what ways is the internet a facilitator for carrying out social research?

CHAPTER SUMMARY

LO1 **Define unobtrusive methods and explain what is meant by reactive and non-reactive research methods.**

Unobtrusive methods are strategies in which the researcher examines evidence of people's behaviour or attitudes, rather than interacting directly with those being studied. A reactive method is one that directly involves a research participant, who may react to being in a study based on how questions are asked (e.g., in a survey) or due to the presence of a researcher (e.g., in an experiment). Non-reactive methods are unobtrusive because the data are obtained without participant involvement.

LO2 **Explain what physical trace analysis is used for and differentiate between erosion and accretion measures.**

Physical trace analysis is the study of products of past behaviour that provide insight into patterns and trends. Erosion measures are signs of selective wear and tear that tell us about human use and non-use (e.g., worn paths that denote desired walkways). Accretion measures are product deposits left behind based on prior activity, such as garbage or graffiti.

LO3 **Differentiate between public and private archives and note a main advantage and disadvantage of archival analysis.**

Public archives are public records prepared specifically to be examined by others, such as annual reports or attendance records. Private archives are created for personal use and include letters and diaries. As with all unobtrusive methods, archival measures are beneficial because they are non-reactive. In addition, archival records are economical and lend themselves well to longitudinal analysis. Drawbacks to this method include selective deposit and selective survival biases, as well as a potential lack of informed consent.

LO4 **Define content analysis and outline the steps for conducting a content analysis.**

Content analysis is a repertoire of methods that allow researchers to make inferences from all kinds of verbal, pictorial, symbolic, and communication data. Steps for carrying out a content analysis include clarifying research objectives, identifying relevant archival sources, employing sampling procedures, coding data in accord with conceptual frameworks, and summarizing and reporting on the findings.

LO5   **Explain what secondary analysis of existing data entails, identify key sources for secondary data analysis, and note a main advantage and disadvantage of secondary data analysis.**

Secondary analysis of existing data involves an examination of data originally collected by someone other than the researcher for a different purpose. Key sources for secondary data analysis include official census data and data obtained through national surveys, as well as data collected in research centres and institutes. Statistics Canada is the main federal government source for secondary data on most topics involving Canadians. One advantage of using data from Statistics Canada is that it includes built-in privacy and informed consent safeguards from when the data were collected. However, data collected for other purposes may be incomplete for the purposes of the current study.

LO6   **Define digital media and explain how the internet has changed the nature of social research and the methods used to study it.**

Digital media refers to all computer-mediated internet and digitally enabled media through which data can be collected, shared, and analyzed. The internet both provides sources of information for social research and entails means for studying it. For example, online communities are subcultures studied by ethnographers, and virtual ethnography is an approach used to study online cultures. The internet also contains tools, such as software that aids in the collection and analysis of online data.

RESEARCH REFLECTION

1. Suggest a physical trace measure that could be employed as one of the main variables for each of the following research topics:
    - Students' use of food service providers on campus
    - Students' typical commute patterns on campus
    - Students' food consumption on campus
    - Students' preferred study space on campus
2. Suggest an appropriate archival or secondary data source for each of the following research topics:
    - Popular vacation spots
    - Fashion trends
    - Crime statistics
    - Canadian documentaries

3. Suppose you wanted to conduct a content analysis on the portrayal of gender in popular general-audience-rated movies.

    a. First, list 10 movies that are rated G, for a general audience, and are suitable for younger children (e.g., *Coco, Frozen 2*, and *Toy Story 4*).

    b. Now consider who or what is likely to constitute the main character in one of these movies. If you had to categorize the main character as one of only five different "types," what would the types consist of to ensure that your categories were mutually exclusive and exhaustive? For example, would all animals of any kind, such as mammals, birds, and fish, be classified together?

    c. Come up with one research question on gender you could examine in a content analysis of popular G-rated movies.

    d. Refer to Smith, S. L., Pieper, K. M., Granados, A., & Choueiti, M. (2010). Assessing gender-related portrayals in top-grossing G-rated films. *Sex Roles, 62*, 774–786. How were the main characters operationalized in this study?

LEARNING THROUGH PRACTICE

Objective: To learn how to code data for a content analysis

Directions:

1. Locate and examine a few online dating sites, such as eHarmony.ca or Zoosk.com.
2. Write down several variables located on the site, such as smoking, height, hobbies, and occupation.
3. Develop three research questions you could examine based on the information provided at the site. For example, how do women seeking relationships with men describe themselves on the site?
4. What exactly would you need to code to explore your research questions?
5. Choose one research question, make up a coding sheet that lists the central variables, and then try coding 10 relevant profiles at the selected site.
6. Did you employ a sampling procedure to obtain relevant profiles? Explain.
7. Are your initial findings what you expected? Why or why not?

RESEARCH RESOURCES

1. For a comprehensive resource on social media, I recommend Burgess, J., Marwick, A., & Poell, T. (Eds.). (2018). *The Sage handbook of social media.* Thousand Oaks, CA: Sage.

2. To learn more about the conceptual foundation of content analysis, content analysis designs, and how to code data, refer to Krippendorff, K. (2019). *Content analysis: An introduction to its methodology* (4th ed.). Thousand Oaks, CA: Sage.

3. For information on conceptualizing digital research, conducting research using digital methods, and assessing digital data, refer to Quinton, S., & Reynolds, N. (2018). *Understanding research in the digital age.* Thousand Oaks, CA: Sage.

4. To learn about ethical considerations in secondary analysis, refer to chapter 22 in Gray, D. E. (2018). *Doing research in the real world* (4th ed.). Thousand Oaks, CA: Sage.

NOTE

1. Note that in Gackenbach et al.'s (2011) study, informed consent was obtained from the young man who posted his dreams and daily activities.

CHAPTER 9

Qualitative Interviewing

Rather than stripping away context, reducing people's experiences to numbers, in-depth interviewing approaches a problem in its natural setting, explores related and contradictory themes and concepts, and points out the missing and the subtle as well as the explicit and the obvious.

—Herbert J. Rubin & Irene S. Rubin, 2012, p. xv

Learning Objectives

After reading this chapter, students should be able to do the following:

LO1   Explain what a qualitative interview is.

LO2   Describe the structure of qualitative interviews and explain why qualitative interviewing is "responsive."

LO3   Identify and explain important considerations that arise in the main steps for conducting a qualitative interview.

LO4   Define and differentiate between main question types.

LO5   Define focus group and compare focus groups to in-depth interviews.

LO6   Describe the main components of a focus group.

INTRODUCTION

In chapters 6 and 7, you learned about two quantitative approaches based on deductive logic, stemming from the positivist paradigm and resting on objective conceptions of social reality (i.e., surveys and experiments). In this chapter, you will learn about a qualitative method known as qualitative interviewing, which is grounded in the interpretive paradigm in its emphasis on naturalism and subjective understanding. A **qualitative interview**, also known as an intensive interview, an in-depth interview, or just a depth interview, is an approach to research that "attempts to understand the world from the subjects' points of view, to unfold the meaning of their experiences, [and] to uncover their lived world prior to scientific explanations" (Kvale & Brinkmann, 2009, p. 1). You are already familiar with the many uses of interviews in the social world as evident in places of employment, where they are regularly relied upon for hiring and promotional purposes. Interviews are an integral part of therapeutic and correctional processes used to assess, monitor, and rehabilitate clients and offenders. Interviews are also employed in everyday life by reporters, historians, and authors who wish to learn more about a person of interest's life, career, or accomplishments. Similarly, qualitative interviewing is an especially popular method among researchers interested in understanding processes, organizations, and events from the perspective of those most knowledgeable about such phenomena—the people who directly experience the processes, who work within the organizations, and/or who undergo or are most impacted by the conditions of interest.

Poulin, Gouliquer, and McCutcheon (2018), for example, conducted in-depth interviews with self-identified gay and lesbian soldiers in the Canadian military to understand how their experiences are impacted by an environment supportive of hyper-masculinity (exaggerated stereotypical male behaviour) and heteronormativity (adherence to binary gender codes). Participants revealed discrimination tied to the policing of masculinity and femininity, as well as the use of various coping strategies, including having to prove they met a "warrior" standard or passing for a heterosexual (Poulin, Gouliquer, & McCutcheon, 2018). As another example, Walsh, Hanley, Ives, and Hordyk (2016) interviewed immigrant women who were newcomers to Montreal, Quebec to learn about housing insecurity. The researchers found insecure housing was linked to various factors, including an ineligibility for government programs due to immigration status, a lack of experience in Canada, and a traumatic migration trajectory such as war or persecution in the country of origin (Walsh, Hanley, Ives, & Hordyk, 2016).

Qualitative interviews share features with everyday conversations.

Source: rawpixel/pixabay.com

QUALITATIVE INTERVIEW STRUCTURE

While quantitative interviewing in the form of a survey tends to be a formal, direct, and highly structured data collection method, qualitative in-depth interviewing is based on informal and flexible approaches to data collection. Qualitative interviews can be **semi-structured** in format, where some of the questions or an outline of potential questions is prepared ahead of time, with room to clarify responses and probe for additional details. The format of qualitative interviews can also be completely **unstructured**, where question wording develops in the moment like a casual conversation consisting of a variety of friendly exchanges between the interviewer and interviewee, with flexibility in choice of topics and issues explored. (See figure 9.1 for a comparison of structured, semi-structured, and unstructured approaches to interviewing.) Since qualitative interviewing relies on listening, understanding, and asking questions, it shares features with everyday conversations, including a fundamental social component. Like two friends having a private conversation, the qualitative interviewer needs to establish trust and rapport, and even needs to be able to "read" unspoken cues evident in nonverbal forms of communication, such as facial expressions or tone of voice. However, a qualitative interview is not a casual conversation because, unlike casual conversations, qualitative interviews have an established purpose, they tend to

Structured	Semi-Structured	Unstructured
• Quantitative • Survey • Questions are prepared ahead of time • Standardized • Often relies on closed-ended response formats • No flexibility (i.e., re: wording of questions or order of questions) • No clarification or follow-up	• Quantitative or qualitative • Survey or in-depth interview • Main questions are prepared ahead of time • Some flexibility (i.e., questions can be clarified, additional questions can included, or earlier items can be omitted) • Can include follow-up/probing questions designed to learn more about a topic raised by the respondent	• Qualitative • In-depth interview • Questions are developed based on respondent answers • Highly flexible (i.e., there is no pre-arranged item wording) • Relies on open-ended questions • Questions can be clarified, modified, and even answered by the interviewer • Incorporates follow-up questions that emerge as a function of reponses provided

Figure 9.1: A Comparison of Interview Structures

Source: Created by author

involve more questioning from the interviewer and more responding from the interviewee, and they deliver much more detail (Rubin & Rubin, 2012).

In addition, while a quantitative survey consists of mainly closed-ended items (see chapter 7), a qualitative interview comprises open-ended questions, where participants are asked to describe their views and personal experiences, however they make sense of those experiences, in their own words. The order of the questions and even the content of any given question can vary from participant to participant, although covering the same topics and even the same questions may be desirable for later comparing the responses across different interviewees. The central underlying feature of qualitative interviewing that makes it unique is its reliance on what Rubin and Rubin (2012) refer to as a "responsive" approach. Responsive interviewing "emphasizes flexibility of design and expects the interviewer to change questions in response to what [they are] learning" (p. 7). The qualitative interviewer's main objective is to listen carefully to what the interviewee is saying to achieve a basic understanding and then, dependent upon what the interviewer hears, subsequently probe the interviewee for verification and for additional details to achieve an even deeper and more thorough understanding. The flexibility of the design is what makes responsiveness possible, rendering in-depth interviews one of the only methods that can be used to truly "get inside a person's head" (Tuckman, 1972) so we can understand "the lived experience" of that person (Seidman, 2006).

Many exploratory topics that begin with the question "What's it like to . . .?" are especially suited to qualitative interviewing. Listed here are some examples that follow from "What's it like to . . .":

- Undergo a transition from a two-year college to a four-year degree-granting university?
- Grieve the loss of a loved one due to an unexpected accident?
- Be a member of an outlaw motorcycle gang?
- Be a professional poker player?
- Live out a life sentence for murder?
- Stay at a shelter after leaving an abusive relationship?

Research on the Net

Forum: Qualitative Social Research
Forum: Qualitative Social Research (FQS) is a peer-reviewed open-access journal for qualitative research that was started in 1999. This multilingual online journal publishes articles based on studies conducted using qualitative methods. Go to qualitative-research.net to learn more about the use of biographies, in-depth interviews, participatory qualitative research, qualitative archives, visual methods, and much more!

Test Yourself

- In what ways does a qualitative interview differ from a quantitative survey?
- In what ways does a qualitative interview differ from a casual conversation?
- In what ways is qualitative interviewing considered to be a reflexive process?

CONDUCTING A QUALITATIVE INTERVIEW

After settling on a topic, narrowing the focus, and developing a research question, as is the case in any research project, main stages for conducting a qualitative interview include determining the type of format to use, selecting a sample, working through ethical considerations, establishing rapport, developing questions ahead

of time and/or while carrying out the interview, coding and analyzing the interview data, and disseminating the findings. Special considerations are associated
with some of these stages, as discussed in the following sections.

Determining the Most Appropriate Structure

Deciding upon the structure for a qualitative interview depends in part on the
nature of the research question and the overall purpose of the study, on the anticipated sample, and on various other considerations, such as the amount of time and
resources available for the project. First, it is important to consider what the interview is designed to accomplish. For example, if the purpose is to assess the needs
and requirements of individuals so they can perhaps receive the most appropriate
therapy or treatment, then a semi-structured interview is likely since specific kinds
of information will be sought. Similarly, if the interview is designed to test an
assumption or more fully explain a process, it is likely to be semi-structured since
the objectives are known in advance. In contrast, an interview designed to identify
processes or relationships that will become the focus of a later study, or an interview
follow-up from another method such as an experiment, used to learn more about
why things happened the way they did, would likely be unstructured. Unstructured
interviews also work best for research designed to get at people's lived experiences.
Ethnographic research that takes place in natural settings heavily relies upon unstructured in-depth interview techniques (see chapter 10). In many cases, the decision about structure boils down to how much control the researcher needs to have
over the type of responses provided by the interviewees (Bernard, 2018).

Sample considerations also impact the structure of an interview. For instance,
if the intended sample comprises a group whose responses will be compared for
similarities and differences, interviews will be more structured than would be the
case if there was only going to be one person interviewed because that person is
perhaps considered to be the starting point, serves as a usual case, or is an extreme
example of some topic of interest. Here, the issue is more one of whether the
researcher wishes to obtain comparable responses, suggesting more structure to
the design, versus a unique understanding, warranting a less structured approach
(Cohen, Manion, & Morrison, 2018).

Overall, unstructured interviews are an excellent means for obtaining rich,
detailed information on a topic of interest from the point of view of the participant. Credibility is likely to be high because the unstructured approach of an
in-depth interview is flexible enough to allow for clarification of questions and
the use of prompts based directly on the responses provided by an interviewee.

This helps ensure that the data obtained are a close approximation of the respondent's construction of reality. However, the researcher still needs to reconstruct or interpret the transcribed data in a manner that is consistent with the respondent's perspective in order to disseminate the findings. While reliability in the "quantitative" sense is likely to be low, especially if the questions were tailored to a participant and may not lend well to replication with different participants, dependability can be high if the researcher is careful to document the research process, including interpretations of the findings and justification for the conclusions reached. See chapter 4 for more information on how rigour is achieved in qualitative research.

Selecting a Sample

Qualitative research is usually more concerned with gaining an in-depth understanding of a phenomenon from those experiencing it than it is with obtaining results that generalize from a large representative sample to a population of interest. As a result, qualitative researchers carefully select for interviewees using techniques such as purposive sampling or snowball sampling to identify and locate the most appropriate participants (see chapter 5 for a discussion of the various sampling techniques). Ideal interviewees are well informed about the research topic (i.e., they have first-hand experience with the event, process, condition, or issue being studied). As Rubin and Rubin (2005) note, finding knowledgeable participants is often not as easy as it first appears to be since "not everyone who *should* know about something is necessarily well informed" (p. 65). In addition,

Participants for in-depth interviews are selected for their unique experiences.

Source: josealmeida1970/pixabay.com

researchers try to select for interviewees who can offer a diverse range of perspectives and opinions on the same topic. For example, to fully appreciate the collective experience of a two-year community college transitioning to a four-year undergraduate degree-granting university, researchers might interview a small number of students, instructors, advisors, support staff, and administrators who were present at the educational institution prior to, during, and after the change in status.

Ethical Considerations

Ethical concerns need to be taken into consideration during the early planning stage of a study. Most social research projects entail at least a minimal risk of harm to participants, and in-depth interviews are no exception. The difficulty with in-depth interviews for both researchers and research ethics review board members lies in anticipating in advance the kinds of risks likely to be experienced by participants, since the questions that evoke emotion or otherwise affect interviewees develop within the research process itself. There are several ways to mitigate for potential risks. First, researchers should be qualified to carry out in-depth interviews. To obtain ethical approval for a study based on qualitative interviews, for example, researchers generally need to validate their qualifications by indicating their prior research experience, by demonstrating their familiarity with the use of qualitative interview techniques, and by providing evidence of completion of the Tri-Council Policy Statement Tutorial (see chapter 3 for a detailed discussion of the TCPS2 on research involving humans as participants). In addition, researchers may be required to provide a detailed project description, a literature review that establishes the scholarly context for the study, and a summary of the methodology including details about the recruitment of participants.

Anticipated risks and benefits to participants are also described in advance to an ethics review board (see chapter 3). Researchers detail potential sources of psychological harm that could result from the type of questions the researcher plans to ask. This is usually accomplished through the creation of an **interview guide**. An interview guide is like an outline, consisting of a series of key questions developed by the researcher after consulting the relevant academic and non-academic literature, and considering any "hunches" about what might be relevant, beyond what is already known (Rapley, 2007). An interview guide helps to frame the interview based on the overall objectives of the study. Although this will only be loosely followed during the actual interview, an interview guide or set of main questions helps to inform the ethics board and potential interviewees about what participation is expected to entail, as part of the informed consent process. Researchers also need to identify specific means for mitigating potential risks posed by the study. For example, a researcher planning on interviewing students about their aggressive driving practices can note that questions about unsafe driving practices will be asked during the interview and can even provide a few sample potential questions. In addition, potential participants can be made aware that they may find some of the questions to be embarrassing or uncomfortable to answer. Finally, a researcher can debrief participants with information that helps them to address their emotions and/or actions beyond the study, such as a listing of local driver education resources and/or anger management resources.

Maintaining privacy is another ethical consideration that necessitates special consideration when planning a study based on qualitative interviewing. Anonymity, as in not knowing who the participant is (see chapter 3), cannot be achieved since an interviewer knows who is being interviewed. Moreover, since the sample size is small for in-depth interview methods, the findings do not get reported as group data in a manner that would obscure the identity of participants as is the case with quantitative survey methods. Instead, the researcher is likely to note themes and use quotes from participants to substantiate the findings. How, then, does a qualitative researcher protect the identity of interviewees? There are several ways to protect the identity of interview subjects. First, a pseudonym or alias name can be attached to the interviewee's comments. In addition, identifying details can be removed or left out of the published findings. For example, in explaining how sociology student Kaitlin Fischer (original name) described her experience within one of the first graduating classes from the Bachelor of Arts program at Algoma University in Sault Ste. Marie, Ontario, the researchers might simply state "a female student taking sociology notes. . . ." But what would happen if the researchers wanted to share information provided by the president of the university or one of the deans? When there are only a few individuals in a given role or the field of study is quite small, it is highly likely that even when names are left off, information made public could inadvertently identify the participant (e.g., there is only one president). Researchers could in this case conceal the role of the participant by generalizing the position to "an administrator" or by broadening the description of the institution, as in "a president at a university in Eastern Canada."

Researchers even need to ensure that others outside the study cannot compromise privacy by gaining access to the data. Since most interviews are recorded, and that information is often stored on the computer of the principal researcher, privacy could be compromised if the researcher's computer was stolen or accessed by someone else. Ethics review boards ask for information on how the data will be collected and stored and who will have access to the data. Password-protected

Researchers are especially likely to face ethical dilemmas regarding privacy while studying individuals who engage in criminal activities.

Source: tommaso79/shutterstock.com

software helps to alleviate concerns about unauthorized access but still might not resolve the issue of data being subpoenaed by the criminal justice system in cases involving interviews that expose criminal activity. Since this cannot always be anticipated ahead of time, researchers need to carefully think through how they will handle sensitive information they may become privy to. As noted in chapter 3, qualitative researchers have been successful in winning court cases based on the need to protect participant confidentiality (e.g., see Samson, 2014).

Establishing Rapport

In all forms of qualitative research, the researcher is the data-gathering instrument. In the case of an in-depth interview, this means the quality and amount of data collected largely rests with the interviewer's ability to establish and maintain rapport with the interviewee. Due to the personalized nature of any given in-depth interview, there are no guaranteed methods for establishing great rapport. An interviewer, however, should try to do whatever is possible, given the circumstances, to make an interviewee feel at ease and valued for whatever contributions may be forthcoming. After all, it is the views of the interviewee that are essential to the study itself. Making the interviewee feel comfortable is not an easy task, as everything about the interviewer, including how an interviewer looks, acts, and conducts the interview, may have an impact on the interviewee, even if indirectly, and influence the success of the interview itself. Just as some instructors are better than others at engaging with their students, some interviewers are more adept at developing rapport. Think about what is likely to happen when a student offers up an incomplete or incorrect answer in class and the instructor's sharp rebuttal makes that student feel embarrassed or ashamed. The student will be less likely to speak up in the future. If, instead, the instructor had thanked the student for responding, clarified the answer, and reassured the student, the same student might be just as willing to try again at another point in time. Similarly, an interviewer needs to create a safe climate where a participant is encouraged to offer up information with an implicit understanding that responses are appreciated and the participant is not being judged by the interviewer.

In the development of this climate, it is even important to consider the physical location in which the interview takes place. The location and setting for an interview should be one that is familiar to the participant and makes the person feel at ease discussing personal issues. Many in-depth interviews take place in the home or workplace of the interviewee, or in a public location, such as a restaurant or coffee shop, that offers privacy and is convenient for the participant. The important consideration in choosing a location for an interview is to make sure it is a place where the interviewee will feel comfortable and can speak freely about the topics raised in the interview.

Lune and Berg (2017) identify three crucial techniques employed by interviewers to help build trust and establish rapport during interviews including tolerating uncomfortable silence, echoing the interviewee, and letting people talk

Qualitative interviews take place in a location that offers privacy and is convenient for the participant.

Source: StockSnap/pixabay.com

(pp. 77–78). "Tolerating uncomfortable silence" means an interviewer should purposely build in long, silent pauses after asking an interviewee a question. Interviewees require time to consider the question, think about how it relates to them and the situation as they understand it, and then try to formulate an answer. As a teaching analogy, I have conducted peer reviews on probationary instructors to provide them with feedback on their teaching. During peer reviews, inexperienced instructors often fail to give students enough time to digest a question posed before the nervous instructor answers it for them. Lune and Berg (2017) recommend waiting for up to 45 seconds before assuming an interviewee truly has nothing to say about a subject.

"Echoing the interviewee" involves acknowledging what the interviewee is saying by repeating back the main idea. This technique conveys interest and understanding. It also helps to establish and maintain rapport because the interviewer is inadvertently encouraging the interviewee to continue (Lune & Berg, 2017). The key to this technique is to keep it brief and only echo back what the interviewee has said, as demonstrated in the following exchange:

Interviewer: "Can you tell me what it was like when you learned your son was highly gifted?"

Interviewee: "When I initially read the results of the intelligence test, I was relieved. The findings gave us an explanation for Brant's disruptive behaviour at school."

Interviewer: "So you were relieved because you had a reason for the disruptive behaviour?"

Interviewee: "Yes. Brant's kindergarten teacher told us that Brant appeared to be low-functioning and easily distracted. Instead, he may have been highly capable but bored by the repetition."

Imagine, instead, how the conversation might have gone if the interviewer was inexperienced and failed to use echoing correctly, inserting a personal viewpoint such as "I know what you mean, I was also a disruptive kid in school." The point of the interview is to obtain needed information from the interviewee, whose perspective needs to remain front and centre throughout the interview process. The underlying goal is to let the participant lead most of the discussion.

Just as the researcher needs to do things to get the participant to feel at ease in order to facilitate the discussion, it is also important to do everything possible to maintain a conversation. "Letting people talk" literally means the interviewer must be careful not to interject at the wrong times. The worst mistake an interviewer can make in this regard is to interrupt an interviewee's thought processing or react in a manner that interferes with an interviewee's response, thereby losing potentially important data (Lune & Berg, 2017). It takes time to develop interviewer skills, and one of the best ways to learn how to conduct great interviews is through first-hand experience and practice. Just as we are apt to make mistakes in some of our exchanges with certain friends and family members, over time we also become more adept at reading cues and figuring out what is working and not working for interviewees.

Accomplished interviewers demonstrate **active listening**. Active listening is a technique in which the interviewer demonstrates an understanding of what is being said and expressed by the interviewee through feedback. Active listening is evident when an interviewer appropriately echoes the interviewee and uses emotional displays based on what the interviewee has expressed. For example, if a participant conveys a happy experience, the interviewer should appear happy by smiling and conversely, if the interviewee appears to be upset, the interviewer should acknowledge this, be empathetic, and possibly even try to console the person (Lune & Berg, 2017). A skilled interviewer is also able to steer an interviewee away from the tendency to answer with "monosyllabic" responses of "yes" or "no" using questioning techniques such as probes and pauses (Lune & Berg, 2017). Probes are defined and discussed in detail in the next section.

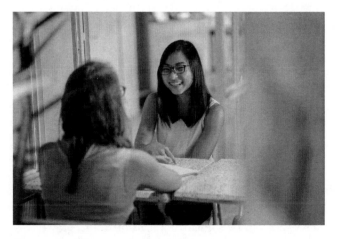

The quality of data collected during an interview rests largely with the interviewer's ability to establish and maintain rapport.

Source: mentatdgt/shutterstock.com

Types of Questions and Interview Sequencing

Various types of questions are routinely used in qualitative interviews. This section describes question types and outlines the order for the sequence of events in a typical interview.

Icebreaker

An interview usually begins with an **icebreaker**, or opening question, that is unrelated to the research topic and is used specifically to establish rapport. The icebreaker can pertain to anything the interviewer feels will be effective for getting the participant talking. For example, the interviewer might begin by asking the participant something about the weather, or, if the interview takes place in the home of the participant, the interviewer might start by asking how long the participant has lived in the home, or by inquiring about a picture that is prominently displayed in the home. The icebreaker should always be a question that is easy for the interviewee to answer.

Informed Consent for Participation

Following the icebreaker, the interviewer can introduce the study by reiterating the overall purpose (e.g., objectives) and procedures. In many cases, the study will consist of a tape-recorded interview that is carried out in the home or workplace of the interviewee. Permission needs to be sought from the participant before starting the recording device. Additional details are also provided ahead of time, such as how long the interview will take and what the questions will pertain to. Also, as part of the consent process, the participant will need to be made aware of the benefits of the research (e.g., how the study will contribute to a better understanding of a particular condition experienced by the participant) and the potential risks (e.g., that the participant might find some of the questions to be embarrassing). Interviewees need to be made aware that participation is voluntary, and even with prior agreement, the participant can refrain from answering questions and can withdraw from the study at any time without penalty. If an interviewee chooses to end the study early, the participant is free to decide whether views provided up to that point will remain as part of the data or will need to be removed from the study. A participant also needs to be informed ahead of time about how privacy will be protected. For example, how will potentially identifying information be stored and who will have access to it? In addition, the participant needs to be informed about how long data will be kept and how records will be destroyed once the study is completed. Finally, the participant needs to know how the findings will be reported (e.g., direct quotes may be used) and what the plans are for dissemination (e.g., findings may be reported at a conference and published in a peer-reviewed journal). These details should be contained in the consent form, which is reviewed with the participant prior to the onset of the interview. Assuming the participant approves of the conditions, signs the consent form, and agrees to be interviewed, the study can officially commence.

Transition Statements

Having established informed consent, the researcher can lead the participant into the focus of the study using a **transition statement**. Transition statements are designed to "move the conversation into the key questions that drive the study" (Krueger & Casey, 2015, p. 45). For example, in a study on teaching, I concluded the consent process with "If you have no further questions or concerns about what the study entails, I'm now going to collect the consent form from you and begin the interview." To transition to the first question, I said, "Take a moment to think about the kinds of things you do to prepare for your classes." After waiting about 45 seconds, I then asked, "What is one of the things you do to prepare for class?"

Essential Questions

Essential questions, also called key or main questions, "exclusively concern the central focus of the study" (Lune & Berg, 2017, p. 63). Essential questions are usually developed in advance of the interview and they form the basis of the interview guide. If demographic information is pertinent to the study, these items will generally be near the beginning of the interview (e.g., questions on age, marital status, and occupational status). Questions that more directly relate to the study topic follow from here, beginning with the least sensitive questions and then moving into the more sensitive ones once rapport is flowing well. Sensitive questions are ones that are most likely to pose the greatest risk of psychological harm by evoking emotions (e.g., asking about the loss of a loved one, asking the participant to retell a painful event, or asking about a private condition the interviewee is deeply affected by).

Probes

Probes are short questions and prompts designed to obtain additional information and details from a participant that will help to further understanding. Interviewees can be encouraged to elaborate on their responses through short prompts, such as "And then what happened?"; "Anything else?"; "How come?"; "Hmm"; "I see"; "Could you tell me more about X?"; "What do you mean by X?"; or "How did that make you feel?" As cultural anthropologist H. Russell Bernard (2018) puts it, "the key to successful interviewing is learning how to probe effectively—that is, to stimulate a respondent to produce more information, without injecting yourself so much into the interaction that you only get a reflection of yourself in the data" (p. 169). For example, suppose an interviewee is asked "Have you ever used illegal drugs while at work?" Assume the participant replies "Yes." The next question can be the probe "Like what?" Note how this prompt enables the interviewee to choose the direction of the ensuing discussion (as opposed to the interviewer stating the name of some drug and waiting for the respondent to answer in the affirmative or negative, thereby leading the creation of the data obtained).

Throw-Away Questions

In cases where it may be difficult for an interviewee to stay focused on a central topic for long periods of time (e.g., because it is stressful or painful to relive), an interviewer can help the interviewee take breaks by asking occasional **throw-away questions**. Throw-away questions are unessential questions that may be un-related to the research. Lune and Berg (2017) highlight the importance of using throw-away questions while probing sensitive issues to "cool out" the participant.

Extra Questions and Follow-Up Questions

One way to examine the reliability and validity of the responses being provided by the interviewee is to include **extra questions** and **follow-up questions**. Extra questions "are those questions roughly equivalent to certain essential ones but worded slightly differently" (Lune & Berg, 2017, p. 63). Extra questions help to assess reliability in responding since the interviewee should discuss similar issues in a consistent manner. Follow-up questions are "specific to the comments that conversational partners have made" (Rubin & Rubin, 2005, p. 136). Follow-up questions help to clarify main ideas or themes that emerge during the interview to ensure that the interviewer has properly understood the intended meaning of the main idea (e.g., Can you tell me more about . . .?). Follow-up questions are similar in nature to probes, but they are usually asked to obtain clarification about an issue central to the overall research objectives. Follow-up questions help to establish validity, since the aim of qualitative interviewing is to understand an issue from the viewpoint of the participant (Miller and Glassner, 2011). Follow-up questions may be asked within an initial interview or they may be asked in subsequent inter-views, after a researcher has had an opportunity to explore the findings to identify themes or concepts that warrant further clarification.

Closing Questions

While there is no set length to a qualitative interview and the actual length will largely be determined by the objectives of the study, the interviewee, and the overall dynamics that develop within the interview process, you can plan, as a general rule of thumb, for an interview to be about 90 minutes in length. Since friendly rapport is established within a new social relationship, it is sometimes difficult for the interviewer to bring the interview to an end. **Closing questions** are designed to help bring closure to the interaction by re-establishing distance between the interviewer and interviewee. (Hennink, Hutter, & Bailey, 2011). Closing questions often consist of slightly reworked earlier statements about data storage and plans for the dissemination of the findings, since these topics reflect late stages of the study and are more technical than personal in nature. The **final question** in an interview asks if the participant has any questions about the research, or anything else to add before the interview concludes. At that point, the participant is thanked for their time and contributions, and the participant is reminded to contact the researcher should any questions about participation arise later. A follow-up interview is sometimes scheduled at the end of the interview. In-depth interviews are generally not a one-time event. In most cases, the participants are interviewed on at least one other occasion. This is because the researcher needs time to analyze the information collected during the first interview (or round of interviews, if multiple people are interviewed for the same project) to determine which of the findings warrant further exploration.

Coding and Analyzing Interview Data

Assuming the interview was properly recorded in some manner, the information obtained during the interview can now be transcribed so that data analysis can take place. **Transcription** is a data-entry process in which the obtained verbal information is transferred verbatim (i.e., word for word), including, where possible, indications of mood, emotion, and pauses into a written (i.e., typed) format. Transcribing interview tapes or sound recordings into text is time consuming, and the longer the time elapsed between the interview and the transcription, the less able a researcher is to capture gestures or indications of special emphasis that took place during an interview (e.g., perhaps the interviewee shrugged their shoulders or fidgeted nervously prior to answering certain questions). As an example, it took students in one of my advanced qualitative methods courses six to eight hours, on average, to transcribe one 90-minute interview for a course assignment. Those who did the transcription right away were able to add in additional insights, such as lengthy pauses and facial expressions used by the interviewee. A few opted to save time using voice-activated software, which transcribed the interview for them with minimal errors. However, the students who transcribed the data themselves benefited from listening repeatedly to what the interviewee was saying, thereby increasing the detail and authenticity of their interpretations of the responses. Reliability can be assessed at the transcription phase using two transcribers, whose verbatim accounts of the interview should end up very similar, provided the audio recording is of adequate quality. Once transcribed, the data can be coded for themes, ideas, and main concepts.

Coding was defined in chapter 8 as means of standardizing data. Coding qualitative data involves "delineating concepts to stand for interpreted meaning of data" (Corbin & Strauss, 2015, p. 220). Recall that the purpose of a qualitative interview is to gain an understanding of a topic from the perspective of someone who has experienced it first-hand. Thus, if you were studying what it is like for someone to parent a highly distracted 10-year-old boy, your research findings

Previously recorded interview data are transcribed word for word into a file for subsequent analysis.

Source: StockSnap/pixabay.com

should help others understand what distractibility means as explained by one of his parents. As you read through the transcription, underline passages that identify main ideas. For example, the parent might note that the child "rarely remembers to bring home his homework," that "teachers continually indicate that the boy cannot complete schoolwork independently," and "that it takes hours upon hours to complete a short piece of homework." These types of comments help to identify what distractibility means in terms of school-related behavioural indicators. The transcript might also contain other indicators of distractibility, such as social implications. For example, the interview transcript might include a comment that "he never gets invited to birthday parties even by the children who attend his party" and "no one ever comes to the door to call on him when the neighbourhood kids are going to the park." The researcher's task is to try to tell the story of distractibility from the perspective of the parent, highlighting main concepts and themes as reflected in the conversation.

In addition to the identification of key concepts, qualitative researchers pay attention to context. **Context** "is a complicated notion. It locates and explains action-interaction within a background of conditions and anticipated consequences. In doing so, it links concepts and enhances a theory's ability to explain" (Corbin & Strauss, 2015, p. 153). In relation to the distracted child, you might be tempted to conclude that the boy probably has something like an attention deficit disorder. However, the researcher would try to make sense of the distractibility in relation to other issues that help to provide a context for understanding why it occurs. For example, the researcher might note that most of the problems are only evident at school and in relation to age-related peers. Careful consideration of the transcript might also reveal that the child has a few close friends who are several years older. In addition, there may be passages indicating that the child has an unusually advanced sense of humour, learns new things very quickly, and is able to retain large amounts of information. These behaviourial traits are associated with giftedness. As noted in an earlier chapter, gifted children are those whose intelligence (as measured by standard IQ tests) is well out of the range of normal (i.e., over 130). Gifted children have a very low tolerance for repetitive tasks; they tend to have what is called sensual and intellectual overexcitability, where they easily become distracted in environments that are not interesting or highly challenging for them (Webb et al., 2005). Trying to make sense of distractibility in the context of giftedness clearly paints a different picture than understanding distractibility in the context of an attention deficit disorder. Qualitative data analysis is discussed in further detail in the final chapter, on report writing.

- Why might a qualitative researcher choose an unstructured interview format?
- Why would a qualitative researcher opt for purposive sampling over a probability-based technique?
- Why is it difficult to anticipate the potential risks stemming from a qualitative interview?
- What three techniques are used during interviews to help establish trust and build rapport?
- What is the purpose of a "throw-away" question?
- What does transcription refer to?
- Why is context important to a qualitative researcher?

FOCUS GROUP INTERVIEWING

A **focus group** is a small discussion group led by a skilled interviewer that is designed to obtain views and feelings about a topic of interest (Krueger & Casey, 2015). Like in-depth interviewing, a focus group is a method for collecting data about people's thoughts, feelings, and behaviours. What sets a focus group apart from an in-depth interview with multiple participants is the additional creation of whole-group data, which become the unit of analysis (Ritchie, Lewis, Nicholls, & Ormston, 2014). For interviews, multiple participants provide independent answers to questions posed by an interviewer. Similarly, individuals in focus groups can provide individual responses that are later examined as participant-based data. However, in a focus group, a moderator creates a small-group discussion and that interactive collaboration also becomes an important source of data collected (Morgan, 1996). Most focus groups consist of between 5 and 10 participants who are selected because they possess certain characteristics in common or are believed to have especially well-informed views on the topic of interest. For example, in advance of a residence being built at a university, focus groups could be conducted with student groups for applied research purposes to learn about the potential impact of a residence on existing campus services. Who better to ask than the primary users of services directed at students and those likely to live in residence? Focus groups can provide insight into how students' current patterns of service use might change if they lived in residence. For example, participants might indicate

The quality of data collected from focus groups rests largely with the skills of the moderator.

Source: Roman Samborskyi/shutterstock.com

that if they lived in an adjacent residence, they would like to be able to access the library after regular hours since they tend to study at night. In addition, they could note that they might be less likely to purchase food to eat on campus, since it would be just as convenient, and now cost saving, to head home between classes to make lunches and snacks. Sometimes focus groups can be extremely beneficial for identifying unanticipated findings. In a focus group I conducted on this topic at the university where I teach, participants identified the need for a special type of "quiet space" or "spiritual room" for prayer on campus. Participants explained that such a space would be especially important for students who pray several times a day.

Like in-depth interviews, focus group topics span an infinite range. When I was seconded from my teaching role by the Office of the Vice President of Resources to serve a two-year term as a resource development planner, I relied heavily upon focus groups to learn more about how students use existing resources and space on campus. I also used focus groups to learn about the ideas and interests of recently retired and soon to be retired faculty and staff members, to see whether and how they might wish to stay connected to their former place of employment. As part of my research on the scholarship of teaching, I've led focus groups with students as participants to learn about study strategies and to determine what they perceive to be effective learning practices. I have similarly interviewed instructors in focus groups to discern how they prepare for courses. Focus groups are especially useful for gaining insight into problems, issues, or processes. Examples of topics studied by Canadian researchers using focus groups include the following:

- The challenge of setting age restrictions for supervised injection facilities (Watson, Strike, Kolla, Penn, & Bayoumi, 2015)
- HIV stigma in the Canadian healthcare system (Wagner, McShane, Hart, & Margolese, 2016)
- Needs of family caregivers of advanced cancer patients (Nissim et al., 2017)
- Positive impacts of technology on young gay men's dating and sexual relationships in Canada (McKie, Lachowsky, & Milhausen, 2015)
- Social casino gaming and online gambling (Kim, Wohl, Gupta, & Derevensky, 2016)

As with an in-depth interview, a focus group is initiated by a skilled interviewer, typically referred to as a moderator or facilitator, who poses questions and attempts to steer an otherwise natural conversation toward the exploration of certain topics. Because the interviewer stands out in a focus group as a moderator who manages group dynamics, leads the group through specific issues and questions, and imposes structure when necessary, a focus group is generally considered to be less natural and more "staged" compared to a one-on-one interview (Morgan, 2001). In addition, participants in focus groups are affected by the presence of others who say things and do things that shift the conversation in directions that might not have occurred had the participants been interviewed individually. This can have positive and negative implications for validity. For example, validity decreases as participants agree with other group members because they think this is the most appropriate response given demand characteristics created by the group. Or, similarly, participants may be unwilling to express divergent viewpoints they possess because they do not want to stand out as being different from the rest of the group (i.e., social desirability bias). Comments made by certain members of the group can also be distracting for other members since they take attention away from what any given individual might have originally stated, had someone else not provided a response first. In other words, listening to one member's response can mean interrupting the thought pattern or potential response of everyone else. On the other hand, comments made by other group members can trigger ideas for greater innovation, or they may help a participant more fully clarify individual responses in a manner that enhances validity.

Compared to in-depth interviews, focus groups can be a relatively inexpensive, time-efficient means for obtaining rich, detailed information from knowledgeable participants. Because group members usually share common characteristics and have specialized knowledge about the topic of interest, their feedback during the focused discussions can be instrumental in producing novel insights for ways to solve issues or create programs tailored to the needs of a specific group. However, much of the data obtained will largely depend on the skill set of the individual moderator, whose role it is to steer the discussion in such a way to produce and maintain group dynamics that yield the most relevant feedback from the participants. In summarizing the most important characteristics of good moderators, Krueger and Casey (2015) point out that the "right" kind of moderator shows their respect for participants, understands the purpose of the study and the topic, communicates clearly, is open and not defensive, and is able to bring about the most useful information from the group.

Research in Action

Focus Groups: Behind the Glass

Focus Groups: Behind the Glass is a short documentary produced and distributed by the Canadian Broadcasting Corporation. This video demonstrates the utility of focus groups in marketing for learning about consumer attitudes and views toward products. Using WorldCat Libraries, you can identify libraries near you that carry a copy of the video. Go to www.worldcat.org and search for "Focus Groups: Behind the Glass."

FOCUS GROUP COMPONENTS

The three most essential elements of a successful focus group are clear objectives, an appropriate group of participants, and a highly skilled moderator.

Clear Objectives

As with any study, a researcher first needs to be clear about the overall purpose and objectives. Like in-depth interviews, a focus group is utilized to learn more about a topic of interest from the perspective of individuals who have first-hand knowledge regarding that process, event, or condition of interest. Beyond an in-depth interview, there is an assumption that through the ensuing discussion, group members will provide a range of views and, ultimately, information and details might emerge beyond what could be obtained in individual interviews.

Participant Groups

Although marketing-based focus groups investigating consumer views often include as many as 12 participants in a session, social researchers recommend 6 to 8 (e.g., Lune & Berg, 2017; Morgan, 2019). If I have a larger potential group (e.g., of 10 or 12 members), I will usually divide it into two separate focus groups (e.g., of 5 or 6 members). However, the actual size of a group is best determined by the overall research purpose and other design considerations, such as the number of potential questions. Krueger and Casey (2015) offer this advice: "If the purpose is to understand an issue or behaviour, invite fewer people. If the purpose is to pilot-test an idea or materials, invite more people" (p. 83). The key is to strike a balance in numbers of participants that will promote discussion and allow the facilitator to fully cover the main issues in a reasonable time frame, anticipating that some of the members will talk more than others. A study may include three or four different focus groups on the same topic to fully explore the issue (Krueger & Casey, 2015). A good indication that "enough" groups have been utilized is when the facilitator can reasonably anticipate what the next group is going to say about the issues during the ensuing discussion (Bryman & Bell, 2016).

In addition to size, a researcher needs to carefully consider the composition of focus groups. Ideally, the more diverse but homogenous (i.e., alike) a group is, with respect to the relevant characteristic of interest, the better. For example, if a researcher is interested in how instructors prepare for courses they have never taught before, the shared characteristic is new-course preparation, but the group could include, for diversity, instructors who teach full- and part-time and those with varied teaching experience. Alternatively, if a researcher is interested in how sessional (i.e., part-time) instructors teaching introductory-level courses prepare for classes, the common elements are instructors with limited-term appointments and introductory level courses. In this case, diversity can be achieved by including instructors who meet the criteria and who are from a variety of disciplines (e.g., sociology, anthropology, and political science).

Participants are typically recruited through a letter of invite sent out via email, as a paper copy, in a newsletter, or as a posting on a Facebook group. The letter of invite is usually less formal than a consent form, and it outlines who the researcher is, what the purpose of the study is, what the expectations are for participants, what the participation incentives are (if any), and what the eligibility criteria are (see figure 9.2).

Term Instructor Focus Group

Dear [term instructor's name],

You are invited to participate in a focus group on teaching preparations.

My name is X and I am an associate professor in the Department of X at X. I am conducting research on teaching introductory X. Since the majority of introductory X courses are taught by term instructors, I would like to learn more about how you go about preparing for your classes and what kinds of resources you find to be useful for instructional purposes.

The focus group will take approximately two hours. If you choose to participate, I will be asking you to comment, as part of an informal discussion with about five other term instructors, on a series of questions related to course preparation. For example, I will be asking you if you use any supplementary resources (e.g., an instructor's manual or test bank), what types of supplementary resources work well for you, and which ones are of little or no value to you. In addition, I will be asking you for any ideas or recommendations you have for resources that might better facilitate introductory-level teaching among term instructors.

Note: This study comprises institutional research and was approved by X's Research Ethics Board. You will be provided with a consent form and an agreement to maintain confidentiality at the session.

Date and Time:
Location:

Light refreshments will be included, and as a token of appreciation, you will receive a $50 gift certificate.

Eligible participants are individuals who are currently teaching at least one course at X and have taught an introductory-level course at least once within the last two years. If you are interested in participating in the focus group, please email me as soon as possible.

Sincerely,

X
X's email address

Figure 9.2: Sample Letter of Invite

Source: Created by author

A Skilled Moderator

A **moderator** "is a trained facilitator used in focus group research who guides the focus group discussion" (Neuman & Robson, 2018, p. 272). A moderator in a focus group is akin to an interviewer in an in-depth qualitative interview. First, a moderator prepares technical and organizational details pertaining to the study. This can include setting up a meeting room (e.g., arranging the chairs so participants can see one another); bringing in refreshments for participants or, at a minimum, providing water for the participants; distributing other necessary materials, such as consent forms and pens; and setting up some type of audio-recording device. An assistant might be included in the session to take some back-up "real-time" notes or to type comments during the session that can later be used to contextualize the transcribed discussion. The main role of a moderator is to welcome the participants, obtain informed consent from the participants, explain the ground rules for the focus group session, get the participants talking, and guide the discussion in a manner that elicits responses from the various participants while covering the essential questions (Krueger & Casey, 2015). In addition, the moderator helps to establish a positive group dynamic by encouraging equitable participation. For example, a moderator must be able to encourage participation by everyone, even the shy participants or people who seem more reluctant to speak out (e.g., by using prompts, by nodding, and by establishing turn-taking rules). Moreover, just as a skilled instructor leads a classroom discussion so that one student doesn't predominate, a moderator also needs to incorporate strategies to help foster equitable group dynamics.

Analyzing Focus Group Data

Akin to the way in-depth interview transcripts are coded for themes using qualitative analysis and how messages in the media are coded for prevalent patterns using content analysis (see chapter 8), focus group data are first transcribed and then examined and coded in stages. This process can be extremely time consuming and complex, especially in studies based on several different focus groups. For example, in a study on parents' and teachers' views on physical activity and beverage consumption in preschoolers, De Craemer et al. (2013) utilized 24 parent-based focus groups and 18 teacher-based focus groups from six different countries (i.e., Belgium, Bulgaria, Germany, Greece, Poland, and Spain). First, each audio-taped focus group discussion was made available in all six countries, where the focus group discussions were transcribed into written text in the local language of each recipient country. Next, the transcriptions were independently coded, using qualitative content analysis, by local researchers. Following this, the main findings from the focus groups were translated into English and forwarded to two principal researchers (who received a total of six versions of the original data). The principal researchers then assessed and compiled the main findings using a qualitative software program called NVivo (see chapter 12 for more information on this software). Finally, the principal researchers summarized the key findings, along with illustrative quotes and excerpts from the original data, in a report that was verified by the organizers (De Craemer et al., 2013).

One of the more interesting findings from this study was a strong opinion by parents that their preschoolers were sufficiently physically active and that they had healthy beverage intakes (e.g., they drank lots of water and only minimal amounts of sugar-laden drinks such as juices, pop, and chocolate-flavoured milk). The parental perspective was not consistent with the conclusions substantiated in the previous literature by more objective methods (e.g., dietary records), suggesting that parents may need more information about existing dietary practices if they are to be motivated to make changes in their own families.

Test Yourself

- What is a focus group?
- In what ways does a focus group differ from a qualitative interview?
- How might the presence of others increase validity in a focus group?
- Why would a researcher run multiple focus groups on the same topic?
- In what ways is focus group composition important?
- What is the role of a focus group moderator?

CHAPTER SUMMARY

LO1   Explain what a qualitative interview is.

A qualitative interview is a technique that is designed to help a researcher understand aspects of the social world from the perspective of the participant who is experiencing them.

LO2   Describe the structure of qualitative interviews and explain why qualitative interviewing is "responsive."

A semi-structured interview is somewhat flexible since questions can be modified and clarified, while an unstructured interview is highly flexible, enabling questioning to develop as a function of exchanges within the interview itself. Qualitative interviewing is responsive because an interviewer asks questions and probes for details based upon what is being said during the interview, rather than just asking questions that are prepared in advance.

LO3 **Identify and explain important considerations that arise in the main steps for conducting a qualitative interview.**

First, a qualitative researcher needs to adopt the most appropriate interview format and try to obtain the most suitable interviewees. In addition, a researcher needs to anticipate potential risks to participants. Since the interviewee is not anonymous, a researcher needs to take special precautions to uphold confidentiality. The interviewer also plays an important role as the research instrument, establishing trust, motivating the interviewee to provide detailed information, and carefully steering the interview in the desired direction.

LO4 **Define and differentiate between main question types.**

An *icebreaker* is an opening statement that is used specifically in order to establish rapport. An *essential question* is one that exclusively concerns the central focus of the study. *Probes* are used to motivate an interviewee to continue speaking. *Throw-away questions* are unrelated to the research and are used to give the interviewee a break. *Extra questions* are equivalent to essential questions and help to assess reliability. *Follow-up questions* are specific to comments and are used to clarify main ideas. *Closing questions* bring the interview to an end by re-establishing distance. The *final question* asks if the participant has any questions about the study or any further comments to make.

LO5 **Define focus group and compare focus groups to in-depth interviews.**

A focus group is a small discussion group led by a skilled interviewer called a moderator. A focus group is somewhat more structured or staged relative to an in-depth interview, and group dynamics can influence individual responses, so they end up different from how someone would normally respond in a one-on-one interview. Focus groups are a relatively inexpensive and efficient means for gaining rich, detailed information from an informed group who likely has first-hand experience with the topic of interest. A disadvantage of a focus group is that the quality of information obtained can be negatively affected by an inexperienced or unskilled moderator.

LO6 **Describe the main components of a focus group.**

The three essential components of a focus group are clear objectives, an appropriate group of participants, and a skilled moderator.

RESEARCH REFLECTION

1. Suppose you are interested in conducting an exploratory study into what it would be like to be married to more than one spouse at the same time (i.e., polygamous or plural marriage). Would an in-depth interview be the most suitable technique for your research project? Why or why not?
2. Develop an interview guide that you could use if you were going to interview a sample of your classmates about their cellphone use.
3. Identify a topic you think would be best addressed using a focus group. Explain your rationale. If you were the moderator for the focus group, what are three essential questions you would ask the group about the topic? Provide one example of an icebreaker you could use to start the session.

LEARNING THROUGH PRACTICE

Objective: To learn how to conduct a focus group

Directions:

1. Suppose you want to learn more about effective study strategies using a focus group.
   a. First, enlist five or six of your classmates.
   b. Next, assign the role of moderator to one member of your group. Also ask for a volunteer to take notes while the group discusses study strategies.
   c. Come up with four essential questions that would help us learn about study strategies.
   d. Identify strategies your group would use to establish rapport and maintain good group dynamics.
2. Try running a 20-minute focus group with the selected moderator as the facilitator.
3. Describe your main findings.
4. How would you improve upon the focus group if you were going to repeat this topic using a different group of participants?

RESEARCH RESOURCES

1. To learn more about qualitative interviewing, I recommend Brinkmann, S., & Vale, S. (2015). *Interviews: Learning the craft of qualitative research interviewing* (3rd ed.). Thousand Oaks, CA: Sage.
2. For a description of feminist interviewing, refer to DeVault, M. L., & Gross, G. (2012). Feminist qualitative interviewing: Experience, talk, and knowledge. In S. N. Hesse-Biber, (Ed.), *The Handbook of feminist research: Theory and praxis* (2nd ed., pp. 173–198). Thousand Oaks, CA: Sage.
3. For information on how to carry out focus group interviews and how to analyze focus group results, see Krueger, R. A., & Casey, M. A. (2015). *Focus groups: A practical guide for applied research* (5th ed.). Thousand Oaks, CA: Sage.
4. For more advanced topics, such as using focus groups in a cross-cultural context and online focus groups, refer to Morgan, D. L. (2019). *Basic and advanced focus groups.* Thousand Oaks, CA: Sage.

CHAPTER 10

Ethnography

Ethnographic knowledge emerges not through detached observation but through conversations and exchanges of many kinds among people interacting in diverse zones of entanglement.
—Danielle Elliott & Dara Culhane, 2017, p. 3

Learning Objectives

After reading this chapter, students should be able to do the following:

LO1 Define ethnography and describe the role of an ethnographer.

LO2 Outline the main features of ethnographic studies.

LO3 Differentiate between the four main roles of ethnographers engaged in fieldwork.

LO4 Describe the main stages of fieldwork.

LO5 Explain the techniques used by ethnographers in order to blend into a group.

LO6 Discuss ethical issues in fieldwork.

INTRODUCTION

Ethnographers "are social scientists who undertake research and writing about groups of people by systematically observing and participating (to a greater or lesser degree) in the lives of the people they study" (Madden, 2017, p. 1). The historical origins of **ethnography** can be traced to naturalistic observation and fieldwork in social and cultural anthropology, and later in the Chicago school of sociology (O'Reilly, 2009). Ethnographers share the assumption that to understand a group, one must engage in fieldwork that involves spending a considerable length of time with the group in its natural setting. This fieldwork includes watching, listening, taking notes, asking questions, and even perhaps directly participating in the activities and conversations as a member of the group being studied. While ethnography is often used interchangeably with the term *participant observation*, ethnography is probably better understood as a multi-method approach to field research that may include any number of qualitative and quantitative data collection techniques undertaken to understand a social group or culture in its natural setting. Data collection in naturalistic settings can be accomplished using systematic observation, participant observation, in-depth interviewing, field notes, surveys, and even visual materials such as drawings and photographs. It is sometimes debated whether ethnography should even be considered a methodology in itself since the purpose of ethnography is intricately tied to the product of fieldwork: the description of a group, culture, or process. From this perspective, "ethnography is about telling a credible, rigorous, and authentic story" (Fetterman, 2010, p. 1). Most importantly, as implied by the opening quote, the knowledge gleaned through ethnography is based on "collaborative" modes of inquiry (Elliot & Culhane, 2017).

Research in Action

William Foote Whyte's (1943) Street Corner Society

As a pioneer in ethnography, William Foote Whyte spent three and a half years in an inner-city Italian district in Boston's North End, dubbed Cornerville, living among, interacting with, and studying various groups, including a gang he refers to as the "corner boys" (Whyte, 1943). In a later book called *Participant Observer: An Autobiography* (1994), Whyte describes how he learned to conduct ethnographic research for his "slum study" through trial and error, beginning with an overly ambitious research topic in which he first hoped to study "the history of the North End, the economics (living standards, housing, marke-ting, distribution, and employment), the politics (the structure of the political organization and its relations to the rackets and the police), the patterns of education and recreation, the church, public health, and—of all things—social attitudes" (p. 64). Following the advice of his mentors, including L. J. Henderson and Talcott Parsons, Whyte narrowed his "ten-man" project into something more manageable for one person lacking in field experience, and then set out to gather information from residents.

As a researcher, Whyte encountered several false starts, beginning with knocking on doors in hopes of surveying tenants about their living conditions. As he surmised, "it would have been hard to devise a more inappropriate way to begin the study I eventually made. I felt ill at ease and so did the people. I wound up the study of the block and wrote it off as a total loss" (pp. 65–66). Next, Whyte tried out a method shared by an economics instructor who claimed it was easy to learn about local women whilst purchasing drinks for them in a bar. This approach proved even worse for Whyte, who was nearly thrown out of a bar that he later learned was never frequented by any North Enders anyway (Whyte, 1994). It was only after Whyte met Ernest Pecci (whom he called Doc) that he understood the fundamental importance of getting to know someone from the community. Among many other insights, Whyte's (1943) early work teaches us that to study a group of interest, a researcher must first find a way to access that group. Knowing someone who is already a member of the group can be extremely helpful in this regard. In addition, the insider can also be of assistance in explaining what is going on and how to conduct oneself within that group to be accepted, to not stand out, and to not offend anyone. Finally, it is of-ten through the establishment of relationships developed while in the field that a researcher begins to gain an insider perspective needed to better understand events from the perspective of those experiencing them.

MAIN FEATURES OF ETHNOGRAPHY

To help you understand what ethnography is and how it is distinct from other research methods used by social scientists, this section describes 10 main features of ethnographic studies, adapted from anthropologist Harry Wolcott's (2010, pp. 90–96) list of what he considers the "essence" of ethnography after more than 50 years of experience in the field.

1. Ethnography takes place in natural settings.
2. Ethnography is context-based.
3. Ethnography relies on participant observation.
4. Ethnography is undertaken by a single principal investigator.
5. Ethnography involves long-term acquaintances.
6. Ethnography is non-judgmental.
7. Ethnography is reflexive.
8. Ethnography is mostly descriptive.
9. Ethnography is case-specific.
10. Ethnography requires multiple techniques and data sources.

Ethnography Takes Place in Natural Settings

First, the research must be conducted in a natural setting. A natural setting, such as a private home, a park, a shopping mall, a daycare, a library, or a lunchroom, is one that is not established for research purposes (Judd, Smith, & Kidder, 1991). The underlying assumption is that behaviour examined in a natural setting is also natural and depicts people as they are in everyday life. In contrast, people's behaviour within the confined parameters of research contexts, such as experimental settings that may bear little resemblance to the participants' real lives, is assumed to not be natural. Moreover, any events or interactions that take place within natural settings are deemed to be the result of naturally occurring causes as opposed to manipulated or controlled independent variables. "Naturalness" in research is beneficial to validity since it is devoid of the participant biases common to survey and experimental methods. For example, "unobtrusively observed behaviours (such as racially integrated seating patterns in a lunchroom) are likely to reflect the desired construct (unprejudiced attitudes) to a greater extent than a questionnaire or other responses obtained for obvious research purposes" (Judd et al., 1991, p. 272).

The internet has changed the way we view natural settings and communities, and the way ethnographers do research. People can be members of all sorts of virtual communities, from friends and followers on social networking sites such as Facebook and Snapchat, to various online support groups, to virtual worlds that are part of interactive games. **Virtual ethnography** is the term for "the in-depth study of a group or culture that exists in an online environment" (D. K. van den Hoonaard, 2019, p. 97). In this case, ethnographic research is undertaken through participation on the internet with other group members as part of a virtual community, such as a discussion group.

Ethnography takes place in everyday, natural settings.

Source: Jacob Lund/shutterstock.com

Ethnography Is Context-Based

To understand social interactions and social processes, an ethnographer also considers the wider context in which the studied phenomenon arises. The context often contains important conditions that help frame problems and can provide clues to why events unfold the way they do. For example, in an evaluation of an educational program, Fetterman (1987) noted that low school attendance should be interpreted within the environment in which the students and their program were situated. In this case, there were insufficient materials within the classroom to meet poor students' needs. For example, even basic supplies, such as paper and pens, were lacking, making it difficult for students to achieve. In addition, there were various competing distractions outside the classroom, including high rates of prostitution, arson, sexual assault, and homicide, that posed special challenges for students.

Ethnography Relies on Participant Observation

Ethnographers often employ a research strategy called **participant observation**, or what anthropologist Clifford Geertz (1998) called "deep-hanging out." In this strategy, the researcher joins a group of interest for an extended period to observe and study its members and functioning first-hand. Participant observation is also sometimes referred to as naturalistic observation and fieldwork, but there are differences between these terms. Fieldwork is the general term for any research

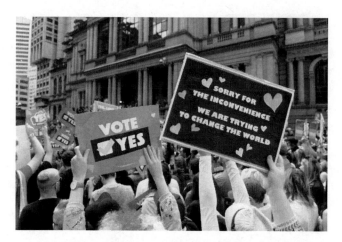

Ethnographers try to understand behaviour within the wider context in which it occurs.

Source: Felman/shutterstock.com

conducted in a natural setting, such as a qualitative researcher conducting in-depth interviews with participants in their homes. Naturalistic observation is a descriptive approach where observations take place in a natural setting (Cozby & Bates, 2018). Participant observation is one of the techniques that may be used to carry out naturalistic observation. Participant observation as a data collection method requires a researcher to join a group of interest and participate in that group over time to study it. Not all observation entails direct participation with group members, as discussed in the following section.

An Ethnographer's Role during Fieldwork

An ethnographer's level of participation while engaged in fieldwork can range from complete observer with no active participation through to complete partici-pation as a member of that community or culture. Gold (1958) identified a contin-uum for participation as illustrated in four ethnographer roles: complete observer (no participation), observer as participant (minimal participation), participant as observer (increased participation), and complete participant (full participation), as shown in figure 10.1.

Complete Observer

As a **complete observer,** the ethnographer's role is to unobtrusively observe a group as a non-member who does not participate with the group in any way.

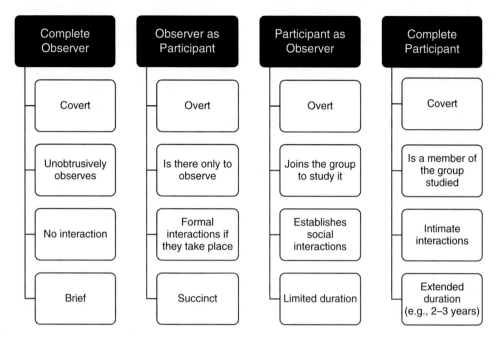

Figure 10.1: An Ethnographer's Role During Fieldwork

Source: Created by author

For example, an ethnographer might set up recording equipment in advance of classes in order to videotape students during class lessons so the videos can be examined as part of an exploration into class dynamics. This example illustrates a qualitative approach if the variables of interest emerge from the observations, such as patterns of interaction that become apparent from content analyses of the videotaped sessions. A complete observer role may also entail systematic observation using a quantitative approach called **structured observation**, which is direct observation "using categories devised before the observation begins" (Bryman & Bell, 2016, p. 127). For example, Zetou, Amprasi, Michalopoulou, and Aggelousis (2011) examined feedback provided by Greek National League volleyball coaches to athletes during the 2010–2011 championships. Researchers videotaped practices and then coded the frequency of the following 12 types of feedback based on a standard instrument called the Revised Coaching Behaviour Recoding Form: technical instructions, tactical instructions, general instructions, motivation, rewards/encouragement, comments, non-verbal punishment, criticism, demonstration, non-verbal reward, humour, and non-coding behaviour. Results indicated that any given practice session included about 279 separate coaching behaviours, with tactical instructions being most prevalent (17.4 percent), followed by general instructions (15.9 percent) (Zetou et al., 2011).

Observer as Participant

In an **observer as participant** role, the researcher's role is brief. For example, an ethnographer might sit in on one or two classes to observe and code student dynamics. During these observational periods, the students will be aware that the researcher is present, but the researcher's role does not entail direct involvement with group members, so it is minimally intrusive. After a few minutes, the students are likely to forget the researcher collecting data and behave as they usually do. In comparison, the complete observer role is wholly unobtrusive.

To carry out structured observations in a complete observer or an observer as participant role, decisions must be made ahead of time with respect to the type of behaviour examined, the way the behaviour will be recorded, and the format in which the data are to be collected and encoded (Judd et al., 1991). Beginning with the selection of the behaviour observed, a researcher might focus on any aspect of an interaction, event, or behaviour deemed to be relevant to the research interest. In the example used earlier, the volleyball coaches' verbal and non-verbal feedback provided to the athletes was selected for systematic observation. Next, it is important to determine whom to sample for the behaviour of interest. In the coaching example, the researchers selected 12 experienced coaches from the top divisions.

It is also important to determine how to observe the behaviour of interest and in what format. In this example, video recordings were made of each training session, with the coaches wearing wireless microphones so the researchers could examine verbal comments and non-verbal gestures. Each training session was recorded in its entirety for the 2010–2011 season of play. The video/audio recordings were then systematically examined for coaching behaviours. Each separate instance of coaching feedback was considered a new event and was encoded into one of the predetermined categories (Zetou et al., 2011). This method of collecting observations is called **continuous real-time measurement** because every instance of the behaviour that occurs during a particular time frame (in this case a practice session) is included in the observations. When it is difficult to determine when a behaviour begins and ends, or behaviour is going to be observed over long periods of time, researchers sometimes opt for **time-interval sampling**, where observations are made "instantaneously at the end of set time periods, such as every ten seconds, or every sixth minute or every hour on the hour, with the number and spacing of points selected to be appropriate to the session length" (Judd et al., 1991, p. 279). In this case, only behaviour taking place at the end of the time interval ends up being included as part of the data collected.

Finally, it is important to decide upon a method for encoding the observations. Like the data-reduction coding schemes used in content analysis, **encoding** is a process used to simplify observations by using categorizations (Judd et al., 1991). Volleyball coach feedback was encoded into 1 of the 12 coaching behaviour categories indicated earlier, including, as one of the categories, "non-coding behaviour" for the few instances that did not fit the other 11 prescribed categories (Zetou et al., 2011).

Participant as Observer

If an ethnographer joins the group to study it over a prolonged time and will interact with that group, then the researcher is engaged in a **participant as observer** role. For example, an ethnographer interested in a subculture such as a weekly poker session might join in, identifying themself as a researcher and as a card-playing member to become immersed in the group over the course of several weeks. In a participant as observer role, the ethnographer directly interacts with members of the group in a somewhat informal role that permits the establishment of communication and relationships while studying group members.

As another example, McNeil, Kerr, Lampkin, and Small (2015) carried out an ethnographic study on an unsanctioned safer smoking room (SSR) in Vancouver, British Columbia, to learn more about how an SSR shapes crack-smoking practices. Researchers conducted 23 in-depth interviews and spent about 50 hours engaged in participant observation with crack cocaine users at an SSR run by the Vancouver Area Network of Drug Users. Findings revealed a high demand for the

An ethnographer assuming the role of a participant as observer joins a weekly poker group.

Source: oneinchpunch/shutterstock.com

SSR due to factors such as homelessness and poverty that otherwise lead addicts to use drugs in unregulated public spaces where they face additional harms, including drug scene violence and crack-pipe sharing.

Complete Participant

Finally, in a **complete participant** role, ethnographers fully immerse themselves in the group as one of the members for a prolonged time to study the group. To lessen reactivity, the research usually takes place covertly in a concealed manner such that the researcher's true identity and purpose are not made known to the members. Researchers engaged in participant as observer and complete participant roles are still interested in observing behaviour (both verbal and non-verbal), people, and patterns of interaction, but the emphasis is more on understanding the subjective meanings of the observed events for the actors themselves, as opposed to coding for behaviours according to pre-established criteria. "Participant observation gives you an intuitive understanding of what's going on in a culture and allows you to speak with confidence about the meaning of the data" (Bernard, 2018, p. 283). For example, anthropologist and motorcyclist Daniel Wolf joined an outlaw motorcycle club called the Rebels to study the group dynamics and activities from within the group for his Ph.D. research while studying at the University of Alberta, in Edmonton (Wolf, 1991). As Wolf (1991) put it, "in order to understand the biker subculture, or any culture for that matter, one must first try to understand it as it is experienced by the bikers themselves. Only then can one comprehend both the meaning of being an outlaw and how that meaning is constructed and comes to be shared by bikers. Only by first seeing the world through the eyes of the outlaws can we then go on to render intelligible the decisions that they make and the behaviours that they engage in" (p. 21).

Data collection *in situ* is very difficult to undertake since it involves finding creative ways to discreetly observe, take notes, and record conversations and events in a manner that is not obvious to those who are present at the time. Imagine what would happen in a conversation with one of your friends if you suddenly pulled out a notebook and starting writing down things the person was saying to you. Field notes, however, are critical in ethnographic research since the notes ultimately become the data that are later used to describe and explain the setting, people, and relationships under investigation. As difficult as it may be to record notes, "*no observation is complete until those notes have been done*" (Palys & Atchison, 2014, p. 211). At a minimum, field notes should detail relevant people, conversations, and events and indicate the date, time, and location for each observation.

Anthropologist Daniel Wolf used participant observation to study an outlaw motorcycle gang for his Ph.D. dissertation.

Source: https://pixabay.com/en/harley-davidson-moto-transport-1241583/

Ethnography Is Undertaken by a Single Principal Investigator

In most cases, ethnographic fieldwork is carried out by a single principal investigator, such as Daniel Wolf's study on the Rebels and William Foote Whyte's study of an Italian slum. More recently, sociologist Fiona Martin (2011), from Dalhousie University in Halifax, Nova Scotia, interviewed 21 habitual drug users who were pregnant or were young mothers, as part of a larger ethnographic study carried out over a two-year period in a treatment clinic for women with substance use issues. Martin (2011) found that, while most addicts were trying to overcome their addictions, they faced various barriers such as established drug identities and the absence of non-drug-using relationships.

Ethnography Involves Long-Term Acquaintances

Since the goal of ethnography is to provide an accurate account of a culture or group, it is important to be around that group long enough to establish relationships with group members. The researcher needs to be in a position that permits an understanding of relationship dynamics and how members view the events and activities they engage in. Not surprisingly, ethnographers tend to spend long periods of time in the field. How long is long enough? The amount of time largely depends on what the research interest entails, including the complexity of the study, how difficult it is to access the setting, how long it takes to get to know people in that setting, and how skilled the researcher is. A study could be carried out in a few weeks, or it could take several years to complete. It is common for field research to take place over a period of about 18 months to two years. During this time, the ethnographer will initiate and develop several contacts, form friendships, and establish intimate relationships. After all, who would you be more likely to disclose personal details of your life to, a stranger or a friend? Getting to know others takes time, so it is probably better to spend more rather than less time in a field setting, for the sake of data quality. H. Russell Bernard (2018) explains:

> It may sound silly, but just hanging out is a skill, and until you learn it you can't do your best work as a participant observer. . . . When you enter a new field situation, the temptation is to ask a lot of questions to learn as much as possible as quickly as possible. There are many things that people can't or won't tell you in answers to questions. If you ask people too quickly about the sources of their wealth, you are likely to get incomplete data. If you ask too quickly about sexual liaisons, you may get thoroughly unreliable responses. Hanging out builds trust, or rapport, and trust results in ordinary conversation and ordinary behaviour in your presence. Once you know, from hanging out, exactly what you want to know more about, and once people trust you not to betray their confidence, you'll be surprised at the direct questions you can ask. (p. 293)

Ethnography Is Non-Judgmental

Although ethnographers can never be truly objective by being completely detached from the research process, and they may even be active, contributing members of groups, they still strive to be analytical and non-judgmental in their opinions and evaluations of groups and group behaviour. As Wolcott (2010) notes, "the ethnographer wants to see how things are, not to judge how they ought to be" (p. 92). According to anthropologists Lavenda, Schultz, and Zutter (2016), we show **cultural relativism** when we are "understanding another culture in its own terms sympathetically enough so that the culture appears to be a coherent and meaningful design for living" (p. 30). Researchers are still going to have their own opinions, and their views are not value-neutral. However, researchers strive to maintain a distinction between their personal views and their perceptions of what is going on in the observational setting. For example, an ethnographer may create several different kinds of field notes about the same event, including quick short-form "jotted notes" taken in the moment; highly "detailed notes" that resemble interview

Using cultural relativism, ethnographers learn about diverse practices such as Holi, a religious festival of colours celebrated by Hindus.

Source: Kristin F. Ruhs/shutterstock.com

transcriptions and include, where possible, direct quotes or words and expressions used by the group members; "analytical notes," where a researcher attempts to give meaning to what was observed; and "personal notes" that are more like journal entries that can include information on a researcher's personal feelings toward members of the group (Wolfer, 2007).

Ethnography Is Reflexive

In ethnographic research, the researcher is the data instrument—that is, it is the researcher who observes, participates, listens, records, and otherwise takes notes of events as they are occurring within the research context. Just as siblings never remember the same event in the same way, no two researchers are likely to see, record, or interpret data in the exact same manner. Juliet Corbin and Anselm Strauss (2015) explain:

> It is impossible to say that there is only one theory that can be constructed from data because qualitative data are inherently rich in substance and full of possibilities. Though participants speak about a topic, they don't determine the perspective or lens through which the analyst will interpret it. It is possible for different analysts to arrive at different conclusions even about the same data because each is examining the data with a different analytic focus or from a different perspective. Furthermore, the same analyst might look at the

same data differently at different times. In other words, data talk to different analysts in different ways. For example, interviews with persons who have chronic illnesses can be examined from the angle of illness management (Corbin & Strauss, 1988), identity and self (Charmaz, 1983), and suffering (Morse, 2001, 2005; Riemann & Schütze, 1991). (p. 68)

Ethnography is reflexive because the product of the research is necessarily influenced by the perceptions of the researcher and the processes enacted by that researcher as part of the data-gathering fieldwork (Davies, 2008). **Reflexivity** is often described as "a turning back on oneself," "a process of self-reference," and/or a "self-reflection" in which an individual researcher considers the ways in which their own subjectivities and values may have influenced the research outcomes (Davies, 2008, p. 7). All qualitative research requires some degree of reflexivity since data on their own are devoid of meaning. Since it is through interpretive data analysis that researchers make sense of their observations, it is important for researchers to recognize their unique perspectives and acknowledge how such perspectives come to bear upon the research process and the meanings that result from it.

Ethnography Is Mostly Descriptive

"Descriptive notes are the meat and potatoes of field work" (Bernard, 2018, p. 316). Most of the techniques used to collect field data generate enormous amounts of information. For example, interviews are transcribed into descriptive field notes. Overheard conversations may be jotted down as notes. Observed practices, customs, processes, and interactions are detailed in descriptive field notes. Wolcott (2010) advises ethnographers to err on the side of "thick" rather than "thin" description because one of the "best ways to be non-evaluative is to be intensively descriptive, to attend to what is, and what those in the setting think about it, rather than become preoccupied with what is wrong, or what ought to be" (p. 103). The goal of the ethnographer is to try to understand the meaning of this data for the participants. To achieve this, Corbin and Strauss (2015) advise researchers to begin examining data as soon as possible, such as after an interview is completed or an initial observation is made. Continuing in this fashion throughout the duration of the study enables "researchers to identify relevant concepts, validate them, and explore them more fully in terms of their properties and dimensions" (Corbin & Strauss, 2015, p. 69). This also prevents the researcher from being overwhelmed with data at the end of a study when it may be too late to further investigate important themes or validate findings. As Fetterman (2010) argues, the very "success or failure of either report or full-blown ethnography depends on the degree to which it rings true to natives and colleagues in the field. These readers may disagree with the researcher's interpretations and conclusions, but they should recognize the details of the description as accurate" (p. 11).

Ethnography Is Case-Specific

Ethnographic research takes place at a particular time, in a particular place, with a particular group within a particular setting. Purposive or theoretical sampling is usually used to obtain the most relevant case (group or setting) given a specific research interest. Alternatively, it could also be that only a certain group is accessible by a given researcher, and this would more closely approximate convenience or availability sampling. Either way, the group is not a representative sample and the results are unlikely to generalize beyond a given case. However, the specific focus on a single case or setting is precisely what facilitates an in-depth study that produces the rich, detailed, and authentic understanding that lies at the heart of ethnography (Hammersley & Atkinson, 2019).

Also, in ethnography, while a case generally refers to the group or setting studied, the researcher is most interested in what goes on within that setting. As a result, data are obtained on individuals, activities, rituals, processes, and so forth, rather than one person, as in a single case. To avoid confusion, Gobo (2011) suggests researchers use the terms *instance* or *occurrence* when describing various events that go on within a given setting.

Ethnography Requires Multiple Techniques and Data Sources

While ethnographic research primarily involves participant observation, details of the group and setting are obtained through any number and combination of specific techniques, including observational analysis, in-depth interviews, field notes, documents, photographs, and visual recordings. Observational analysis and field notes have already been discussed in detail in earlier sections of this chapter, while in-depth interviewing is the subject matter of chapter 9 and documents are part of the unobtrusive measures in chapter 8. Photographs are used in various ways in ethnographic research. A researcher might take a picture of a group, event, or setting to visually depict certain aspects of the stimuli that might not be captured as eloquently by descriptive notes, such as the implications of crowding, the extent of cultural diversity, or the elaborate detail on clothing. However, photographs are much more than visual aids, and anthropologists and other researchers rely upon visual ethnography as a means for understanding human behaviour and culture.

For example, John Collier Jr. and Malcolm Collier (1986) explain how photographs can be used within data collection methods such as in-depth interviewing to help facilitate communication:

> Psychologically, the photographs on the table performed as a third party in the interview session. We were asking questions of the photographs and the informants became our assistants in discovering the answers to the questions in the realities of the photographs. We were exploring the photographs *together*. Ordinarily, note taking during interviews can raise blocks to free-flowing information, making responses self-conscious and blunt. Tape recorders sometimes stop interviews cold. But in this case, making notes was totally ignored, probably because of the triangular relationship in which all questions were directed at the photographic content, not at the informants. (pp. 105–106)

Skilled ethnographers sometimes incorporate photographs into interviews as focal points to help establish rapport and to keep interviews on track, much in the same manner as transition questions and probes.

Visual ethnography is a term used to describe the visual representation of a culture as depicted in film. Ethnographers may use visual recordings for various types of observational analyses, such as structured observation in a complete observer role, as discussed earlier. Video recordings can also be used to capture and represent a culture on film. Ethnographic documentaries are a popular means for portraying a culture or group in its natural setting through visual representations and participant accounts.

Research in Action

People of a Feather
People of a Feather, produced by Joel Heath and the community of Sanikiluaq in 2011, is a multiple-award-winning documentary about the way of life of the Inuit peoples on the Belcher Islands in the Hudson Bay area. This visual ethnographic study of the Arctic takes place over seven winters. Learn how the residents live and survive challenges, especially those arising from the hydro-electric dams that have implications for sea currents and the ecosystems tied

intricately to them. You can find out more about this ethnography by visiting peopleofafeather.com.

People of a Feather is a visual ethnography of the way of life of Inuit Peoples on the Belcher Islands.

Source: People of a Feather, peopleofafeather.com

Test Yourself

- What is the main assumption shared by ethnographers?
- What 10 features exemplify an ethnographic study?
- Which of the four ethnographer roles identified by Gold (1958) involve the researcher as a member of the group?
- Why is ethnography considered to be reflexive?

ETHNOGRAPHIC FIELDWORK

While ethnographic research will vary depending on the research interest, the group studied, and the methods used during fieldwork, the main stages of any ethnographic field project will include accessing the field, dealing with gate-keepers, establishing relations, becoming invisible, collecting data, and exiting the field.

Accessing the Field

First, a researcher must be able to enter the group of interest for a study. Depending on the nature of a group or setting, as well as the researcher's own characteristics, access can be a relatively open, straightforward, and uneventful process, or it may be a highly restricted, difficult, and even dangerous process. Entering the field of study is crucial for the researcher to be able to examine the group in its natural setting and for the researcher to establish relationships needed to begin to acquire an insider's view of what is going on.

In 1965, R. A. Laud Humphreys embarked upon a field study of illegal and impersonal homosexual exchanges among males in park public washrooms for his doctoral research. Because Humphreys was interested in learning about the practices and rules surrounding the heterosexual behaviour of men who otherwise had no "homosexual identity," he needed to find a way to be included in the secret exchanges designed to maintain privacy (Humphreys, 1970). To accomplish this, Humphreys posed as a "voyeur-lookout"—someone interested in homosexual exchanges but not a direct participant, who could help alert the participants to potential detection by police or unsuspecting passersby. Thus, Humphreys carried out observational analyses in the field as a covert deviant. In his role as a participant observer, Humphreys discovered that silence was the main feature of the environment used to uphold privacy. That is, the men who had impersonal sex in tearooms (the name for public washrooms in which known exchanges took place) did so in silence specifically to ensure that the interaction was limited to that secret exchange and would not in any way impede on their regular lives, which included wives, children, and so on.

Note that, even before he ever posed as a voyeur, Laud Humphreys had to learn about homosexual men so that he would be able to later pass himself off as one. He notes that "homosexuals have developed defenses against outsiders" (Humphreys, 1970, p. 24) and he therefore underwent considerable preparation to learn about what was then considered to be a "deviant subculture" so that he would be able to join it. For example, while in clinical training at a psychiatric hospital, he got to know homosexual patients, and while serving as a pastor in parishes in Oklahoma, Colorado, and Kansas, he counselled "hundreds of homosexuals of all sorts and conditions." He also visited "gay bars" and observed "pick-up operations in the parks and streets" (see Humphreys, 1970, pp. 23–26).

One of the more straightforward (and less time-consuming) means for accessing a group and navigating within in it is through one of the existing group members. Fetterman (2010) claims an "introduction by a member is an ethnographer's best ticket into the community." Regardless of who the specific member is in terms of social standing or specific role, as long as the person has some "credibility with the group—either as a member or as an acknowledged friend or associate . . . the trust the group places in the intermediary will approximate the trust it extends to the ethnographer at the beginning of the study" (p. 36). This was the fortune of William Foote Whyte, who had an automatic entry into the group through Doc, as Doc explains: "You won't have any trouble. You come in as my friend. When you come in like that, at first everybody will treat you with respect. You can take a lot of liberties, and nobody will kick. After a while, when they get to know you, they will treat you like anybody else—you know, they say familiarity breeds contempt. But you'll never have any trouble" (Whyte, 1994, p. 68).

In cases where it is not possible to first get to know an existing member of the group who can serve as an entrance guide, a researcher might need to assume a more covert role, pretending to be a full member to gain inside acceptance based on membership status (Lune & Berg, 2017).

Dealing with Gatekeepers

Most groups and research settings are formally or informally "policed" by **gate-keepers**. Gatekeepers refer to "people who have power to grant or deny permission to do a study in the field" (Bailey, 1996, p. 149). Gatekeepers can control access to a setting in a formal or informal capacity, and there may be several gatekeepers in any given setting. For example, when I conducted my dissertation research on low self-control among sex offenders, as identified by information contained in patient files for inmates who had previously undergone treatment for sexual offending at Alberta Hospital Edmonton, formal gatekeepers included the institutional manager, the program supervisor, and the psychiatrist in charge of sex offender treatment. In addition, once I gained approval from the formal gatekeepers and was granted ethical approval from the hospital and the University of Alberta, I still had to negotiate access to the data from an informal gatekeeper who managed the research database containing variables I wished to include in my study, as well as

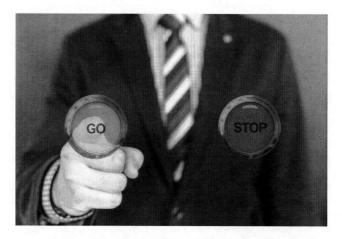

Gatekeepers are individuals who have the power to grant or deny permission to do a study in the field.

Source: TheDigitalArtist/pixabay.com

an informal gatekeeper who managed the records department where I needed to verify information contained in the database against original documents.

Whenever possible, interactions with gatekeepers should be honest and overt. Even in the case of covert participation roles, gatekeepers are generally fully aware of who the ethnographer is and what the research objectives are. This is an important consideration, as gatekeepers are in positions where they can vouch for the researcher's presence, aiding in the establishment of relations within the field (Wolfer, 2007).

Establishing Relations

Even with an introduction into the community and the successful negotiation past gatekeepers, the intricacies of fieldwork have barely begun. To gain a true insider perspective, an ethnographer must spend a considerable amount of time in a setting and be skilled at establishing and maintaining relations with various group members while living alongside them or spending time in that setting. Gaining the acceptance of a group will be dependent on any number of considerations, including a researcher's personal characteristics, such as age, sex, or ethnicity, as well as professional attributes, such as experience, social skills, and/or demeanour.

Cultures and subcultures tend to develop their own patterns, rituals, rules, and specialized language that may not be readily understood by an outsider, even by someone who is specifically attempting to learn the language and customs to gain an insider's view. **Key insiders**, also called sponsors, can be especially helpful to an ethnographer who is learning who people are and how things operate. A key insider is "a member of the setting who is willing to act as a guide or assistant within the setting" (Bailey, 1996, p. 55). Key insiders are often people who initially befriend the ethnographer and are willing to help the ethnographer understand the nuances of the setting, such as informal norms and specialized jargon. Ernest Pecco, known as Doc, helped William Foote Whyte understand all the intricacies of the world he was immersed in, as evident in his warning admonishment: "Go easy on that 'who', 'what', 'why', 'when', 'where' stuff, Bill. You ask those questions and people will clam up on you. If people accept you, you can just hang around, and you'll learn the answers in the long run, without even having to ask the questions" (Whyte, 1994, p. 75).

Due to their existing status within the culture or group, insiders are invaluable for helping the ethnographer to better understand the setting and the roles of the individuals in it.

Becoming Invisible

The primary goal of the ethnographer is to observe and describe the setting and its participants without affecting them. To accomplish this, a researcher needs to find a way to blend in with the group they are studying so that members will act naturally around the researcher and view the researcher as an insider. Stoddart (1986) suggests the ethnographers immerse themselves within the community using an invisible presence that is created through disattending or misrepresentation. Stoddart goes on to describe six potential ways to achieve invisibility while engaged in fieldwork (1986, pp. 109–113), which are adapted as follows:

1. *Disattending with time.* Recall that most field studies are carried out over a considerable length of time. When a researcher first joins a group, their presence is obvious and visible. However, over time, members will begin to accept the researcher's presence and will eventually habituate to their presence, failing to take special notice. When members fail to notice the researcher, we can say they are "disattending" and that the researcher now has invisible status within the community.

2. *Disattending by not standing out.* Stoddart (1986) claimed it was important for an ethnographer to fit in with the group members by making sure there was "no display of symbolic detachment" (pp. 109–110). This means an ethnographer needs to look, act, and sound like the rest of the group to fit in. An ethnographer wearing a suit is less likely to fit in with a group of

children on a playground than someone who is dressed more appropriately for digging in the sand or playing soccer. Similarly, someone who wishes to study street prostitutes would need to be familiar with the language, norms, and practices of the sex trade.

3. *Disattending by participating in the group.* In addition to trying not to stand out, an ethnographer can achieve invisibility by participating with the group members in their everyday routines. For example, an ethnographer studying school-aged children can become a playground supervisor during recess, a lunch hour classroom monitor, or an assistant for art projects.

4. *Disattending by establishing personal relationships.* In this case, ethnographers can elicit information and support from group members on a personal, rather than professional, level. As Stoddart (1986) put it, "the ethnographer was invisible insofar as informants suspended concern with the research aspect of [the ethnographer's] identity and liked [them] as a person" (p. 111).

5. *Misrepresentation involving the research purpose.* Another way that researchers can achieve invisibility is using deception. An ethnographer may, for example, identity themself as a researcher but fail to disclose all the study's details, or an ethnographer may misrepresent details about the true nature of the study.

6. *Misrepresentation involving the researcher's identity.* In some ethnographic studies, the researcher adopts a covert participant observation role, perhaps posing as a potential recruit to the group, a new hire to the organization, or a returning member of the existing community.

While becoming invisible supports an ethnographer's need to blend into the environment to better study the setting and its inhabitants, an ethnographer's role as an observer also warrants ongoing consideration while engaged in fieldwork. Recall the earlier discussion of the ethnographer as the data collection instrument and ethnography as a reflexive method. Reinharz (2011) suggests that there are three main selves operating simultaneously in the field, including a "research self," a "personal self," and a "situational self" (p. 5). The research self largely reflects the ethnographer role, which is focused on gathering data. The personal self consists of individual characteristics, such as age, gender, and existing belief systems that the researcher brings to the setting. Such characteristics influence the kinds of relationships that develop while in the setting, and they can even affect how events and observations are interpreted by the ethnographer. The situational self is the

An ethnographer can achieve invisibility by regularly participating with group members.

Source: geralt/pixabay.com

insider or member position that develops in response to specific events and group interactions that take place while immersed in the setting. Reinharz (2011) notes that by recognizing these selves in her own field research on aging in a kibbutz (an agriculture-based community in Israel), she was also able to recognize who she was not. "For example, in this study of aging, I, myself, was not an elderly woman. This fact probably affected what I understood and how people related to me" (p. 205).

Collecting Data

While the essence of ethnography is listening and observing in the field in an ongoing and extensive capacity to achieve understanding, the final product of ethnographic research is generally a written document. Hence, an ethnographer records detailed **field notes** at every available opportunity. Field notes are detailed records about what the researcher hears, sees, experiences, and thinks about while immersed in the social setting. To an ethnographer, "field notes are the qualitative equivalent to quantitative researchers' raw data" (Warren & Karner, 2015, p. 114). After taking the initial field notes, an ethnographer reviews the notes and records additional reflexive thoughts and observations on a regular basis, using audio recordings as well as further journal entries. To distinguish field notes from analytic notes that a researcher makes as they begin to interpret the data, Schatzman and Strauss (1973) recommend preparing three different kinds of notes, including (1) observational notes, which are the highly detailed notes written about the actual events made while still in the field; (2) theoretical notes, which are based on the researcher's interpretation of events, including hunches, analytical insights, and initial attempts to classify the information into concepts; and (3) methodological notes, which are procedural details about how observations were carried out.

To accompany their field notes, researchers may conduct various informal interviews that are later transcribed or summarized in a written format. While in the field, researchers may even supplement or substantiate information obtained in interviews with data gathered through other methods, such as focus groups or surveys. Ethnographers can also employ visual aids—such as photographs, video recordings, sketches, and maps—to describe the setting and provide details of interactions, processes, and events going on in that setting.

Data analysis often begins while still in the field as an ethnographer examines and re-examines notes, looking for ways to best describe processes, to locate ideas within existing theoretical frameworks, and to identify emerging ideas, patterns, and themes. Data analysis continues long after the ethnographer has exited the field.

Exiting the Field

Just as entering the field and establishing relationships must be carefully negotiated, ending relationships and leaving the group is also a process that can be relatively smooth or highly problematic. An ethnographer will often plan for a gradual disengagement or look for a natural ending to a process or project occurring within the community to provide closure to the various relationships involving the ethnographer. Warren and Karner (2015) suggest, as a rule of thumb, that it is time to leave the field when "your observations are no longer yielding new and interesting data" (p. 96). Although an ethnographer may realize from an objective, data-driven perspective that it is time to leave the field, disengaging from the setting and people with whom one has spent a great deal of time can be difficult on a more personal and social level.

Test Yourself

- Why is it important to identify gatekeepers?
- How do key insiders help researchers establish relations?
- What four techniques can be used to achieve disattending?
- How does misrepresentation help a researcher to become invisible in the field?

Research on the Net

The Journal for Undergraduate Ethnography

The Journal for Undergraduate Ethnography (JUE) is an online journal that publishes ethnographies carried out by undergraduate students in a variety of disciplines as part of their course work. The journal was started in 2011. In its first issue, you can learn about a community, based on an ethnographic study of a historical cemetery; why people engage in "freeganism," where they eat and recycle garbage from dumpsters; how sex offenders view themselves; and how women in relationships with incarcerated men view the criminal justice system, among other interesting topics. Visit undergraduateethnography.org.

ETHICAL CONSIDERATIONS

Informed Consent and Deception

In contrast to methods such as experiments and surveys, where participants sign an informed consent statement outlining the main features of study, including expectations regarding the participants' role and the true purpose of the study, informed consent in ethnographic fieldwork is not always possible ahead of time. This poses special challenges for ethnographers and members of research ethics boards who need to weigh out the potential risk to participants of withholding information against the need to use deception to establish natural relations with group members.

On the one hand, it can be argued that informed consent is not necessary or even desirable in the case of fieldwork. This is because fieldwork takes place in a natural setting, and the behaviours and processes are going to take place irrespective of whether a researcher is studying them (Bailey, 1996). In addition, a covert approach may be preferable to lessen the potential for research-induced reactivity (Douglas, 1979). Finally, since deception exists in real-life interactions, it may also be necessary in research to study groups, particularly ones engaged in illegitimate activities (Bailey, 1996).

On the other hand, we ask ourselves, is it ethical or morally acceptable to knowingly deceive participants to study them? Bailey (1996) notes that, for example, "a premise of a feminist ethical stance is that the process and outcomes of field research are greatly affected by the reciprocal relationships that develop between the field researcher and those in the setting" (p. 13). From this perspective, it would be unethical to use deception to achieve what a researcher hopes will become open and honest relationships with group members. Moreover, if a researcher is upfront about their position and objectives, it may be even more likely that a group will come to trust the researcher. Since outsider status is often obvious to group members, attempts to cover the newcomer's identity may lead to mistrust and inhibit the establishment of relationships. A researcher's outsider status may even afford group members the additional liberty to ask naïve or blunt questions, or to provide highly insightful responses that would not be characteristic of insider relations (Bailey, 1996).

One way to resolve the dilemma of choosing between informed consent versus the need for deception in field research is to conceptualize consent as an ongoing process rather than an initial step or one-time document. In this case, there may be alternatives, such as an **alteration of documentation of informed consent**, which refers to "an informed consent discussion with every subject" as opposed to a written, signed statement of informed consent listing all risks and requirements of participation in a study (Scott & Garner, 2013, p. 61). Another option is a **step-wise consent process** in which you (as the researcher) "describe roughly how you're going to enter the community or group, how and when you're going to first describe what you're doing and what their involvement will consist of as subjects, and so forth" (Scott & Garner, 2013, p. 61).

Maintaining Privacy

Due to the personal nature of the insider information collected during fieldwork, an ethnographer needs to carefully consider how issues of privacy relate to the research project in its entirety and what the researcher's own accountability is when it comes to maintaining the privacy of respondents. First, while a researcher may attempt to maintain confidentiality by leaving out names or by using pseudonyms for information that will appear in print, the descriptions, quotes, or illustrations used may still identify participants or groups to others based on the nature of the information revealed. In such cases, researchers may have to take further measures to disguise the identity of participants by changing the age and sex of the participants or by modifying their roles to protect them from potential privacy violations and subsequent harm.

In describing globalizing feminist research, Mendez (2009) points out that privacy and accountability issues can be especially problematic because "there is no single homogenous community to which the researcher is accountable, but rather multiple groups, communities, organizational and international levels, and conflicting interests. It is within these often intersecting and sometimes conflicting communities that the researcher and those she is studying must negotiate mechanisms of accountability" (p. 87). For example, while studying labour mobility,

Mendez encountered women whose undocumented immigration status, if known, would result in incarceration or deportation. She also spoke with outreach workers who were highly sensitive about their lack of decision-making authority within the larger organizations, and higher-level administrators who were reluctant to share information that would negatively reflect on their own or other organizations. Given established relations at various levels within and between groups, an ethnographer needs to keep in mind what information is obtained, how that information will be shared, how that information will be received, and what the repercussions might be as a result.

Risk of Harm to the Researcher

Field research, because of its inherent naturalness, presupposes a level of unpredictability that can pose a risk of harm to researchers. An ethnographer who infiltrates an outlaw motorcycle club known for its reliance on violence as a means for resolving conflict is going to be at risk for physical danger. Similarly, an ethnographer who joins a travelling carnival to understand what life is like for members of that subgroup is likely entering a setting that contains many yet-to-be-discovered illegal behaviours and questionable practices that may inadvertently pose risks to any insider. Then again, it is precisely the use of first-hand observation in a natural setting that produces highly valid representations and conclusions.

Test Yourself

- Why might an ethnographer question the need for informed consent?
- What are two alternatives to obtaining informed consent prior to the onset of fieldwork?

Research in Action

Why Not Dad?
Why Not Dad? (2009), produced and directed by Monique Derenia, is an ethnographic study of four stay-at-home dads in San Francisco. Find out how these men experience parenthood and gender stereotypes as they get together each week at the playground. You can learn more about this documentary and even watch it by visiting whynotdad.com.

CHAPTER SUMMARY

LO1 **Define ethnography and describe the role of an ethnographer.**
Ethnography is a methodology for studying a social group or culture based on observation. An ethnographer systematically studies a group by observing it and by participating in it.

LO2 **Outline the main features of ethnographic studies.**
Ethnographic studies usually include the following 10 features:
1. Ethnography takes place in natural settings.
2. Ethnography is context-based.
3. Ethnography relies on participant observation.
4. Ethnography is undertaken by a single principal investigator.
5. Ethnography involves long-term acquaintances.
6. Ethnography is non-judgmental.
7. Ethnography is reflexive.
8. Ethnography is mostly descriptive.
9. Ethnography is case-specific.
10. Ethnography requires multiple techniques and data sources.

LO3 **Differentiate between the four main roles of ethnographers engaged in fieldwork.**
As a *complete observer*, an ethnographer observes a group but is not in the group and does not participate with the group in any way. In an *observer as participant* role, the researcher systematically observes a group but is not a group member and only interacts indirectly with the group. A researcher in a *participant as observer* role systematically observes a group by becoming a member to establish relationships and interact with group members. Finally, in *complete participation*, a researcher is already a group member at the onset of the research or becomes a group member to covertly study that group as a fully participating member over a prolonged time.

LO4 **Describe the main stages of fieldwork.**
To conduct fieldwork, ethnographers need to access the field, often through the introduction of existing members. In addition, ethnographers must identify and gain permission from gatekeepers, establish relations with group members, and become invisible so members stop viewing the ethnographer as a researcher and start accepting them as a group member. While in the field, researchers also collect data through a variety of techniques and eventually exit the field by disengaging from ongoing activities and relationships with group members.

LO5   **Explain the techniques used by ethnographers to blend into a group.**

The main method used to blend into a group is to achieve invisibility. This can occur in a variety of ways. For example, if a researcher spends a considerable amount of time with a group, the members will habituate to the researcher's presence (i.e., disattending with time). In addition, a researcher can become invisible by not standing out, by participating in everyday routines, and by establishing personal relationships. A researcher may even use deception or adopt a covert participation role to achieve invisibility.

LO6   **Discuss ethical issues in fieldwork.**

Various ethical considerations arise in fieldwork, beginning with initial decisions pertaining to the need to obtain informed consent versus the use of deception in order to be accepted as a group member. Other ethical considerations relate to privacy and how to keep information provided by members confidential but still meet the research objectives and maintain accountability to various groups and individuals with sometimes competing or conflicting interests. Finally, researchers need to be aware of ongoing personal risks of harm incurred through participation in the group.

RESEARCH REFLECTION

1. Over the course of a week, keep a "reflective" journal that you can use to record entries that describe conversations you had with your close friends and family members. Try to jot down details of the conversation using "thick description" (adapted from Watt, 2010).
2. At the end of the week, go back over the journal entries and review the descriptions. Using "reflexivity," identify several ways in which the conversations resulted from or show evidence of your own personal interests, values, and points of view (adapted from Watt, 2010).
3. Now suppose you are an ethnographer studying group dynamics. In what ways could you change your future behaviour during interactions with the individuals described in your reflective journal to be less directing and more neutral during the conversations?

LEARNING THROUGH PRACTICE

Objective: To learn how to conduct fieldwork

Directions:

1. Choose a well-known service provider on campus (e.g., a food provider, a library service, computer help desk).

2. Visit the service provider to examine the setting from the perspective of an ethnographer planning to do a field study.
    a. Draw a map of the physical setting.
    b. Identify gatekeepers and describe the process you would need to go through to gain access to the setting for research purposes.
    c. Provide a description of any individuals you think might serve as key insiders. If you don't know anyone in the setting, indicate who might be a potential key insider. For example, if you were studying the library borrower services, one of the employees at the circulation desk would be a potential key insider.
3. Of the four roles ranging from complete observer to complete participation, which do you feel would be most appropriate, given your selected site? Justify your response.
4. Describe a technique you think would assist you in becoming invisible in this environment.
5. Visit your selected service provider/location a total of four times on two different days at two different times. Take notes each time you go and see if you can detect changes in the environment at different times or on one of the days. Describe your observations.
6. What ethical issues are raised by observational studies? What can be done to address these considerations?

RESEARCH RESOURCES

1. For a comprehensive guide to ethnography, I recommend Atkinson, P. (2017). *Thinking ethnographically*. Thousand Oaks, CA: Sage.
2. For a comprehensive guide to fieldwork, I recommend Bailey, C. A. (2017). *A guide to qualitative fieldwork* (3rd ed.). Thousand Oaks, CA: Sage.
3. Senior lecturer Rachela Colosi's interest in women's roles in deviant and unregulated occupations informed her research on lap-dancing described in Colosi, R. (2010). *Dirty dancing? An ethnography of lap-dancing*. New York, NY: Willan.
4. Associate Professor Vincent Lyon-Callo describes his insider view of homeless sheltering in Lyon-Callo, V. (2008). *Inequality, poverty, and neoliberal governance: Activist ethnography in the homeless sheltering industry*. Toronto, ON: University of Toronto Press.

CHAPTER 11

Mixed Methods and Multiple Methods

Mixed methods research recognizes, and works with, the fact that the world is not exclusively quantitative or qualitative; it is not an either/ or world, but a mixed world, even though the researcher may find that the research has a predominant disposition to, or requirement for, numbers or qualitative data.
—Louis Cohen, Lawrencee Manion, & Keith Morrison, 2018, p. 31

Learning Objectives

After reading this chapter, students should be able to do the following:

LO1   Compare and contrast quantitative and qualitative approaches.

LO2   Define mixed-methods approach, explain why a researcher might opt for a mixed-methods design, and differentiate between mixed-methods designs.

LO3   Define case study research and explain why a researcher might choose a single-case design over a multiple-case study.

LO4   Define evaluation research and explain what an evaluation design entails.

LO5   Define action research, describe the underlying logic of action research, and identify the steps in an action research cycle.

INTRODUCTION

In earlier chapters, you learned to distinguish between qualitative and quantitative approaches to social research. In this chapter, you will learn about the merits of mixing qualitative and quantitative approaches for adding depth and breadth to our understanding of just about any social topic. In addition, you will learn about various ways to combine multiple methods in a single study.

How the Approaches Differ

Recall how quantitative approaches tend to stem from the positivist tradition, which emphasizes objectivity and the search for causal explanations, while qualitative approaches can often be traced to a more interpretive framework, with an emphasis on the socially constructed nature of reality. In addition, while quantitative approaches are usually rooted in deductive reasoning and include research questions framed into hypotheses with operationalized variables, qualitative methods often incorporate inductive reasoning and research questions that are broader or take the form of exploratory statements about concepts of interest. There are always exceptions to these patterns, as in the case of qualitative research that is designed to test theories or quantitative research that is inductive. However, it is fair to say that the methods used by quantitative researchers often consist of experiments, surveys, or unobtrusive measures such as the analysis of secondary data, while qualitative researchers are more apt to rely upon in-depth interviews, participant observational approaches, or ethnography to examine a phenomenon in its natural setting.

Acknowledging differences between qualitative and quantitative approaches does not imply that there must be a division between them, so much as it helps to illustrate the ways in which the approaches are complementary. That is, the strengths of one approach tend to be the weaknesses of the other and vice versa. For example, a survey in the form of a questionnaire can be used to obtain a great deal of data from a large representative sample, and the measures on the questionnaire might be considered highly reliable and valid using quantitative criteria such as inter-item reliability and construct validity. However, from a qualitative perspective, the findings still might not be genuine, since they are based on predetermined categories and highly structured questions—meaning respondents cannot provide additional details or explain the issue from their own perspective. In addition, respondents may choose not to answer certain items and may provide less truthful, albeit socially desirable, answers. Conversely, the rapport established in an in-depth qualitative interview can uncover a wealth of information from the perspective of an interviewee. The insightful discoveries are deemed to be credible because of the trustworthy processes used to obtain the data, as well as the rigour used to verify the findings, such as through member checks and peer debriefing. However, from a quantitative perspective, the same results are going to be viewed as having limited reliability, due to the small sample size and a lack of generalizability. Figure 11.1 provides a highly simplified comparison of the key differences between quantitative and qualitative methods. For a more detailed discussion of the various ways to assess reliability and validity in qualitative and quantitative studies, refer to chapter 4.

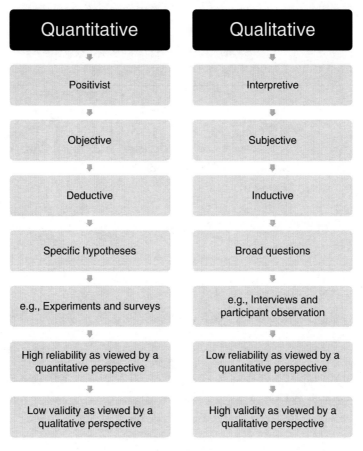

Figure 11.1: Comparing Quantitative and Qualitative Approaches

Source: Created by author

How the Approaches Are Similar

Although it may appear that quantitative and qualitative approaches are opposites, there is one main similarity shared by the approaches when it comes to their overall orientation to research: both qualitative and quantitative approaches rely on empirical methods. Both approaches are geared toward empirical observations even though they rely upon different techniques to obtain them. Although different methods are used, the processes undertaken follow systematic procedures that are recognized by other researchers. Qualitative researchers, for example, carry out in-depth interviews in standardized ways, by first obtaining ethical approval, by obtaining consent from the interviewee, by using opening remarks to break the ice and establish rapport, and by utilizing various types of questions and prompts. Similarly, quantitative researchers administer a questionnaire in standardized ways, by first obtaining ethical approval, by obtaining consent from the participants, by including clear instructions for completing the questionnaire, and by developing a questionnaire instrument that avoids the use of jargon and technical language. In the same way, quantitative researchers carefully create instruments so they constitute highly reliable and valid measures, while qualitative researchers go to great lengths to ensure their approaches to data collection are trustworthy and credible and that the data obtained are accurate. Moreover, when it comes to the dissemination or sharing of research findings, all researchers describe the procedures they followed to undertake the study in such detail that others can check on and verify the processes and, in some cases, even replicate the study based on how it was described. Thus, one approach is not better or worse than another—the two are just different, as required for different purposes.

Combined Approaches Are Not New

Research in the social sciences is highly complex, particularly when the goal is to accurately describe a group, explain a process, or explore an experience. Relying on either quantitative or qualitative methods exclusively can be unnecessarily limiting. For example, Padgett (2012) points out that while "surveys supply much-needed aggregate information on individuals, households, neighborhoods, organizations, and entire nations . . . they fall short in assessing individuals as they live and work *within* their households, neighborhoods, organizations, and nations" (p. 9). Wouldn't it make sense to combine approaches to achieve a more complete understanding? Research utilizing combined approaches is common in a variety of disciplines, including education, healthcare and nursing, library science, political science, psychology, and sociology (Terrell, 2012). Some approaches to research are always based on a combination of methods. Ethnography, for example, is routinely carried out using a combination of qualitative methods of equal importance within the overall design of a study, such as participant observation and qualitative interviewing, or qualitative interviews combined with elements of photography (see chapter 10). Further, methods that are primarily quantitative sometimes include a qualitative component, such as structured questionnaires that include closed- and open-ended items (see chapter 7). Some methods are conducive to both qualitative and quantitative approaches, such as content analysis and observational analysis. Finally, triangulation in qualitative research necessitates attempts to locate a point of convergence or agreement in findings as based on multiple observers, multiple data sources, or the use of multiple methods (see chapter 4). There are endless possibilities for combining methods and approaches in a single study. Methods were introduced in singular forms in earlier chapters mainly for the sake of simplicity, so you would first be able to understand their underlying logic and unique contributions. As noted in the opening quote, using a combination of approaches has the potential to describe and explain phenomena more fully and completely than could ever be the case if researchers limited themselves to only one quantitative or qualitative method.

Test Yourself

- Why are qualitative approaches considered to be empirical?
- In what ways are qualitative and quantitative approaches complementary?

MIXED-METHODS APPROACHES

Distinct from the use of multiple methods of any kind, a **mixed-methods approach** always entails an explicit combination of qualitative and quantitative methods as framed by the research objectives. This can involve designing a study to include a qualitative and quantitative method undertaken at the same time, such as obtaining existing data for an organization for secondary analysis while at the same time interviewing members of that organization. A mixed-methods approach can also include the use of two or more methods at different times, such as seeking participants for qualitative interviews based on the findings from the secondary analysis of existing data.

Research on the Net

Journal of Mixed Methods Research

The *Journal of Mixed Methods Research* (JMMR) is an interdisciplinary quarterly publication that focuses on empirical, theoretical, and/or methodology-based articles dealing with mixed methods in a variety of disciplines. In the articles found in JMMR, you can learn more about types of mixed-methods designs, data collection and analysis using mixed-methods approaches, and the importance of inferences based on mixed-methods research. You can visit the home page at mmr.sagepub.com.

Why Researchers Mix Methods

Researchers combine qualitative and quantitative methods for any number of reasons. The most commonly cited reason for mixing methods pertains to the benefits that can only be obtained through a combination of different but complementary approaches. For example, after employing one method, researchers can elaborate upon or clarify the results obtained, using additional methods (Green, Caracelli, & Graham, 1989). Faye Mishna and colleagues at the University of Toronto (2018) first examined the nature and extent of cyber-aggression among university students via responses provided by 1,350 students who completed an online survey. Survey findings, for example, indicated that about one-quarter of the respondents had had a video or photo shared without their permission and that perpetrators tended to be friends of the victims. The researchers later conducted a series of focus groups and interviews to better understand respondents' concerns and identified themes of perceived anonymity and the practice of sexting as contributors to on-line "attacks," and discovered cumulative mental health consequences (Mishna et al., 2018).

A second, related reason for combining approaches is to capitalize on the benefits of both approaches, while minimizing or offsetting their associated drawbacks (Bryman & Bell, 2016). Recall that an experiment is conducted in a controlled environment that lends itself to high internal validity but may be so artificial that is not representative of a real-life setting. In-depth interviews with participants can help to determine whether the findings have external validity. Finally, a researcher might also use mixed methods for development purposes where the findings from one method (e.g., qualitative) are used to help design the second method (e.g., quantitative) (Green et al., 1989). This kind of development usually takes place in what Creswell and Creswell (2018) refer to as sequential designs, where one method is used in the first phase of a study and the results then inform a different method that is used in a later phase. For example, a researcher may start off with a focus group or in-depth interviews to establish categories or to develop items that will be later utilized in a structured survey.

Mixed-Methods Designs

There are various ways to mix methods within a research study, based on the order or sequence in which the methods are employed and the point (or points) at which the data are combined. Three mixed-methods designs are discussed in this section to illustrate customary ways to combine qualitative and quantitative methods within a single study.

Convergent Design

In a **convergent design** (also known as a convergent parallel design), both qualitative and quantitative methods are employed at the same time, with equal priority (Creswell & Creswell, 2018). For example, secondary analysis of existing data might coincide with interviews during the same phase of a research study. Using a convergent design, researchers carry out independent data collection and analyses where the secondary analysis is done separately from the interviews. Only at the end stage of the research are findings from the qualitative and qualitative components compared and integrated as part of the overall interpretation (see figure 11.2). Note that convergent designs are used in triangulation strategies, where more than one method is employed to see if the results converge. However, in such cases, the two methods are likely to both be qualitative, as opposed to qualitative and quantitative.

Wilson et al. (2012) employed a mixed-methods convergent design to understand the implications of care-setting transitions during the last year of life for

Figure 11.2: Convergent Design

Source: Created by author

rural Canadians. They used quantitative secondary analysis to describe and compare healthcare transitions between rural and urban residents based on in-patient hospital and ambulatory care information on Albertans that was contained in databases. At the same time, the researchers used an online survey to collect information from individuals who could provide details on rural Canadians who had died in the last year. Respondents were asked to provide information on the number of moves, the location of the moves, and the impact of care moves undertaken by the now deceased. Researchers also conducted qualitative interviews with bereaved family members, located through notices posted in rural newspapers and in community settings (e.g., grocery store bulletin boards), to learn about the moves and the family members' experiences over the last year. Findings from the secondary data revealed that rural decedents had undergone more healthcare-setting transitions for in-patient hospital care than urban patients had. Survey data indicated that the deceased had undergone an average of eight moves in the last year of life, and that a great deal of travelling was required to take the now deceased individuals to and from appointments, generally at different hospitals in various locations. Main themes that emerged from interviews included the point that necessary care was scattered across many places, that travelling was difficult for the terminally ill and their caregivers, and that local services were minimal (Wilson et al., 2012).

Explanatory Design

Recall that one of the main reasons for combining methods is to clarify the results of one method through the utilization of a second method. In an **explanatory design** (also known as an explanatory sequential design), a quantitative method is employed first and then the findings are followed up on, using a qualitative method (see figure 11.3). For example, a researcher might administer a survey to understand the general views of a sample on an issue of interest. After the survey data are collected and analyzed, researchers might conduct in-depth qualitative interviews with a few respondents to better understand and explain results obtained in the earlier, prioritized quantitative phase.

Figure 11.3: Explanatory Design

Source: Created by author

In a study on the interrelationships between bisexuality, poverty, and mental health, Ross and colleagues (2016) first examined quantitative survey data stemming from a sample of 302 bisexual individuals from Ontario. The quantitative data provided descriptive information on the sample, including demographics (e.g., age, gender identity, education, and relationship status), and the data was used to develop a context for understanding poverty and mental health by examining the effect of low income, as measured by the Canadian Low Income Cut-Off (LICO), on mental health indicators such as depression and anxiety. For example, 76 participants (25.7%) were below the LICO, and of those, individuals who identified as "trans" were over-represented. Those below the LICO also showed higher scores for psychological distress and discrimination compared to those above the LICO (Ross et al., 2016). The researchers later followed up with 41 participants through qualitative interviews, to learn more about how bisexuality, poverty, and mental health interrelate through pathways. For example, one pathway concerned early life experiences related to bisexuality that directly or indirectly impacted income and mental health, as was the case for participants who lost middle-class status when they left their families of origin due to conflicts relating to their sexuality, or those who turned to substance abuse as a means for dealing with their feelings (Ross et al., 2016, p. 67).

Exploratory Design

In an **exploratory design** (also known as an exploratory sequential design), a qualitative method is prioritized and then, based on the findings from the qualitative study, a quantitative method is developed and subsequently employed (see figure 11.4). For example, themes emerging from transcribed data based on a small number of in-depth interviewees can help to create categories and constructs included in a questionnaire for use with a much larger, more representative sample of respondents.

Moubarac, Cargo, Receveur, and Daniel (2012) used a two-stage exploratory mixed-methods design to examine the situational context associated with the

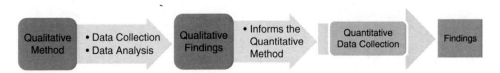

Figure 11.4: Exploratory Design

Source: Created by author

consumption of sweetened food and drink products in a Catholic Middle-Eastern Canadian community in Montreal. In stage 1, the researchers conducted semi-structured interviews with 42 individuals to learn more about sweetened food and drink consumption. Specifically, the convenience sample was asked to think about their consumption of sweetened drinks and foods, and they were provided with examples. Interviewees were then directed to comment on the last three times they consumed sweetened products, noting conditions and circumstances associated with consumption, such as time of day and location. In addition, the interviewees were asked to name their favourite sweetened product and to note conditions and circumstances associated with it. Finally, they were asked about customary consumption of sweetened products in different locations, such as at work and at home. A content analysis of the transcribed interview data revealed 40 items and 6 main themes associated with consumption of sweetened products, including energy (i.e., sweets provide energy); negative emotions, or tendency to eat sweets when sad; positive emotions, such as a reward; social environment (e.g., offered at someone's house); physical environment or availability; and constraints (e.g., eating out at restaurants) (Moubarac et al., 2012).

Findings from stage 1 were then used to construct the Situational Context Instrument for Sweetened Product Consumption (SCISPC), a self-report questionnaire used in stage 2 of the study. Stage 2 consisted of a cross-sectional study in which 192 individuals (105 women and 87 men) completed the SCISPC. The participants also completed a food frequency questionnaire that included a listing of sweet products such as brownies, cakes, candy, cookies, muffins, and soft drinks along with the associated total sugar content, a questionnaire on socio-demographics, and items on self-reported weight and height. Quantitative analyses revealed seven situational factors related to the consumption of sweets, including emotional needs, snacking, socialization, visual stimuli, constraints, energy demands, and indulgence (Moubarac et al., 2012).

Test Yourself

- In what ways is a qualitative approach similar to a quantitative one?
- What distinguishes a mixed-methods approach from other ones using multiple methods?
- For what reasons might a researcher choose a mixed-methods design?
- In which kind of mixed-methods design does a researcher begin with quantitative data collection and analysis?

RESEARCH USING MULTIPLE METHODS

Within the social sciences, certain types of studies are routinely carried out using multiple methods, such as ethnography, as discussed in chapter 10. Three areas of research that typically employ multiple methods (but not necessarily mixed methods) are case study research, evaluation research, and action research.

Case Study Research

Recall from chapter 4 that a case study pertains to research on a small number of individuals or an organization carried out over an extended period. A case study is an intensive strategy that employs a combination of methods such as archival analysis, interviews, and/or direct observation to describe or explain a phenomenon of interest in the context within which it occurs. As Yin (2018) puts it, a case study is most relevant when a "how" or "why" research question is being asked about a contemporary set of events over which the investigator has little control (p. 9). The focus of a case study can be a person, a social group, an institution, a setting, an event, a process, or even a decision. In addition, the scope of a case study can be narrow, as in an examination of one person's journey through a single round of chemotherapy treatments, or it can be broad, as in a case study of chemotherapy as an available treatment option for cancer patients. What sets case study research apart from other forms of research is that it is a strategy that intensively "investigates a contemporary phenomenon (the 'case') in depth and within its real-world context, especially when the boundaries between phenomenon and context may not be clearly evident" (Yin, 2018, p. 15).

By holistically examining one person undergoing chemotherapy treatment, for example, a researcher can gain insight into the greater context of how other variables, such as interactions with doctors and hospital staff, travel arrangements, family dynamics, and pain management all contribute in various ways to the overall experience for that individual. Case study research relies upon multiple methods of data collection, with the goal of uncovering converging evidence that will help to explain or describe the phenomenon of interest. If the goal of a case study is to understand a person's experience while undergoing chemotherapy, a researcher is likely to interview that person on several occasions and speak to primary caregivers close to that person, such as a spouse, parent, sibling, and/or child. In addition, the researcher might examine archival documents, such as postings on Facebook or entries in a personal diary, to get a sense of what the experience means to the person undergoing treatment. While most often employing qualitative methods, case studies are not inherently qualitative in nature and can include

A case study might examine a person's experience over the course of a major illness such as cancer.

Source: ABO PHOTOGRAPHY/shutterstock.com

quantitative methods or a combination of qualitative and quantitative data collection techniques.

Single- versus Multiple-Case Study Designs

Single-Case Design

Case study research is based on either a single-case or a multiple-case design. A **single-case design** refers to case study research that focuses on only one person, organization, event, or program as the unit of analysis as emphasized by the research objectives. Yin (2018) offers several reasons why researchers might choose a single-case design. First, a single-case design might be selected by a researcher if the case represents a critical case that represents all criteria necessary for testing a theory of interest. A single-case design might also be preferred if the case represents an extreme situation or event, since an outlier is likely to provide insights that are unanticipated. However, a single-case design is also likely to be chosen if a case can be identified that is highly representative or common among a larger range of phenomena, to convey what is typical. In addition to features of the case itself, a single-case design might be selected largely because of the unique opportunity it affords to investigate an area. For example, a case study of a patient with a rare disorder can help medical practitioners and families to more accurately describe the disorder, find appropriate interventions, and reveal new insights. This is usually called a revelatory case (Yin, 2018, p. 50). Finally, if the goal of a study is to determine how a person, organization, or process changes over time, a single-case study is a good choice, as this design is especially suited to longitudinal analysis.

As an example of a single-case strategy focused on one person, Nunes, Harr, Dunn, and Price (2011) examined the utility of household task participation for improving other activities, such as work opportunities, in a 20-year-old disabled male who was born with spina bifida. The study included a period of initial assessment, an intervention period designed to promote autonomy and independence as a function of successes experienced through the completion of household chores (e.g., doing the dishes on a regular basis), and a subsequent post-intervention re-assessment. Quantitative measures included standardized assessment instruments such as a self-determination scale, a chores instrument, and an occupational performance measure. Separate qualitative interviews were also conducted with the young man and his father (the primary caregiver) at regular intervals over the period of study to gauge perceived progress. Results of this quasi-experiment showed that performance and satisfaction increased from pre- to post-assessment. The young man also demonstrated increased participation at home and in the community following the intervention. In addition, qualitative data highlighted additional benefits, including improved communication between father and son.

As another example, Hamm, MacLean, Kikulis, and Thibault (2008) focused their single-case study research on a long-standing Canadian non-profit sports organization to examine value congruence between the employees and the organization. First, the researchers collected and examined existing documents, such as policy statements, meeting notes, and emails. The next phase of the study involved non-participant observation in meetings and activities. In the third phase, employees rated their personal employee values by completing the Rokeach Value Survey. Finally, employees identified as having the highest and lowest value congruence, based on the survey findings, were then interviewed to learn more about their opinions and experiences. Overall, the findings indicated a significant discrepancy or incongruence between organization and employee values. For example, while the organization emphasized "wisdom" and "equality," the employees rated "accomplishment" and "family security" as being much more important. Moreover, while the organization highly valued "equality," the employees did not feel that they were treated with equality. In addition, the organization heavily promoted their five core values (i.e., "leadership," "open," "listen," "responsive," and "relevant"), but none of the interviewed employees mentioned these as values they felt they shared with the organization (Hamm et al., 2008).

Multiple-Case Design

A **multiple-case design** is a case study strategy that involves more than one case studied concurrently for the explicit purpose of comparison. According to Yin (2018), a small number of cases are specifically chosen for use in multiple-case study designs because they are expected to produce similar findings, akin to replication in experimental research. Alternatively, two or more cases might also be selected because they are expected to show contrasting findings, as predicted by relevant theoretical assertions. It is important to note that the logic underlying the inclusion of additional cases cannot be likened to the sampling logic used in quantitative survey research to obtain representative samples or generalizable findings. However, it can approximate the control obtained in experimental research if the two selected cases are virtually identical except for the feature that becomes the focus of a controlled comparison (George & Bennett, 2005).

As an example of a multiple-case design, Sussman et al. (2011) sought to identify factors associated with positive palliative care outcomes through a comparison of four healthcare systems from different regions of Ontario. To identify factors contributing to positive outcomes, they used purposive extreme case sampling so that their unit of analysis would consist of the healthcare systems with the highest and lowest cancer-related acute care deaths and emergency department visits within the last two weeks of life. Based on qualitative and quantitative data analyses, findings revealed main differences between the regions' three measures: capacity, such as available funding for palliative care services; access to after-hours service and mechanisms for palliative care identification; and coordination for things such as formalized reporting structure and location-of-death planning. Sussman et al. (2011) also identified the presence of various features in superior care systems, including 24/7 palliative-care-team access and the use of a common chart to facilitate care provider communication.

Research on the Net

Research Strategy: Case Study

To better understand how a case study differs from an experiment and to appreciate the differences between single-case and multiple-case designs, you can view Robert Barcik's video on case study research, uploaded on March 17, 2016, to YouTube. You can find the video on youtube.com by searching "Research Strategy: Case Study."

Evaluation Research

Another form of research that relies upon the use of multiple methods for data collection and analysis is evaluation research. Recall from chapter 1 that evaluation research is undertaken to assess whether a program or policy is effective in reaching its desired goals and objectives. Social science evaluation research includes "the application of empirical social science research to the process of judging the effectiveness of . . . policies, programs, or projects, as well as their management and implementation for decision making purposes" (Langbein, 2012, p. 3). Virtually every government department and every funded social program or intervention undergoes evaluation. For example, evaluation research was used to determine the effectiveness of Parks Canada's Law Enforcement Program (Parks Canada, 2017), a master of science program in anatomical sciences at Queen's University (Kolomitro, MacKenzie, Wiercigroch, & Godden, 2018), the Aboriginal Head Start in Urban and Northern Communities program (Health Canada & the Public Health Agency of Canada, 2017), and a sexual assault training program for emergency department staff in Ontario (Du Mont, Solomon, Kosa, & Macdonald, 2018). The potential topics for evaluation research are endless.

Types of Evaluation Research

There are different kinds of evaluation research, depending on where a program is in terms of its existence and overall life course. For example, *before* a program is developed, evaluation research is informative for diagnosing what is required in the way of a program. "The main form of diagnostic research that centers on problems is the **needs assessment**. In needs assessment, the focus is on understanding the difference between a current condition and an ideal condition" (Stoecker, 2013, p. 109). Goals of a needs assessment typically centre on identifying a problem, finding out who is affected by that problem and coming up with a program to address the problem. Sample questions include the following:

- What is the nature of the problem affecting this community (or group)?
- How prevalent is this problem?
- What are the characteristics of the population most affected by this problem?
- What are the needs of the affected population?
- What resources are currently available to address this problem?
- What resources are required to more adequately address this problem?

Needs assessments are largely focused on obtaining information that will help in the early planning and eventual development of a program. To learn as much as possible about members of a target community, researchers are likely to rely upon a range of tools and methods, including existing documents, survey methods, observational analyses, and interviews (Sullivan, 2001).

Evaluation research that is conducted to examine and monitor *existing* programs is usually called **program evaluation** or program monitoring. The over-arching question in a program evaluation is likely to take the form of "Does the program work?" Evaluation directed at answering the question of whether a program, policy, or project works usually entails a large-scale research project that combines multiple methods, such as site visits, the examination of existing program documents, and in-depth interviews with employees. The purpose is to gauge how well the major program components link up with the corresponding program goals.

Sample questions include the following:

- Is this program working? (Why or why not?)
- Is this program operating as it was intended?
- Are program objectives being met?
- Are the services reaching the intended target population?
- Were the program goals achieved?
- Did the program result in positive outcomes for the clients?

Program evaluations have historically relied on some form of system's model (see figure 11.5). The model describes the program by depicting its organizational

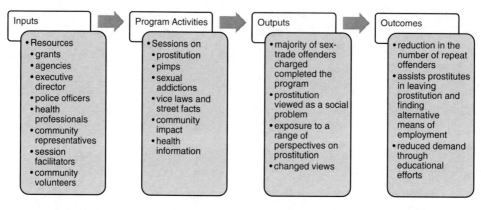

Figure 11.5: A System's Model of an Educational Program for Sex-Trade Offenders

Source: Created by author

structure in terms of interconnected inputs, including resources put into the program, such as funding, other agency involvement, and certified staff; activities, including program offerings, such as counselling sessions or skill development classes; outputs or results, including who attended the program; and outcomes, including the overall goals and benefits, such as reduced recidivism or increased social development. While this might come across as a straightforward approach to evaluation, it is anything but. Many programs are not amenable to evaluation because they do not have clearly articulated goals and objectives, or the goals and objectives are not realistic or measurable. Wholey (1994) suggests first employing an evaluability assessment to see if minimum criteria can be met before embarking on a full-scale evaluation of a program. An evaluability assessment includes (1) a description of the program's overall model; (2) an assessment of how amenable that model is to evaluation, such as whether the goals and objectives are clearly stated and whether performance measures can be obtained; and (3) additional details on stakeholder views of the purpose and use of the evaluation findings, where possible (Rossi, Lipsey, & Henry, 2019, p. 61).

The purpose of the evaluability assessment is to gauge whether a program can be meaningfully evaluated. For example, programs designed to reduce the incidence of prostitution (i.e., the purchasing of sexual services), through educational efforts, also known as John School (see Symbaluk & Jones, 1998), are regularly criticized for having unclear or unmeasurable goals. For instance, how would it be possible to show that there was a reduced demand for prostitution? Yet this is a claim frequently made by proponents of these programs as evidence of their success (Coté, 2009). It is possible, however, to show a reduction in the number of complaints about street prostitution to the police by business and community members in a location, or to measure whether known sex trade offenders reoffend. Except, in both cases, this still is not evidence that the program was effective, because it could be that offenders are less likely to get caught a second time or that they learn to be more discreet, resulting in fewer complaints. An exemplary evaluability assessment template, an evaluation handbook, guidelines for selecting evaluators, and guidelines for an evaluation report can be downloaded from the United Nations Office on Drugs and Crime (go to unodc.org and search for "Evaluability Assessment Template").

Because programs are typically very costly to operate, questions concerning whether a program is effective sometimes translate into a **cost-benefit analysis**. A cost-benefit analysis is a method for systematically assessing the overall costs incurred by the program, including the ongoing costs needed to run the program such as wages paid to employees, rent for the building, and materials, versus outputs or program results, such as who benefited and how they benefited. Is the cost

of the program justified, given the overall benefit to the clients or to the wider society? For example, the cost-benefit analysis of a sex-trade offender program might
account for the financial costs of running the program for one year, including
educational resources such as skilled facilitators, police personnel, and rental space
for the classroom, in relation to the risk of the same number of men reoffending in
the absence of the educational program. Or, a cost-benefit analysis might compare
the financial costs and outcomes incurred by this program to other alternatives,
such as criminal charges, fines, and vehicle seizures, to see whether the costs are
warranted, given the benefits achieved. Sample questions include the following:

- How costly is this program (i.e., operating costs)?
- Are there ways to quantify the benefits of the program (e.g., into dollars
  saved)?
- How do various operating costs compare to alternative resources (e.g., wages)?
- How do the overall costs of the program compare to alternatives to the
  program?
- Are the costs of the program justified, given the overall benefits of the
  program?
- How do the costs and benefits of this program compare to alternate meth-
  ods for dealing with the underlying social problem?

Carrying Out Evaluation Research

The process for carrying out evaluation research will vary depending on the type of
evaluation, the exact program, and the evaluation objectives. However, an evaluation is generally going to proceed through these five stages as simplified here and
depicted in figure 11.6:

1. Engage with stakeholders who provide valuable input.
2. Clarify the research problem—what questions are to be addressed in this
   evaluation?
3. Establish evaluation criteria (the criteria the program is being evaluated
   against), including standards for indicating whether the program meets or
   fails to meet these criteria.
4. Assess the program, including the selection of appropriate methods, data
   collection, and data analysis undertaken in order to measure performance
   against the established criteria.
5. Provide the outcome, or the assessment or conclusion reached in the
   evaluation.

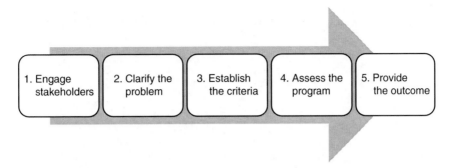

Figure 11.6: Steps for Carrying Out Evaluation Research

Source: Created by author

Engaging with Stakeholders

Because a program is generally set up to provide a social service or resolve a particular social issue, a number of social relationships and roles exist within that program. For example, managers and other decision-makers supervise staff members who are responsible for delivering program services to intended target recipients. Social relationships involve **stakeholders** who need to be considered as part of the evaluation. Stakeholders include any individuals, groups, and/or organizations that are directly or indirectly involved with or impacted by the program of interest. For example, the target recipient of an intended service or intervention would be considered a primary stakeholder, as would employees involved in the operation of the program and groups that fund the program, such as program sponsors and donors. Stakeholders play a vital role in the creation, operation, and success of a program, and they are usually identified early on so that their input can be sought at various stages throughout an evaluation (Rossi et al., 2019).

For example, in an evaluation of a Canadian workplace-disability prevention program called Prevention and Early Active Return-to-work Safely (PEARS), Maiwald, de Rijk, Guzman, Schonstein, and Yassi (2011) sought feedback from three main groups of stakeholders: program designers, deliverers, and workers. The researchers used a variety of qualitative methods, including semi-structured interviews, participatory observations, and focus group sessions. Although the three groups of stakeholders defined the causes of workplace disability similarly, they placed emphasis on different aspects. For example, the deliverers explained disability largely in terms of risk factors and individual-level causes, while workers emphasized the importance of the workplace and organization contributors. In addition, while they agreed on the importance of workplace safety and the belief that workplace interventions can have a positive effect on work disability, stakeholders had very different ideas about how the intervention should work in

Stakeholders are individuals or organizations impacted by the program undergoing evaluation.

Source: geralt/pixabay.com

practice. Deliverers, for example, largely targeted individual-directed measures, while workers felt these measures offered only short-term benefits, rather than a sustainable long-term return-to-work solution.

From this example, it becomes apparent that while all stakeholders have a vested interest in how a program or initiative operates, they are unlikely to view the program similarly. While different perspectives clearly help an evaluator gain a richer understanding, they also add to the complexity of the evaluation, as it becomes less clear which features should be changed and which ones should be retained. Guba and Lincoln (1994) suggest that one of the primary purposes of an evaluation is to facilitate negotiations among stakeholders so that they can come to a common or shared construction of the social program. In addition, Rossi, Lipsey, and Freeman (2004) point out that "even those evaluators who do a superb job of working with stakeholders and incorporating their views and concerns in the evaluation plan should not expect to be acclaimed as heroes by all when the results are in. The multiplicity of stakeholder perspectives makes it likely that no matter how the results come out, someone will be unhappy" (p. 43). While a necessary and vital element in all program evaluations, stakeholders also constitute one of the main challenges in evaluation research.

Evaluator's Role in Relation to Stakeholders

Evaluation research designs can be quite simple or highly complex, depending on the nature of the program and the objectives of the evaluation. At a minimum, the design should specify the questions the evaluator seeks to answer, the methods that will be employed to answer the questions, and the nature of the relationship between the evaluator and the stakeholders. An evaluator is likely to assume one of two main roles in an evaluation. Either the evaluator works directly with the stakeholders, who are part of the evaluation team with the evaluator acting as the team lead, or the program evaluator conducts research independently from the stakeholders but still consults with them at various points to establish the evaluation criteria and to obtain information used in the evaluation. In the case of the former, the research is often called participatory action research, collaborative research, or community-based research because the researcher is literally partic-ipating with the stakeholders to help them evaluate their own program. While there are some obvious disadvantages to this approach—as stakeholders, who are typically the greatest proponents of the program, are now in charge of evaluating it—there are also merits. People with a vested interest are also likely to be those willing to commit their time and resources to a process that they feel is useful and is likely to lead to welcomed improvements. Compare this to an approach in which (often) underpaid and overworked stakeholders are asked to commit additional time and resources on behalf of an outsider who is paid to assess their program and then tell them what their issues are (Stoecker, 2013).

A program evaluation most often takes the form of an **independent evalua-tion**. An independent evaluation is one led by a researcher who is not part of the organization and who has no vested interested in that organization. The evaluator is not a stakeholder but a commissioned researcher who designs the study, conducts the evaluation, and shares the findings with stakeholders (Rossi et al., 2019). Al-though the evaluator is not a stakeholder, they will still need to work closely with various stakeholders since stakeholders provide valuable data and inadvertently set the agenda for the program evaluation through their vested interests. For example, funding agencies are interested in cost-benefit analyses and outcome measures since they want to know if a program is run efficiently from a cost perspective and whether the program meets its intended objectives. In contrast, program managers are more concerned with questions pertaining to program monitoring since their vested interest has to do with how the program operates. Finally, in some cases, programs are examined and evaluated to determine where changes can and should be made, as discussed in a later section on action research. As a final comment on evaluation research, it is important to be aware of how evaluation research takes place within a larger political framework that ultimately influenced how that pro-gram came to be, why it is currently being evaluated, and what will happen once the assessment is made available.

Research on the Net

Canadian Evaluation Society

The Canadian Evaluation Society (CES) is a multidisciplinary association based on the advancement of evaluation theory and practice. The CES hosts an annual conference that serves as a forum for discussing current issues in evaluation. In addition, the CES and the Canadian Evaluation Society Educational Fund (CESEF) jointly host an annual Case Competition. In this student learning opportunity, teams compete for prizes and a trophy by first completing a preliminary round involving the analysis of a case file. Each team has five hours to complete their evaluation and submit it for judging. The three highest-rated teams are invited to participate in the final round, held at the annual conference, where they receive a new case to evaluate and present their findings to a live audience. For more information, visit the CES website at evaluationcanada.ca.

Action Research

Action research, as its name implies, is a research strategy that attempts to better understand an area of interest in order to implement change within that area of interest. Greenwood and Levin (2007) define action research as "social research carried out by a team that encompasses a professional action researcher and the members of an organization, community, or network ('stakeholders') who are seeking to improve the participants' situation" (p. 3). For example, action research is routinely employed in education, where it serves as a transformational methodology used to determine how to optimize learning strategies and programs so that they work best for students with a range of learning needs and skills. Multiple methods used to explore an issue can include interviews, focus groups, surveys, archival analysis, and the secondary analysis of existing data.

As a simplified illustration, a teacher might begin by identifying a problem or concern, such as students are having difficulty understanding an important concept, as evidenced by their grades on standard assessments as well as comments they have made in class. Once the problem is articulated via discussions with the class and in-depth interviews with a sample of students, the teacher needs to identify potential ways to resolve the issue. For example, other teachers might recommend strategies that have worked in their classrooms, there may be recommended strategies in the literature, and there may be potential solutions identified in the minutes from professional development meetings. After a period of reflection in

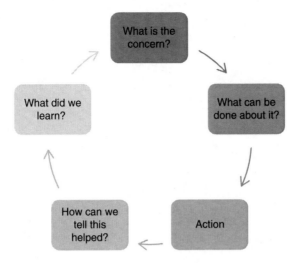

Figure 11.7: The Underlying Logic of Action Research

Source: Created by author

which the teacher will consider potential options, they will then determine the course of action most suitable for this class and then implement it for a trial period. Following this, the teacher will need to evaluate the success of the strategy by reassessing students' level of understanding on objective measures such as tests as well as through informal discussions with the students. Once the evaluation has occurred, the teacher can begin to consider how to change or modify future instruction based on what worked and did not work. See figure 11.7 for a summary of the logic underlying action research.

Action research is a continuous reflective, cyclical process that begins with observation, is followed by reflection, action, evaluation, modification, and then subsequent observation (McNiff, 2017). In this sense, action research generally involves a series of cycles as opposed to one phase of research. Going back to the earlier example, a teacher might try a learning strategy and then discover that it was only effective for certain students. In this case, another action cycle will begin. The second cycle will retain successes of the first phase and add in a new course of action to try to further improve upon the learning environment. For instructors who strive to continuously improve upon their teaching, the action cycle can continue indefinitely (see figure 11.8).

The purpose of action research is not only to improve conditions, but to empower participants, since it is the stakeholders who participate directly in identifying the issues and means for resolving them. For this reason, action research is sometimes referred to as participatory action research. McKenzie, Seidl, and Bone (2010) relied

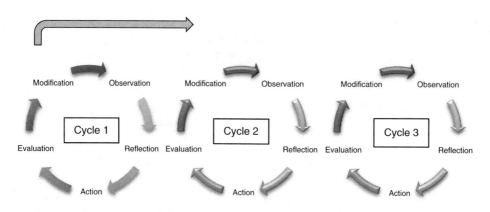

Figure 11.8: Action Research Cycles

Source: Adapted from McNiff & Whitehead, 2006, pp. 9, 37.

upon participatory action research to examine child welfare problems and practices in eight Manitoba First Nations communities. During the first phase of the study, focus groups and interviews were conducted with more than two hundred individuals, including Elders, Chiefs, and Council members; biological parents, foster parents, and homemakers; local child and family service committee members as well as community staff members; and youth between the ages of 13 and 18. After common themes were identified in the responses provided, the researchers engaged in a second round of consultation in order to evaluate and validate the findings.

Consistent with the literature on Indigenous people, one of the common themes that emerged from this study was a traditional extended view of family that included aunts, uncles, cousins, and grandparents. In addition, along with concerns about the provision of good emotional and physical care and guidance, participants identified the common need to include the teaching of traditional values, language, and customs as part of the definition of what is in the "best interests of the child." Another main finding was that in cases where there are indicators of inadequate care, support should be provided to that family such that potential solutions are enacted within the family setting (McKenzie et al., 2010).

Research on the Net

The Canadian Journal of Action Research

The Canadian Journal of Action Research is a free full-text journal dedicated to action research for educators. Here, instructors and administrators share articles, book reviews, and notes from the field. You can find this journal on Nipissing University's site at http://cjar.nipissingu.ca.

Test Yourself

- What is case study research?
- For what reasons might a researcher choose a single-case study design over a multiple-case design?
- What is an independent evaluation?
- Why is it important to consult stakeholders in evaluation research?
- What is action research?
- What questions can be posed to depict the underlying logic of action research?
- What are the main steps in the process for carrying out an action research cycle?

CHAPTER SUMMARY

LO1   **Compare and contrast quantitative and qualitative approaches.**

Quantitative approaches are based in the positivist paradigm and tend to be focused on objective methods that are based on deductive reasoning. Research questions are usually stated as hypotheses, and data collection is carried out in experiments, surveys, or certain forms of unobtrusive methods, such as the analysis of existing data. Quantitative methods are highly reliable but may be lacking in validity since findings from highly controlled experiments are difficult to generalize to the real world. Qualitative approaches, in contrast, tend to be based in the interpretive paradigm that emphasizes subjectivity and inductive reasoning. Research questions tend to be broad, and methods for data collection can include in-depth interviews, participant observations, and focus groups, as well as various forms of unobtrusive methods, such as content analysis. Qualitative methods tend to be higher in validity but lack reliability.

LO2   **Define mixed-methods approach, explain why a researcher might opt for a mixed-methods design, and differentiate between mixed-methods designs.**

A mixed-methods approach always entails an explicit combination of qualitative and quantitative methods, as framed by the research objectives. Mixed methods can be useful for establishing the validity of measures and findings. For example, the results obtained in an experiment might be clarified by the results obtained via qualitative interviewing. In addition, mixed methods are useful for development purposes, such as when a researcher uses focus group findings to help inform categories that will later be used on a questionnaire. In a *convergent design*, both qualitative and quantitative methods are employed at the same time with equal priority. In an *explanatory design*, a quantitative method is employed first and then the findings are followed up on using a qualitative method. In an *exploratory design*, a qualitative method is prioritized and then, based on the findings from the qualitative study, the researcher develops and subsequently employs a quantitative method.

LO3 **Define case study research and explain why a researcher might choose a single-case design over a multiple-case study.**

Case study research is research on a small number of individuals or an organization carried out over an extended period. A researcher might opt for a single-case study if the case selected represents a critical case for testing a theory, if the case is common, if the case represents an extreme, if the case constitutes a rare opportunity, or if the researcher wishes to conduct a longitudinal analysis.

LO4 **Define evaluation research and explain what an evaluation design entails.**

Evaluation research is research undertaken to assess whether a program or policy is effective in reaching its desired goals and objectives. At a minimum, an evaluation design outlines the questions of interest, the methods for obtaining answers, and the nature of the relationship between researchers and stakeholders.

LO5 **Define action research, describe the underlying logic of action research, and identify the steps in an action research cycle.**

Action research is a research strategy that directly involves stakeholders to better understand an area of interest and to bring about improvement. The logic underlying action research centres on identifying a concern, determining what can be done about it, implementing an action, determining whether the action helped, and evaluating what was learned as a result. The process for carrying out action research entails observation, reflection, action, evaluation, and modification.

RESEARCH REFLECTION

1. Suppose you are interested in studying one program that is specifically geared toward students at the school you are currently attending. As a case study, provide rationale for examining this program using a single-case design.
2. If you were going to conduct an organizational case study of the school you are currently attending, describe two methods that you would use to collect suitable data.
3. If you were going to conduct a Bachelor of Arts degree program evaluation, what three questions would you pose to help focus the evaluation? In other words, what three questions do you think should be answered in the evaluation?
4. Thinking of the community in which you live, identify one main social issue that could be examined using participatory action research. Create a list of stakeholders you would include in a study designed to help address the social issue.

LEARNING THROUGH PRACTICE

Objective: To learn how to conduct case study research

Directions:

1. Identify a local restaurant or coffee shop that you enjoy going to.
2. Describe some of the features that lead you to enjoy this restaurant.
3. Thinking of other restaurants or similar service providers, is this a typical case or more of an outlier? Explain your answer.
4. Visit the restaurant and conduct an observation to see if there is anything else you wish to add to your description.
5. Now suppose you have been asked by the owners to write a verifiable report on what makes this restaurant enjoyable.
   a. How could you go about proving your claims?
   b. How could you find out if others share similar views?
6. List and describe three methods you could use to help substantiate your description of what makes this restaurant special.
7. Based on the methods you selected and the potential order in which you could employ these methods, would your resulting design be best described as a mixed-methods design or a design that includes the use of multiple methods?

RESEARCH RESOURCES

1. For information on more advanced mixed-methods designs, see Creswell, J. W., & Creswell, J. D. (2018). *Research design: Qualitative, quantitative, and mixed method approaches* (5th ed.). Thousand Oaks, CA: Sage.

2. To learn more about designing case study research and analyzing case study evidence, refer to Yin, R. K. (2018). *Case study research and applications* (6th ed.). Thousand Oaks, CA: Sage.

3. For a comprehensive overview of evaluation research and to learn how to become an evaluator, see Podems, D. R. (2019). *Being an evaluator: Your practical guide to evaluation*. New York, NY: Guilford Press.

4. For more information on the purposes of action research and methods used to carry it out, I recommend McNiff, J. (2017). *Action research: All you need to know*. Thousand Oaks, CA: Sage.

Writing Up Research and the Dissemination of Findings

Writing Research Proposals and Reports

Research is of no use unless it gets to the people who need to use it.
— Chris Whitty[1]

Learning Objectives

After reading this chapter, students should be able to do the following:

LO1   Outline the main components of a research proposal.

LO2   Explain the purpose of a method section in a research proposal.

LO3   Identify key ethical considerations that need to be addressed in a research proposal.

LO4   Outline the structure and format of a scholarly research report.

INTRODUCTION

Just as research is conducted for a variety of purposes, such as to explore or to explain a phenomenon of interest, as discussed at the start of this book, research is also carried out with its eventual target audience in mind, as implied by the opening quote to this chapter. Basic research is generally undertaken for an academic audience, and research findings are disseminated (communicated) in reports that form the basis of conference talks or published works such as books, chapters, or journal articles read by scholars in affiliated disciplines. Disciplines recommend their own writing style for academic papers and reports. Three common documentation styles used in the social sciences throughout North America are American Psychological Association (APA) format, Modern Language Association (MLA) style, and the American Sociological Association (ASA) style. All three provide direction for quoting and paraphrasing the work of others, for setting up the format of documents (e.g., spacing, headers, and the presentation of material in tables and figures), and for referencing sources. APA format is based on the most current edition of the *Publication Manual of the American Psychological Association*. MLA style is based on the most current edition of the *MLA Handbook for Writers of Research Papers*, and ASA is based on the *American Sociological Association Style Guide*. Consult your instructor, your course syllabus, your library's writing resources, or the instructions for contributors at a journal to determine the exact style you should use for preparing course work, research proposals, or research reports.

Research Proposals versus Reports

Most everyone who takes a research methods course or who plans to carry out basic research for an honours project, an independent study, or graduate studies (e.g., master's research or a research-based dissertation for a doctorate degree) is expected to develop a research proposal. Similarly, researchers and other academics who wish to carry out studies at universities, in community settings, and in the private or business sector typically submit a research proposal to an ethics board and/or to a funding agency prior to beginning the research project. A **research proposal** is a comprehensive plan, created in advance of carrying out research, that details what a research project is about and what the process entails for obtaining the data needed to address the research questions and objectives. Included in the proposal is a description of the relevant literature, the main research questions or hypotheses the study hopes to address, the methods for obtaining data, and anticipated ethical considerations. A **research report**, in contrast, is written after research is conducted. The report is a detailed account that describes the area of

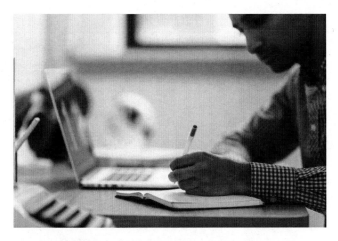

A research proposal is a comprehensive plan for a research project.

Source: StockSnap/pixabay.com

interest, provides the specific research questions or hypotheses addressed in the study, spells out the methods used to obtain the data, and communicates the main results from the study. In addition, a research report discusses the findings in relation to the wider literature on the subject matter, indicates any limitations of the study, and offers suggestions for future research on that topic. The next section provides you with some guidance for what to include in a research proposal.

THE RESEARCH PROPOSAL

A research proposal is meant to address two primary questions: (1) What purpose does the research serve? and (2) How will the research be carried out to meet the intended objective? The research purpose is articulated in the introduction section and the planned process for carrying out the research is detailed in the method section. A research proposal is usually divided into five main sections consisting of an introduction, a method section, a section on data analysis and dissemination, a section on ethical considerations, and a listing of prospective references. These sections are described in detail below.

Introduction

To explain the research purpose in a manner that is accessible to a wide audience of readers, a researcher should frame the general research interest within a theoretical context, briefly describe what other researchers have done and found on the topic, state the current research interest, and explain how the present study will contribute to the literature by posing specific research questions and/ or by testing hypotheses. Begin with a broad opening statement that identifies the area of interest. For example, a student of mine who planned to compare the portrayal of masculinity in the lyrics of country versus hip-hop songs began with "Hip-hop (or rap, the two terms are now used interchangeably) and country music are increasingly popular genres of music" and went on to point out the earnings and prevalence of the two genres in order to introduce the general topic (Holub, 2012). After introducing the general topic, a researcher can begin to narrow the topic by linking the topic to previous research on the proposed area of interest. This is where central concepts are discussed and the theoretical context is established. Continuing with the previous example, my student went on to point out prevalent masculinity themes identified in previous research on lyrics of music from the two genres. The same student ended the introduction by noting that her proposed study would compare depictions of masculinity across genres to see if there were common underlying features. A qualitative study with an exploratory focus is going to include a general question, such as "Are there similarities in the way masculinity is depicted in country and hip-hop music lyrics?" In contrast, a quantitative study with a more descriptive focus would likely include a directional hypothesis, such as "H_1: The proposed study predicts that masculinity will be more evident in hip-hop than in country music lyrics." Ask yourself the following questions as you prepare the introductory section:

- What is my broad area of interest?
- Did I identify a narrow focus within this area of interest?
- Did I summarize the relevant literature in this area?
- Did I include clear conceptual definitions for the main concepts?
- Is a theoretical context established for my study?
- What will my research contribute to this area?
- What is my research question or hypothesis?

Method

The method section outlines who the participants will be and how they will be selected. In addition, the method section includes details about the setting and materials needed to conduct the study, the procedures for carrying out the study, and the main variables examined in the study, as discussed in more detail below.

Participants and How They Will Be Obtained or Sample Selection

First, if the study will include research participants, such as interview participants, survey respondents, or experimental subjects, a researcher needs to detail who the potential research participants will be and how they will be identified and recruited. In addition, the researcher should note any relevant criteria that may be used to include or exclude participants. For example, an honours student working under my supervision examined the prevalence of aggressive and dangerous forms of driving in a sample of three hundred university students (Haje & Symbaluk, 2014). In his ethics application, Bruno Haje proposed that participants would be recruited from the university's research subject pool in accordance with the department's procedures for online survey research participation. He also pointed out that since this study was specifically about driving behaviours, participants would need to be volunteers who drive a motor vehicle at least on occasion.

Note that not all forms of research involve research participants. A researcher planning to use unobtrusive methods, such as physical trace analysis, or wanting to carry out a content analysis would instead describe proposed units of analysis. Recall Gackenbach et al.'s (2011) study on the video game player's online dream diary. Although there was a person to whom the dreams belonged, it was the content of 447 of his 831 dream postings that constituted the units of analysis. In a qualitative study, this section is usually titled sample selection. Here, a researcher articulates how the sample (e.g., of dream postings) will be obtained, including any inclusion or exclusion criteria that will determine eligibility (Padgett, 2012). For example, of the 831 posted dreams, a dream was included in the analysis if it was more than 50 but fewer than 500 words, had a clear date as to when it occurred, included an activity blog entry from the night before the dream, and fit one of the defined dream categories, resulting in a sample of 447 dreams (Gackenbach et al., 2011).

A research sample might consist of visual or textual content obtained from the internet.

Source: 472301/pixabay.com

Setting and Materials

In addition to describing the participants and how they will be recruited or the units of analysis, the method section also indicates the proposed setting or location for data collection and any materials needed to carry out the study. Research is often carried out at a university where the primary researcher holds a faculty position. However, if the study is an in-depth qualitative interview, the setting may be the respondent's place of residence or a public location that the respondent feels comfortable in and one that provides some degree of needed privacy, such as a booth in a local coffee shop. Similarly, if the study involves ethnographic fieldwork, the research setting is likely to be wherever that group or process is located and can best be examined from within a natural context.

Materials for a study include items that need to be purchased ahead of time to carry out the study. For example, to carry out my master's research on pain perception and endurance, I needed to purchase a heart rate monitor to assess participants, for health and safety reasons, throughout the exercise. I also needed equipment that could be used to assist in the measurement of pain endurance. Specifically, participants performed an isometric sitting exercise above a box with a pressure plate. A participant who was too tired to continue sat down on the box, thereby activating the pressure plate to stop a timer that recorded endurance.

As another example, an online ethnography might require a computer, internet access, and possibly some kind of registration or software needed to gain access to a group of interest, such as through a membership or user account. Finally, a researcher conducting an interview-based study might wish to use incentives to compensate interviewees for their time and would therefore need to purchase gift cards or prepare some comparable remuneration in advance of the study.

Main Variables

Next, researchers describe the main variables or measures of interest. If the approach is quantitative, as in the case of an experimental method, this section describes the dependent variables. (The independent variables are discussed as part of the procedures for how the manipulation will be carried out.) For example, in the pain study, the main dependent variable was pain endurance, defined as the length of time a participant was able to maintain an isometric sitting exercise in minutes and seconds. Each dependent variable should be listed, along with the operational definition for how it will be measured. For a quantitative survey, each main variable is likely to be measured using a question or multiple questions on a self-report questionnaire. For example, in a study on aggressive driving, aggressive behaviour might be measured using Deffenbacher, Lynch, Oetting, and Swaim's

(2002) shortened version of the Driver Anger Expression Inventory, consisting of 21 items. The inventory assesses verbally aggressive behaviour (e.g., yelling at other drivers), physically aggressive behaviour (e.g., giving someone the finger), and/or constructive expressions of anger (e.g., thinking about other things). Survey items are usually summarized in this section and the full inventory is included in an appendix. If the measures are already established, you can report on the reliability and validity of the measure as described in the literature.

Alternatively, if a study is based on a qualitative content analysis, an in-depth interview, or an unstructured observation, this section elaborates on how the researcher plans to identify main themes and patterns from the data once they are collected and transcribed, as opposed to operationalizing variables ahead of time. This section is sometimes called coding procedures and it can take the place of the main variables and procedures sections. For example, a researcher who wishes to examine a television series for depictions of violence enacted by the main characters might indicate a plan to use an open coding scheme to detail every separate and distinct act of violence committed by a main character as a first-cycle coding method. This can be followed by a second phase of coding directed at identifying main themes and categorizing the patterns to the violence identified in the first round of coding. Similarly, an ethnographer might plan to use descriptive coding for field notes and documents collected on a group of interest that will be later subjected to a more structured coding process. A qualitative researcher might also adopt existing coding schemes from the established literature to conduct a content

Published journal articles based on similar forms of research serve as examples for how to structure reports and write method sections.

Source: fritsdejong/pixabay.com

analysis. When possible, the researcher should articulate the coding schemes and tie them back to the theoretical context in which they developed. Since the content of any method section is going to vary considerably depending on the approach and methodology (e.g., quantitative survey versus qualitative interview), you should examine published journal articles based on the same methodology you plan to use for a more definitive sense of what you need to include here.

Procedures

Finally, the procedures section outlines the detailed plan for carrying out the study as the last main component of the method section. This section needs to include enough detail that a reader could replicate the study exactly, based on how it is described in writing. For example, if a researcher intends to conduct online survey research, the procedures will detail how the participants are to access the online survey through a link they receive in an email invitation sent to their university email account. Once a participant clicks on the study link, what happens next? The procedures walk the reader through the study. For an online survey, the first page that is likely to appear on the screen following the link to the study is the informed consent statement. The procedures will then go into detail about how the online consent form describes the study, provides details about what is expected of participants, notes the benefits and risks of participation, indicates that participation is voluntary, and explains how privacy will be maintained and what the plans are for dissemination of findings. The procedures also indicate how consent is obtained. In the case of an online survey, potential participants are likely to be asked to click on a box that reads something like "I agree to participate in this study" or "I do not agree to participate in this study." Procedures can also note that upon agreeing to participate in the study, the participants then receive the first screen page of the survey. What happens to those who choose not to participate? The procedures should also note that participants who do not consent to participate instead receive a debriefing statement that provides additional details about the study and contact information for the principal researcher.

In addition to describing the process leading up to survey access, the procedures also describe the survey instrument by noting how many questions are on the questionnaire, indicating whether questions are grouped into sections, noting the topic of each section, and listing the order in which the information will be received by the participant. For example, perhaps the questionnaire begins with 10 items that assess background information, followed by a 5-item personality scale or a 12-item behaviour inventory. The procedures also note what happens once participants complete the survey. In most cases, after completing an online survey, participants will receive the debriefing statement mentioned above. Finally, a copy of the questionnaire in its entirety, along with the consent form and debriefing statement, should be attached at the end of the proposal as an appendix.

Again, I would advise you to look at how the procedures are described in a couple of published journal articles based on studies like the one you are planning, for additional ideas on what you need to include as necessary steps. Ask yourself the following questions as you prepare the method section:

- Did I indicate who the target participants will be and how I plan to obtain them?
- If I don't have participants, did I explain what my units of analysis will be and how I plan to sample for them?
- Did I explain any relevant inclusion or exclusion criteria for selection?
- Have I noted where the proposed study will take place?
- Have I identified all materials that need to be obtained in advance of the study?
- For a quantitative study, have I listed and operationalized all main variables I plan to examine in my study?
- For a qualitative study, have I explained how I plan to code or categorize the information I will be collecting?
- Have I explained all steps I will undertake to carry out the study?

Data Analysis and Dissemination

In addition to describing the main variables and/or coding procedures, a research proposal also includes a brief section outlining the plan for data analysis and dissemination of findings. A quantitative study is likely to include statistical analysis using a software package especially designed for the social sciences, such as IBM SPSS or Stata statistical software. Data analysis in a qualitative study may be carried out by developing codes through transcription and textual analysis, or it can be assisted through specialized software programs such as NVivo, which helps to manage data by treating units of analysis as cases and organizing ideas, concepts, and themes into codes so that patterns and trends can be made apparent (Jackson & Bazeley, 2019). Here researchers can also indicate any strategies they plan to use to establish reliability, including inter-rater reliability and methods for obtaining rigour. Finally, a proposal outlines the plan for what will be done with the data once they are collected. Perhaps the researcher intends to report on the findings at an upcoming conference or submit the main findings to a journal for peer review and possible publication.

Ethical Considerations

If a researcher plans to undertake a study that will include university students (or any humans) as research participants, as in the case of an experimental design, a survey project, an in-depth qualitative interview, or a focus group, the researcher would need to first obtain ethical approval through a university's research ethics board. Even in the case of non-reactive research, if a researcher wishes to carry out a project that will in some way involve a university's assets (directly or indirectly), as in the case of non-participatory observation in public spaces on campus, ethical approval will need to be sought from that university's research ethics board. A research proposal always includes relevant ethical concerns along with the ways in which the planned study will address the concerns.

Minimal Risk for Harm

Recognizing that all research involving humans has at least a minimum potential for harm, a researcher should identify whether the proposed study can be judged as a minimal risk. While it is up to the research ethics board to determine whether the study is deemed minimal risk, a researcher can and should provide rationale for why the proposed project should be assessed as such. For example, a researcher who plans to conduct a survey on driving may indicate that there are no anticipated risks associated with participating in the proposed study. However, since the participants are disclosing information about their own driving habits, there is a minimal risk that participants may experience psychological discomfort when answering questions about the extent to which they engage in dangerous or aggressive driving practices. Specifically, participants could feel remorse or embarrassment while responding to certain questions. In addition, participants could later reflect on responses given and regret having disclosed information about their driving.

Mitigating Minimal Risk of Harm

To help mitigate this potential likelihood of harm, a researcher can include explicit information in the initial consent form to give the potential participants an idea of the type of questions they can anticipate being asked during the survey. For example, participants might be informed that they will be asked to report on safe and unsafe driving practices. In addition, the researcher can even include examples of specific items on the survey (e.g., Question #25 asks "How often do you send or receive text messages while stopped at a red light?").

Researchers can also include a statement within the questionnaire itself that reiterates that participation is voluntary, that participants may skip over questions they do not want to answer, and that they can choose to end their participation at any time without penalty. Finally, a researcher can include additional self-help resources with the debriefing statement, such as resources for driver education and training.

Addressing Beneficence

Recall from chapter 3 the importance of designing a study in a manner that minimizes harm while maximizing the overall benefit of the research. Where possible, a research proposal should include a statement about the benefits of the proposed study for the researcher. For example, might the research help to fulfill the requirements for an honours project or a master's thesis? In addition, it is important to list potential benefits for the participants, such as the opportunity to learn more about themselves or research processes. Finally, the proposal should also indicate benefits to the wider research community and/or society more generally. For example, may the proposed study contribute toward our understanding of some group, phenomenon, or process?

Upholding Privacy and Confidentiality

A researcher also needs to detail the planned procedures for upholding privacy through the anonymity of participants, how safe and secure storage of data will be achieved, and how confidentiality will be upheld in the disclosure of findings. For example, a researcher will need to note whether any personally identifying information is going to be collected and, if so, how the researcher plans to safeguard the identity of individual participants. Note that participants need to be made aware of this prior to providing consent.

Part of the process of ensuring privacy includes a consideration and disclosure of who is going to participate in data collection (e.g., Will research assistants help to collect information?); who is expected to access the collected data (e.g., Will anyone other than the principal researcher assist in the transcription or coding?); and whether data are going to be stored (e.g., Will the data be transferred onto a computer file that will be kept on a password-protected computer in a locked office of the principal researcher? Will field notes be kept in a locked cabinet in the secure office of the principal researcher?). A research ethics board will ask for information on these items, as well as additional information, including how long the data will need to be stored (the recommended length being about two years) and how the data will eventually be disposed of (e.g., Will the notes be shredded?).

Data stored on a computer should be password-protected.

Source: mohamed_hassan/pixabay.com

Prospective References

Finally, a research proposal ends with a list of relevant references. References included in a research proposal help to establish a scholarly context for the planned study. The references help identify, for example, the appropriate and relevant theories, theorists, and concepts that inform the proposed research. In addition, references can help to validate the proposed methodology. For example, perhaps the researcher plans to use a grounded theory approach such as the one described by Barney G. Glaser in 1992.

References are listed on a separate page in a standard citation format such as the one provided by the sixth edition of the *American Psychological Association's Publication Manual* (APA format). In APA format, an author of a book is listed by last name, followed by first initials, year of publication, title, place, and then the publisher according to specific rules for style and punctuation. As illustrated here, in APA format, only the first word of the title of a book is capitalized, and the title appears in italics. MLA and ASA format are similar, as shown below.

APA format:
Glaser, B. G. (1992). *Grounded theory analysis: Emergence vs forcing.* Mill Valley, CA: Sociology Press.

MLA format:
Glaser, Barney. *Grounded Theory Analysis: Emergence vs Forcing.* Mill Valley, CA: Sociology Press, 1992.

ASA format:
Glaser, Barney. 1992. *Grounded Theory Analysis: Emergence vs Forcing.* Mill Valley, CA: Sociology Press.

Test Yourself

- What are the two primary questions addressed by a research proposal?
- Does the introduction section in a research proposal begin with a broad or narrow statement?
- In which section of a research proposal would you expect to find information on the setting and materials for a study?
- Which subsection of a research proposal walks the reader through the study?
- What suggestions might researchers propose to mitigate the risk of harm to participants?

THE RESEARCH REPORT

A research report is a formalized summary of a completed research project. A research report is written in a standard format that you can use to describe the research you have carried out for an undergraduate research class, an honours project, an independent study, or a field placement. Whether you are writing up the research for class marks, to give to a supervisor or instructor as proof that you have completed your project, or you hope to submit the work to an academic journal for possible publication, these guidelines serve as a template for your finished product. A research report is structured so that it includes standard components or features that are recognized by other researchers and academics in the field. This format, also required for publication in most professional journals, includes a title page, an abstract, an introduction, a method section, a results section, a discussion section, references, tables, figures, and an appendix, as described in detail in this section. Also, refer to the appendix of this book for a sample research report that conforms to this format, written by a former student as part of the requirements for an undergraduate introduction to research methods course.

Title Page

The title page is much more than just a placeholder for the title of the study—it not only identifies what was studied, it provides additional information that helps to locate and establish the study within the greater context of the discipline in which it is situated. First, a title page includes a *long title* that summarizes what the study was about. There is no required minimum or maximum word length; however, the title should contain enough information to give the reader a sense of the specific research objectives. For example, "Sleep Quality" as a title would help identify the area of interest, but not what the study was about. In contrast, Semplonius and Willoughby's (2018) full title, "Psychosocial Adjustment Throughout University: A Longitudinal Investigation of the Roles of Sleep Quality and Emotion Dysregulation," informs readers that the relationship between sleep and emotions is being studied over time.

In addition to the full title, a title page usually includes a *running head*, which is a shortened version of the title that appears in the header of the manuscript once it is published (e.g., in a journal). A sample running head for Semplonius and Willoughby's 2018 study is "Sleep Quality and Emotion Dysregulation." Finally, a title page includes a short list of relevant *key words*, which are concepts used to locate the article via database searches once it is in print. Key words also give the reader additional insight into the study. For example, readers interested in the interrelations between *sleep*, *depression*, *emotion dysregulation*, and *alcohol* might benefit from reading Semplonius and Willoughby's study.

A title page also includes additional details, including a recognition statement for the source of any relevant funding and how to correspond with the principal researcher for more information about the study. The recognition statement cites the source of support for the study, such as an external research grant (e.g., the Social Sciences and Humanities Research Council) or an internal source of funding (e.g., a research fund from within a department or school, or a university's research office). The correspondence statement lists the name and email address of the main contact person or the principal researcher for the study so that interested readers and other researchers can reach the person for more information about the study.

Abstract

Located at the beginning of a research project, an **abstract** is a brief overview of the research project. It summarizes what the research is about, how many participants there were and how they were obtained (or what the units of analysis were), what the procedures were for carrying out the study, what the design consisted of, and what the main findings were. This can be considered the most important section in the entire report, as it is generally the first and sometimes the only section that is read by other academics and researchers conducting searches for relevant articles of interest. Although it appears at the beginning of a report, it should be the last thing the researcher writes, to ensure that it is both succinct (i.e., usually less than 120 words) and comprehensive. This is one of the most difficult sections to write, as it needs to include a lot of information in what amounts to only about six to eight sentences. A good strategy for writing an abstract that is under 120 words is to first write an abstract that includes all relevant information (this will likely be about 300 words on your first try), and then rework it a few times, paring it down word by word, until it is as concise as possible.

Always write an abstract last because it provides a comprehensive overview of what the research was about and found.

Source: Alexas_Fotos/pixabay.com

Introduction

An introduction section follows the abstract. Like the research proposal, an introduction in a research report should include a general opening and a broad discussion of the research interest and area, followed by a narrowing of the research topic. In addition, the research topic should be situated within the relevant literature, and the theoretical context and key concepts should all be well articulated. After summarizing the relevant literature, the introduction ends with a statement of the research problem, key question(s), issues explored, and/or hypotheses tested.

For example, in a research project on pain that I conducted for my master's research, the broad opening statement in the journal article I published was "Pain is a fundamental fact of life" (Symbaluk, Heth, Cameron, & Pierce, 1997, p. 258). From there, the introduction narrowed to discuss forms of acute and chronic pain in everyday life. It further narrowed as we brought in the social psychology of pain and established how monetary incentives and social modelling have been used in experimental research to increase pain endurance. It continued to narrow as we identified gaps in the literature and explained how this experiment was the first to look at the role of self-efficacy and pain perception as potential mediators for the anticipated effects of money and modelling on pain endurance. The introduction ended with specific hypotheses, including one predicting that pain endurance would increase as a function of money for participants who were exposed to pain-tolerant social models.

Note that the introduction section for a qualitative research project also summarizes the relevant literature and ties that literature to the research interests of the present study. However, in lieu of hypotheses, this section is likely to conclude with a statement of the research objective or the main question (or questions) explored in the study that follows logically from the literature review (Pyrczak & Bruce, 2017). For example, a qualitative study conducted by one of my students in an introduction to research methods course focused on the reproduction of common stereotypes in popular media. Finlay's (2012) research question was "Does the popular television series *Crime Scene Investigation* promote or resist common stereotypical media representations of gender?"

Method

The method (sometimes called methodology) section of the research report is next. The method section is generally the longest in a report, as it contains subsections on the participants or selection of a sample, setting and materials, procedures or coding scheme, dependent or main variables, and data analysis.

Participants and How They Were Obtained or Sample and Sample Selection

For research involving humans as participants, this section notes how many participants were included in the study, who the participants were, and how they were obtained. For example, Sabbane, Bellavance, and Chebat's (2009) experiment on the effects of anti-smoking warnings on attitudes and smoking intentions included 178 teenagers as participants. Specifically, participants were males and females between the ages of 12 and 17 who were non-smokers (N = 158) or occasional smokers (N = 15) recruited, with parental consent, from classes in a Montreal secondary school.

As a second example, Boyd, Jardine, and Driedger (2009) analyzed the content of media representations of bovine spongiform encephalopathy (BSE), more commonly known as "mad cow disease" for the first 10 days following an outbreak in Alberta on May 20, 2003. Their sampling frame consisted of *The Globe and Mail* and the *National Post* (as leading national papers), as well as

The Lethbridge Herald (as a local Alberta newspaper) and the *Edmonton Journal* (as a regional newspaper). The sampling procedure involved online searches of these papers for articles on mad cow disease identified through key words. From this potential sample, articles were included if they met additional criteria. For example, articles that only peripherally mentioned BSE (i.e., it was not the focus of the study) were excluded, resulting in 309 articles in the sample used (Boyd et al., 2009).

Finally, as a third example, Dr. Rosemary Ricciardelli interviewed 14 men as part of a study on the role of hair in self-identification. The interviewees were recruited through convenience sampling via four means of advertising the study, including business card advertisements for the study given out and left in coffee shops and shopping centres in the Greater Toronto Area, an email invitation sent out to students in a small suburban university, an advertisement in *Fab* magazine, and an ad in a free gay publication (Ricciardelli, 2011).

Setting and Materials

As addressed under research proposals, the setting refers to the location where the data collection takes place. For example, in a study looking at the meaning of recovery from the perspective of Canadian consumers receiving mental health services, Piat et al. (2009) conducted interviews at major mental health service sources, including the Wellington Centre of the Douglas Mental Health University Institute, the Canadian Mental Health Association Waterloo/Wellington-Dufferin branches, and at the Programme d'encadrement clinique et d'hébergement. If the setting does not apply, as might be the case if the study was conducted over the internet, then this section would refer to materials only.

The materials refer to the main instruments and supplies used to carry out the procedures of the study. In an experiment, whatever is manipulated as the independent variable likely constitutes a material that requires preparation in advance of the study. For example, in a study on social-information processing as a function of psychopathic traits, Wilson, Demetrioff, and Porter (2008) showed participants artificially created characters and then examined recall and recognition. The characters were profiles developed ahead of time that consisted of eight stimulus characters created with images of faces from the Pictures of Facial Affect (POFA) series put together with descriptions that contained a name, an occupation, and a set of likes and dislikes.

Note that indexes, scales, and other items used to compose a questionnaire given as part of survey research are generally described as main variables or measures after the procedures (not as materials needed to carry out the study).

Procedures

The procedures section of a research report details how the study was carried out. This subsection within the methods is written in the past tense, and it includes a description of all phases of the study, beginning with any instructions given to participants and the consent process, followed by details on the type of techniques employed to gather and later examine the data. For example, if interviews were conducted, the researcher needs to indicate how many times each participant was interviewed and the time frame over which data collection (interviewing) took place. Alternatively, if observations occurred, when, where, and under what conditions did these take place? As another example, if an experiment was employed, how did participants experience the independent variable? Instead, if the study was based on ethnography, how did the researcher access the setting? Who were the gatekeepers and how was the gatekeeping process navigated? How was rapport with group members established? What role did the researcher engage in for data collection purposes (e.g., participant observation)? What methods were used to collect data? How did the researcher disengage from the setting at the completion of the study?

Note that if the study was based on content analysis, instead of procedures, a research report could include a section on coding procedures or a coding scheme. Similarly, if the study was based on secondary analysis of existing data, this section would outline why and how that source was selected and obtained, and how the archival material was organized and synthesized for subsequent data analysis (Neuman & Robson, 2018).

Main Variables or Measures

A research report always includes a section that outlines the main variables examined in the study. If the study is an experiment, the dependent variables are listed along with their operationalized definitions. For example, in the pain experiment I conducted for my master's research, *pain perception* was operationalized as the time elapsed prior to the first sensation of pain in seconds, and *pain endurance* referred to how long a participant held an isometric sitting position in minutes and seconds (Symbaluk et al., 1997).

As another example, in a study looking at alcohol content as a mediating factor for brand preference, Segal and Stockwell (2008) employed measures of intoxication and enjoyment completed by participants after they drank two low-alcohol or two regular-alcohol-content beers. Their measures section included a description of an objective variable based on blood-alcohol content assessed using a standard instrument called the Alco-Sensor IV, and it included a description of three subjective measures. Each subjective measure was listed along with appropriate citations for the originating source and an account of the measure. For example, one measure was The Sensation Scale, which they note was originally developed by Maisto, Conners, Tucker, McCollam, & Adesso (1980) and consists of 31 items about the effects of alcohol. The measures section also notes that participants scored the items using Likert responses ranging from 0 (not at all) to 9 (extremely), with the higher ratings referring to higher intoxication.

If the study is based on qualitative research, as would be the case for in-depth interviews or most focus group sessions, the research report might not have a section for the main variables or measures. This is because concepts, themes, and main ideas may emerge during data collection and analysis in response to open-ended questions. However, if interviews or focus-group sessions are more structured, a researcher may include the questions or describe items that compose an interview guide as part of a section titled interview guide (in lieu of main variables).

Data Analysis

The last part of the method section of a research report details how data analysis was carried out. For example, if content analyses employed the frequency of occurrence of certain categories of events, how were the categories developed? Specifically, did the researcher use categories already established in the literature, modify categories based on previous literature, or develop new ones? Were categories counted once or every time there was an instance of that category? And how was reliability assessed? Did the researchers employ inter-coder reliability and, if so, what was the reliability rate achieved?

As another example, the process for data analysis in an ethnographic study of young homeless men in Calgary was described as follows: "Interviews were transcribed verbatim and checked for accuracy against the digital recordings. A thematic framework was agreed upon by the authors (SP and LM), based on the reported significance of daily routines, coping strategies and access to services. This was used along with an open coding strategy to recursively analyze these findings using NVivo 7, a qualitative analysis software (QRS International 2007). Data analysis was concurrent with data collection and uncovered common themes among the interviewees" (Persaud, McIntyre, & Milaney, 2010, p. 345).

Results

The results section of a research report outlines the main findings of the study in the appropriate technical terms. If there are several dependent variables or measures, each variable might be listed as a subheading in this section. Note that the results section states only facts, as succinctly as possible. In the case of quantitative research, the results section for an experiment is likely to report on findings based on tests of differences between means using t-tests for two groups or analysis of variance for variation between and within more than two groups or categories. The results section for quantitative survey research is likely to describe main variables (e.g., using measures of central tendency and variability), as well as report on tests for associations between variables of interest, such as correlations, regression analysis, or nonparametric measures of correlation.

Coding and the Development of Categories

In a qualitative research report, results typically document the findings from the coding methods employed in the study. The coding methods involve stages or phases, beginning with initial codes. As described in various earlier chapters, data obtained in a study are assigned labels or codes. Specifically, a code "is most often a word or short phrase that symbolically assigns a summative, salient, essence-capturing, and/or evocative attribute for a portion of language-based or visual data" (Saldaña, 2016, p. 4). Recall that qualitative data includes a range of information, from narrative and text based on interviews and field notes to drawings and images presented in magazine ads, shown through character portrayals on television, and so on. A posting on RateMyProfessor.com, for example, might contain the passage "She really knows her stuff," coded as "instructor" and "knowledge" since the passage refers to the instructor and it contains a comment about an attribute of the instructor. To begin with, each unit of data is usually assigned its own specific code.

After the initial codes are determined, the next phase includes going back over the data to determine if there are patterns in the data that can be coded into categories based on their common elements. For example, perhaps lots of comments refer to the instructor. Some of the comments might pertain to instructor attributes, such as comments about the instructor's knowledge of the subject matter and comments about the instructor's willingness to help students. Other items might have to do with an instructor's grading, such as "The instructor is a hard marker" or "The instructor grades fairly." Finally, other comments might pertain to assignments in the course, such as "This course has a lot of papers!" One large category to emerge from this data might be "comments about the instructor." Another category might be "comments about the course content." Within the "comments about the instructor" category, other subcategories could also be identified. For example, there may be a subcategory for "instructor attributes." Within the subcategory for "instructor attributes," researchers could also list codes for "clarity," "helpfulness," "knowledge," and so on.

Qualitative data analysis is a lengthy process that eventually culminates in the development of themes. As Saldaña (2016) points out, "a theme is an outcome of coding, categorization, and analytic reflection, not something that is, in itself, coded" (p. 15). Results from qualitative studies, then, highlight main themes or claims that are descriptive outcomes identifying the main overall findings that emerged from the data collection and analysis processes. To substantiate the results, qualitative researchers need to carefully articulate each of the coding stages and categories that developed within each stage. Each main theme is generally discussed within its own subsection in the results, similar to how each main dependent variable is discussed for a quantitative study.

Figures

Results from research studies are often depicted in **figures**. Figures are charts or graphs used to display results based on how a variable is measured. A pie chart, for example, is used to depict the results in a picture format for a single, qualitative variable that is measured at the nominal level. For example, a researcher doing a content analysis on gender portrayals in the media might use a pie chart to convey that there are more males than females depicted as central characters on television. Or a researcher conducting an online survey on attitudes toward healthcare might use a pie chart to describe the respondents who completed the survey. Perhaps the largest slice of the pie indicates that many participants were married, followed by single, common-law, divorced, and separated (see figure 12.1). If none of the respondents claimed they were in a category (e.g., widowed), that category would not be included in the pie chart.

If it is important to indicate the frequency distribution for the categories of a variable, a bar graph would be used instead of a pie chart, since it emphasizes the number of respondents in each category of a variable and it can even be used to show the concurrent pattern of findings for two variables measured at the nominal level. In figure 12.2 we can still determine that more than half of the participants in this fictitious study on the effectiveness of a drug treatment program were married (86 + 11 = 97 out of 183). However, we can also note that there may be a relationship between treatment completion and marital status, since a higher proportion of respondents who were in a relationship (married or common-law) completed treatment relative to participants who were single or divorced.

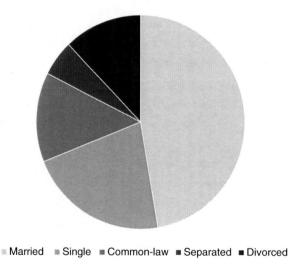

▨ Married   ▨ Single   ▪ Common-law   ▪ Separated   ▪ Divorced

Figure 12.1. Sample Pie Chart: Marital Status

Note: N = 183 participants

Source: Created by author

Figure 12.2. Sample Bar Graph: Frequencies for Treatment Completion by Marital Status

Source: Created by author

Bar graphs can also be used to display the distributions of responses across or within categories of a nominal variable, shown in percentages. For example, figure 12.3 shows the percentage of respondents in each marital status category who completed or failed to complete treatment. This figure more clearly illustrates the relationship between relationship status and treatment completion, as it is now obvious to the reader that the clear majority of those in relationships completed

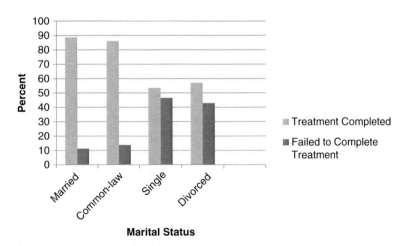

Figure 12.3. Sample Bar Graph: Percentage of Treatment Completers by Marital Status

Source: Created by author

treatment, whereas those who are not in relationships appear to have just slightly higher than a 50–50 chance of success (see figure 12.3).

Tables

Tables are typically summaries of the main findings from quantitative research, such as the percentage of respondents who gave answers in each category of a variable on a questionnaire or the differences in means between groups on dependent measures. For example, Symbaluk and Howell's (2010) study showed that students gave higher ratings to teaching-award winning instructors than to research-award winners on the popular website RateMyProfessors.com. In the results section, a table compared teaching-award and research-award recipients by listing the mean rating given by students for easiness, helpfulness, and clarity for the two groups of instructors (see table 12.1). Tables are also especially useful for indicating patterns in data over time (Nardi, 2006).

Discussion

In the discussion section of a research report, researchers summarize and elaborate on the main findings, highlight the importance of the findings, and tie them

Table 12.1. Comparison between Teaching-Award and Research-Award Recipients on Student Ratings of Easiness, Helpfulness, and Clarity

Rating Variable	Teaching-Award Recipients	Research-Award Recipients
Easiness		
M	3.29	2.84
SD	.61	.81
Helpfulness		
M	4.10	3.42
SD	.76	1.07
Clarity		
M	4.10	3.51
SD	.72	1.10

Note: Means and standard deviations are based on sample sizes of 120 for teaching-award recipients and 119 for research-award recipients. Ratings were made on five-point scales, with higher scores reflecting greater ease, helpfulness, or clarity.

Source: Adapted from Symbaluk & Howell, 2010, p. 80.

back into the wider literature. In addition, the discussion section notes limitations of the current study and identifies directions for future research. Since the results section focuses only on the findings, the discussion section is where the researcher can indicate what the results mean and whether the results are consistent with prior expectations, previous research, and/or the hypotheses tested in the study. In addition, researchers can elaborate on what the findings mean, why they are important, and how they can best be interpreted within the context of existing literature. A research report is often described as having the overall shape of an hourglass. Just as the introduction section began broad and narrowed to the focus of the current study, wherein the methods and the results sections are exclusive to the present study, the discussion broadens again until it finally generalizes back to the wider topic of interest.

After discussing the results in relation to the original research questions and wider literature, limitations are raised and suggestions for improvements are provided. All studies have strengths and weaknesses. Usually, a researcher will point out a few of the methodological limitations of the current study. Perhaps the sample size was smaller than desired, or perhaps the sampling method used was not ideal but was necessary under the present circumstances. Even if the most appropriate sampling method was used, as might be the case for a sample of convenience employed in an interview-based study on centenarians (people who live to be more than one hundred years of age), inherent limitations such as the resulting inability to generalize the findings should be mentioned in the discussion. If secondary sources are used, there may be restrictions in terms of what can be explored given the different originating purpose of data collection. Usually, a researcher will indicate ways to improve on the present study or offer suggestions for future studies given the limitations discussed. A discussion typically ends with a statement of direction for academics interested in conducting further research in this area. Note that some authors choose to include a conclusion section as a separate section to end the report. A conclusion section summarizes the contributions of the present study and provides suggestions for future research and/or includes directives for policy initiatives.

References

The last section of a research report is a list of the sources cited throughout the report. The list is generally double-spaced in accordance with the rest of the report and is written in a standard style, such as the one provided by the most current version of the American Psychological Association (APA) format discussed earlier on.

Research on the Net

APA Style

For questions you might have on how to cite special sources such as Facebook or interviews, visit the American Psychological Association's APA Style webpage at apapstyle.org. You will find quick answers to frequently asked questions about referencing, such as how to cite Twitter and Facebook, as well as quick answers to questions about formatting tables, figures, or table of contents. In addition, you can view a tutorial on the basics of APA style where you will learn more about how to apply the style in headings or for citing references in-text, for example.

Test Yourself

- What seven sections compose a standard academic research report?
- Why is an abstract so important?
- What is provided at the end of an introduction?
- What five subsections are described in the method section of a research report?
- Which section includes figures or tables?
- Where would a researcher indicate whether the findings obtained were the ones anticipated prior to the onset of the study?

OTHER ITEMS

Other optional items that may be included in a research report are an appendix and a list of acknowledgements.

The Appendix

The appendix is a section where a researcher can include additional information that may be relevant to other researchers, such as a scale or index used to construct questionnaire items, an interview guide used to assist a moderator in a focus group, a set of instructions provided to participants in an experiment, or a coding scheme adapted from the literature for use in a content analysis. Since the appendix is an extra section, it is generally not included in the page count for a research report.

List of Acknowledgements

A list of acknowledgements is included to pay tribute to individuals and organizations that helped to support the research. For example, research assistants, graduate students, or paid assistants who are not primary researchers or contributing authors are generally acknowledged at the end of the report. The researcher can also list agencies, groups, or organizations that provided funding in the form of grants, scholarships, and/or awards, along with any individual or organization that provided necessary materials, such as meeting space, for carrying out the study.

Test Yourself

- Why is a list of acknowledgements important to include in a research report?

CHAPTER SUMMARY

LO1 **Outline the main components of a research proposal.**
A research proposal includes five main sections: an introduction, a method section, a section on data analysis and dissemination, a section on ethical considerations, and a listing of prospective references.

LO2 **Explain the purpose of a method section in a research proposal.**
The method section outlines who the participants will be and how they will be selected or how the sample will be obtained. In addition, a method section includes information on the setting and materials needed to conduct the study, the procedures for carrying out the study, and the main variables that are examined in the study.

LO3 **Identify key ethical considerations that need to be addressed in a research proposal.**
If a researcher plans to conduct research using humans as participants, the proposal should indicate why the study can be deemed minimal risk and how the minimal risk will be mitigated. The proposal should also include a statement that outlines the benefits of the study for participants, for the researchers, and for the wider academic community. Finally, the proposal should also include a discussion about how privacy and confidentiality will be upheld in the planned study.

LO4   **Outline the structure and format of a scholarly research report.**
A research report includes a title page, an abstract, an introduction, a method section, a results section, a discussion section, and references. The method section includes subsections on participants and how they were selected or the sample and how it was obtained, the setting and materials, the main variables or measures, and how data analysis was conducted.

RESEARCH REFLECTION

1. Suppose you are interested in studying the prevalence of texting while driving. What method do you think would be most suitable for examining this phenomenon? If you were going to use that method to study texting while driving, what ethical considerations would you need to address in a research proposal?

2. Suppose you are interested in learning about effective strategies used by university students to prepare for final exams. Indicate what you would include in a research proposal in the section on participants. Specifically, who would your sample comprise and how you would go about obtaining participants?

3. Suppose you want to explore the ways in which people treat their pets in comparison to how they treat members of their immediate family, in an exploratory study for your master's thesis. What kind of method would you employ to study this topic? Based on your choice of method, what sorts of information would you need to include in the results section of a research report based on the findings?

LEARNING THROUGH PRACTICE

Objective: To develop a research outline

Directions:

1. Suppose you plan to carry out your course-assigned research project on gender portrayals in the mass media. Try to use the following questions and steps to develop an outline that is two to three pages long that could serve as a starting point for a research proposal on this topic.
   a. First, decide on one area of the mass media where you wish to examine gender, such as music, television, magazines, or on the internet.
   b. Next, identify relevant secondary sources for data on gender within the selected area of the mass media. For example, if you want to study gender

in music, a relevant source would be music lyrics in songs within a genre, such as rap.

    c. Develop one or two general research questions that you could (potentially) examine using the secondary source identified in the previous step.

    d. Explain whether your study will be based on qualitative or quantitative research. Justify your approach.

    e. Describe the main method you plan to use to examine your question of interest. For example, will you be conducting a content analysis?

2. Conduct a database search and locate one research article that examines gender and is relevant in some way to your proposed research topic.

    a. Describe a main research question or hypothesis examined in the article.

    b. Describe the method or methods used to answer the question of interest.

    c. Explain whether this article has provided you with any ideas or guidance for how to develop your own study in the area.

3. Locate one secondary source of potential data for your study, such as finding and printing the lyrics to one song.

    a. Do you think this source of data is a good one to include in your eventual sample? Why or why not?

    b. Describe the sampling procedure you would use to conduct your planned study.

    c. Examining the secondary source of data with your research questions in mind, what kind of data analysis do you think you would need to do? Explain the procedures for how you would carry out this analysis on a larger scale in your eventual study.

RESEARCH RESOURCES

1. For step-by-step instructions on how to write research proposals and reports, refer to chapters 6 and 7 in Symbaluk, D., Hall, R., & Champoux, G. (in press). *Navigating an undergraduate degree in the social sciences: Tips and strategies.* Edmonton, AB: MacEwan University Open Press.

2. For more information on ways to code qualitative data (e.g., descriptive coding, process coding, emotion coding, axial coding, theoretical coding), refer to Saldaña, J. (2016). *The coding manual for qualitative researchers* (3rd ed.). Thousand Oaks, CA: Sage.

3. To learn how to code qualitative data using NVivo software, refer to Jackson, K., & Bazeley, P. (2019). *Qualitative data analysis with NVivo* (3rd ed.). Thousand Oaks, CA: Sage.

4. To learn about data analysis based on qualitative, quantitative, and mixed methods, refer to Bergin, T. (2018). *An introduction to data analysis: Quantitative, qualitative and mixed methods*. Thousand Oaks, CA: Sage.

NOTE

1. Opening quote by Professor Chris Whitty, chief scientific advisor for the Department of Health, retrieved January 29, 2019, from the National Institute for Health Research home page at nihr.ac.uk.

A title should be interesting enough to gain a reader's attention and be detailed enough to describe the main topic. It may even include a reference to the research method(s) employed and/or the units of analysis.

Body Image in an Online Environment: A Content Analysis of Reactions to a Body Positive Post on Facebook

An author is anyone who contributed significantly within the research process (e.g., to the project conception, design, data collection, data analysis, and/or report writing).

by
Jessica Gillard
MacEwan University

Articles that appear in scholarly journals include the date the article was first received, the date it was revised (if necessary), and the date of final acceptance.

Date submitted: April 05, 2018

The author note includes any relevant funding source as well as contact information for the principal researcher, who is listed first when there are multiple authors.

Author Note

This research was made possible through funding provided by the Department of Sociology at MacEwan University, Edmonton, Alberta, Canada. For more information, direct correspondence to Jessica Gillard (gillardj8@mymacewan.ca).

Include as key words main constructs and concepts examined in the study along with other relevant terms that would appear in database searches for scholarly articles with similar content.

Keywords: body image, self-esteem, weight stigmatization, obesity, social media, Facebook

An abstract provides a comprehensive overview of what the research is about, how the study was carried out, what the study found, and what the findings mean, in less than 120 words.

ABSTRACT

This study examined public reactions to a Facebook post depicting Taz Jane's love for her "before" and "after" body where her before self was a thin young model versus a current and older average-sized nude. A content analysis on the 150 most recent comments about Taz Jane's contribution to the positive Body Image Movement identified seven themes including physical appearance, body standards, children and family life, gender, health and fitness, media, and self-esteem. The most prevalent theme was physical appearance, comprising approximately 48.7% of the comments. While mainly encouraging towards Taz Jane's current body and efforts, the views also emphasized ways in which females continue to be negatively impacted by society's preoccupation with weight and unrealistic body image ideals.

The first main section of the report is the introduction, and it begins with a broad opening statement that identifies the general topic.

INTRODUCTION

Appearance plays an important role in the formation of first impressions, and weight is a salient component of appearance that contributes to the overall judgements made about individuals including perceptions of their own body image. In Western society, the physical ideal is to be thin if you are female and fit if you are male. The quest to achieve socially constructed weight standards prompts gendered weight-loss and weight-control practices as well as moral panic over obesity (Broom & Dixon, 2008). Alongside attempts to manage weight is corresponding widespread body dissatisfaction and weight stigma directed at those who fail to achieve or maintain targeted weight loss (Puhl, Moss-Racusin, Schwartz, & Brownell, 2008).

Puhl, Moss-Racusin, Schwartz, and Brownell (2008) examined self-reported forms of weight bias (i.e., negative attitudes towards individuals based on their weight) and weight stigmatization experiences in a sample of overweight and obese men and women. Responses to open-ended questions indicated that participants experienced various forms of weight bias from a range of sources such as spouses, peers, family members, and health professionals with most reporting that their worst experience involved verbal bias including ridicule, intentional negative comments, and insults (Puhl, Moss-Racusin, Schwartz, & Brownell, 2008). Obese and overweight individuals are routinely subject to a range of weight-based stereotypes and negative attributions including commonly held notions that they are lazy and eat too much. Participants also mentioned that stigma associated with weight-based stereotypes had a profound negative impact on their mental well-being, and that interpersonal relationships suffered even when peers and loved ones voiced negative assumptions out of concern or a desire to promote health (Puhl, Moss-Rascusin, Schwartz, & Brownell, 2008).

This report is based on a class assignment for an introductory course in research methods where students were asked to locate a minimum of four articles on a topic of interest. If you were carrying out research of a greater scope, the literature review would be much more extensive and thorough, especially as it pertains to weight-based stereotypes and weight stigma, and the implications of weight bias for body image, mental health, and subsequent eating practices such as dieting and binging.

While weight stigma is often expressed verbally with the intent to motivate an overweight individual toward weight-loss, the actual outcome produced may be more harmful than helpful when stereotypes become internalized by those who are stigmatized. The impacts of internalized weight-based stereotypes on eating habits and mental health were examined in a study by Puhl, Moss-Racusin, and Schwartz (2007). Participants were asked to identify weight-based stereotypes that pertain to obese individuals and they were asked whether they believed the stereotypes to be true or false. Participants also reported on their experiences with weight stigma, whether and how often they used coping strategies, and they completed measures assessing their emotional well-being and binge-eating tendencies. Findings showed that participants who believed stereotypes about obese individuals were true were more likely to cope with stigma by binge eating and avoiding diets. Believing in weight stigma was not related to stigma experienced or emotional well-being (Puhl, Moss-Racusin, & Schwartz, 2007).

In addition to avoiding attempts at weight-loss, weight stigmatization may contribute to unsuccessful weight-loss maintenance for obese individuals who lose weight.

Puhl, Quinn, Weisz, and Suh (2017) looked at the relationship between weight stigma and weight loss maintenance in a sample of weight-loss maintainers and weight gainers. Weight stigma was measured by the amount of stigma previously experienced, internalized stigma assessed using a weight bias scale, and subjective stigma where participants gauged themselves as (1) "very underweight," (2) "underweight," (3) "just about right," (4) "overweight," and (5) "very overweight" (p. 757). Hierarchical logistic regression analyses showed that the odds of maintaining weight-loss decreased with increasing levels of stigma, especially in the form of subjective weight categorization (Puhl, Quinn, Weisz, & Suh, 2017).

Weight stereotypes and weight stigmatization are reinforced in traditional forms of mass media such as television and cinema in various ways from the overrepresentation of celebrities who conform to ideal body types and promote unrealistic body images, to the underrepresentation and shaming of individuals who fail to meet the ideal. Himes and Thompson (2007) conducted a content analyses to learn more about the nature of fat stigmatization in a sample of 135 vignettes from popular television shows and films containing overweight-based stigma as part of the plot (e.g., humour). Findings showed that most fat shaming took the form of verbal commentary, and adults were most likely to make fat comments towards other adults. Overweight men and women were equally likely to receive derogatory comments, while men were three times as likely to use fat commentary compared to females (Himes & Thompson, 2007). It is unclear from the findings of this study how viewers might feel about the fat shaming they are exposed to in television shows and feature films, but there are likely to be negative repercussions for individuals who identify with the characters, particularly if they internalize weight stigma and believe weight stereotypes to be true.

Newer forms of media made possible by the Internet are perceived to have the potential for positive and negative effects on body image and weight-based ideals. Youtube, as an example, provides a creative platform where individuals can bypass the reach of the traditional media ownership to display a wider array of viewpoints and perspectives, potentially challenging existing stereotypes (e.g., see Burgess & Green, 2009). Marchant et al. (2017) systematically reviewed existing literature to gauge the impacts of different types of internet use on younger individuals who engage in self-harming and suicidal behaviours. Results revealed a range of positive, negative, and mixed outcomes for participants across forty-six studies. For example, public forums can provide support and resources for those who are depressed and are considering self-harm activities, while video and image sharing tends to glorify and encourage self destructive behaviors, as opposed to describing recovery processes and how to seek help. In general, social media was found to facilitate the expression, and potentially the normalization, of poor self-esteem and thoughts about suicide. Overall, high internet use and internet addiction was associated with negative psychological outcomes including a higher risk for suicide (Marchant et al., 2017). Activity online, especially in high amounts, has the potential to encourage harmful messages, and this carries serious impacts for users' emotional and physical well-being. As a result, there are implications for the effect of internet use on body image and self-esteem specifically.

Given the popularity of social network sites, the effects of social media on physical appearance and body image is especially pronounced for adolescents. Research by de Vries, Peter, de Graaf, and Nikksen (2016) explored adolescents' use of social media and its effect on self-worth and body dissatisfaction. The longitudinal study found that females were more likely to experience feedback about appearance, and they were more dissatisfied with their bodies compared to males (de Vries, Peter, de Graaf, & Nikksen, 2016). Regression analyses showed that social media use in general increased body dissatisfaction over time, but body dissatisfaction did not influence the use of social media in the first place and peer-related feedback about appearance did not account for increased body dissatisfaction (de Vries, Peter, de Graaf, & Nikksen, 2016). While it may not be the peer attention itself that had a negative impact on body image (or there may have been a range of effects not captured by this study), the use of social media in general has been shown to adversely effect self-worth, typically through the internalization of harmful body standards and weight-based attitudes voiced online.

Since social media is both a powerful tool for presenting body standards and a potential source of support or harm, it would be important to learn whether the self-worth of users can be enhanced by portrayals of body positive images or debunked stereotypes in the social media realm. As a step in this direction, the present qualitative study contributes to the existing literature by exploring how online users react to a body positive post on Facebook through comments made in response to Taz Jane's positive narrative regarding a love for her "before" and "after" body as shown in photos where her before self is a younger, thin model and her after self is a more current, normal weight representation.

> The introduction section should conclude with the aims of the present study.

METHOD

> The method section details how the study was carried out. It contains information on the participants or sample, participant recruitment or sample selection, units of analysis, setting and materials, procedures, main variables (if quantitative), and design.

Sample

The sample consisted of Facebook comments posted in reaction to photos and commentary shared by "Taz Jane," whose actual name is Taryn Brumfitt. Brumfitt is the founder of *Body Image Movement*, an organization directed at ending body shaming through the promotion of body loving (Body Image Movement, 2018). *Body Image Movement* was identified through an online search using keywords, including: "self-esteem," "body positive," and "body image" on Facebook. Facebook was selected as the data source because it is a leading social networking platform that is easily accessible by the public and allows users to share opinions through posted comments. *Body Image Movement* features photos, videos, and status updates about body positivity, self-esteem, and health. With a diverse audience able to access the posts of this page, viewers often engage in discussion surrounding societal standards of beauty and health, especially in relation to females. With over 250,000 likes, *Body Image Movement* provides a platform to analyze attitudes towards weight-based issues and experiences.

Sample Selection

The Facebook status examined in this study was posted by *Body Image Movement* on April 21, 2013 at 6:14 am. The post by "Taz Jane" was selected because it had the highest number of "shares" (i.e., it was shared by Facebook users nearly 19,000 times), demonstrating that the message was impactful enough to spread amongst peers and initiate discussion. Within the chosen post is a non-traditional "before" and "after" photo that features weight gain, rather than weight loss as a challenge to prevailing standards. Specifically, Taryn Brumfitt posted a "before" picture of her younger self as a thin model in a swimsuit alongside an "after" more current picture of herself as a nude illustration depicting normal weight and natural signs of body changes over time (e.g., following the birth of her children). In addition to the photos, Brumfitt included a narrative that challenged traditional portrayals and explained how she loved her body in both cases and accepted how it has changed over time. A total of 2,879 user comments were made in response, with the last one received on July 20, 2017 at 5:21 A.M. The specific post can be found at the following address: https://www.facebook.com/bodyimagemovement/photos/a.209208695873480.46106.207017289425954/314574818670200/?type=3&theater

INCLUSION AND EXCLUSION CRITERIA

All 150 of the most recent comments made to the Facebook status were included in the analysis. This means the study included individual comments made directly in response to Taz Jane's post as well as additional responses posted to comments made as part of an online discussion between individuals.

Units of Analysis

The units of analysis for this study were the words and phrases contained in the 150 comments made in reaction to Taz Jane's positive Body Image Movement contribution posted to Facebook.

Setting and Materials

Data collection took place in the principal researcher's home. Access to the internet was necessary to collect the data, as the comments were posted online to the *Body Image Movement* Facebook page. Since the page is publicly available, a Facebook account was not necessary to view the user comments included for the purposes of this study.

> Students and researchers alike tend to struggle with data analysis. Where possible, a researcher should explain how data analysis was carried out, including the type of coding process used in qualitative research or the type of statistical tests performed in quantitative research.

Coding Procedures

Each comment was examined individually and open-coded for key words, phrases or constructs that captured the meaning or intent of the statement. Comments tagging other Facebook users to view the status were coded as "miscellaneous." In cases where comment meaning could not be readily discerned either because of brevity, ambiguousness, or the use of a language other than English, further inferences were not made about the comment. Coded comments were then re-evaluated for the presence of general themes such as an emphasis on body standards.

> The results section provides a succinct overview of the main findings. Save interpretation of the results (re: what they show or mean) for the discussion. If the study is qualitative, the results section will be longer than if the study were quantitative because main themes will be described and substantiated, often in separate paragraphs with sub-headings, as shown here.

Design

A content analysis was used to identify recurring themes contained in the reactions to a positive body contribution posted to Facebook.

RESULTS

Results indicated a range of topics identified in the 150 comments made in reaction to the body positive post.

Men and women posted comments that provided feedback about Taz Jane's narrative, her self-photos, or her initiative to promote body love. Some commenters reflected openly about themselves or people they knew in terms of weight-related issues or body standards. Others commented about aging in general and how bodies undergo similar transformations over time. Some brought up topics such as "self-love," the importance of being "natural," and what it means to be "healthy." Seven more general themes were evident in the individual topics raised in the comments including in order of prevalence, a focus on: 1) physical appearance, 2) self-esteem, 3) body standards, 4) gender, 5) health and fitness, 6) media, and 7) children (see Figure 1). Characteristics of these groupings are discussed in more detail below.

Physical appearance referred to comments regarding the figures in the Facebook post's photo, or to specific body parts and looks in general. This was the most common category, as it encompassed approximately 48.7% of the sample (n=150). These responses typically involved praise or criticism of the woman depicted in the "before" and "after" post. For example, one individual stated: "Beautiful in both pictures but do you know what? I prefer the 2nd one." Other respondents discussed their own bodies instead, often with positive or negative evaluations of their appearance. This is evident in a comment stating, "im chubby and im proud. Im a size 14ish, and even though i hit the gym twice a week … i love me. I love my mummy belly, my wobbly arms and jelly legs."

Self-esteem consisted of responses that mention self-worth and body image, either generally or as the personal perspective of the commenter. This theme was the second most prevalent, comprising approximately 28.7% of the sample. The category includes comments such as: "Confidence is what makes a woman beautiful. <3 nothing more and nothing less. But it's even harder to find than the so called 'perfect' body shape."

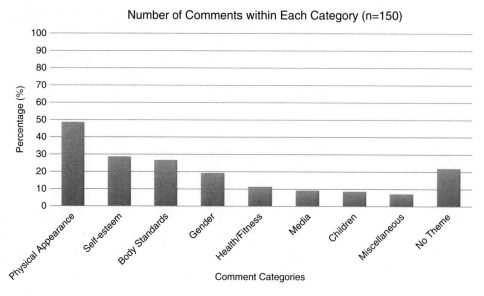

Figure 1: Percentage of Comments by Theme Category

> Figures usually consist of bar graphs, pie charts, or images such as photos that convey key patterns and trends in the data.

Body standards involved explicit and implicit references to societal norms on what constitutes the ideal body shape. This was the third most prevalent theme, as it was referenced in 26.7% of the responses. Explicit statements included a commentary on the state of societal norms themselves: "We should be comfortable in our own skin and create a body that we are happy with – free of what society or others have led us to believe is beautiful." Implicit statements involved assumptions that originate from societal norms, such as, "She's not gross but if looking average is your goal than good for you."

Out of the total comments, 19.3% included references to attitudes or experiences of *gender*. For instance, one respondent posted that, "It is a question of what has had more influence on misogynists today. Was it society or were their fathers misogynists? When did they first realize that they feared women? When did they realize that they hated women? These men raise insecure daughters which perpetuates the cycle."

Another popular topic was *health and fitness*. Health and fitness involved any comments about physical health, mental health, and exercise. An example of this comment is as follows: "There is a world of difference between having a few extra kilograms and stretch marks and being obese. The first is natural and healthy, the second is not."

Media refers to any comments about forms of media that contribute to societal norms about body size, either positively or negatively. For example, one individual stated, "I have no issues with my body image. I want to drag women out of the dark ages and to see that the advertised 'perfect' female body is manufactured and that sad little misogynists such as yourself have no real power over the female psyche."

Lastly, *children and family* refers to comments about childbirth, raising children, or family life in general. This theme comprised 8.7% of the comments. As an example, one commenter posted: "I love this page and recently got enough confidence to wear a bikini to the beach then my 5 year old told me my legs were getting big… Obviously I need to watch what I say around her and stop criticizing myself to ensure she has a positive body image when she grows up!!" Additional examples of the key themes are provided in Table 1.

Table 1: Examples of Facebook Comments by Theme

Themes Present	Comment Examples
Physical Appearance	"You look better with curves, (after pic)"
Body Standards	". . . The ideals most women are forced to subscribe to are often a) photoshopped b) unhealthy and c) quite frankly ridiculous . . ."
Children/ Family	". . . I went from being a size 0 to my current size 6 after childbirth. I much prefer having curves and a booty. My stretch marks are proof I've held a star and she thinks they're beautiful . . ."
Gender	". . . The media and men place so much importance on the way a woman should look. Men need to back off and let women be real without all the plastic surgery which creates falseness."
Health/ Fitness	". . . too often we are encouraging people to be happy with a body that isn't healthy for them. A lot of extra weight is a health risk, not having muscular tone at all is a health problem . . ."
Media	"To promote positive natural female body image, one thing that we can do is insist that advertisers use real, unaltered models for their products . . ."
Self-esteem	"Size isn't important if the people around us add to our confidence we are bombarded with so much criticism everywhere . . ."

The discussion usually begins by reiterating the purpose of the study. The discussion includes interpretations of the main findings and links the findings back to the literature and broader theoretical context within which the study was framed. The discussion section also includes mention of limitations of the present study and directions for future research.

DISCUSSION

The majority of comments made in reference to Taz Janes' positive body post on Facebook were supportive in nature by default as highly negative reactions were deleted by the moderators of Body Image Movement, potentially limiting the topics observed, such as the use of weight stereotypes and stigmatizations. Despite this, the present study explored the nature of reactions provided to determine what sort of discussion ensues when a post breaks with tradition to present self-love and body acceptance in the face of weight gain. The most predominant theme identified was physical appearance, as nearly half of the comments analyzed made references to either the body and looks depicted in the Facebook post, or of other individuals, including the commenters themselves. These findings indicate the importance of physical appearance as a sought-out value, as many of the comments praised the photo figures as being "beautiful," "stunning," and "gorgeous." Not all comments were of a praising nature, as evident in responses like "gross," and "out of shape." Negative attitudes were self-inflicted, as well, with responders expressing body dissatisfaction and envy that they were not proudly displaying their own "after" photo. While this is not a study aimed at adolescents, these results reflect existing research that social media and other internet spaces can promote peer rivalry, negative self-esteem, and poor body image (e.g., see de Vries, Peter, de Graaf, & Nikken, 2016; Marchant et al., 2017).

Among the comments, issues of body dissatisfaction, societal criticism, and pressure to be healthy were expressed as part of the female experience. Facebook users, including both males and females, repeatedly mentioned the pressures women face to maintain body ideals. This extended into discussions of children and family life, as respondents felt that their children, some as young as 5 years old, were already internalizing poor body image. Along with this, men were often cited as a source of harmful weight-based attitudes, with extreme comments describing them as "misogynists" with "nothing to offer other than abuse and insults." These findings parallel the tendency for men to be the instigators of appearance-related criticism in film and television, suggesting that this may reflect views within the general public, as well (e.g., see Himes & Thompson, 2007, p. 715). An interesting comment concerning this gender dynamic involved giving praise that the woman in the photo "sacrificed the perfect body" and yet her "husband still thinks [she's] beautiful." There are many implicit messages within this comment, including what the ideal female form is, as well as perceived male attitudes towards the appearance of women, including relationship partners.

To build upon this topic further, the source of these weight-based attitudes, beyond simply a social media post, should be discussed. Broom and Dixon (2008) refer to the concept of an obesophobic environment, in which health is deemed critically important. A portion of the Facebook comments analyzed reflect this worldview, as some consider the post to simply "justify being out of shape." Other respondents emphasized the difference between body sizes, noting "there is a world of difference between having a few extra kilograms and stretch marks and being obese," and "the first is natural and healthy, [while] the second is not." Another comment stressed that focussing on looks is not ideal and instead health should be the goal, while implying in the same comment that appearance equates to one's level of healthiness. The perception that different body sizes are incompatible with fitness goes along with another weight-based stereotype observed in the data: obesity is associated with laziness. This is evident in a comment that the woman in the photo may be considered overweight, but this "does not mean she is fat." The respondent further explained that the woman depicted "obviously ... is hardworking." Comments such as this refer to the weight-based stereotype that obese individuals are unmotivated and unproductive (Puhl, Moss-Racusin, & Schwartz, 2007). Therefore, opinions that are expressed on social media may reflect attitudes held by the public overall.

There are several limitations to the study that must be addressed when considering the research findings. For practical purposes, the sample size consisted of only 150 comments representing only a fraction of the overall comments made in reaction to the post. Additionally, it is unknown how many negative comments were removed by the authors of the Facebook post, and this may have affected the themes and attitudes that could have been observed otherwise. The non-neutral nature of the post itself – which could be viewed as controversial or supportive of body positivity, may have motivated respondents to reply in specific ways. For instance, commenters may have a belief system that aligns with the Facebook page, and are therefore self-motivated to share their perspective. On the other hand, the provocative nature of the post may have provoked input from others who hold contrasting views. Finally, this content analysis only examined one social media post by a single Facebook page. While there are limits to applications of this study, previous literature suggests that widespread societal beliefs about body size, weight, and appearance in general can have potential negative effects on self-esteem, eating habits, and self-harming behaviors. As a result, further research should investigate the ways in which online body positive messages might be used to challenge weight stigmatizations and promote self-acceptance and well-being.

References are provided on a separate page at the end of the report and they are listed in a standard format, such as APA.

REFERENCES

Body Image Movement. (2018). *What is the body image movement?* Retrieved April 1, 2018 from https://bodyimagemovement. com/about/

Broom, D. H., & Dixon, J. (2008). The sex of slimming: Mobilizing gender in weight-loss programmes and fat acceptance. *Social Theory & Health, 6*(2), 148–166.

Burgess, J., & Green, J. (2009). *YouTube: Online video and participatory culture.* Digital Media and Society Series. Cambridge, UK: Polity.

de Vries, D. A., Peter, J., de Graaf, H., & Nikken, P. (2016). Adolescents' social network site use, peer appearance-related feedback, and body dissatisfaction: Testing a mediation model. *Journal of Youth & Adolescence, 45*(1), 211–224.

Himes, S. M., & Thompson, J. K. (2007). Fat stigmatization in television shows and movies: A content analysis. *Obesity, 15*(3), 712–718.

Marchant, A., Hawton, K., Stewart, A., Montgomery, P., Singaravelu, V., Lloyd, K., . . . John A. (2017). A systematic review of the relationship between internet use, self-harm and suicidal behavior in young people: The good, the bad and the unknown. *PLOS ONE, 12*(8), 1–26.

Puhl, R. M., Moss-Racusin, C. A., & Schwartz, M. B. (2007). Internalization of weight bias: Implications for binge eating and emotional well-being. *Obesity, 15*(1), 19–23.

Puhl, R. M., Moss-Racusin, C. A., Schwartz, M. B., & Brownwell, K. D. (2008). Weight stigmatization and bias reduction: Perspectives of overweight and obese adults. *Health Education Research, 23*(2), 347–358.

Puhl, R. M., Quinn, D. M., Weisz, B. M., & Suh, Y. J. (2017). The role of stigma in weight loss maintenance among U.S. adults. *Annals of Behavioral Medicine, 51*(5), 754–763. doi:10.1007/ s12160-017-9898-9

APPENDIX

An appendix includes additional materials that were central to the study, such as the Facebook post that produced the comments analyzed in the present study. Note that the post includes a photo of an identifiable person. Although the post was in the public domain, it was necessary from an ethical perspective to obtain permission to reproduce this image from its originator (see acknowledgements at the end).

If the report is for an instructor in a research methods class, the appendix might include additional information on how the sample was selected, how the data were collected or compiled, or even include the raw data. Generally, an appendix includes additional material that would be beneficial to readers and other researchers. For example, if the study was based on interviews, interview guidelines might be included in the appendix so the reader has access to the essential questions.

 Body Image Movement is with Taz Jane.
April 20, 2013 · ⏱ · 🌐

Here is my non traditional before and after photo. Traditionally when we see a "before" photo, the person is represented as sad, overweight and quite miserable. (sometimes even holding a newspaper!) Miraculously in the "after" photos once they have shed a few pounds they are blissfully happy, confident and self assured.

Have we become conditioned to thinking that we should only love our bodies when it's in "perfect condition"?

I just wanted to share with you that I loved my body on the stage, prancing around in a bikini as much as I loved my body sitting butt naked in my girlfriends studio.

Our bodies will go through many changes in our life. Our bodies change through ageing, pregnancy, illness, weight loss, weight gain the list goes on. One thing we must learn to do is love our bodies before, during and after....

Be loyal to your body, love your body, it's the only one you've got.

www.bodyimagemovement.com.au

👍 Like   💬 Comment   ↗ Share

A list of
acknowledgements
is included to pay
tribute to individuals
and/or organizations
that were integral to
the research project.

Acknowledgements

The researcher wishes to express gratitude to Taryn Brumfitt, founder of The Body Image Movement, person shown in the photos, and originator of the Facebook post that produced the comments analyzed in this study. Taryn Brumfitt provided permission to include the post containing her pictures in this sample report and accompanying sample poster.

MacEwan UNIVERSITY

Body Image in an Online Environment
A Content Analysis of Reactions to a Body Positive Post on Facebook
Jessica Gillard

Abstract

This study examined public reactions to a Facebook post depicting Taz Jane's love for her "before" and "after" body where her before self was a thin young model versus an older average-sized nude. A content analysis on the 150 most recent comments about Taz Jane's contributions to the positive Body Image Movement identified seven themes including: physical appearance, body standards, children and family life, gender, health and fitness, media, and self-esteem. The most prevalent theme was physical appearance, comprising approximately 48.7% of the comments. While mainly encouraging towards Taz Jane's current body and efforts, the views also emphasised ways in which females continue to be negatively impacted by society's preoccupation with weight and unrealistic body image ideals.

Introduction

Weight-related Stereotypes

Body image ideals that permeate Western society emphasize thinness, and this is reflected in the stigma that overweight individuals experience (Puhl, Moss-Racusin, Schwartz, & Brownell, 2008). The expression of negative weight-based assumptions increases the likelihood of individuals developing poor self-esteem and disordered eating habits.

The Role of Media

Through analyzing popular media, fat stigmatization has been found in television and film media, with most taking the form of verbal comments originating with male characters (Himes & Thompson, 2007). Internet use, while it can provide mental health support, is generally associated with negative psychological outcomes and poor adolescent self-worth (de Vries, Peter, de Graaf, & Nikkan, 2016; Marchant et al. 2017).

The Present Study

A content analysis was conducted to examine the nature of Facebook reactions made in comments to a post challenging weight stigma and depicting body love as part of the Body Image Movement.

Method

The Facebook status examined in this study was posted by Body Image Movement on April 21, 2013 at 6:14 am. The post by Taz Jane was selected because of its high number of "shares" (19,000), demonstrating an impactful message that would initiate discussion. The post (shown on the left) contains a non-traditional "before" and "after" photo that features weight gain, rather than loss as a challenge to the prevailing standards. A total of 2,879 comments were made in response.

The units of analysis for this study were the words and phrases in the most recent 150 comments made in reaction to Taz Jane's positive body contribution. Each comment was examined individually and open-coded for key words, phrases or constructs that captured the meaning or intent of the statement. Comments were then re-evaluated for the presence of general themes.

Results

Findings

Results indicated a range of topics in reactions to the body positive post from feedback about the narrative and photos, to self disclosures, and statements made about society more broadly on issues about weight, gender, and body image (see Table 1). Within the comments, seven overall main themes emerged:

Physical Appearance: comments about body parts and looks, either in reference to the image or in general.

Body Standards: refers to explicit and implicit societal norms regarding perceived ideal body types.

Children and Family: discusses childbirth, childrearing, and family life more broadly.

Gender: refers to the experiences of men and women.

Health and Fitness: includes comments about physical and mental health.

Media: consists of references to media sources.

Self-esteem: responses that reflect self-worth and body image.

User responses predominantly discussed physical appearance (see Figure 1), often including positive or negative personal evaluations of body parts.

Table 1: Examples of Comments by Theme

Figure 1: Percentage of Comments by Theme

Conclusion

Social Media and Body Image

The most predominant theme identified in this study was physical appearance, and comments tended to include evaluations of the physical appearance of the person in the Facebook post, themselves, or appearance more generally. This finding illustrates the societal value of looking a particular way, often in accordance with a normative ideal.

Gendered Experiences

Issues pertaining to body dissatisfaction, societal criticism, and pressure to be healthy were overwhelmingly described as a part of the female experience. Concerns were raised that these issues affect adolescents at young ages. In contrast, men were discussed, most often negatively, as being the evaluators of female appearance.

Weight in Relation to Health

The relationship between physical health and body size was a common debate. Weight was described as an indicator of how fit and motivated an individual is, reflecting stereotypes of obesity (Puhl, Moss-Racusin, & Schwartz, 2007). Literature suggests the detrimental effects of these assumptions, and therefore further research aimed at changing weight-based attitudes may better promote physical and mental wellbeing.

References

de Vries, D. A., Peter, J., de Graaf, H., & Nikken, P. (2016). Adolescents' social networks site use, peer appearance-related feedback, and body dissatisfaction: Testing a mediation model. *Journal of Youth & Adolescence, 45*(1), 211-224.

Himes, S. M., & Thompson, J. K. (2007). Fat stigmatization in television shows and movies: A content analysis. *Obesity, 15*(3), 712-718.

Marchant, A., Hawton, K., Stewart, A., Montgomery, P., Singaravelu, V., Lloyd, K., ... John A. (2017). A systematic review of the relationship between internet use, self-harm and suicidal behaviour in young people: The good, the bad and the unknown. *PLOS ONE, 12*(8), 1-26.

Puhl, R. M., Moss-Racusin, C. A., & Schwartz, M. B. (2007). Internalization of weight bias: Implications for binge eating and emotional well-being. *Obesity, 15*(1), 19-23.

Puhl, R. M., Moss-Racusin, C. A., Schwartz, M. B. & Brownell, K. D. (2008). Weight stigmatization and bias reduction: Perspectives of overweight and obese adults. *Health Education Research, 23*(2), 347-358.

Puhl, R. M., Quinn, D. M., Weisz, B. M., & Suh, Y. J. (2017). The role of stigma in weight loss maintenance among U.S. adults. *Annals of Behavioral Medicine, 51*(5), 754-763.

Acknowledgements

- The mentorship of Dr. Diane Symbaluk in Sociology 315 (Winter 2018).
- Taz Jane's Body Image Movement Post was reprinted with the explicit permission of the originator/individual shown in the photos, Taryn Brumfitt.

ABOUT THE AUTHOR

I am a professor in the Department of Sociology at MacEwan University in Alberta, where I teach a range of courses, including second-year lecture-based classes (e.g., criminology, social psychology), third- and fourth-year classes (social research methods, advanced qualitative methods), a senior seminar, and an advanced social psychology seminar.

I earned all three of my degrees at the University of Alberta, where I was fortunate enough to be mentored by professors with expertise in a range of methods, including behaviourists who conducted experiments (Drs. W. David Pierce and the late W. Frank Epling), demographers who specialized in survey research (Drs. Frank Trovato and Parameswara Krishnan), criminologists who worked with data on risk assessment and offenders or studied victims and vulnerable populations (Drs. Robert Silverman, Leslie W. Kennedy, Helen Boritch, and James Creechan), sociologists recognized for their contributions in evaluation research (Dr. John Gartrell) and human factors research (Dr. W. Andrew Harrell), and an educational psychologist who helped me understand the merits of using a statistical methodology called meta-analysis (Dr. Judy Cameron).

I introduced social research methods in the winter of 1997 and added advanced qualitative methods to the course offerings in 2010. While I have conducted experiments, designed surveys, carried out observational studies, moderated focus groups, and administered in-depth interviews as part of my own scholarly activity and service, my primary passion is teaching. As a result, most of my published research emphasizes features of teaching and learning, culminating in pedagogical tools designed to aid instructors and students, including textbooks, manuals, engagement activities, study guides, test banks, PowerPoints, chapter resources, homework modules, and online supplements. For more information on my research interests and recent work, visit my home page at https://tinyurl.com/y5v6gyqs.

GLOSSARY

abstract—a brief overview of a research project, which describes the participants or units of observation, the design, the procedures, and the main findings in 120 words or less

accretion measures—patterns of selective use and non-use based on accumulation

action research—social research carried out by a team that encompasses a professional action researcher and the members of an organization, community, or network (stakeholders) who are seeking to improve the participants' situation

active listening—a technique in which the interviewer demonstrates an understanding of what is being said and expressed through appropriate feedback

alteration of documentation of informed consent—an informed consent discussion that takes place with each participant in the setting in lieu of a signed informed consent statement

anonymity—a state of being unknown. In the case of research, this means a researcher cannot link any individual response to its originator

applied research—scientific research that is conducted to address a problem or issue

archives—historical documents, records, or collections detailing the activities of businesses, agencies, institutions, governments, groups, or individuals

attitude questions—questions designed to measure points of view toward an attitude object, such as a person or an event

audit trails—attempts made by a researcher to carefully document the research process in its entirety

authority—a source of information that is perceived to possess specialized knowledge

basic experimental design—an experimental design that includes random assignment, an experimental and a control group, the manipulation of an independent variable, and a post-test measurement of the dependent variable

basic research—scientific research that is conducted to advance knowledge

behaviour questions—questions designed to find out more about the respondent's activities

beneficence—a moral principle outlining that in the planning and conducting of research with human participants, the researcher maximizes the possible benefits and minimizes the potential harms from the research

between-subjects design—a type of design in which the experimental group is exposed to only one level of the independent variable

case study—research on a small number of individuals or an organization carried out over an extended period

classic experimental design—an experimental design that includes random assignment, an experimental and a control group, a pre-test measure of a dependent variable, the manipulation of an independent variable, and a post-test measure of the same dependent variable

closed-ended questions—a question prompting an answer selected from a pre-determined set of responses provided

closing questions—questions used to bring closure to the interview by re-establishing distance between the interviewer and interviewee

cluster sampling—a probability-based method for selecting groups for a sample, based on their geographic location

codebook—a detailed listing of how each variable is coded in the data set, along with information on the methodology underlying the original study

coding—the process of transforming raw data into a standardized form

cohort study—research on the same category of people carried out at multiple points in time

common sense—practical knowledge based on adaptive forms of prior learning

complete observer—a participant observation role in which the researcher covertly observes a group but is not a group member and does not participate in any way

complete participant—a covert participant observation role in which the researcher systematically observes a group as a full member whose identity and research purpose is unknown to the group members

computer-assisted telephone interviews (CATI)—a telephone-based interview method in which the interviewer inputs survey responses directly into a software program

concepts—abstract mental representations of important elements in our social world

conceptualization—the process where a researcher explains what a concept means in terms of a research project

concern for welfare—steps taken to protect the welfare of research participants, in terms of both harm and other foreseeable risks associated with participation in a given study

confidence interval—an estimated range that is likely to contain the true population value based on the sample value

confidentiality—the process of maintaining privacy. In research, this means even when a participant's identity is known to the researcher, steps are taken to make sure it is not made public

construct—intangible idea that does not exist independent of our thinking

construct validity—assesses the extent to which an instrument is associated with other logically related measures of the intended construct

content analysis—a repertoire of methods that allows researchers to make inferences from all kinds of verbal, pictorial, symbolic, and communication data

content validity—assesses the extent to which an instrument contains the full range of content pertaining to the intended construct

context—a complicated notion that locates and explains action-interaction within a background of conditions and anticipated consequences

contingency question—a question prompting additional information about a previous item identified as relevant for the respondent

continuous real-time measurement—an observation-based data coding method in which every separate and distinct instance of a variable is recorded during a set observation period

control group—the group that does not experience the independent variable in an experiment

convenience sampling—a non-probability method used to obtain a sample based on availability

convergent design—a mixed-methods design in which qualitative and quantitative methods are employed concurrently, with independent data collection and analysis compared in the final interpretation

cost-benefit analysis—a method for assessing the overall costs incurred by a program relative to outcome measures

coverage error—a type of error that results when the list from which sample members are drawn does not accurately represent the population on the characteristic(s) one wants to estimate with the survey data

credibility—an assessment of the goodness of fit between the respondent's view of reality and a researcher's representation of it

criterion validity—assesses the extent to which an instrument holds up to an external standard, such as the ability to predict future events

critical paradigm—a worldview that is critical of paradigms that fail to acknowledge the role of power in the creation of knowledge and that aims to bring about empowering change

cross-sectional research—research conducted at a single point in time

cultural relativism—an ability to understand another culture in its own terms sympathetically enough so that the culture appears to be a coherent and meaningful design for living

data—information gathered through research techniques

data format—the statistical format in which data are saved or stored

data structure—the number and organizational nature of distinct files that compose a data collection and the relationship among those data

data triangulation—the reliance on multiple data sources in a single study

debriefing—the full disclosure and exchange of information that occurs upon completion of a study

decolonization—a process of conducting research in such a way that the worldview of those who have suffered a long history of oppression and marginalization are given space to communicate from their frames of reference

deductive reasoning—a theory-driven approach that typically concludes with empirical generalizations based on research findings

demographic questions—questions designed to collect facts about a respondent's age, race/ethnicity, education, job, gender, marital status, geographic place of residence, type of residence, size of family, and so on

dependability—an assessment of the researcher's process as well documented and verifiable

dependent variable—the variable that is measured in an experiment and is the outcome

descriptive research—research undertaken to identify the main traits or characteristics of a population or phenomenon of interest

digital media—all computer-mediated internet and digitally enabled media through which data can be collected, shared, and analyzed

disproportionate sampling—a sampling method used deliberately to obtain a different ratio of relevant characteristics than what exists in the population

double-barrelled question—a question prompting a single answer to a combination of questions

empirical methods—data collection techniques carried out using systematic procedures that are widely recognized by other researchers and produce verifiable findings

encoding—a data-reduction method used to simplify observations by using categorizations

erosion measures—patterns of selective use based on wear

essential questions—questions that exclusively concern the central focus of the study

ethics—conduct that is considered "morally right" or "morally wrong," as specified by codified and culturally ingrained principles, constraints, rules, and guidelines

ethnographers—social scientists who undertake research and writing about groups of people by systematically observing and participating (to a greater or lesser degree) in the lives of the people they study

ethnography—a multi-method approach to field research that is used to study a social group or culture in its natural setting over time

exhaustive—comprehensive enough to include all likely responses

experience—first-hand observations or recollections of first-hand events that serve as sources of knowledge

experiment—a research method in which a researcher manipulates an independent variable to examine its effects on a dependent variable

experimental group—the group that experiences the independent variable in an experiment

experimental mortality—the course of participant drop-out over time

experimenter bias—the tendency for researchers to influence the behaviour of research participants in a manner that favours the outcomes they anticipate

explanatory design—a mixed-methods design in which a quantitative method is employed first and then the findings are followed up on using a qualitative method

explanatory research—research undertaken to clarify the variation found between groups on some dimension of interest

exploratory design—a mixed-methods design in which a qualitative method is employed first and then the findings are used to help develop a subsequent quantitative-method–based phase

exploratory research—research undertaken to find out more about an area of interest

external validity—the generalizability of an experimental effect

extra questions—questions roughly equivalent to essential ones that are used to assess reliability

evaluation research—research undertaken to assess whether a program or policy is effective in reaching its desired goals and objectives

face validity—assesses the extent to which an instrument appears to be a good measure of the intended construct

field experiment—a naturally occurring experiment that takes place in a real-life setting

field notes—detailed records about what a researcher hears, sees, experiences, and thinks about while immersed in the social setting

figures—charts or graphs used to display results based on how a variable is measured

final question—the last interview question, in the form of a general inquiry to determine if the participant has any questions about the study or further comments to make

focus group—a small discussion group led by a skilled interviewer that is designed to obtain views and feelings about a topic of interest through group interaction

follow-up questions—questions specific to comments made that are used to clarify main ideas

garbology—the study of behaviour based on the analysis of waste

gatekeepers—people who have power to grant or deny permission to do a study in the field

graffiti—a form of visual communication, usually illegal, involving the unauthorized marking of public space by an individual or group

grounded theory—theory discovered from the systematic observation and analysis of data

history—changes in the dependent measure attributed to external events outside the experiment

hypothesis—a testable statement that contains at least two variables

icebreaker—an opening question that is used specifically to establish rapport

illogical reasoning—faulty decision making based on a failure to consider the most appropriate sources of information

imprecise observations—everyday errors made as a function of our limited ability to perceive, store, and later accurately recall information

independent evaluation—an evaluation that is headed up by a researcher who is not a primary stakeholder for the program under consideration

independent variable—the variable that is manipulated in an experiment and is presumed to be the cause of some outcome

index—a composite measure of a construct comprising several different indicators that produce a shared outcome

indicator—a measurable quantity that in some sense stands for or substitutes for something less readily measurable

Indigenous knowledges—diverse learning processes that come from living intimately with the land and working with the resources surrounding the land base and the relationships that it has fostered over time and place

inductive reasoning—a bottom-up approach beginning with observations and ending with the discovery of patterns and themes informed by theory

informed consent—a process where potential participants are provided with all relevant details of the study needed to make a knowledgeable judgment about whether to participate in it

instrumentation—differences produced by changes in the way the dependent variable is measured

inter-item reliability—demonstrated associations among multiple items representing a single concept

internal validity—the capacity to demonstrate an experimental effect and to rule out rival explanations for that effect

interpretive paradigm—a worldview that rests on the assumption that reality is socially constructed and must be understood from the perspective of those experiencing it

inter-rater reliability—consistency between the same measures for a variable of interest provided by two independent raters

interval level of measurement—a level of measurement in which the distance between categories of the variable of interest is meaningful

interview guide—a series of key questions that provide the framework for an interview

justice—a moral principle of rightness claiming that in the course of research, researchers behave and make decisions in a manner that demonstrates social responsibility in relation to the distribution of harm versus benefits

key insider—a member of the setting who is willing to act as a guide or assistant within the setting

knowledge questions—questions designed to gauge whether respondents can retrieve and correctly report on facts about some area of interest

latent content—implied meaning inferred by the message

longitudinal research—research conducted at multiple points in time

macro level—the level of broader social forces

manifest content—content stated in the message itself

maturation—changes in the dependent measure that result from naturally occurring processes within the research participants themselves over the period of treatment

member checks—attempts made by a researcher to validate findings by testing them with the original sources of the data

micro level—the level of individual experiences and choices

mixed-methods approach—a research design that includes an explicit combination of qualitative and quantitative methods as framed by the research objectives

moderator—a trained facilitator used in focus group research who guides the focus group discussion

multiple-case design—a case study strategy that focuses on two or more persons, organizations, events, or programs selected for the explicit purpose of comparison

mutually exclusive—response categories that are separate and distinct from each other

needs assessment—a systematic evaluation focused on improving an existing condition through the identification of a problem and a means for addressing it

negative question—a question comprising the negative form of a statement

nominal level of measurement—a level of measurement used to classify cases

non-probability sampling—a method in which the chance of selection of an individual or element in the population is unknown

non-response error—the difference between the estimate produced when only some of the sampled units respond compared to when all of them respond

Nuremberg Code—a set of ethical directives for human experimentation

observer as participant—an overt participant observation role in which the researcher systematically observes a group but is not a group member and only interacts indirectly with the group

one-shot case study—a quasi-experimental design lacking a control group, in which one group is examined following a treatment

open-ended questions—a question prompting any response deemed appropriate in the participant's own words

operationalization—the process whereby a concept or construct is defined so precisely that it can be measured

order effects—differences in the dependent variable that result from the order in which the independent variable is presented

ordinal level of measurement—a level of measurement used to order cases along some dimension of interest

overgeneralization—the tendency to assume the existence of a general pattern based on a limited number of observed cases

panel study—research on the same unit of analysis carried out at multiple points in time

paradigm—a theoretical perspective including a set of assumptions about reality that guide research questions

participant as observer—an overt participant-observation role in which the researcher systematically observes a group by becoming a group member to establish relationships and interact directly with the group

participant observation—a research method in which the researcher is involved with the group being observed over an extended period

participant reactivity—the tendency for research participants to act differently during a study simply because they are aware that they are participating in a research study

peer debriefing—attempts made by a researcher to authenticate the research process and findings through an external review provided by an independent researcher

periodicals—publications that contain articles written by different authors and are released at regular intervals

physical traces—the remnants, fragments, and products of past behaviour

population—the total collection of all cases in which the researcher is interested and that they wish to understand better

positivist paradigm—a worldview that upholds the importance of discovering truth through direct experience using empirical methods

pragmatic paradigm—a worldview that rests on the assumption that reality is best understood in terms of the practical consequences of actions undertaken to solve problems

premature closure—the tendency to stop searching for necessary observations due to an erroneous belief that the answer has already been determined

primary research—first-hand data collection and data analysis that are undertaken to answer an original research question

private archives—personal records that are usually directed at a small known target or are produced only for use by the originating author

probability sampling—a method in which every individual or element in the population has a known chance of being selected

probes—questions used to motivate an interviewee to continue speaking or to elaborate on a topic

program evaluation—a systematic method for collecting and analyzing information used to answer questions about a program of interest

public archives—public records that are prepared specifically to be examined by others

purposive sampling—a non-probability method in which a researcher uses a combination of techniques to obtain all possible cases that possess the desired characteristics of the population of interest

qualitative interview—a technique used to understand the world from the subjects' point of view, to unfold the meaning of their experiences, and to uncover the world prior to scientific explanations

qualitative research method—a technique that seeks to explore, interpret, explain, or evaluate a phenomenon of interest and produces non-numerical data

quantitative research method—a technique that seeks to describe, explain, or evaluate a phenomenon of interest and produces numerical data

quasi-experimental designs—an experimental design that lacks one or more of the basic features of a true experiment, including random assignment or a control group

questionnaire—a survey data collection instrument consisting of a series of questions or items to which a respondent provides responses containing the information of interest to the researcher

quota sampling—a non-probability method used to obtain a similar proportion of some characteristic of interest in a sample as exists in the population

random assignment—a method for assigning cases in which chance alone determines receipt of the experimental manipulation

random digit dialing—a technique used to generate a random sample of phone numbers from a sampling frame created using the assigned area codes for a given location

random errors—measurement miscalculation due to unpredictable mistakes

rate of response—the percentage of those sampled for whom data are collected

ratio level of measurement—an interval level of measurement with an absolute zero

reflexivity—a self-reflection process in which researchers consider the ways in which their own subjectivities may have influenced the research outcomes

regression—differences produced by the tendency for extreme scores to become less extreme

reliability—consistency in measurement

representative sample—a sample with the same aggregate characteristics as the population from which it was selected

research design—the plan or blueprint for a study, outlining the who, what, where, when, why, and how of an investigation

research ethics—an array of considerations that arise in relation to the morally responsible treatment of humans in research

research ethics board—a committee whose mandate is to review the ethical acceptability of research on behalf of the institution, including approving, rejecting, proposing modifications to, or terminating any proposed or ongoing research involving humans

research methods—techniques for carrying out research to answer questions of interest

research proposal—a comprehensive plan created in advance of carrying out research that details what the purpose of the project is and what the process will be for obtaining data

research report—a detailed account, following research, that describes the research interest, questions or hypotheses addressed, methods used, and findings from the study

respect for human dignity—a value necessitating that research involving humans be conducted in a manner that is sensitive to the inherent worth of all human beings and the respect and consideration that they are due

respect for persons—a moral principle stressing that researchers respect the human participants in their investigations as persons of worth whose participation is a matter of autonomous choice

rigour—a means for demonstrating integrity and competence in qualitative research

sample—a subset of the population of interest that comprises the unit of analysis in a study

sampling—the technique or process used to acquire the unit of analysis from a population of interest

sampling error—the difference between the sample statistic and the population parameter

sampling frame—the complete list of individuals or elements making up the population

sampling interval—the fixed interval used to select every nth case listed after a random starting point is obtained

scale—a composite measure of a construct consisting of several different indicators that stem from a common cause

secondary analysis of existing data—examination of data originally collected by someone other than the researcher for a different purpose

secondary research—the summation or analysis of research already collected by others

selection—methods used to obtain groups that can result in differences prior to the experimental manipulation

selection by maturation interaction—a combined effect of maturation and initial differences in the groups at the onset of the study

selection by treatment interaction—a threat to external validity produced by the self-selection of participants susceptible to the independent variable

selective deposit—a bias resulting from the greater likelihood of establishing certain physical traces over others

selective observation—the tendency to assume a general pattern exists based on factors other than objective frequency

selective survival—a bias resulting from the greater likelihood of certain physical traces persisting over time

semi-structured interview—a somewhat flexible interview format in which main questions are prepared ahead of time but the questions can be modified or clarified based on participant feedback

simple random sampling—a probability-based method used to obtain individuals or cases that make up a sample, based on chance alone

single-case design—a case study strategy that focuses on only one person, organization, event, or program as the unit of analysis, as emphasized by the research objectives

snowball sampling—a non-probability method used to obtain a sample based on one available case, followed by associated referrals

social domain personal archive—personal information that is posted to public arenas using social media such as Facebook or Twitter

social research—a process in which people combine a set of principles, outlooks, and ideas with a collection of specific practices, techniques, and strategies to produce knowledge

social research question—a question about the social world that is answered through the collection and analysis of first-hand, verifiable, empirical data

split-half reliability—consistency between both halves of the measure for a variable of interest

stakeholders—an individual, group, or organization that is directly or indirectly involved with or impacted by the program of interest

static group comparison—a quasi-experimental design lacking random assignment in which two groups are compared following a treatment

step-wise consent process—a consent process that takes place in stages following the establishment of relationships within a group

stratified sampling—a probability-based method used to obtain a sample, based on known population characteristics

structured observation—a quantitative approach in which behaviour is observed and coded using pre-determined categories

survey—an information collection method used to describe, compare, or explain individual and societal knowledge, feelings, values, preferences, and behaviours

survey interview—a highly structured data collection method consisting of a series of prescribed questions or items asked by an interviewer who records the answers provided by the respondent

systematic errors—miscalculation due to consistently inaccurate measures or intentional bias

systematic sampling—a probability-based method used to obtain a sample based on a fixed interval representing every *n*th case listed

tables—summaries of main findings from quantitative research, such as the percentage of respondents who gave answers in each category of a variable on a questionnaire or the differences in means between groups on dependent measures

testing—changes in the dependent measure that result from experience gained on the pre-test

test-retest reliability—consistency between the same measures for a variable of interest taken at two different points in time

theoretical frameworks—a perspective based on core assumptions

theoretical sampling—a concept-driven method for obtaining data used in qualitative research

theory—a set of propositions intended to explain a fact or phenomenon

throw-away questions—questions unrelated to the research topic that are used to take breaks in the conversation

time-interval sampling—an observation-based data coding method in which variables are recorded at the end of each set time interval throughout a set observation period

time-series study—research on different units of analysis carried out at multiple points in time

tradition—a familiar compilation of beliefs and practices passed down from one generation to the next

transcription—a data-entry process in which the obtained verbal information is transferred verbatim into text

transition statement—statements that move the conversation into the essential questions

triangulation—the use of multiple methods or sources to help establish rigour

unit of analysis—the object of investigation

unobtrusive research methods—strategies in which the researcher examines evidence of people's behaviour or attitudes rather than interacting directly with those being studied

unstructured interview—a highly flexible interview format based on questions that develop during the interaction as a result of participant feedback

validity—the extent to which a study examines what it intends to

variable—a categorical concept for properties of people or events that can differ and change

virtual ethnography—an in-depth study of a group or culture that exists in an online environment

visual ethnography—representations of culture as depicted in photographs and film documentaries

within-subjects design—a type of design in which the experimental group is exposed to all possible levels of the independent variable

REFERENCES

Abel, E. L., & Buckley, B. E. (1977). *The handwriting on the wall: Toward a sociology and psychology of graffiti*. Westport, CT: Greenwood.

Adair, J. G. (2001). Ethics of psychological research: New policies; continuing issues; new concerns. *Canadian Psychology, 42*(1), 25–37.

Alberta Fishing Guide. (2019). Fishing zones. Retrieved from http://www.albertafishingguide.com

Alberta's Tomorrow Project. (2018a). All about Alberta's Tomorrow Project. Calgary, AB: Alberta Health Services. Retrieved from https://myatp.ca/about-atp/our-history

Alberta's Tomorrow Project. (2018b). Common questions from our participants. Calgary, AB: Alberta Health Services. Retrieved from https://myatp.ca/for-participants/faqs

Allen, A. (1999). *The power of feminist theory: Domination, resistance, solidarity*. Boulder, CO: Westview Press.

Alonso, A. (1998, February 14). *Urban graffiti on the city landscape*. Paper presented at the Western Geography Graduate Conference, San Diego State University. Retrieved from www.streetgangs.com/academic/alonsograffiti.pdf

Anderson, E. E., & Corneli, A. (2018). *100 questions (and answers) about research ethics*. Thousand Oaks, CA: Sage.

Annenberg Learner. (2017). Random sampling. Data analysis, statistics, & probability. Session 1, part D: Bias in sampling. Annenberg Foundation. Retrieved from http://www.learner.org/courses/learningmath/data/session1/part_d/random_noflash.html

Ardévol, E. (2012). Virtual/visual ethnography: Methodological crossroads at the interaction of visual and internet research. In S. Pink (Ed.), *Advances in visual methodology* (pp. 74–93). Thousand Oaks, CA: Sage.

Aronson, E., Wilson, T. D., Fehr, B., & Akert, R. M. (2017). *Social psychology* (6th Can. ed.). Toronto, ON: Pearson Education Canada.

Asch, S. E. (1946). Forming impressions of personality. *Journal of Abnormal Social Psychology, 41*(3), 258–290.

Atkeson, L. R., & Alvarez, R. M. (2018). *The Oxford handbook of polling and survey methods*. New York, NY: Oxford University Press.

Atkinson, P. (2017). *Thinking ethnographically*. Thousand Oaks, CA: Sage.

Auschwitz-Birkenau State Museum. (2019). Medical experiments in Auschwitz. In *History*. Oświęcim, PO: Państwowe Muzeum Auschwitz-Birkenau w Oświęcimiu. Retrieved from http://en.auschwitz.org/h/index.php?option=com_content&task=view&id=12&Itemid=10&limit=1&limitstart=0

Babbie, E., & Roberts, L. W. (2018). *Fundamentals of social research* (4th Can. ed.). Toronto, ON: Nelson Education.

Babbie, R. (1990). *Survey research methods* (2nd ed.). Belmont, CA: Wadsworth.

Bachrach, C. (2007). Taking stock: Do surveys of men's fertility deliver? In S. L. Hofferth & L. M. Casper (Eds.). *Handbook of measurement issues in family research* (pp. 325–332). Mahwah, NJ: Lawrence Erlbaum Associates.

Bailey, C. A. (1996). *A guide to field research.* Thousand Oaks, CA: Pine Forge Press.

Bailey, C. A. (2017). *A guide to qualitative fieldwork* (3rd ed.). Thousand Oaks, CA: Sage.

Banks, M., & Zeitlyn, D. (2015). Visual methods in social research (2nd ed.). *Visual methods in social research.* Thousand Oaks, CA: Sage.

Bansal, H., & Eiselt, H. A. (2004). Exploratory research of tourist motivations and planning. *Tourism Management, 25*(3), 387–396.

Battiste, M. (2000). *Reclaiming Indigenous voice and vision.* Vancouver, BC: UBC Press.

Battiste, M. (2013). *Decolonizing education: Nourishing the learning spirit.* Saskatoon, SK: Purich.

Baumrind, D. (1964). Some thoughts on ethics of research: After reading Milgram's "Behavioral Study of Obedience." *American Psychologist, 19*(6), 421–423.

Bedi, R. P., Young, C. N., Davari, J. A., Springer, K. L., & Kane, D. P. (2016). A content analysis of gendered research in the Canadian Journal of Counselling and Psychotherapy. *Canadian Journal of Counselling and Psychotherapy, 50*(4), 365–383.

Beins, B. C. (2017). *Research methods: A tool for life* (3rd ed.). Cambridge, UK: Cambridge University Press.

Belanger, Y. D. (2018). *Ways of knowing: An introduction to Native studies in Canada* (3rd ed.). Toronto, ON: Nelson Education.

Bell Media. (2018). About us. Retrieved from https://www.bellmedia.ca/about-bellmedia

Bendriss, N. (2014). *Report on the practice of forced marriage in Canada: Interviews with frontline workers: Exploratory research conducted in Montréal and Toronto in 2008.* Ottawa, ON: Department of Justice Canada.

Bergin, T. (2018). *An introduction to data analysis: Quantitative, qualitative and mixed methods.* Thousand Oaks, CA: Sage.

Bernard, H. R. (2018). *Research methods in anthropology: Qualitative and quantitative approaches* (6th ed.). Lanham, MD: Rowman & Littlefield.

Berscheid, E., & Reiss, H. T. (1998). Attraction and close relationships. In D. Gilbert, S. Fiske, & G. Lindzey (Eds.), *The handbook of social psychology* (4th ed., pp. 193–281). New York, NY: McGraw-Hill.

Bianchi, S. (2011). Family change and time allocation in American families. *Annals of the American Academy of Political and Social Sciences, 638*(1), 21–44.

Blair, J., Czaja, R. F., & Blair, E. A. (2014). *Designing surveys: A guide to decisions and procedures.* Thousand Oaks, CA: Sage.

Bloch, A. (2013). The labour market experiences and strategies of young undocumented migrants. *Work, Employment and Society, 27*(2), 272–287.

Bogardus, E. S. (1933). A social distance scale. *Sociology and Social Research, 17*(3), 265–271.

Boulianne, S., Loptson, K., & Kahane, D. (2018). Citizen panels and opinion polls: Convergence and divergence in policy preferences, *Journal of Public Deliberation, 14*(1). Retrieved from https://www.publicdeliberation.net/cgi/viewcontent.cgi?article=1504&context=jpd

Bouma, G. D., Ling, R., & Wilkinson, L. (2016). *The research process* (3rd Can. ed.). Don Mills, ON: Oxford University Press.

Bowman, T. (1997). Facing loss of dreams: A special kind of grief. *International Journal of Palliative Nursing, 3*(2), 76–80.

Boyd, A. D., Jardine, C. G., & Driedger, S. M. (2009). Canadian representations of mad cow disease. *Journal of Toxicology & Environmental Health, 72*(17/18), 1096–1105.

Brace, I. (2018). *Questionnaire design: How to plan, structure and write survey material for effective market research* (4th ed.). London, UK: Kogan Page.

Bradburn, N., Sudman, S., & Wansink, B. (2004). *Asking questions: The definitive guide to questionnaire design.* San Francisco, CA: John Wiley & Sons.

Brinkmann, S., & Vale, S. (2015). *Interviews: Learning the craft of qualitative research interviewing* (3rd ed.). Thousand Oaks, CA: Sage.

Bryman, A. (2008). Why do researchers integrate/combine/blend/mix/merge/fuse quantitative and qualitative research? In M. M. Bergman (Ed.), *Advances in mixed methods research: Theories and applications* (pp. 87–100). Thousand Oaks, CA: Sage.

Bryman, A., & Bell, E. (2016). *Social research methods* (4th Can. ed.). Don Mills, ON: Oxford University Press.

Bull, J. (2016). A two-eyed seeing approach to research ethics review: An Indigenous perspective. In W. C. van den Hoonaard & A. Hamilton (Eds.), *The ethics rupture: Exploring alternatives to formal research-ethics review* (pp. 167–186). Toronto, ON: University of Toronto Press.

Burger, J. M. (2009). Replicating Milgram: Would people still obey today? *American Psychologist, 64*(1), 1–11.

Burgess, J., Marwick, A., & Poell, T. (Eds.). (2018). *The Sage handbook of social media.* Thousand Oaks, CA: Sage.

Cabanac, M. (1986). Money versus pain: Experimental study of a conflict in humans. *Journal of the Experimental Analysis of Behavior, 46*(1), 37–44.

Callan, M. J., Ellard, J. H., Shead, N. W., & Hodgins, D. C. (2008). Gambling as a search for justice: Examining the role of personal relative deprivation in gambling urges and gambling behavior. *Personality and Social Psychology Bulletin, 34*(11), 1514–1529.

Campbell, D. T., & Stanley, J. C. (1963). *Experimental and quasi-experimental designs for research.* Chicago, IL: Rand McNally.

Canadian Council on Learning. (2009, February 18). Why don't boys like to read: Gender differences in reading achievement. *Lessons in Learning.* Retrieved from http://www.eric.ed.gov/PDFS/ED519285.pdf

Canadian Institutes of Health Research, Natural Sciences and Engineering Research Council of Canada, & Social Sciences and Humanities Research Council of Canada. (2014, December). *Tri-council policy statement: Ethical conduct for research involving humans.* Her Majesty the Queen in Right of Canada. Catalogue No: RR4-2/2014E-PDF.

Canadian Medical Association. (2004). *CMA code of ethics.* Ottawa, ON: Author. Retrieved from http://www.cpsa.ca/wp-content/uploads/2019/01/CMA_Policy_Code_of_ethics_of_the_Canadian_Medical_Association_Update_2004_PD04-06-e.pdf

Canadian Psychological Association. (2017). *Canadian code of ethics for psychologists* (4th ed.). Ottawa, ON: Author. Retrieved from https://www.cpa.ca/docs/File/Ethics/CPA_Code_2017_4thEd.pdf

Canadian Radio-television and Telecommunications Commission. (2018). Ownership chart. Québecor profile. Retrieved from https://crtc.gc.ca/ownership/eng/cht156.pdf

Canadian Sociological Association. (2012). *Statement of professional ethics.* Mississauga, ON: Author. Retrieved from https://www.csa-scs.ca/files/www/csa/documents/codeofethics/2012Ethics.pdf

CBC News. (2004, May 12). Vets exposed to mustard gas receive compensation. In Canada: Calgary. CBC News online. Retrieved from http://www.cbc.ca/news/canada/calgary/story/2004/05/12/ca_suffield20040512.html

Chambliss, D. F., & Schutt, R. K. (2019). *Making sense of the social world: Methods of investigation* (6th ed.). Thousand Oaks, CA: Sage.

Charlesworth, R. (2016, Winter). *Inequalities and resiliency among young Indigenous mothers.* Unpublished Final Report for the Community-Based Sociology Project. MacEwan University and iHuman Youth Society.

Charmaz, K. (1983). Loss of self: A fundamental form of suffering in the chronically ill. *Sociology of Health and Illness, 5*(2), 168–195.

Chawla, R. K., & Uppal, S. (2012). Household debt in Canada. Statistics Canada. Retrieved from http://www.statcan.gc.ca/pub/75-001-x/2012002/article/11636-eng.htm

Chilisa, B. (2012). *Indigenous research methodologies.* Thousand Oaks, CA: Sage.

Cho, Y. J., Thrasher, J. F., Swayampakala, K., Lipkus, I., Hammond, D., Cummings, K. M., . . . Hardin, J. W. (2018). Does adding information on toxic constituents to cigarette pack warnings increase smokers' perceptions about the health risks of smoking? A longitudinal study in Australia, Canada, Mexico, and the United States. *Health Education & Behavior, 45*(1), 32–42.

Cohen, J. (1960). A coefficient of agreement for nominal scales. *Educational and Psychological Measurement, 20*(1), 37–46.

Cohen, L., Manion, L., & Morrison, K. (2018). *Research methods in education* (8th ed.). New York, NY: Routledge.

Collier, J. Jr., & Collier, M. (1986). *Visual anthropology: Photography as a research method.* Albuquerque, NM: University of New Mexico Press.

Colosi, R. (2010). *Dirty dancing? An ethnography of lap-dancing.* New York, NY: Willan.

Corbin, J., & Strauss, A. (1988). *Unending work and care.* San Francisco, CA: Jossey-Bass.

Corbin, J., & Strauss, A. (2015). *Basics of qualitative research* (4th ed.). Thousand Oaks, CA: Sage.

Coté, J. (2009, September 20). Prostitution program badly flawed, audit finds. *San Francisco Chronicle*, p. C1. Retrieved from http://ehis.ebscohost.com.ezproxy.macewan.ca/eds/detail?vid=2&sid=ad169edb-4b67-48bb-85ac-ddef1d40d81a%40sessionmgr12&hid=17&bdata=JnNpdGU9ZWRzLWxpdmUmc2NvcGU9c2l0ZQ%3d%3d#db=bwh&AN=44239304

Cozby, P. C., & Bates, S. (2018). *Methods in behavioral research* (13th ed.). New York, NY: McGraw-Hill.

Creswell, J. W., & Creswell, J. D. (2018). *Research design: Qualitative, quantitative, and mixed method approaches* (5th ed.). Thousand Oaks, CA: Sage.

Cronbach, L. J. (1951). Coefficient alpha and the internal structure of tests. *Psychometrika, 16*(3), 297–334.

Czaja, R., & Blair, J. (1996). *Designing surveys: A guide to decisions and procedures.* Thousand Oaks, CA: Pine Forge Press.

David, M., & Sutton, C. D. (2011). *Social research: An introduction* (2nd ed.). Thousand Oaks, CA: Sage.

Davies, C. A. (2008). *Reflexive ethnography: A guide to researching selves and others* (2nd ed.). New York, NY: Routledge.

Decker, S. H., & Curry, G. D. (2017). Graffiti. *Encyclopaedia Britannica Online.* Retrieved from https://www.britannica.com/art/graffiti-art

De Craemer, M., De Decker, E., De Bourdeauhuij, I., Deforche, B., Vereecken, C., Duvinage, K., . . . Cardon, G. (2013). Physical activity and beverage consumption in preschoolers: Focus groups with parents and teachers. *BMC Public Health 2013, 13*(1), 1–13. Retrieved from http://www.biomedcentral.com/1471-2458/13/278

Deffenbacher, J. L., Lynch, R. S., Oetting, E. R., & Swaim, R. C. (2002). The driving anger expression inventory: A measure of how people express their anger on the road. *Behaviour Research and Therapy, 40*(6), 717–737.

DeJean, D., Giacomini, M., Schwartz, L., & Miller, F. A. (2009). Ethics in Canadian health technology assessment: A descriptive review. *International Journal of Technology Assessment in Health Care, 25*(4), 463–469.

Denzin, N. K., & Lincoln, Y. S. (Eds.). (2018). *The Sage Handbook of Qualitative Research* (5th ed.). Thousand Oaks, CA: Sage.

DeVault, M. L., & Gross, G. (2012). Feminist qualitative interviewing: Experience, talk, and knowledge. In Hesse-Biber, S. N. (Ed.), *The handbook of feminist research: Theory and praxis* (2nd ed., pp. 206–236). Thousand Oaks, CA: Sage.

DeVellis, R. F. (2017). *Scale development: Theory and applications* (4th ed.). Thousand Oaks, CA: Sage.

Dillman, D. A., Smyth, J. D., & Christian, L. M. (2014). *Internet, mail, and mixed-mode surveys: The tailored design method* (4th ed.). Hoboken, NJ: John Wiley & Sons.

DiscoverText. (2019). About our text analysis and data science software. Amherst, MA: Author. Retrieved from https://discovertext.com/

Djikic, M. (2011). The effect of music and lyrics on personality. *Psychology of Aesthetics, Creativity, and the Arts, 5*(3), 237–240.

Dorsten, L. E., & Hotchkiss, L. (2005). *Research methods and society: Foundations of social inquiry.* Upper Saddle River, NJ: Pearson Education.

Douglas, J. (1979). Living morality versus bureaucratic fiat. In C. B. Klockars & F. W. O'Connor (Eds.), *Deviance and decency* (pp. 13–33). Thousand Oaks, CA: Sage.

Dow, J., & Jacques, A. (2012). Educating doctors on evaluation of fitness to drive: Impact of a case-based workshop. *Journal of Continuing Education in the Health Professions, 32*(1), 68–73.

Downie, J., & Chandler, J. A. (2018). *Interpreting Canada's medical assistance in dying legislation.* Retrieved from http://irpp.org/wp-content/uploads/2018/03/Interpreting-Canadas-Medical-Assistance-in-Dying-Legislation-MAiD.pdf

Du Mont, J., Solomon, S., Kosa, S. D., & Macdonald, S. (2018). Development and evaluation of sexual assault training for emergency department staff in Ontario, Canada. *Nurse Education Today, 70*, 124–129.

EBSCO Industries. (2018). Academic Search Premier. Retrieved from https://www.ebsco.com/products/research-databases/academic-search-premier

Elliott, D., & Culhane, D. (2017). *A different kind of ethnography: Imaginative practices and creative methodologies.* Toronto, ON: University of Toronto Press.

Emmel, N. (2013). *Sampling and choosing cases in qualitative research: A realist approach.* Thousand Oaks, CA: Sage.

Engel, U., Jann, B., Lynn, P., Scherpenzeel, A., & Sturgis, P. (Eds.) (2015). *Improving survey methods: Lessons from recent research.* New York, NY: Routledge.

Evans, J. (2020). Counting crime. In R. Linden (Ed.), *Criminology: A Canadian perspective* (9th ed., pp. 91–120). Toronto, ON: Nelson Education.

Eysenck, S. B. G., Eysenck, H. J., & Barrett, P. (1985). A revised version of the psychoticism scale. *Personality and Individual Differences, 6*(1), 21–29.

Ferris, J., & Wynne, H. (2001). *The Canadian Problem Gambling Index: Final report.* Ottawa, ON: Canadian Centre on Substance Abuse.

Fetterman, D. M. (1987). Ethnographic educational evaluation. In G. D. Spindler (Ed.), *Interpretative ethnography of education: At home and abroad* (pp. 81–106). Hillsdale, NJ: Lawrence-Erlbaum.

Fetterman, D. M. (2010). *Ethnography* (3rd ed.). Thousand Oaks, CA: Sage.

Fink, A. (2003). *How to ask survey questions* (2nd ed.). Thousand Oaks, CA: Sage.

Fink, A. (2017). *How to conduct surveys: A step-by-step guide* (6th ed.). Thousand Oaks, CA: Sage.

Finlay, J. (2012). *Portrayals of gender stereotypes in crime scene investigation*. Unpublished report submitted as part of the course work for Introduction to Social Research Methods, Fall 2012.

Fischer, B., Rudzinski, K., Ivsins, A., Gallupe, O., Patra, J., & Krajden, M. (2010, August). Social, health, and drug use characteristics of primary crack users in three mid-sized communities in British Columbia, Canada. *Drugs: Education, Prevention, and Policy, 17*(4), 333–353.

Flick, U. (2014). *An introduction to qualitative research* (5th ed.). Thousand Oaks, CA: Sage.

Flynn, D. (2011, November 4). The rich kids of occupy Wall Street. *FrontPage Magazine*. Retrieved from http://frontpagemag.com/2011/11/04/the-rich-kids-of-occupy-wall-street/

Foster, J. B., Clark, B., & York, R. (2010). *The ecological rift: Capitalism's war on the earth*. New York, NY: Monthly Review Press.

Fowler, F. J. (2014). *Survey research methods* (5th ed.). Thousand Oaks, CA: Sage.

Frey, B. S. (1997). *Not just for the money: An economic theory of personal motivation*. Gloucestershire, UK: Edward Elgar.

Gackenbach, J., Sample, T., Mandel, G., & Tomashewsky, M. (2011). Dream and blog content analysis of a long-term diary of a video game player with obsessive compulsive disorder. *Dreaming, 21*(2), 124–147.

Gallagher, K. (Ed.). (2018). *The methodological dilemma revisited: Creative, critical, and collaborative approaches to qualitative research for a new era*. New York, NY: Routledge.

Garner, D. M., & Garfinkel, P. E. (1979). The Eating Attitudes Test: An index of the symptoms of anorexia nervosa. *Psychological Medicine, 9*(2), 273–279.

Geertz, C. (1998, October 22). Deep hanging out. *New York Review of Books, 45*(16), 69–72.

Genome British Columbia. (2018). Genome Canada programs: 2018 large-scale applied research project competition: Genomics solutions for agriculture, agrifood, fisheries and aquaculture. Retrieved from https://www.genomebc.ca/funding-opportunity/2018-large-scale-applied-research-project-competition-genomics-solutions-for-agriculture-agrifood-fisheries-and-aquaculture/

George, A. L., & Bennett, A. (2005). *Case studies and theory development in the social sciences*. Cambridge, MA: MIT Press.

Giwa, S., & Chaze, F. (2018). Positive enough? A content analysis of settlement service organizations' inclusivity of LGBTQ immigrants. *Journal of Gay and Lesbian Social Services*. doi: http://dx.doi.org/10.1080/10538720.2018.1463889

Glaser, B. G. (1992). *Grounded theory analysis: Emergence vs forcing*. Mill Valley, CA: Sociology Press.

Glaser, B. G., & Strauss, A. L. (2007). *The discovery of grounded theory: Strategies for qualitative research*. Piscataway, NJ: Aldine Transaction.

Globerman, J. (1996). Motivations to care: Daughters- and sons-in-law caring for relatives with Alzheimer's disease. *Family Relations, 45*(1), 37–45.

Gobo, G. (2011). Ethnography. In D. Silverman (Ed.), *Qualitative methods* (3rd ed., pp. 15–34). Thousand Oaks, CA: Sage.

Gold, R. L. (1958). Roles in sociological field observations. *Social Forces, 36*(3), 217–223.

Gosling, S. D., & Johnson, J. A. (2010). *Advanced methods for conducting online behavioral research*. Washington, DC: American Psychological Association.

Gosselin, J., & Gosselin, N. (2016). Women's maternal experiences in Canadian stepfamilies: An exploratory study. *Journal of divorce and remarriage, 57*(6), 389–410.

Gottfredson, M. R., & Hirschi, T. (1990). *A general theory of crime*. Stanford, CT: Stanford University Press.

Gould, K., Pellow, D. N., & Schnaiberg, A. (2008). *The treadmill of production: Injustice and unsustainability in the global economy*. Boulder, CO: Paradigm.

Government of Canada. (2016). A backgrounder on poverty in Canada. Retrieved from https://www.canada.ca/en/employment-social-development/programs/poverty-reduction/backgrounder.html

Government of Canada. (2017a). Open data 101. Retrieved from https://open.canada.ca/en/open-data-principles

Government of Canada. (2017b). Prepare for the citizenship test. Retrieved from https://www.canada.ca/en/immigration-refugees-citizenship/services/canadian-citizenship/become-canadian-citizen/citizenship-test.html

Government of Canada. (2018). Panel on research ethics. Ottawa, ON: http://www.pre.ethics.gc.ca/eng/policy-politique/initiatives/tcps2-eptc2/chapter1-chapitre1/#toc01-1b

Graber, M. L., Franklin, N., & Gordon, R. (2005). Diagnostic error in internal medicine. *Archives of Internal Medicine, 165*(13), 1493–1499.

Gray, D. E. (2018). *Doing research in the real world* (4th ed.). Thousand Oaks, CA: Sage.

Gray, F. D. (1998). *The Tuskegee syphilis study*. Montgomery, AL: NewSouth Books.

Gray, G., & Guppy, N. (1994). *Successful surveys: Research methods and practice*. Toronto, ON: Harcourt Brace.

Green, J. C., Caracelli, V. J., & Graham, W. F. (1989). Toward a conceptual framework for mixed-method evaluations designs. *Educational Evaluation and Policy Analysis, 11*(3), 255–274.

Greenwood, D. J., & Levin, M. (2007). *Introduction to action research: Social research for social change* (2nd ed.). Thousand Oaks, CA: Sage.

Groves, R. M. (1989). *Survey errors and survey costs.* Hoboken, NJ: John Wiley & Sons.

Guba, E. G. (1996). What happened to me on the road to Damascus. In L. Heshusius & K. Ballard (Eds.), *From positivism to interpretivism and beyond: Tales of transformation in educational and social research* (pp. 43–49). New York, NY: Teachers College Press.

Guba, E. G., & Lincoln, Y. S. (1994). Competing paradigms in qualitative research. In N. K. Denzin & Y. S. Lincoln (Eds.), *Handbook of qualitative research* (pp. 105–117). Thousand Oaks, CA: Sage.

Guppy, N., & Gray, G. (2008). *Successful surveys: Research methods and practice* (4th ed.). Toronto, ON: Nelson.

Guppy, N., & Luongo, N. (2015). The rise and fall of Canada's gender-equity revolution. *Canadian Review of Sociology, 52*(3), 241–265.

Hagan, F. E. (2018). *Research methods in criminal justice and criminology* (10th ed.). Upper Saddle River, NJ: Pearson Education.

Hägelli, P. (2005). *Winter backcountry use trend estimates for Western Canada.* Revelstoke, BC: Canadian Avalanche Association.

Hagen, C. A., Ender, M. G., Tiemann, K. A., & Hagen, C. O. (2005). Graffiti on the great plains: A social reaction to the Red River Valley flood of 1997. In K. J. Strand & G. L. Weiss (Eds.), *Experiencing social research: A reader* (pp. 181–190). Boston, MA: Pearson Education.

Haines-Saah, R. J., Mitchell, S., Slemon, A., & Jenkins, E. K. (2018). "Parents are the best prevention"? Troubling assumptions in cannabis policy and prevention discourses in the context of legalization in Canada. *International Journal of Drug Policy.* https://doi.org/10.1016/j.drugpo.2018.06.008

Haje, B. E., & Symbaluk, D. G. (2014). Personal and social determinants of aggressive and dangerous driving. *Canadian Journal of Family and Youth, 6*(1), 59–88.

Hamm, S., MacLean, J., Kikulis, L., & Thibault, L. (2008). Value congruence in a Canadian nonprofit sport organization: A case study. *Sport Management Review, 11*(2), 123–147.

Hammersley, M., & Atkinson, P. (2019). *Ethnography: Principles and practice* (4th ed.). New York, NY: Routledge.

Hammond, D., Reid, J. L., & Zukowski, S. (2018). Adverse effects of caffeinated energy drinks among youth and young adults in Canada: A web-based survey. *CMAJ Open, 6*(1), E19–E25.

Hancock, K., Keast, H., & Ellis, W. (2017). The impact of cyber dating abuse on self-esteem: The mediating role of emotional distress. *Cyberpsychology: Journal of Psychosocial Research on Cyberspace, 11*(2), 45–57.

Haney, C., Banks, C., & Zimbardo, P. (1973). Interpersonal dynamics in a simulated prison. *International Journal of Criminology and Penology, 1*(1), 69–97.

Healey, J. F., Prus, S. G., & Lieflander, R. (2019). *A tool for social research* (4th Can. ed.). Toronto, ON: Nelson Education.

Health Canada and the Public Health Agency of Canada. (2017). *Evaluation of the Aboriginal Head Start in Urban and Northern Communities Program 2011–2012 to 2015–2016.* Ottawa, ON: Office of Audit and Evaluation. Retrieved from https://www-deslibris-ca.ezproxy.macewan.ca/ID/10095754

Heberlein, T. A., & Baumgartner, R. (1978). Factors affecting response rates to mailed questionnaires: A quantitative analysis of the published literature. *American Sociological Review, 43*(4), 447–462.

Hennick, M., Hutter, I., & Bailey, A. (2011). *Qualitative research methods.* Thousand Oaks, CA: Sage.

Hesse-Biber, S. H. (Ed.) (2012). *The handbook of feminist research: Theory and praxis.* Thousand Oaks, CA: Sage.

Hine, C. (2000). *Virtual ethnography.* Thousand Oaks, CA: Sage.

Hine, C. (Ed.). (2013). *Virtual research methods* (Four volume set). Thousand Oaks, CA: Sage.

Holub, J. (2012). *Themes surrounding masculinity within hip-hop and country music: Portrayals of hegemonic masculinity common within each domain.* Unpublished report submitted as part of the course work for Introduction to Social Research Methods, Fall 2012.

Howell, A. J., & Symbaluk, D. G. (2001). Published student ratings: Reconciling the views of students and faculty. *Journal of Educational Psychology, 93*(4), 790–796.

Hudson, C. C., Lambe, L., PREVNet National Youth Advisory Committee, Pepler, D. J., & Craig, W. M. (2016). Coping while connected: The association among cybervictimization, privacy settings, and reporting tools in youth. *Canadian Journal of School Psychology, 31*(1), 3–16.

Humes, E. (2012). *Garbology: Our dirty love affair with trash.* New York, NY: Avery.

Humphreys, R. A. L. (1970). *Tearoom trade: Impersonal sex in public places.* Chicago, IL: Aldine.

iscience. (2019). Home page. Retrieved from iscience.deusto.es

Ivory, J. D., Williams, D., Martins, N., & Consalvo, M. (2009). Good clean fun? A content analysis of profanity in video games and its prevalence across game systems and ratings. *Cyberpsychology & Behavior, 12*(4), 457–460.

Jackson, K., & Bazeley, P. (2019). *Qualitative data analysis with NVivo* (3rd ed.). Thousand Oaks, CA: Sage.

Jackson, W., & Verberg, N. (2007). *Methods: Doing social research* (4th ed.). Toronto, ON: Pearson Education Canada.

Janke, J. (2012). The contract year myth: Do NHL players produce at a higher level during the final year of their contracts? Poster session. Sociology Undergraduate Symposium. MacEwan University, Edmonton, Alberta, April 10.

Jansen, H. (2010). The logic of qualitative survey research and its position in the field of social research methods. *Forum Qualitative Sozialforschung/Forum: Qualitative Social Research, 11*(2), Art. 11. Retrieved from http://nbn-resolving.de/urn:nbn:de:0114-fqs1002110

Janssen, P. A., Henderson, A. D., & Vedam, S. (2009). The experience of planned home birth: Views of the first 500 women. *Birth, 36*(4), 297–304.

Johnson, J., Guerrero, M. D., Holman, M., Chin, J. W., & Signer-Kroeker, M. A. (2018). An examination of hazing in Canadian intercollegiate sports. *Journal of Clinical Sport Psychology, 12*(2), 144–159.

Johnson, M. (2007). The theoretical and social context of research ethics. In T. Long & M. Johnson, *Research ethics in the real world: Issues and solutions for health and social care* (pp. 29–46). Philadelphia, PA: Churchill Livingstone.

Jones, J. H. (1993). *Bad blood: The Tuskegee syphilis experiment.* New York, NY: The Free Press.

Judd, C. M., Smith, E. R., & Kidder, L. H. (1991). *Research methods in social relations* (6th ed.). Fort Worth, TX: Harcourt Brace Jovanovich.

Karamouzian, M., Dohoo, C., Forsting, S., McNeil, R., Kerr, T., & Lysyshyn, M. (2018). Evaluation of a fentanyl drug checking service for clients of a supervised injection facility, Vancouver, Canada. *Harm Reduction Journal, 15*(46). https://doi.org/10.1186/s12954-018-0252-8

Kim, H. S., Wohl, M. J. A., Gupta, R., & Derevensky, J. (2016). From the mouths of social media users: A focus group study exploring the social casino gaming–online gambling link. *Journal of Behavioral Addictions, 5*(1), 115–121.

Kintz, B. L., Delprato, D. J., Mettee, D. R., Persons, C. E., & Shappe, R. H. (1965). The experimenter effect. *Psychological Bulletin, 63*(4), 223–232.

Kirk, R. E. (2013). *Experimental design: Procedures for the behavioral sciences* (4th ed.). Thousand Oaks, CA: Sage.

Knish, B. (2018). *The nature of Youtube comments responding to music videos featuring sexually objectified women.* Unpublished research report. MacEwan University, Edmonton, Alberta.

Kolomitro, K., MacKenzie, L. W., Wiercigroch, D., & Golden, L. (2018). The design and evaluation of a master of science program in anatomical sciences at Queen's University Canada. *Anatomical Sciences Education, 11*(6), 613–622.

Kovach, M. (2010). *Indigenous methodologies: Characteristics, conversations, and context.* Toronto, ON: University of Toronto Press.

Kovach, M. (2018). Doing Indigenous methodologies: A letter to a research class. In N. K. Denzin & Y. S. Lincoln (Eds.), *The Sage handbook of qualitative research* (5th ed., pp. 214–234). Thousand Oaks, CA: Sage.

Krippendorff, K. (2019). *Content analysis: An introduction to its methodology* (4th ed.). Thousand Oaks, CA: Sage.

Krueger, R. A., & Casey, M. A. (2015). *Focus groups: A practical guide for applied research* (5th ed.). Thousand Oaks, CA: Sage.

Kuhn, T. S. (1962). *The structure of scientific revolutions.* Chicago, IL: Chicago University Press.

Kvale, S., & Brinkmann, S. (2009). *Interviews: Learning the craft of qualitative research interviewing* (2nd ed.). Thousand Oaks, CA: Sage.

Lagnado, L. M., & Dekel, S. C. (1991). *Children of the flames: Dr. Joseph Mengle and the untold story of the twins of Auschwitz.* New York, NY: William Morrow.

Lake, S., Kerr, T., Nosova, E., Milloy, M. J., Wood, E., & DeBeck, K. (2018). Patterns of non-injection drug use associated with injection cessation among street-involved youth in Vancouver, Canada. *Journal of Urban Health, 9*(2), 267–277.

Landis, J. R., & Koch, G. G. (1977). The measurement of observer agreement for categorical data. *Biometrics, 33*(1), 159–174.

Landry, A. (1934). *La révolution démographique.* Paris, France: Sirey.

Langbein, L. (2012). *Public program evaluation: A statistical guide* (2nd ed.). Armonk, NY: M. E. Sharpe.

Lasswell, H. (1927). *Propaganda techniques in the world war.* New York, NY: Knopf.

Lavenda, R. H., Schultz, E. A., & Zutter, C. (2016). *Anthropology: What does it mean to be human?* (Can. ed.). Don Mills, ON: Oxford University Press.

Lemert, E. M. (1951). *Social pathology: A systematic approach to the study of sociopathic behavior.* New York, NY: McGraw-Hill.

Leos-Toro, C., Rynard, V., & Hammond, D. (2017). Prevalence of problematic cannabis use in Canada: Cross-sectional findings from the 2013 Canadian tobacco, alcohol, and drugs survey. *Canadian Journal of Public Health, 108*(5–6), e516–e522.

Lerman, B. I., Lewis, S. P., Lumley, M., Grogan, G. J., Hudson, C. C., & Johnson, E. (2017). Teen depression groups on Facebook: A content analysis. *Journal of Adolescent Research, 32*(6), 719–741.

Levy, P. S., & Lemeshow, S. (2011). *Sampling of populations: Methods and applications* (4th ed.). Hoboken, NJ: John Wiley & Sons.

Lewin, K. (1951). *Field theory in social science: Selected theoretical papers.* D. Cartwright (Ed.). New York, NY: Harper & Row.

Liamputtong, P. (2013). *Qualitative research methods* (4th ed.). Don Mills, ON: Oxford University Press.

Library and Archives Canada. (2017). About the collection. Retrieved from http://www.collectionscanada.gc.ca/collection/003-300-e.html

Lincoln, Y. S., Lynham, S. A., & Guba, E. G. (2018). Paradigmatic controversies, contradictions, and emerging confluences, revisited. In N. K. Denzin & Y. S. Lincoln (Eds.), *The Sage handbook of qualitative research* (5th ed., pp. 108–150). Thousand Oaks, CA: Sage.

Lombard, M., Snyder-Duch, J., & Bracken, C. C. (2002). Content analyses in mass communication: Assessment and reporting of intercoder reliability. *Human Communications Research, 28*(4), 587–604.

Lowe, M. E., & McClement, S. E. (2011). Spousal bereavement: The lived experience of young Canadian widows. *OMEGA, 62*(2), 127–148.

Lune, H., & Berg, B. L. (2017). *Qualitative research methods for the social sciences* (9th ed.). New York, NY: Pearson.

Lyon-Callo, V. (2008). *Inequality, poverty, and neoliberal governance: Activist ethnography in the homeless sheltering industry.* Toronto, ON: Higher Education University of Toronto Press.

MacEwan University. (2018). Evaluating information sources. Retrieved from https://library.macewan.ca/research-help/evaluating

Madden, R. (2017). *Being ethnographic: A guide to the theory and practice of ethnography* (2nd ed.). Thousand Oaks, CA: Sage.

Maisto, S. A., Conners, G. J., Tucker, J. A., McCollam, J. B., & Adesso, V. J. (1980). Validation of the sensation scale: A measure of subjective physiological responses to alcohol. *Behavior Research and Therapy, 18*(1), 37–43.

Maiwald, K., de Rijk, A., Guzman, J., Schonstein, E., & Yassi, A. (2011). Evaluation of a workplace disability prevention intervention in Canada: Examining differing perceptions of stakeholders. *Journal of Occupational Rehabilitation, 21*(2), 179–189. doi: 10.1007/s10926-010-9267-z

Marczyk, G., DeMatteo, D., & Festinger, D. (2005). *Essentials of research design and methodology.* Hoboken, NJ: John Wiley & Sons.

Marion, J. S., & Crowder, J. W. (2013). *Visual research: A concise introduction to thinking visually.* London, UK: Bloomsbury Academic.

Martin, F. S. (2011). Deep entanglements: The complexities of disengaging from drug use for young mothers. *Contemporary Drug Problems, 38*(3), 335–336.

McConville, K. M. V., & Virk, S. (2012). Evaluation of an electronic video game for improvement of balance. *Virtual Reality, 16*(4), 315–323.

McDonald, L., Conrad, T., Fairtlough, A., Fletcher, J., Green, L., Moore, L., & Lepps, B. (2009). An evaluation of a groupwork intervention for teenage mothers and their families. *Child and Family Social Work, 14*(1), 45–57.

McDonald, S. M., & Reeder, B. A. (1997, July 1). Obesity in Canada: A descriptive analysis. *Canadian Medical Association Journal, 157*(1 Suppl.), S3–S9.

McIntyre, L., Glanville, N. T., Raine, K. D., Dayle, J. B., Anderson, B., & Battaglia, N. (2003). Do low-income lone mothers compromise their nutrition to feed their children? *Canadian Medical Association Journal, 168*(6), 686–691.

McIsaac, J. L. D., Penney, T. L., Ata, N., Munro-Sigfridson, L., Cunningham, J., Veugelers, P. J., . . . Kuhle, S. (2017). Evaluation of a health promoting schools program in a school board in Nova Scotia, Canada. *Preventative Medicine Reports, 5*(March), 279–284.

McKenzie, B., Seidl, E., & Bone, N. (2010). Child and family service standards in First Nations: An action research project. *Child Welfare League of America, 74*(3), 633–653.

McKie, R. M., Lachowsky, N. J., & Milhausen, R. R. (2015). The positive impact of technology on young gay men's dating and sexual relationships in Canada: Results from a focus group study. *Journal of LGBT Youth, 12*(1), 19–38.

McLaren, L., Patterson, S., Thawer, S., Faris, P., McNeil, D., Potestio, M. L., & Shwart, L. (2017). Exploring the short-term impact of community water fluoridation cessation on children's dental caries: A natural experiment in Alberta, Canada. *Public Health, 146*(May), 56–64.

McNeil, R., Kerr, T., Lampkin, H., & Small, W. (2015). "We need somewhere to smoke crack": An ethnographic study of an unsanctioned safer smoking room in Vancouver, Canada. *International Journal of Drug Policy, 26*(7), 645–652.

McNiff, J. (2017). *Action research: All you need to know.* Thousand Oaks, CA: Sage.

McNiff, J., & Whitehead, J. (2006). *All you need to know about action research.* Thousand Oaks, CA: Sage.

Mead, E., Gittelsohn, J., Kratzmann, M., Roaches, C., & Sharma, S. (2010). Impact of the changing food environment on dietary practices of an Inuit population in Arctic Canada. *Journal of Human Nutrition and Dietetics, 23*(Suppl. 1), 18–26.

Melhorn, J. J., & Romig, R. J. (1985). Rest room graffiti: A descriptive study. *Emporia State Research Studies, 34*(2–3), 29–45.

Mendez, J. B. (2009). Globalizing feminist research. In M. K. Huggins & M. L. Glebbeek (Eds.), *Women fielding danger: Negotiating ethnographic identities in field research* (pp. 67–96). Plymouth, UK: Rowman & Littlefield.

Merton, R. K. (1938). Social structure and anomie. *American Sociological Review, 3*(5), 672–682.

Mezzana, D., Lorenz, A., & Kelman, I. (2012). Islands and islandness in rock music lyrics. *Island Studies Journal, 7*(1), 69–98.

Milgram, S. (1961). Nationality and conformity. *Scientific American, 205*(6), 45–51.

Milgram, S. (1963). Behavioral study of obedience. *Journal of Abnormal and Social Psychology, 67*(4), 371–378.

Miller, J., & Glassner, B. (2011). The "inside" and the "outside": Finding realities in interviews. In D. Silverman (Ed.), *Qualitative research: Issues of theory, method and practice* (3rd ed., pp. 131–148). Thousand Oaks, CA: Sage.

Milner, H. (2007). *Political knowledge and participation among young Canadians and Americans* (Institute for Research on Public Policy Working Paper number 2007-01). Montreal, QC: IRPP.

Mishkind, M. E., Rodin, J., Silberstein, L. R., & Striegel-Moore, R. H. (1986). The embodiment of masculinity: Cultural, psychological, and behavioral dimensions. *American Behavioral Scientist, 29(5)*, 545–562.

Mishna, F., Regehr, C., Lacome-Duncan, A., Daciuk, J., Fearing, G., & Van Wert, M. (2018). Social media, cyber-aggression and student mental health on a university campus. *Journal of Mental Health, 27*(3), 222–229.

Mitchell, M., & Jolley, J. (1996). *Research design explained* (3rd ed.). Orlando, FL: Harcourt Brace.

Montgomery, D. C. (2001). *Design and analysis of experiments.* New York, NY: John Wiley & Sons.

Morgan, D. L. (1996). Focus groups. *Annual Review of Sociology, 22*, 129–152.

Morgan, D. L. (2001). Focus group interviewing. In J. F. Gubrium & J. A. Holstein (Eds.), *Handbook of interview research: Context & method* (pp. 141–159). Thousand Oaks, CA: Sage.

Morgan, D. L. (2019). *Basic and advanced focus groups.* Thousand Oaks, CA: Sage.

Morisano, D., Hirsch, J. B., Peterson, J. B., Pihl, R. O., & Shore, B. M. (2010). Setting, elaborating, and reflecting on personal goals improves academic performance. *Journal of Applied Psychology, 95*(2), 255–264.

Morse, J. M. (2001). Toward a praxis theory of suffering. *Advances in Nursing Science, 24*(1), 47–59.

Morse, J. M. (2005). Creating a qualitatively derived theory of suffering. In U. Zutler (Ed.), *Clinical practice and development in nursing* (pp. 83–91). Aarhus, Denmark: Centre for Innovation in Nurse Training.

Moubarac, J. C., Cargo, M., Receveur, O., & Daniel, M. (2012). Describing the situational contexts of sweetened product consumption in a Middle Eastern Canadian community: Application of a mixed-method design. *PLoS ONE, 7*(9), 1–9.

Moulden, H. M., Firestone, P., Kingston, D. A., & Wexler, A. F. (2010). A description of sexual offending committed by Canadian teachers. *Journal of Child Sexual Abuse, 19*(4), 403–418.

Nardi, P. M. (2006). *Interpreting data: A guide to understanding research.* Toronto, ON: Pearson Canada.

National Commission for the Protection of Human Subjects of Biomedical and Behavioral Research. (1979, April 18). *The Belmont report: Ethical principles and guidelines for the protection of human subjects of research.* Department of Health, Education, and Welfare. Washington, DC: US Government Printing Office.

Neuendorf, K. A. (2002). *The content analysis guidebook.* Thousand Oaks, CA: Sage.

Neuman, T. R., Pfefer, R., Slack, K. L., Hardy, K. K., Raub, R., Lucke, R., & Wark, R. (2003). *National Cooperative Highway Research Program report 500: Guidance for implementation of the AASHTO Strategic Highways Safety Plan. Volume 1: A guide for addressing aggressive-driving collisions.* Washington, DC: Transportation Research Board.

Neuman, W. L., & Robson, K. (2018). *Basics of social research: Qualitative and quantitative approaches* (4th Can. ed.). Toronto, ON: Pearson Canada.

Nissim, R., Hales, S., Zimmerman, C., Deckert, A., Edwards, B., & Rodin, G. (2017). Supporting family caregivers of advanced cancer patients: A focus group study. *Family Relations, 66*(5), 867–879.

Norvig, P. (2012). Warning signs in experimental design and interpretation. Retrieved from http://norvig.com/experiment-design.html

Notestein, F. (1945). Population: The long view. In Theodore W. Schultz (Ed.), *Food for the world* (pp. 36–57). Chicago, IL: University of Chicago Press.

Nowrouzi-Kia, B., Li, A. K. C., Nguyen, C., & Casole, J. (2018). Heart disease and occupational risk factors in the Canadian population: An exploratory study using the Canadian Community Health Survey. *Safety and Health at Work, 9*(2), 144–148.

Nunes, I. L., Harr, N., Dunn, L., & Price, P. (2011). Case study on effect of household task participation on home, community, and work opportunities for a youth with multiple disabilities. *Work, 39*(4), 445–453.

Nuremberg Code. (1949). In *Trials of war criminals before the Nuremberg Military Tribunals under Control Council Law No. 10* (Vol. 2, pp. 181–182). Washington, DC: US Government Printing Office.

Ochoo, B., Valcour, J., & Sarkar, A. (2017). Association between perceptions of public drinking water quality and actual drinking water quality: A community-based exploratory study in Newfoundland (Canada). *Environmental Research, 159*, 435–443.

O'Dell, K. (2016). *Savage or sexual: The representation of Aboriginal women in Halloween costumes.* Poster. Student Research Week. MacEwan University, Edmonton, Alberta, January 26.

Ontario Ministry of Transportation. (2018). Distracted driving. Retrieved from https://www.ontario.ca/page/distracted-driving

O'Reilly, K. (2009). *Key concepts in ethnography.* Thousand Oaks, CA: Sage.

Orne, M. T. (1962). On the social psychology of the psychological experiment: With particular reference to demand characteristics and their implications. *American Psychologist, 17*(11), 776–783.

Padgett, D. K. (2012). *Qualitative and mixed methods in public health.* Thousand Oaks, CA: Sage.

Palys, T., & Atchison, C. (2014). *Research decisions: Quantitative and qualitative perspectives* (5th ed.). Toronto, ON: Nelson Education.

Parks Canada. (2017). *Evaluation of Parks Canada's law enforcement program: Final report.* Gatineau, QC: Office of Internal Audit and Evaluation. Catalogue No: R62-470/2017E-PDF.

Persaud, S., McIntyre, L., & Milaney, K. (2010). Working homeless men in Calgary, Canada: Hegemony and identity. *Human Organization, 69*(4), 343–351.

Pfeiffer, S. I., Petscher, Y., & Kumtepe, A. (2008). The gifted ratings scales-school form: A validation study based on age, gender, and race. *Roeper Review, 30*(2), 140–146.

Piat, M., Sabetti, J., Couture, A., Sylvestre, J., Provencher, H., Botschner, J., & Stayner, D. (2009). What does recovery mean for me? Perspectives of Canadian mental health consumers. *Psychiatric Rehabilitation Journal, 32*(3), 199–207.

Pienta, A. M., McFarland O'Rouke, J., & Franks, M. M. (2011). Getting started: Working with secondary data. In K. H. Trzesniewski, M. B. Donnellan, & R. E. Lucas (Eds.), *Secondary data analysis [electronic resource]: An introduction for psychologists.* Washington, DC: American Psychological Association. Retrieved from http://ehis. ebscohost.com.ezproxy.macewan.ca/ehost/detail?sid=0e86d55d-4979-4768-9935-383cdd4eb836%40sessionmgr198&vid=1&hid=105&bdata=JnNpdGU9ZWhvc-3QtbGl2ZSZzY29wZT1zaXRl#db=pzh&jid=201009298

Pila, E., Mond, J. M., Griffiths, S., Mitchison, D., & Murray, S. B. (2017). A thematic content analysis of #cheatmeal images on the social media: Characterizing an emerging dietary trend. *International Journal of Eating Disorders, 50*(1), 698–706.

Pink, S. (2001). *Doing visual ethnography.* Thousand Oaks, CA: Sage.

Podems, D. R. (2019). *Being an evaluator: Your practical guide to evaluation.* New York, NY: Guilford Press.

Poulin, C., Gouliquer, L., & McCutcheon, J. (2018). Violating gender norms in the Canadian military: The experiences of gay and lesbian soldiers. *Sexuality Research and Social Policy, 15*(1), 60–73.

PPG. (2018). Automotive color trends. Retrieved from http://corporate.ppg.com/Color/Color-Trends/Automotive-Color-Trends.aspx

Pyrczak, F., & Bruce, R. R. (2017). *Writing empirical research reports: A basic guide for students of the social and behavioral sciences* (8th ed.). New York, NY: Routledge.

Quinton, S., & Reynolds, N. (2018). *Understanding research in the digital age.* Thousand Oaks, CA: Sage.

Rapley, T. (2007). Interviews. In C. Seale, G. Gobo, J. F. Gubrium, & D. Silverman (Eds.), *Qualitative research practice* (pp. 15–33). Thousand Oaks, CA: Sage.

Rathje, W., & Murphy, C. (2001). *Rubbish: The archeology of garbage.* Tucson, AZ: University of Arizona Press.

Rawlinson, F., & Farrell, P. (2010). Construction site graffiti: Discourse analysis as a window into construction site culture. In C. Egbu (Ed.), *Proceedings of the 26th annual ARCOM conference* (pp. 361–370), September 6–8, 2010, Leeds, UK: Association of Researchers in Construction Management.

Rea, L. M., & Parker, R. A. (2005). *Designing and conducting survey research: A comprehensive guide* (3rd ed.). San Francisco, CA: Jossey-Bass.

Reinharz, S. (2011). *Observing the observer: Understanding ourselves in field research.* New York, NY: Oxford University Press.

Reiss, A. J., & Rhodes, A. L. (1964). An empirical test of differential association theory. *Journal of Research in Crime and Delinquency, 1*(1), 5–18.

Ricciardelli, R. (2011). Masculinity, consumerism, and appearance: A look at men's hair. *Canadian Review of Sociology, 48*(2), 181–201.

Ricciardelli, R., & White, P. (2011). Modifying the body: Canadian men's perspectives on appearance and cosmetic surgery. *The Qualitative Report, 16*(4), 949–970.

Richardson, J. E. (2007). *Analysing newspapers: An approach from critical discourse analysis.* New York, NY: Palgrave Macmillan.

Riemann, G., & Schütze, F. (1991). "Trajectory" as a basic theoretical concept for analyzing suffering disorderly social process. In D. R. Maines (Ed.), *Social organization and social process* (pp. 333–357). New York, NY: Aldine de Gruyter.

Ritchie, J., Lewis, J., Nicholls, C. M., & Ormston, R. (2014). *Qualitative research practice: A guide for social science students and researchers* (2nd ed.). Thousand Oaks, CA: Sage.

Ritter, L. A., & Sue, V. M. (2007). *Using online surveys in evaluation.* San Francisco, CA: Jossey-Bass.

Ritzer, G., & Stepnisky, J. (2018). *Classical sociological theory* (7th ed.). Thousand Oaks, CA: Sage.

Rooney, B. J., & Evans, A. N. (2019). *Methods in psychological research* (4th ed.). Thousand Oaks, CA: Sage.

Rosenthal, R., & Rosnow, R. L. (1975). *The volunteer subject.* New York, NY: John Wiley & Sons.

Rosnow, R. L., & Rosenthal, R. (2013). *Beginning behavioral research: A conceptual primer* (7th ed.). Toronto, ON: Pearson Education.

Ross, L. E., O'Gorman, L., MacLeod, M. A., Bauer, G. R., MacKay, J., & Robinson, M. (2016). Bisexuality, poverty and mental health: A mixed methods analysis. *Social Science & Medicine, 156*, 64–72.

Rossi, P. H., Lipsey, M. W., & Freeman, H. E. (2004). *Evaluation: A systemic approach* (7th ed.). Thousand Oaks, CA: Sage.

Rossi, P. H., Lipsey, M. W., & Henry, G. T. (2019). *Evaluation: A systematic approach* (8th ed.). Thousand Oaks, CA: Sage.

Royal Canadian Mounted Police. (2018a). Police officer careers. Retrieved from http://www.rcmp-grc.gc.ca/en/police-officer-careers

Royal Canadian Mounted Police. (2018b). Strategic priorities. Retrieved from http://www.rcmp-grc.gc.ca/prior/index-eng.htm

Rubin, H. J., & Rubin, I. S. (2005). *Qualitative interviewing: The art of hearing data.* Thousand Oaks, CA: Sage.

Rubin, H. J., & Rubin, I. S. (2012). *Qualitative interviewing: The art of hearing data* (3rd ed.). Thousand Oaks, CA: Sage.

Russell, N. J. C. (2010). Milgram's obedience to authority experiments: Origins and early evolution. *British Journal of Social Psychology, 50*(1), 140–162.

Sabbane, L. I., Bellavance, F., & Chebat, J. C. (2009). Recency versus repetition priming effects of cigarette warnings on nonsmoking teenagers: The moderating effects of cigarette-brand familiarity. *Journal of Applied Social Psychology, 39*(3), 656–682.

Saldaña, J. (2016). *The coding manual for qualitative researchers* (3rd ed.). Thousand Oaks, CA: Sage.

Samson, N. (2014, March 5). Québec ruling supports confidentiality of researchers' interviews. *University Affairs.* Retrieved from https://www.universityaffairs.ca/news/news-article/quebec-ruling-supports-confidentiality-of-researchers-interviews/

Sandler, T. (2012, March 2). "People keep falling sick": How poor Indians are recruited for clinical drug trials. NBC News. Retrieved from http://openchannel.msnbc.msn.com/_news/2012/03/02/10561824-people-keep-falling-sick-how-poor-indians-are-recruited-for-clinical-drug-trials?chromedomain=insidedateline

Sapsford, R. (2006). Indicator. In V. Jupp (Ed.), *The Sage dictionary of social research methods.* doi: 10.4135/9780857020116

Saris, W. E., & Gallhofer, I. N. (2014). *Design, evaluation, and analysis of questionnaires for survey research* (2nd ed.). Hoboken, NJ: John Wiley & Sons.

Schatzman, L., & Strauss, A. L. (1973). *Field research: Strategies for a natural sociology.* Englewood Cliffs, NJ: Prentice-Hall.

Schnaiberg, A. (1980). *The environment: From surplus to scarcity.* New York, NY: Oxford University Press.

Schutt, R. K. (2019). *Investigating the social world: The process and practice of research* (9th ed.). Thousand Oaks, CA: Sage.

Scott, G., & Garner, R. (2013). *Doing qualitative research: Designs, methods, and techniques.* Upper Saddle River, NJ: Pearson Education.

Segal, D. S., & Stockwell, T. (2008). Low alcohol alternatives: A promising strategy for reducing alcohol related harm. *International Journal of Drug Policy, 20*(2), 183–187.

Seidman, R. (2006). *Interviewing as qualitative research: A guide for researchers in education and the social sciences* (3rd ed.). New York, NY: Teacher's College Press.

Semplonious, T., & Willoughby, T. (2018). *Psychosocial adjustment throughout university: A longitudinal investigation of the roles of sleep quality and emotion dysregulation. Journal of Youth and Adolescence, 47*(6), 1267–1278.

Shaffer, S. L. (1993). *Young widows: Rebuilding identity and personal growth following spousal loss.* Unpublished doctoral dissertation. California: University of San Francisco.

Shaughnessy, J. J., Zechmeister, E. B., & Zechmeister, J. S. (2015). *Research methods in psychology* (10th ed.). New York, NY: McGraw-Hill.

Shier, M., Graham, J. R., & Jones, M. E. (2009). Barriers to employment as experienced by disabled people: A qualitative analysis in Calgary and Regina, Canada. *Disability and Society, 24*(1), 63–75.

Shigeta, N., Ahmed, S., Ahmed, S. W., Afzal, A. R., Qasqas, M., Kanda, H., . . . Turin, T. C. (2017). Content analysis of Canadian newspapers articles and readers' comments related to schizophrenia. *International Journal of Culture and Mental Health, 10*(1), 75–81.

Sieber, J. E. (1992). *Planning ethically responsible research.* Newbury Park, CA: Sage.

Singer, B. D. (1982). Minorities and the media: A content analysis of native Canadians in the daily press. *Canadian Review of Sociology and Anthropology, 19*(3), 348–360.

Slaunwhite, A. K., Ronis, S. T., Sun, Y., & Peters, P. A. (2017). The emotional health and well-being of Canadians who care for persons with mental health or addictions problems. *Health and Social Care in the Community, 25*(3), 840–847.

Smith, L. T. (2012). *Decolonizing methodologies: Research and Indigenous Peoples* (2nd ed.). London, UK: Zed Books.

Smith, S. L., Pieper, K. M., Granados, A., & Choueiti, M. (2010). Assessing gender-related portrayals in top-grossing G-rated films. *Sex Roles, 62*(11–12), 774–786.

Smyth, J. D., & Pearson, J. E. (2011). Internet survey methods: A review of strengths, weaknesses, and innovations. In M. Das, P. Ester, & L. Kaczmirek (Eds.), *Social and behavioral research and the internet* (pp. 11–44). New York, NY: Routledge.

Social Sciences and Humanities Research Council. (2018). About SSHRC. Retrieved from http://www.sshrc-crsh.gc.ca/about-au_sujet/index-eng.aspx

Spithoven, A. (2011). It's the institutions, stupid! Why U.S. health care expenditure is so different from Canada's. *Journal of Economic Issues, 45*(1), 75–95.

Stat Trek. (2019). Random number generator. Retrieved from https://stattrek.com/statistics/random-number-generator.aspx#error

Statistics Canada. (2015). *Canadian tobacco alcohol and drugs (CTADS): 2013 summary.* Ottawa, ON: Author. Retrieved from https://www.canada.ca/en/health-canada/services/canadian-tobacco-alcohol-drugs-survey/2013-summary.html

Statistics Canada. (2016a). Mandate and objectives. Retrieved from https://www.statcan.gc.ca/eng/about/mandate

Statistics Canada. (2016b). Median annual earnings of women and men aged 25 to 64 who worked full time and full year as paid employees, by highest level of education and province or territory, 2015. Retrieved from https://www12.statcan.gc.ca/census-recensement/2016/as-sa/98-200-x/2016024/98-200-x2016024-eng.cfm

Statistics Canada. (2017a). Previous standard—ethnicity. In *Definitions, data sources, and methods*. Ottawa, ON: Author. Retrieved from http://www.statcan.gc.ca/concepts/definitions/previous-anterieures/ethnicity-ethnicite2-eng.htm

Statistics Canada. (2017b). Winnipeg, CY [Census subdivision], Manitoba and Canada [Country] (table). Census Profile. 2016 Census. Statistics Canada Catalogue no. 98-316-X2016001. Ottawa. Released November 29, 2017. Retrieved from https://www12.statcan.gc.ca/census-recensement/2016/dp-pd/prof/details/Page.cfm?Lang=E&Geo1=CSD&Code1=4611040&Geo2=PR&Code2=01&Data=Count&SearchText=Mission&SearchType=Begins&SearchPR=01&B1=All&wbdisable=true

Statistics Canada. (2018a). Canadian Community Health Survey—Annual component (CCHS). In *Data sources and methodology*. Ottawa, ON: Author. Retrieved from http://www23.statcan.gc.ca/imdb/p2SV.pl?Function=getSurvey&SDDS=3226#a2

Statistics Canada. (2018b). Census program. Retrieved from https://www12.statcan.gc.ca/census-recensement/index-eng.cfm

Statistics Canada. (2018c). Concept: Census family. In *Definitions, data sources, and methods*. Ottawa, ON: Author. Retrieved from http://www23.statcan.gc.ca/imdb/p3Var.pl?Function=Unit&Id=32746

Statistics Canada. (2018d). Data sources. Retrieved from http://www.statcan.gc.ca/pub/85-002-x/2012001/sources-eng.htm

Statistics Canada. (2018e). Data tables and definitions. In *Health indicators*. Ottawa, ON: Author. Retrieved from https://www150.statcan.gc.ca/n1/pub/82-221-x/2017003/dd-tdd-eng.htm

Statistics Canada. (2018f). Homicide victims, primary methods used to commit homicide. CANSIM. Table 35-10-006901, and Homicide Survey, Canadian Centre for Justice Statistics. Retrieved from https://www150.statcan.gc.ca/t1/tbl1/en/tv.action?pid=3510006901

Statistics Canada. (2018g). Labour force survey. Retrieved from http://www23.statcan.gc.ca/imdb/p2SV.pl?Function=getSurvey&SDDS=3701

Statistics Canada. (2018h). Pension plans in Canada. Retrieved from http://www23.statcan.gc.ca/imdb/p2SV.pl?Function=getSurvey&SDDS=2609

Statistics Canada. (2018i). Results and documentation of surveys and statistical programs. In *Surveys and statistical programs*. Ottawa, ON: Author. Retrieved from https://www150.statcan.gc.ca/n1/en/type/surveys

Statistics Canada. (2018j). Uniform crime reporting survey. Retrieved from http://www23.statcan.gc.ca/imdb/p2SV.pl?Function=getSurvey&SDDS=3302&lang=en&db=imdb&adm=8&dis=2

Stebbins, R. A. (2001). *Exploratory research in the social sciences: Qualitative research methods series 48*. Thousand Oaks, CA: Sage.

Stockemer, D., & Rocher, F. (2017). Age, political knowledge and electoral turnout: A case of Canada. *Commonwealth & Comparative Politics, 55*(1), 41–62.

Stoddart, K. (1986). The presentation of everyday life: Some textual strategies for adequate ethnography. *Urban Life, 15*(1), 103–121.

Stoecker, R. (2013). *Research methods for community change: A project-based approach*. Thousand Oaks, CA: Sage.

Stoltz, J. M., Shannon, K., Kerr, T., Zhang, R., Montaner, J. S., & Wood, E. (2007). Associations between childhood maltreatment and sex work in a cohort of drug-using youth. *Social Science and Medicine, 65*(6), 1214–1221.

Strand, K. J., & Weiss, G. L. (Eds.). (2005). *Experiencing social research: A reader*. Boston, MA: Pearson Education.

Stryker, J. (1997, April 13). Tuskegee's long arm still touches a nerve. *New York Times*. Retrieved from http://www.nytimes.com/1997/04/13/weekinreview/tuskegee-s-long-arm-still-touches-a-nerve.html

Sullivan, T. J. (2001). *Methods of social research*. Orlando, FL: Harcourt.

Sussman, J., Barbera, L., Bainbridge, D., Howell, D., Yang, Y., Husain, A., . . . Walker, H. (2011). Health system characteristics of quality care delivery: A comparative case study of patients in four regions in Ontario, Canada. *Palliative Medicine, 26*(4), 322–335.

Sutherland, E. H. (1947). *Principles of criminology*. Philadelphia, PA: J. B. Lippincott.

Symbaluk, D., & Bereska, T. M. (2019). *Sociology in action: A Canadian perspective* (3rd ed.). Toronto: Nelson Education.

Symbaluk, D., Hall, R., & Champoux, G. (in press). *Navigating an undergraduate degree in the social sciences: Tips and strategies*. Edmonton, AB: MacEwan University Open Press.

Symbaluk, D., Heth, C. D., Cameron, J., & Pierce, W. D. (1997). Social modeling, monetary incentives, and pain endurance: The role of self-efficacy and pain perception. *Personality and Social Psychology Bulletin, 23*(3), 258–269.

Symbaluk, D., & Howell, A. J. (2010). Web-based student feedback: Comparing teaching-award and research-award winners. *Assessment and Evaluation in Higher Education, 35*(1), 71–82.

Symbaluk, D., & Jones, K. M. (1998). Prostitution offender programs: Canada finds new solutions to an old problem. *Corrections Compendium, 23*(11), 1–2, 8.

Telefilm Canada. (2006). *The blonde mystique*. A. Mehler & L. Nault (Producers). Vancouver, BC: Paperny Films.

Terrell, S. R. (2012). Mixed-methods research methodologies. *The Qualitative Report, 17*(1), 254–280.

Thyer, B. A. (2012). *Quasi-experimental research designs.* Oxford Scholarship Online: doi: 10.1093/acprof:oso/9780195387384.003.0001

Tobin, G. A., & Begley, C. M. (2004). Methodological rigour within a qualitative framework. *Journal of Advanced Nursing, 48*(4), 388–396.

Tuckman, B. W. (1972). *Conducting educational research.* New York, NY: Harcourt Brace Jovanovich.

Turnbull, C. (1973). *The mountain people.* London, UK: Jonathan Cape. (Original work published 1972).

Tuskegee Syphilis Study Legacy Committee. (1996, May 20). Final report of the Tuskegee Syphilis Study Legacy Committee. In *Historical collections.* Charlottesville, VA: Claude Moore Health Sciences Library. Retrieved from http://www.hsl.virginia.edu/historical/medical_history/bad_blood/report.cfm

Tuskegee University. (2019). *Coverage of the apology.* Tuskegee, AL: Tuskegee University. Retrieved from https://www.tuskegee.edu/about-us/centers-of-excellence/bioethics-center/coverage-of-the-apology

Tversky, A., & Kahneman, D. (1973). Availability: A heuristic for judging frequency and probability. *Cognitive Psychology, 5*(2), 207–232.

UNESCO. (2017). *What is local and Indigenous knowledge?* Paris, France: Author. Retrieved from http://www.unesco.org/new/en/natural-sciences/priority-areas/links/related-information/what-is-local-and-indigenous-knowledge/

Unger, D. (2011). *The Canadian bioethics companion: An online textbook for Canadian ethicists and health care workers.* Retrieved from http://canadianbioethicscompanion.ca

University of Toronto. (2018). Facts and figures. Retrieved from https://www.utoronto.ca/about-u-of-t

van den Hoonaard, D. K. (2019). *Qualitative research in action: A Canadian primer* (3rd ed.). Don Mills, ON: Oxford University Press.

van den Hoonaard, W. C. (2019). Ethics on the ground: A moral compass. In D. K. van den Hoonaard. *Qualitative research in action: A Canadian primer* (3rd ed., pp. 55–74). Don Mills, ON: Oxford University Press.

Van Dijk, T. (Ed.). (1997). *Discourse studies: A multidisciplinary introduction (Volume 1: Discourse as structure and process; Volume 2: Discourse as social interaction).* London, UK: Sage.

Vehovar, V., Manfreda, K. L., & Berzelak, J. (2019). About. Retrieved from http://www.websm.org//c/1888/About/

Vettese, F. (2013). Why Canada has no retirement crisis. *Rotman International Journal of Pension Management, 6*(1), 32–38.

Wada, M., Clarke, L. H., & Rozanova, J. (2015). Constructions of sexuality in later life: Analyses of Canadian magazine and newspaper portrayals of online dating. *Journal of Aging Studies, 32,* 40–49.

Wagner, A. C., McShane, K. E., Hart, T. A., & Margolese, S. (2016). A focus group qualitative study of HIV stigma in the Canadian health care system. *Canadian Journal of Human Sexuality, 25*(1), 61–71.

Wallace, W. (1971). *The logic of science in sociology.* Hawthorne, NY: Transaction.

Walsh, C. A., Hanley, J., Ives, N., & Hordyk, S. R. (2016). Exploring the experiences of newcomer women with insecure housing in Montréal Canada. *Journal of International Migration and Integration, 17*(3), 887–904.

Warren, C. A. B., & Karner, T. X. (2015). *Discovering qualitative methods: Field research, interviews, and analysis* (3rd ed.). New York, NY: Oxford University Press.

Warrior, R. A. (1995). *Tribal secrets: Recovering American Indian intellectual traditions.* Minneapolis, MN: University of Minnesota Press.

Watson, T. M., Strike, C., Kolla, G., Penn, R., & Bayoumi, A. M. (2015). "Drugs don't have age limits": The challenge of setting age restrictions for supervised injection facilities. *Drugs, Education, Prevention, and Policy, 22*(4), 370–379.

Watt, S. (2010). Leaving the field: A reflexive journey. In J. S. Jones & S. Watt (Eds.), *Ethnography in social science practice* (pp. 187–196). New York, NY: Routledge.

Webb, E. J., Campbell, D. T., Schwartz, R. D., & Sechrest, L. (2000). *Unobtrusive measures* (Rev. ed.). Thousand Oaks, CA: Sage.

Webb, J. T., Amend, E. R., Webb, N. E., Goerss, J., Beljan, P., & Olenchak, F. R. (2005). *Misdiagnosis and dual diagnosis of gifted children and adults: ADHD, bipolar, OCD, Asperger's, depression, and other disorders.* Scottsdale, AZ: Great Potential Press.

Webb, J. T., Gore, J. L., Amend, E. R., & DeVries, A. R. (2007). *A parent's guide to gifted children.* Scottsdale, AZ: Great Potential Press.

Weitzer, R., & Kubrin, C. (2009). Misogyny in rap music: A content analysis of prevalence and meanings. *Men and Masculinities, 12*(1), 13–29.

Weschler, D. (2003). *Weschler Intelligence Scale for children (WISC-IV)* (4th ed.). Toronto, ON: Pearson Education.

Wholey, J. S. (1994). Assessing the feasibility and likely usefulness of evaluation. In J. S. Wholey, H. P. Hatry, & K. E. Newcomer (Eds.), *Handbook of practical program evaluation* (pp. 15–19). San Francisco, CA: Jossey-Bass.

Whyte, W. F. (1943). *Street corner society: The social structure of an Italian slum.* Chicago, IL: Chicago University Press.

Whyte, W. F. (1994). *Participant observer: An autobiography.* Ithaca, NY: Cornell University.

Willis, J. W. (2007). *Foundations of qualitative research: Interpretive and critical approaches.* Thousand Oaks, CA: Sage.

Wills, J., Datta, K., Evans, Y., Herbert, J., May, J., & McIlwaine, C. (2010). *Global cities at work: New migrant divisions of labour.* London, UK: Pluto.

Wilson, K., Demetrioff, S., & Porter, S. (2008). A pawn by any other name? Social information processing as a function of psychopathic traits. *Journal of Research in Personality, 42*(6), 1651–1656.

Wilson, D. W., Thomas, R., Burns, K. K., Hewitt, J. A., Osei-Waree, J., & Robertson, S. (2012). Canadian rural-urban differences in end-of-life care setting transitions. *Global Journal of Health Services, 4*(5), 1–13. http://dx.doi.org/10.5539/gjhs.v4n5p1

Wilton, S., & Ross, L. (2017). Flexibility, sacrifice and insecurity: A Canadian study assessing the challenges of balancing work and family in academia. *Journal of Feminist Family Therapy, 29*(1–2), 66–87.

Wolcott, H. F. (2010). *Ethnography lessons: A primer.* Walnut Creek, CA: Left Coast Press.

Wolf, D. (1991). *The rebels: A brotherhood of outlaw bikers.* Toronto, ON: University of Toronto Press.

Wolfer, L. (2007). *Real research: Conducting and evaluating research in the social sciences.* Boston, MA: Pearson Education.

Wood, R. T., & Williams, R. J. (2007). Problem gambling on the internet: Implications for internet gambling policy in North America. *New Media Society, 9*(3), 520–542.

Yang, W. (2017). Does "compulsory volunteering" affect subsequent behavior? Evidence from a natural experiment in Canada. *Education Economics, 25*(4), 394–405.

Yin, R. K. (2018). *Case study research and applications* (6th ed.). Thousand Oaks, CA: Sage.

Zaric, G. S., Brennan, A. W., Varenbut, M., & Daiter, J. M. (2013). The cost of providing methadone maintenance treatment in Ontario, Canada. *The American Journal of Drug and Alcohol Abuse, 38*(6), 559–566.

Zetou, E., Amprasi, E., Michalopoulou, M., & Aggelousis, N. (2011). Volleyball coaches behavior assessment through systematic observation. *Journal of Human Sports Exercise, 6*(4), 585–593.

Zimbardo, P. G. (2004). A situationist perspective on the psychology of evil: Understanding how good people are transformed into perpetrators. In A. G. Miller (Ed.), *The social psychology of good and evil* (pp. 21–50). New York, NY: Guilford Press.

Zimbardo, P. G., Maslach, C., & Haney, C. (2000). Reflections on the Stanford Prison Experiment: Genesis, transformations, consequences. In T. Blass (Ed.), *Obedience to authority: Current perspectives on the Milgram paradigm* (pp. 193–237). Mahwah, NJ: Erlbaum.

Zweig, J. M., Lachman, P., Yahner, J., & Dank, M. (2014). Correlates of cyber dating abuse among teens. *Journal of Youth and Adolescence, 43*(8), 1306–1321.

INDEX